East-West Dialogues in Educational Philosophy and Theory

This series, published by Beijing Normal University, is geared toward developing approaches to intercultural philosophy in education, especially in the Chinese and Western cultures. The first series of its kind produced by a Chinese university, it addresses open problems in the analysis and structure of the ethics of self-cultivation, clarifies the differences between respective cultures' approaches to philosophy, and equips readers to handle complex ideas in the context of moral education.

Zhuran You • Yingzi Hu

Philosophy and Civilization: How the Idea of Moral Cultivation Shaped China

Springer

Zhuran You
School of Education and Psychology
Shaoxing University
Shaoxing, Zhejiang, China

Yingzi Hu
Provost Office, Rm 323
Shaoxing University
Shaoxing, Zhejiang, China

ISSN 2661-8753 ISSN 2661-8761 (electronic)
East-West Dialogues in Educational Philosophy and Theory
ISBN 978-981-95-5659-5 ISBN 978-981-95-5660-1 (eBook)
https://doi.org/10.1007/978-981-95-5660-1

This Springer imprint is published by the registered company Springer Nature Singapore Pte Ltd.
The registered company address is: 152 Beach Road, #21-01/04 Gateway East, Singapore 189721, Singapore

No. 1: "We in the West are used to thinking of moral cultivation as a fortuitous and fortunate add-on of upbringing and education, but not as an essential part of either the nature of human beings or human societies. In a uniquely original contribution to the history of ethical ideas, the authors argue that moral cultivation has been, in contrast, a central organizing principle of Chinese civilization through history, and they elicit the implications of this insight for various ontological, psychological, educational, and political issues that are of relevance both for Chinese modern society and for the world at large. Highly recommended reading."
—Professor Kristján Kristjánsson, *University of Birmingham, UK. Editor of Journal of Moral Education.*

No. 2: "*Philosophy and Civilization: How the Idea of Moral Cultivation Shaped China* is a refreshing journey through the history of philosophy and its significance in China. It is outstanding in its clarity in bringing complex ideas to life in a way that is both authentic and true to traditional sources, while also inviting readers in who come from other philosophical and cultural backgrounds. This is essential reading for anyone seeking to better understand Chinese thought and society."
—Liz Jackson, *Karen Lo Eugene Chuang Professor in Diversity and Equity, University of Hong Kong*

No. 3: "This new study by Zhuran You and Yingzi Hu powerfully extends their earlier history of moral cultivation in China by showing how this guiding idea has shaped philosophy, education, arts, and politics. By foregrounding 'moral cultivation' rather than the somewhat misleading term 'self-cultivation'— they clarify that the aim of education in China was never the cultivation of isolated selves, but the formation of humane persons responsive to shared norms within the community. In our era of hyper-vocational universities with shrinking programs in the humanities, this book makes the case for reviving reading and discussion of formative texts to a common moral horizon. It is learned, timely, and deeply constructive for educators."
—Leonard Waks, *Distinguished Professor at Qufu Normal University and Professor Emeritus of Educational Leadership at Temple University.*

Beholding the grandeur of the cosmos, yet still I cradle the green of the humble leaves.—Ma Yifu

Foreword: Civilization as Moral Cultivation

The term "civilization" is both evocative and contested. It conjures images of monumental achievements and sophisticated institutions, yet it is also burdened with a history of hierarchy, exclusion, and imperial ambition. Too often, it has served as a rhetorical tool to distinguish the "civilized" from the "barbaric," providing ideological cover for colonization and conquest. In our contemporary global discourse, "civilization" functions as a battleground concept—mobilized in debates over cultural identity, political legitimacy, and moral authority. To invoke civilization today is to enter a deeply charged discursive terrain.

It is precisely against this backdrop that *Philosophy and Civilization: How the Idea of Moral Cultivation Shaped China* makes a critical intervention. This work by Zhuran You and Yingzi Hu does not merely analyze civilization from an academic distance—it performs a philosophical reclamation. It strips civilization of its triumphalist pretensions and returns it to a more essential and humanistic meaning: not the scale of a society's power, but the depth of its ethical commitments; not the number of its inventions, but the cultivation of its people.

At the heart of this reframing is the central concept of *xiuyang* (修养), or moral cultivation. The authors argue—persuasively and elegantly—that Chinese civilization, in its most enduring and coherent expression, is best understood as a civilizational project rooted in the continuous cultivation of virtue. Civilization, in this vision, is not an endpoint but a process, a collective striving toward ethical refinement, grounded in lived practice rather than abstract doctrine. Philosophy here is not divorced from daily life; it is the animating force of a culture's ethical imagination.

This book offers a powerful thesis: that Chinese civilization is unified not by a single dogma or political regime, but by a long-standing commitment to moral education as the cornerstone of human development. This idea is deeply embedded in the metaphysical notion of the "unity of Heaven and humanity" (天人合一), a foundational paradigm that sees the cosmos as inherently moral and humans as capable of harmonizing with its rhythms. This unity is not mystical escapism but an existential directive: to shape oneself, one's society, and one's world in accordance with cosmic virtue. In doing so, moral cultivation becomes both the method and the goal of civilization itself.

The book's most compelling contribution is its articulation of moral cultivation as the cultural DNA that weaves together the diverse threads of Chinese philosophical thought. The Confucian aspiration to become a *junzi* (君子)—a person of noble character—through *li* (ritual) and *ren* (humaneness); the Daoist ideal of *wuwei* (non-coercive action) in alignment with the natural order; the Buddhist commitment to inner awakening and the realization of *Buddha-nature*—each of these represents a distinct yet complementary path toward the refinement of the self. Rather than framing these traditions as competing ideologies, the authors show how they converge on a shared civilizational ethos: the elevation of character through ongoing, embodied ethical practice.

This vision stands in sharp contrast to dominant Western paradigms, especially those shaped by Enlightenment rationalism and industrial modernity. While the West has made immense strides in scientific and technological progress, its civilizational narrative has often been one of external conquest rather than internal cultivation. Individual rights, economic growth, and technological innovation—though undeniably significant—do not constitute civilization in themselves. When untethered from ethical purpose, they risk producing a society that is materially advanced but spiritually impoverished, efficient but alienated, powerful but predatory.

By contrast, the Chinese tradition, as reconstructed in this volume, offers an alternative orientation: one in which true progress is measured not by accumulation, but by attunement; not by domination, but by harmony. The metaphor of "sculpting jade" is apt—a vision of moral development as slow, deliberate, and beautiful. The self, in this framework, is never isolated but always relational—embedded in a matrix of responsibilities to family, society, nature, and cosmos. Self-cultivation is thus inseparable from world cultivation.

Importantly, this work does not promote a triumphalist or chauvinistic vision of Chinese civilization. It does not offer a new form of civilizational exceptionalism. Rather, it invites a more pluralistic and integrative global dialogue in which different traditions can learn from one another. The challenge it sets forth is universal: How can we build civilizations that nurture virtue, sustain balance, and cultivate the moral imagination necessary for co-flourishing?

In our time—marked by ecological degradation, spiritual malaise, technological disorientation, and deepening geopolitical divisions—this call to re-center moral cultivation is both urgent and transformative. The questions posed by this tradition are no longer simply Chinese questions; they are human questions. How do we foster the *Greater Self* (大我) that transcends egoism and embraces mutual flourishing? How can our institutions, from education to politics, be recalibrated to encourage virtue rather than merely regulate vice? Can we imagine progress not as a race to the top, but as a return to harmony?

This book does not offer easy answers. Instead, it provides a philosophical architecture—rooted in millennia of thought and practice—through which we might begin to ask the right questions. It shows that the future of civilization depends not only on our capacity to innovate, but on our willingness to cultivate.

Ultimately, *Philosophy and Civilization* is a work of bridge-building. It connects ancient wisdom with contemporary crises. It fosters dialogue between East and West, past and present, self and other. And perhaps most importantly, it builds a bridge within each of us—between who we are and who we might become through the patient work of self-cultivation.

This is a vision of civilization as an open horizon, not a closed chapter; as an ethical process, not a political possession. It is a vision we urgently need—and one we must now strive to realize together.

Tairua, New Zealand
17 September, 2025

Michael A. Peters

Acknowledgments

We extend our profound gratitude to Michael A. Peters, Emeritus Professor at the University of Illinois at Urbana–Champaign and Distinguished Visiting Professor at Tsinghua University, and to A. G. Rud, Distinguished Professor Emeritus of Washington State University, for their invaluable guidance, scholarly insight, and unwavering support.

Our sincere thanks also go to Alice Xie, our editor at Springer, for her invaluable guidance and support throughout the publication process.

The book is funded by the Humanities and Social Sciences Project of the Ministry of Education in China [20YJA880075] "The philosophical system of traditional Chinese moral education and its cultural implication."

Competing Interests The authors have no competing interests to declare that are relevant to the content of this manuscript.

Contents

Part I
The Philosophy of Moral Cultivation

Chapter 1
Moral Cultivation in Chinese Philosophy and Civilization

Every great civilization is a conversation—an ongoing dialogue with itself about what it means to be human. Philosophy is that dialogue made conscious, the moment a people pauses to examine its noblest ideals and darkest flaws. Without such reflection, no civilization—however mighty or vast—can ever attain true flourishing. Imagine a world without Confucius' humaneness (ren), Mencius' sprouts of virtue, or Lao Tzu's Dao. Now erase Plato's Republic, Aristotle's Ethics, and Kant's Categorical Imperative. What is left? A hollow civilization stripped of its moral compass: adrift, unanchored, and bereft of the very ideas that teach us how to live, how to govern, and why justice and goodness are worth pursuing.

Ancient China exemplified one of history's most profound fusions of philosophy and civilization, where moral cultivation served as the heartbeat of cultural life, shaping its ethical norms and social fabric. Unlike many Western traditions that sought metaphysical heights through reason or revelation, Chinese philosophies remained grounded in the art of living: practical wisdom of social bonds, self-perfection through ritual, and attunement to the rhythms and patterns of nature. Philosophy was not for solitary enlightenment but for the well-being of the whole, achieved through patient character refinement. Yet, beneath these East-West particularities lies a shared aspiration: the refinement of human nature, the alchemy transforming instinct into virtue, and the struggle to align microcosm with macrocosm. It is within this very tension, the struggle between intimate duties and the higher calling toward shared flourishing, that our inquiry finds both its origin and its enduring urgency.

Z. You, Y. Hu, *Philosophy and Civilization: How the Idea of Moral Cultivation Shaped China*, East-West Dialogues in Educational Philosophy and Theory,
https://doi.org/10.1007/978-981-95-5660-1_1

1.1 Philosophy as a Civilizing Force

Philosophy constitutes humanity's rigorous interrogation of its own existence—the foundational grammar that structures all meaningful thought—whether scientific, artistic, political, or cultural. By cultivating critical consciousness and ethical clarity, philosophy remains globally indispensable for steering civilization toward greater justice, wisdom, and social harmony.

1.1.1 Philosophy as an Agent of Civilization

Across civilizations, philosophy has stood as both mirror and architect of human culture, reflecting humanity's deepest questions while shaping the contours of its destiny. In classical Greece, a constellation of brilliant minds laid the bedrock of Western thought. In ancient India, the wisdom of Brahmin masters and the transformative teachings of the Buddha swept across the subcontinent. Meanwhile in China, Confucius, and Lao Tzu offered contrasting yet complementary visions of social harmony and cosmic order—each tradition reshaping the very worldview of its civilization.

The intricate bond between human development and philosophical articulation allows us to understand, explain, and even compare civilizations across vast spans of time and space. This perspectivist method, which views history as culture and culture as built on values (Nobre, 2006), has been widely used to identify the defining characteristics of a civilization over the past century. Max Weber (2001), for instance, analyzes civilizations through the lens of religious ethics, suggesting that Protestant ethics played a role in creating the capitalistic spirit. Similarly, Samuel Huntington (1996) defines civilization as a broad cultural construct, including "values, norms, institutions, and modes of thinking" (p. 41) passed down through generations, and argues that in the post–Cold War world, cultural and religious identities will be the primary source of civilizational conflict.

This cultural lens positions philosophy, alongside religion, as a key to unraveling a civilization, offering profound insights into its core beliefs, values, and, ultimately, its identity. As John Dewey (1931) emphasizes, philosophy itself is a cultural phenomenon, "its connection with social history, with civilization, is intrinsic" (p. 3). As such, philosophy can be used to identify and understand civilizations. Dewey illustrates this by showing how the idea of pragmatism reflects the characters, values, institutions, and ways of thinking, behaviors, scientific thought, and social organizations of the American people (Dewey, 1931, p. 3). Similarly, Maurice De Wulf underscores the close relationship between medieval philosophical and religious thought and the broader landscapes of Western medieval civilization (De Wulf, 2008). Bertrand Russell takes it a step further, arguing for a reciprocal relationship: "if we need to understand a nation or an age, we need to understand its philosophy," for "the circumstances of men's lives do much to determine their philosophy, but, conversely, their philosophy does much to determine their circumstances" (Russell, 2013, p. 5).

Philosophy's influence on civilization extends beyond the intellectual sphere. A truly advanced civilization, as reflected in enduring philosophical traditions, is measured not only by achievements in culture, technology, or institutions but also by its deep moral commitment. Reverence for nature and life, fidelity to promises, tolerance for diversity, the defense of justice, and compassion for the vulnerable are all widely recognized hallmarks of a civilized society. True progress, then, depends heavily on the cultivation of these moral virtues, which foster collective well-being and the harmonious development of human society.

1.1.2 The Role of Philosophy in Chinese Civilization

Throughout history, philosophical and religious traditions have profoundly shaped human societies, offering frameworks of belief and value that bolstered social structures, guided ethical guidelines, and informed answers to fundamental existential questions about the world, consciousness, and the meaning of life. Christianity, for example, has molded the Western world, not only through its doctrines and institutions, but also through its impact on art, science, politics, and everyday life. While European thought often draws a distinction between faith (revealed theology) and reason (natural theology), the two have historically been closely intertwined, especially in the realm of ethics (Branson, 2020), as illustrated by Max Weber's argument that the spirit of capitalism was largely rooted in Protestant moral values.

As one of the world's oldest and most enduring major civilizations, China presents a remarkable case where its culture and values were profoundly shaped by a confluence of Confucianism, Daoism, Buddhism, and other influential traditions. Western scholarship has historically grappled with classifying Confucianism, often characterizing it as occupying a liminal space between philosophy and religion—a categorization that, while increasingly contested, reflects its hybrid nature, as seen in frequent comparisons with major world religions in efforts to understand the distinctive features of Chinese civilization.

Whereas Western culture often draws a sharper line between abstract philosophical reasoning and religious concerns about daily life and salvation, traditional Chinese thought tends to blur boundaries between philosophy, ethics, social theory, and what Western perspectives might classify as religion. Confucianism, Daoism, and even syncretic Chinese Buddhism are deeply interwoven with social order, governance, personal conduct, and daily rituals, fueling ongoing debate about their true nature. Confucianism, for instance, functions as a philosophy of moral development, encompassing various rituals, ceremonies, and ethical practices reminiscent of religious observances. Its influence on education, governance, and family life is often likened to that of organized religion, despite its grounding in this-worldly ethical cultivation rather than divine authority or salvation.

That said, Confucianism should be primarily considered a social and ethical philosophy. While Confucian teachings provide guidance on life, virtues, and even a kind of belief system, its abstract concept of Heaven (天) lacks the personalized deities, divine revelations, or focus on the afterlife commonly associated with religion (Kennedy & Lee, 2020). Without a creator god, it centers instead on moral principles that guide human relationships and governance; its ultimate aim lies not in theological doctrine but in the cultivation of practical ethics and the pursuit of social harmony.

The emphasis on the earthly well-being and the deep integration of philosophy with social practices helps explain why indigenous Chinese philosophical traditions played a central role in shaping Chinese civilization. Confucianism deeply influenced social structures and daily life, while other schools of thought—such as Classical Daoism, with its focus on harmony with natural order, and Legalism, with its emphasis on law and statecraft—provided complementary perspectives (henceforth, Daoism specifically refers to Classical Daoism). Even Buddhism, with its rich philosophical and ethical dimensions, is often regarded as much a philosophy as a religion. This grounding of philosophy in lived experience is the reason the book is titled "*Philosophy and Civilization*": It explores the core beliefs and enduring values of Chinese civilization through a philosophical lens.

1.1.3 Why Chinese Philosophy and Civilization Matter

China, alongside Western and Islamic cultures, stands as one of the major cultural traditions with a rich history and significant global influence. After a prolonged period of backwardness and foreign dominance, China is now undergoing a remarkable resurgence, characterized by growing political influence, economic dynamism, technology development, and the reaffirmation of a distinct cultural identity. As its presence on the world stage steadily expands, the international community is witnessing the reemergence of China as a key global force.

China's rise on the world stage has elicited a spectrum of reactions, from optimism and anticipation to unease and skepticism. This mixed response arises from two main factors: First, a limited grasp of its vast history and cultural intricacies renders it an enigma; second, its distinct political and ideological systems—diverging sharply from Western paradigms— prompt some to perceive it as a potential threat. From a cultural and geopolitical standpoint, scholars offer divergent perspectives. Samuel P. Huntington (1996) foresees civilizational clashes in the post–Cold War era, warning that China's rise would test the foundations of the international order. Martin Jacques (2009) contends that China is not merely a nation-state but a civilization-state, whose unique historical trajectory ensures that its global influence will unfold in ways unfamiliar to the West. Peters and Meier (2025) further envision two parallel world regimes—the United States and China—where competing cultural values, political systems, and economic models vie for global influence. While these scholars posit the potential for civilizational conflict, others, like Bergsten et al. (2008), frame China's rise as both a disruptive force and a transformative opportunity for the United States and the broader world.

This book, however, does not wade into the heated debates over whether a rising China presents an opportunity or a threat to the West, nor does it engage in the contentious discourse surrounding superpower succession. Instead, it turns to the deeper cultural foundations that have sustained Chinese civilization through the ages, allowing readers to develop their own understanding. This exploration addresses the core questions that inspired this project: What defines traditional Chinese culture? What are its essential qualities? How have these traits influenced the development of Chinese civilization? And what enduring significance might they hold for navigating the challenges and opportunities of our contemporary world?

Among the many dimensions of culture, this inquiry centers on the concept of moral cultivation to deepen our understanding of Chinese philosophy and civilization. This concept, emphasizing self-improvement, ethical conduct, and social harmony, forms the bedrock of mainstream Chinese thought—especially within Confucianism. Echoing this enduring tradition, contemporary writer Liang Xiaosheng (2005) eloquently distills Chinese culture into four guiding pillars: moral cultivation rooted in the heart, self-awareness without the need for reminders, freedom grounded in self-restraint, and, ultimately, empathetic consideration for others.[1] Collectively, these principles express a foundational Chinese tenet regarding moral cultivation as crucial for both individual realization and collective harmony.

The idea of moral cultivation plays a dual role. First, it functions as a conceptual key for unlocking traditional Chinese philosophy—a formidable task complicated not only by linguistic barriers but also by the cultural diversity, intricacy, and ambiguity inherent in this philosophical heritage. This makes moral cultivation an essential focal point, precisely because it provides the unifying thread that connects, distinguishes, and ultimately weaves China's diverse philosophical traditions into a plural yet coherent framework.

Second, moral cultivation—the core of a pragmatic Chinese philosophy—serves as both a lens for understanding ancient Chinese civilization and a catalytic force actively shaping its evolution. Grasping this interplay is essential, for neglecting the foundational worldviews and ethical ideals that guided Chinese society risks producing shallow or distorted interpretations. Similarly, examining Chinese philosophy apart from its social manifestations renders it abstract and meaningless. An integrated approach is particularly significant today as it not only illuminates the past, but also offers crucial perspective on, as French (2017) perceptively notes, "what kind of global power China stands to become—and how to interact wisely."

[1] Liang Xiaoshen, lecture at Shaoxing University in 2005.

1.2 Moral Cultivation as a Foundation for Chinese Philosophy and Civilization

Prior to further discussion, it is essential to situate Chinese philosophy within a global context and to recognize the ethical character of its civilization. While Western philosophical traditions have long dominated global discourse, other ancient systems of thought—particularly those of China and India—developed equally profound yet distinctive approaches to understanding human existence. These traditions not only constitute essential chapters in the story of world philosophy but have fundamentally shaped the development of their respective civilizations.

1.2.1 The Ethical Roots of Chinese Civilization

Ancient China ranks among one of the most prominent civilizations in human history. From its early origin millennia ago, China has weathered countless upheavals, time and again renewing itself with remarkable vitality. This resilience is rooted in a unique cultural DNA of moral cultivation, ritual practice, and a deep reverence for shared lineage. A compelling example is the long-standing tradition of ancestor worship, epitomized by the continued public veneration of the Yellow Emperor, a symbolic and legendary sovereign and cultural hero, across successive dynasties. This persistent and widespread practice highlights the profoundly ritualistic and ethical character of Chinese civilization.

Unlike some ancient civilizations that were primarily rooted in religion, China developed largely as a humanistic, ethical, and secular society. The centrality of family and ancestral lineage in Chinese society laid a strong foundation for moral cultivation, which, in turn, served as a compass guiding individuals and communities toward social harmony and collective well-being, nurturing a sense of unity and purpose across generations. At the heart of this tradition lies the conviction that true civilization rests on principles like respect, responsibility, justice, and compassion, a view memorably expressed by Albert Schweitzer (1923), who argues that the ultimate goal of civilization is the spiritual and moral perfection of individuals.

The term "civilization" generally refers to complex human societies that thrive both spiritually and materially, encompassing the development of languages, cities, institutions, organizational forms, technology, art, architecture, religions, and ideology. Despite their vast diversity, civilizations share a cultural core, often described as a constellation of "economic provision, political organization, moral tradition, and the pursuit of knowledge and the arts" (Durant, 2014, p. 1). From a philosophical perspective, however, the essence of civilization is more ontological than functional: affirming the intrinsic value of humanity. An ethical foundation is thus indispensable, serving as the critical criterion for a society to be deemed a true civilization.

Given the centrality of ethics in defining a civilization, this book centers on the ethical and cultural dimensions of Chinese civilization. It examines how moral cultivation, as both a philosophical idea and a social practice, shaped its foundations: belief systems, ways of life, art and literature, national identity, social norms, and governance structures capable of integrating diverse peoples. In this light, Chinese civilization emerges as a worldview of All under Heaven, embodying harmony, universal ethical principles, and social order. Its enduring commitment to humanistic values and moral ideals serves as a defining expression of a fully developed civilizational ethos.

For this purpose, the book adopts a "thick" philosophical paradigm or a philosophy of civilization, rather than a "thin" philosophical approach. While thin philosophy, often associated with purely analytical or conceptual studies, seeks knowledge for its own sake, thick philosophy expands the scope of inquiry to engage with concrete events, cultural practices, and civilizational patterns (Chen, 2019). In this context, "thickness" signifies the inclusion of historical depth, cultural complexity, and the lived realities of a civilization, a perspective exemplified by intellectual giants like Max Weber, John Dewey, and Albert Schweitzer in their studies of the intricate relationship between philosophy and civilization.

Although ancient China possessed spiritual traditions, its governance remained predominantly secular, grounded in humanistic and ethical principles derived from Confucianism, Daoism, Mohism, and Legalism—among which Confucianism played the most pivotal role in shaping Chinese society and political institutions. These philosophies functioned both as a diverse array of ideas and beliefs and as systematic solutions through which communities organized social life, fostered harmony or administrative efficiency, and responded to the challenges of maintaining order and prosperity. Hence, exploring the richness of Chinese philosophy reveals valuable insights into the characteristics of its ancient civilization.

That said, labeling ancient China as a "Confucian civilization" risks oversimplification. While Confucianism exerted a profound influence, it was by no means the only shaping force. Daoism, for instance, contributed significantly with its naturalistic and harmony-centered worldview. Over time, diverse influences blended into a distinctive cultural synthesis, often described as a fusion of Confucianism, Daoism, and Buddhism. Recognizing this complexity, Samuel Huntington (1996) adopted the term "Sinic civilization" in his book *The Clash of Civilizations*, replacing the "Confucian civilization" he had employed in his previous article (1993), a revision that better reflects the pluralistic nature of Chinese intellectual tradition.

1.2.2 Moral Cultivation as the Foundational Principle Structuring Chinese Civilization

Generally speaking, Chinese philosophical traditions are deeply grounded in the metaphysical framework of "unity of Heaven and humanity" (天人合一), which inspires individuals to pursue moral perfection by aligning with the cosmic order. It holds that all things, from the humblest pebble to the grandest mountain, partake in the same supreme principle—one embodied in Heaven or the Dao. Individuals "are ontologically and spiritually linked to the universe, therefore their moral actions are simultaneously cosmic and metaphysical" (Redmond & Hon, 2014). Given that Heaven is perceived as inherently virtuous and humanity intrinsically linked to it, the pursuit of virtue becomes not only an external imperative but an inner call. As such, this principle stands as a foundational pillar of moral cultivation in Chinese thought.

This convergence of metaphysical principles and lived reality is perhaps most evident in Confucianism, where human virtues are understood as reflections of the grand moral force that animates Heaven and Earth, generating and nurturing all beings without seeking acknowledgment (Confucius, 2016a). This perspective calls for a conscious reawakening of one's inherent moral nature for social harmony. The pursuit of moral perfection becomes both the journey and the destination, leading to a philosophy where the subjective and objective realms converge, and the phenomenal world is seamlessly fused with the noumenal world. Moral cultivation is consequently not just an abstract ideal but a tangible path for both individuals and communities, which involves continuous learning, practice, self-discipline, and peer influence as individuals strive to fully realize their inherent virtuous potential, ultimately returning to a state of cosmic harmony.

Ancient China's remarkable endurance was deeply rooted in a robust system of moral cultivation, demonstrating the crucial role of moral principles in civilizational longevity. It is no coincidence, then, that for much of its history, China placed a premium on nurturing and preserving moral values. Erosion of this moral foundation could spell disaster, even dynastic collapse. This insight finds echoes in Western thought, as illustrated by Edward Gibbon (2001) in *The History of the Decline and Fall of the Roman Empire*, where he posited that Rome's fall was driven partly by the decline of civic virtues, including public spirit and political freedoms. China presents a more nuanced case. While dynasties inevitably rose and fell, Chinese civilization itself endured. Frequently, a dynasty's downfall was accompanied by moral decay. Yet, the succeeding dynasty, renewing its commitment to core values, revived the civilization.

Throughout history, philosophy and religion have served as the bedrock of civilizations, molding their values, beliefs, and social structures. These belief systems have enabled societies to navigate challenges by facilitating collaboration, mediating disputes, and reinforcing collective identity. Chinese philosophy operates within this broad framework, yet distinguishes itself by favoring experiential wisdom, intuitive insight, and holistic understanding over abstract reasoning and analysis. This distinctive orientation fosters a supple, context-sensitive approach to ethics and social relations—most notably through its focus on moral cultivation to harmonize intricate human systems. Examining this philosophical dynamic unveils the profound underpinnings of Chinese civilization, illuminating its shared beliefs, moral values, ways of life, and signature traits, all of which serve to define its lasting cultural heritage. In this sense, Chinese civilization emerges as a project fundamentally shaped and continuously guided by the principle of moral cultivation.

1.2.3 Distinctive Characteristics of Chinese Morality

Morality (de) represents both a personal conviction about proper human conduct and a social compact governing the distribution of resources and exercise of power, safeguarding both collective welfare and individual dignity. More than mere rules of behavior, morality constitutes a civilization's living pursuit of human flourishing—a constantly evolving ideal shaped by historical experience and cultural values. This pursuit extends beyond material considerations to encompass ethical principles, communal harmony, and transcendent aspirations that give meaning to human existence.

A nuanced understanding of de (德) is essential for comprehending moral cultivation in Chinese culture, as the term encompasses both collective morality and individual virtue. While these translations—morality and virtue—offer a starting point for cross-cultural understanding, they fall short of conveying the term's full depth and complexity. In effect, "de" carries a wide range of meanings, ranging from celestial blessings and ancestral favor to inner strength, ethical conduct, and a kind of spiritual power derived from the Dao (Wang, 2015). Although both "de" and the Western idea of "virtue" engage with the notion of right and wrong, their core connotations differ in subtle yet significant ways. Western "virtue" primarily concerns reasoning, autonomy, justice, and public good, whereas "de" is infused with emotive and relational qualities such as harmony, humaneness, compassion, and humility. While Western virtue often leans toward individualism, "de" reflects a more integrated framework of collectivist values and cosmic resonance.

While Chinese philosophical schools present nuanced connotations of morality and virtue—from normative consensus and ritual propriety to spontaneous virtue and universal care—they all affirm its guiding role in personal development and the pursuit of social harmony. For example, Confucian morality extended beyond individual virtues to encompass social consensus, virtuous leadership, ethical oversight, and the concern for the greater good. In this sense, Confucian morality functions somewhat similarly to a social contract in Western thought that binds society through shared norms and mutual obligations. This system fulfills the Confucian ideal of "ruling by virtue," a refined model of governance, where moral authority complements institutional power, shaping conduct through the subtle but pervasive influence of ethical norms rather than coercion alone.

Another characteristic of Chinese mainstream morality lies in its relational orientation. The Confucian virtue of humaneness highlights the interconnectedness of individual flourishing and the well-being of others, prioritizing harmonious human relationships. Even Daoist ethics, though distinct in style, are relational—emphasizing attunement with the Dao as the natural order. Furthermore, morality is not seen as a static set of rules but as a developmental process, a valuable and dynamic pursuit involving the continuous internalization of ethical principles in alignment with one's authentic nature. This transformative path involves "becoming virtuous" through sustained self-reflection, social practice, and the active cultivation of communal virtuous qualities. Thus, moral cultivation, driven by both internal commitment and external influences, becomes integral to life—a lifelong pursuit of moral excellence.

1.2.4 The Dual Dimensions of Moral Cultivation

Moral cultivation is a simple phrase with profound meaning. It encapsulates a core belief on "de" and its practical realization, "by which one attempts to direct the course of moral development either of oneself or others" (Prior, 2007, p. 49). This idea resonates with Aristotle's emphasis on habitual practice, the lived experience of virtue, and the cultivation of phronesis for navigating moral complexities. While the pursuit of moral excellence is a universal human endeavor, evident in traditions from ancient Greece to classical India, Chinese philosophy distinguishes itself through its unparalleled historical emphasis on this lifelong moral journey, making it the cornerstone of its cultural tradition.

1.2.4.1 Moral Cultivation in Cross-Cultural Context

Notably, although the term "moral cultivation" exists in both Chinese and English, its significance is nuanced. In Chinese thought, moral cultivation is a central and pervasive concept deeply embedded in classical texts. By contrast, in English-language discourse, the term is rarely used and lacks comparable cultural resonance or philosophical weight.

In English, "cultivation" often evokes images of gardeners tending crops or refining skills, not necessarily the arduous journey of building moral character (Stone, 2018). Still, the phrase surfaces in many scholarly works on traditional Chinese philosophy and even in Western philosophical reflections on moral development. For example, the American Transcendentalist Ralph Waldo Emerson employed the term to describe his ideal society: "if you have a nation of men who have risen to that height of moral cultivation that they will not declare war or carry arms, for they have not so much madness left in their brains, you have a nation of lovers, of benefactors, of true, great, and able men" (Emerson, 1904, pp. 168–169).

The reason the term "moral cultivation" is relatively uncommon in Western discourse is that many ethical theories often "overlook or undervalue the developmental aspects of moral activity, instead favoring criterial matters of moral judgment" (Stroud, 2006, p. 100). In comparison, Confucianism centers on the cultivation of virtues over abstract conceptual analysis. For Confucius, individuals are not morally complete, but must actively engage in a process of moral development, through their own efforts and the help of others. Thus, "cultivation" aptly captures the dynamic, ongoing process of moral character formation, a concept central to Confucian thought.

The concept of moral cultivation in Chinese thought originates in two key concepts: "道德修养 (xiu-yang)," denoting the continuous personal agency to refine and enhance one's moral character, and "道德教化 (jiao-hua)," emphasizing the dual process of external moral education and internal transformation. Broadening this perspective, the English phrase moral cultivation can also be literally translated into Chinese as "育德 (yu-de)," meaning to cultivate virtues. This linguistic formulation implies a moral seed or innate moral potential within each individual that can be cultivated through conscious self-cultivation and proper environmental conditioning.

This book privileges "xiu-yang" (修养) and "yu-de" (育德) over the conventional use of "jiao-hua" (教化) as the preferred translation for "moral cultivation," arguing that the former two more fully capture the concept's rich, multifaceted, and dynamic nature of ethical development within Chinese thought. While "jiao-hua," often associated primarily with Confucian ethics, provides a vital foundation for moral cultivation, particularly in its state-guided forms, "xiu-yang" and "yu-de" convey a more expansive vision shared across major Chinese traditions, highlighting individual resolve and grassroots efforts, and offering perspectives that both challenge and enrich orthodox understandings.

1.2.4.2 Unity of Self-Cultivation and Social Moral Cultivation

Chinese philosophical traditions conceive moral cultivation as an inherently integrative process, seamlessly blending internal and external dimensions. While self-cultivation remains foundational, it is inseparably connected to external influences, including social support networks and the broader environment. This dialectical approach reflects the characteristically Chinese worldview that emphasizes holistic interconnection and mutually constitutive relationships in moral development.

Self-cultivation (修身), a central theme across Chinese philosophical traditions, refers to an inward path of personal refinement and moral perfection through a holistic process of integrated learning, disciplined practice, self-reflection, and mindful living (Barbalet & Barbalet, 2017; Lai, 2017). While the term literally translates as "cultivating the body," its philosophical significance extends far beyond mere physical exercise to embrace moral and spiritual development, reflecting Chinese thought of the body-mind unity, where physical and mental states are deeply interdependent. Thus, to cultivate the body is also to cultivate the mind: Refining one's appearance, conduct, and demeanor can enhance moral character, just as a cultivated mind can guide and elevate outward behavior. Aligned with the modern psychological concept of embodied cognition, which emphasizes the interplay between physical experience and mental processes, self-cultivation involves refining both body and mind in the pursuit of moral excellence. It is akin to sculpting a piece of jade: External influences, such as social interactions and moral education, serve as the tools, while internal discipline and self-reflection act as the artist's hand, shaping one's character over time. Virtue, therefore, is not forged in isolation but emerges through a dynamic synergy between inner effort and outer context.

The belief that moral character is inextricably tied to the social environment stands in contrast to many Western perspectives, which tend to emphasize individual autonomy and self-determination. Rather, traditional Chinese culture integrates substantial collective efforts with self-cultivation, manifesting in two primary approaches—whether by nurturing an inherent goodness, as Mencius (2016) suggests, or by correcting potentially unruly impulses through ritual and discipline, as Xunzi (2015) emphasizes. Within this framework, education, mentorship, peer influence, family values, and even state policies collectively constitute an interconnected moral ecosystem, which supports and refines one's ethical development, ensuring that self-cultivation is not an isolated process but one deeply integrated with the broader social and cultural dynamics.

From this perspective, the notion that Confucians pursue moral development solely through self-cultivation can be misleading and has raised doubts about its practicality. Michael Slote (2016), for instance, contends that Confucian moral self-cultivation through one's own efforts is psychologically unrealistic due to people's insufficient intrinsic motives to maintain consistent self-discipline. This analysis logically leads to the recognition that external structures and communal support are indispensable for continuous ethical growth.

In reality, Confucian moral cultivation emphasizes the vital role of social engagement within the relational and collective framework of Chinese society. Given that moral challenges often arise in human relationships, this approach legitimizes external influences as an essential complement to self-cultivation (Wong, 2014). Alongside inner motivation like self-reflection and self-discipline, external factors such as guidance from elders, participation in rituals, learning from exemplars, encouragement, and a sense of belonging are essential for moral self-cultivation. These experiences, in turn, prepare individuals to take on responsibility of teaching and influencing others, within their families, communities, and the broader society, contributing to the formation of a virtuous community and state. In this context, moral cultivation becomes a reciprocal process as it "occurs both in what one learns and what one teaches" (Foust, 2017, p. 29). Together, these two pillars—inner cultivation and outward engagement—form a comprehensive, systemic approach to spiritual transformation and ethical development, serving as a cornerstone of ancient Chinese culture and society.

This inherent relationality repositions Confucianism beyond a mere ethics of self-cultivation to reveal its profound commitment to environmental shaping and collective moral responsibility. It advances a holistic worldview where the "self" and the "other" are not opposites, but collaborative partners in the formation of moral character. That said, Confucianism should not be misconstrued as a rigid system where virtue is solely determined by external conditions. While environmental factors undeniably influence moral development, self-cultivation remains central to Confucian ethics. Individuals retain the agency to choose to become a junzi (gentleman) or a small person, regardless of their circumstance—underscoring a vital Confucian affirmation of self-determination within a relational moral framework.

The phrase "moral cultivation" aptly reflects its metaphorical connection to "unity of Heaven and humanity," where individual efforts align with the broader cosmic and social order, revealing the intrinsic link between individual growth and communal harmony in moral development. Unlike the ancient Greek idea of moral development through knowledge acquisition, reasoning, and habit formation, many ancient Chinese traditions highlight the cultivation of an inherent goodness, a "moral seed" bestowed by Heaven or the Dao. Nonetheless, both sides share a transcendent premise: For many Greek philosophers, the path to virtue through knowledge presupposes that humans possess divine reason; for many Chinese philosophers, the moral potential embedded in human nature also implies a form of moral rationality, and its cultivation requires both cognitive understanding and the development of virtuous habits. Thus, even with a belief in innate goodness, learning and practice remain essential for moral flourishing.

A common misconception about "moral cultivation" is that it operates as a two-tiered system: self-cultivation is reserved for the elite, while external influence is designated to the masses. This interpretation finds apparent support in Confucius's teaching that the junzi, through their own moral refinement, should serve as exemplars for the broader community, with their virtues influencing the common people, like the wind bending the grass (Confucius, 2016a). Yet this metaphor captures only one facet of a more complex ideal. Traditional Chinese philosophy conceives of moral development as a holistic process—one requiring both inner reflection and external guidance, accessible to all individuals regardless of status. While societal structures played a pivotal role in shaping the moral development of the general population, the attainment of self-initiated virtue was nonetheless regarded as within their reach. Conversely, even elites, scholars and rulers alike, were not solely reliant on introspection; their cultivation was also influenced by the wisdom of sages, the guidance of teachers, peer oversight and encouragement, and societal expectations. This inclusive understanding is affirmed by Mencius (2016), who believed in the universal potential for sagehood, and Xunzi (1997), who argued that anyone could attain it through effort and education. Ultimately, moral cultivation emerges as a generative process of mutual nourishment between the individual and society, the internal and the external, morality and culture—an inclusive way of life that shaped ancient China.

1.2.5 Philosophical Traditions of Moral Cultivation

Moral cultivation is a global theme across many philosophical and religious traditions, including Confucianism, Buddhism, Hinduism, Stoicism, Christianity, and Islam. In ancient China, it found particularly fertile ground in Confucian thought. Therefore, this exploration centers on the profound impact of Confucian moral cultivation on Chinese civilization. That said, it is crucial to acknowledge that moral cultivation is not exclusive to Confucianism. Other philosophical schools and religious traditions, such as Daoism, Mohism, and Buddhism, offer unique perspectives on this theme, which, whether converging with or diverging from Confucian ideas, enrich our understanding of moral cultivation. Consequently, this discussion will incorporate insights from these schools, recognizing their significant contributions to the cultural landscape of China and their role in shaping the moral values and ethos of the Chinese people.

1.2.5.1 Daoist and Confucian Paths to Virtue

Though often misconstrued as amoral, Daoism offers a nuanced ethical framework grounded in natural virtues such as simplicity, "wuwei" (noncoercive action), and harmony (Kohn, 2004). The principle of "wuwei," central to Daoist thought, does not imply passivity but rather attuning oneself to the natural order. In contrast to Confucianism's emphasis on ritual and prescriptive norms, Lao Tzu (2010) envisions a profound virtue (玄德) that transcends conventional rules. This virtue enables individuals to act effortlessly yet effectively by aligning themselves with the Dao's spontaneous rhythms, accomplishing tasks without coercion through the practice of wuwei, the art of "acting through non-action."

In this light, Lao Tzu (2010) champions a natural vision of moral cultivation. His critique targets not moral cultivation itself, but rather the rigid structures of Confucian moral indoctrination—its dependence on artificial norms and prescribed virtues like humaneness, righteousness, ritual propriety, and wisdom. In contrast, Lao Tzu offers an alternative ethical framework grounded in the Dao, emphasizing virtues such as compassion, frugality, and humility, which emerge organically through wuwei and tacit guidance, and are embodied in a way of life characterized by simplicity, non-contention, and harmony with nature's rhythms.

While often perceived as opposing philosophies, Daoism, in fact, complements Confucianism in cultivating a harmonious life, collectively shaping a Chinese cultural ethos that aligns human endeavor with natural laws. Rather than imposing rigid moral codes, Lao Tzu (2010) advocates for a spontaneous moral cultivation and governance where the leader's moral example is paramount. Through their virtuous presence, others are inspired to transform themselves. It is the intrusion of greed or ambition, especially among rulers, that distorts this organic process. Thus, even if Daoist moral cultivation objects Confucianism's emphasis on rigid rituals and social norms, its ultimate aspiration concurs with Confucianism: to build a peaceful, stable, and ethically grounded world (Cai, 2016).

Even Confucianism's emphasis on moral cultivation—extending from the individual to the family, state, and world—finds a parallel in Daoism. In Lao Tzu (2010)'s words: "Cultivate it in your person, and the character you develop will be genuine; cultivate it in your family, and its character will be abundant; cultivate it in your village, and its character will be enduring; cultivate it in the state, and its character will flourish; cultivate it in the world, and its character will be all-pervading" (Chap. 54). This ideal of Daoist moral cultivation, though rooted in a natural framework rather than prescriptive norms, echoes Confucianism's broader vision of building a flourishing and harmonious society.

Contemporary researchers have extensively examined the ethical implications of Daoism (see Kjellberg & Ivanhoe, 1996; Lai, 2007; Kemmerer, 2009; Nelson 2009; Chen, 2019; among others). Lai suggests that wuwei and ziran (spontaneity) together constitute an ethical framework that supports individual freedom beyond the constraints of conventional norms. Chen Guying (2012) challenges the widespread view that humanism is exclusively Confucian, maintaining that Daoism's conception of nature mostly refers to a humanistic nature and is socially relevant, as "nature and cultivation, or the Dao of Heaven and the Dao of human affairs, were always understood as being mutually inclusive in Pre-Qin era" (p. 108). Building on this perspective, Chen further asserts that Confucian and Daoist models continuously enrich one another throughout Chinese intellectual history.

In conclusion, Confucianism and Daoism function in a complementary manner within the tradition of moral cultivation. Whereas Confucianism focuses on individuals' familial and social responsibilities, Daoism emphasizes cultivating natural virtues and resisting excessive normalization and institutionalization. In contrast to Daoist spontaneity, Confucianism is renowned for its proactive and energetic attitude for life and politics, as reflected in *the Commentary on Changes*: "Heaven, in its motion, (gives the idea of) strength. The superior man, in accordance with this, nerves himself to ceaseless activity" (Confucius, 2016b, Appendix II). Yet this unrelenting drive can also produce tension and psychological strain, potentially leading to fatigue or insincerity, as it places considerable demand on individual ability and effort in a world of uncertainty.

This is where Daoism offers a crucial counterbalance. By embracing spontaneity and non-coercive action, Daoism acts as a safety valve against the rigidity and relentless pursuit of success that can distort human nature. Rather than measuring virtue solely by social conformity or ritual performance, Daoism redirects focus toward living authentically in harmony with the Dao, cultivating inner tranquility as the foundation of genuine moral character. This perspective helps guard against the moral hypocrisy that arises when excessive ethical demands or ostentatious displays of "virtue" overshadow sincere self-cultivation. Moreover, Daoism's philosophical influence profoundly shaped Confucian moral philosophy, which adopted concepts such as the "unity of Heaven and humanity" and the ideal of the "inner sage and outer king." These ideas enriched Confucianism's ethical framework with deeper metaphysical grounding while preserving its moral orientation.

In imperial China since the Han Dynasty, while Confucianism was officially upheld as the foundation of governance and education, rulers and intellectuals alike often incorporated elements of Classical Daoism to temper and augment mainstream Confucian thought, creating a dynamic of Confucianism and Daoism complementing each other (Zhang, 2016). This interplay was reflected in the lives of many Confucian scholar-officials, who embodied a dual identity often described as "external Confucianism and internal Daoism." Publicly, they upheld Confucian ideals of duty, order, and scholarship; privately, they often turned to Daoist solace, seeking spiritual freedom, inner peace, and attunement to the Dao (Tao & Guo, 2012). Thus, Confucianism and Daoism, while distinct, can be perceived as the two sides of the same coin in the pursuit of moral and spiritual development. If Confucianism acts as the engine driving societal progress, Daoism serves as the brake and shock absorber—moderating that drive and preserving individual well-being. Therefore, any meaningful discussion of Confucian moral cultivation must also consider its profound and inseparable connection to Daoist thought.

1.2.5.2 Buddhist, Mohist, and Legalist Perspectives on Moral Cultivation

Introduced from ancient India, Buddhism profoundly enriched Chinese culture by offering a path to spiritual liberation closely intertwined with ethical development. Core Buddhist concepts such as emptiness, causality, karma, Buddha nature, and sudden enlightenment deepened and broadened the metaphysical and ethical horizons of Chinese moral cultivation. For example, the doctrine of karma reinforced notions about moral responsibility, while the concept of emptiness offered a framework for detaching from selfish desires. The pursuit of ultimate liberation emphasizes compassion, altruism, and interdependence, which encourage kindness not just to loved ones, but toward all sentient beings, thereby broadening the scope of moral concern in Chinese thought. By gradually assimilating indigenous values, such as filial piety, faithfulness, and ancestor veneration, Buddhism deeply influenced the cultivation of virtues, the harmonization of human relationships, and the stabilization of social order in ancient China.

Mohism contributed to the discourse on moral cultivation by introducing the principle of impartial caring, or universal love, which, contrary to Confucianism's emphasis on graded love, proposes an equal ethical obligation toward all individuals. Another concept embodying impartial care is "the Heaven's Will," an impersonal cosmic justice that rewards moral conduct and punishes wickedness. Mozi argues that true virtue required aligning oneself with this universal order by extending equal concern to all people, regardless of personal relationships. Rejecting ritual-based ethics, he grounds moral development in introspection, authenticity, and utilitarian outcomes. Though Mohism eventually faded as a dominant philosophical school, its legacy persisted. The Han Dynasty Confucian scholar Dong Zhongshu notably integrated "heaven's will" into his synthesis of correlative cosmology, infusing Confucian ethics with a transcendent moral framework. This synthesis, while reinforcing the ethical imperative of moral cultivation in Confucianism, exemplifies the enduring cross-pollination among rival philosophical traditions.

Even Legalism offers an important counter-narrative, deepening our understanding of the complex political-ethical landscape of Chinese civilization. Unlike Confucian or Daoist emphasis on cultivation of virtue, Legalism reduces morality to a political tool designed to advance state objectives and serve the ruler's ambitions. Through its "carrot-and-stick" approach to governance, Legalism manipulates self-interest and fear to concentrate power, creating a hyperefficient bureaucracy geared toward three uncompromising ends: state wealth, military power, and social control. Although its tenure as a dominant ruling doctrine was brief, as seen in the swift collapse of the Qin dynasty, Legalism serves as a cautionary reminder that political order pursued without ethical grounding can devolve into systemic oppression. This tension between ethical idealism and political pragmatism remained a recurring feature in Chinese statecraft throughout history.

Still, Legalism is indispensable to understanding the evolution of Confucian moral-political thought, as its institutional principles were strategically assimilated by later Confucian reformers. Dong Zhongshu, for instance, deftly grafted Legalist techniques such as rule by law and centralized authority onto Confucian governance in exchange for imperial patronage. His hybrid model employed legal codes and rites as complementary instruments to promote humaneness and righteousness, while pragmatically supporting state consolidation— a characteristically Legalist priority. That said, he firmly adhered to Confucian ethical stance, holding that the virtue of humaneness should offer reassurance to others, whereas righteousness ought to be employed for self-correction, embodying Confucian principle of strict self-discipline and leniency towards others. This synthesis allowed Dong Zhongshu to reconcile Legalist methods with core Confucian principles, ultimately grounding governance in both moral cultivation and institutional control.

Far from disappearing after Qin Empire, Legalist principles endured as a pragmatic counterweight to Confucian idealism throughout imperial China. Where moral cultivation alone proved insufficient to prevent misconduct, Legalist-inspired penal systems provided crucial deterrents. More importantly, Legalism's institutional toolkit enabled structural reforms, particularly in challenging entrenched power blocs. Historical records reveal that many Confucian scholar-officials, during times of crisis, adopted Legalist-style measures—reforming land taxation, centralizing fiscal authority, and curbing concentrations of power and wealth that threatened dynastic stability. This dynamic highlights Confucianism's often-overlooked adaptive capacity, which echoed the Legalist approach of reforming existing structures to enhance efficiency and weaken the dominance of powerful elites. Thus, while Confucian moral cultivation prioritized social harmony, it also exhibited the flexibility to pursue measured reforms when circumstances demanded.

In conclusion, moral cultivation serves as a practical philosophy for navigating the complexities of a densely populated, agrarian society. For scholars, it charts a path toward moral integrity, political discernment, and even spiritual enlightenment. For rulers, it offers a framework for legitimate and effective governance, enabling them to educate the populace, uphold order, and mediate diverse interests. For ordinary people, it is more about a way of life that allows them to establish roots, raise families, and live together in harmony. This philosophical tradition has been central to the development of Chinese civilization, deeply shaping its values, institutions, and social fabric.

1.2.6 The Philosophical Nature of Moral Cultivation

Traditional Chinese philosophical thought is characterized by its fluidity and integrative nature, lacking the clear boundaries and specialized subfields typical of Western philosophy. Its rich philosophical inquiry is interwoven across a wide range of texts, necessitating a holistic approach and hermeneutical sensitivity to discern its underlying coherence and structure (Feng, 1983). Themes such as cosmology, epistemology, ethics, education, politics, and religion (Hu, 2016) are dispersed throughout prose, literature, and political discourse. Among these, the concept of moral cultivation emerges as a unifying thread—a valuable lens through which to understand the distinctive nature of Chinese philosophy. As the thread connecting diverse schools—from Confucian moral perfection to Daoist natural attunement—it reveals Chinese philosophy's fundamental concern: the transformative integration of cosmic principles, social harmony, and personal virtue.

The markedly different path of traditional Chinese philosophy from its Western counterpart led early Western thinkers, such as Hegel, to dismiss Confucius's Analects as mere commonplace morality and Lao Tzu's teachings as rudimentary (Hegel, 1837/2009). Such judgments, however, arose from a failure to recognize the distinctive nature and profound contributions of Chinese thought. Whereas much of Western philosophy emphasizes abstract logic and systematic reasoning, Chinese philosophy centers on a lived philosophy—one that applies ethical principles to real-world situations, guiding individuals in navigating social relationships and cultivating harmony and virtue in everyday life. This contrast raises fundamental questions: How did a philosophical tradition so distinct from the Greek-influenced model support a civilization as enduring as China? And what foundational principles have given Chinese philosophy its remarkable resilience?

This apparent paradox—that Chinese philosophy, while rich and comprehensive, often defies easy categorization within Western philosophical frameworks— compels us to move beyond surface comparisons and appreciate it on its own terms: Rather than critiquing it for lacking elements familiar to Western traditions, we should recognize it as a distinct and valuable branch within the global philosophical landscape. For three millennia, China developed an intricate system of thought with its own internal logic, methods of classification, and evolving trajectory. While the Western emphasis on conceptual reasoning and analytical dissection paves the way for scientific and epistemological progress, traditional Chinese philosophy forges a different yet equally profound mode of thinking. It integrates subjectivity and objectivity into a holistic worldview, blurring conventional boundaries between self and other, individual and collective, and humans and nature, all grounded in the harmony between Heaven and humanity.

Although this philosophical tradition did not develop a Western-style epistemology, it gave rise to the ethical-epistemological framework of "gongfu"—a disciplined, lifelong pursuit of moral excellence in alignment with cosmic principles. Emphasizing action and experience over pure reason and logic, gongfu explores how individuals acquire and embody moral virtues through learning, disciplined practice, reflection, and enlightenment. This process of moral cultivation is a cornerstone of Chinese philosophy, present not only in Confucianism but also in Daoism and Buddhism, all of which prioritize the process of "becoming" over "being." Individual moral cultivation, therefore, is understood as an ongoing journey of self-transformation.

Collectively, these three schools offer a comprehensive framework of philosophical inquiry and moral development, integrating intellectual contemplation with practical ethical engagement. In this context, traditional Chinese philosophy can be understood through the lens of moral cultivation, which emphasizes conscious efforts toward moral progress, the dissemination of ethical values, and the realization of political ideals. Through this ongoing practice, individuals develop virtue that radiates outward—shaping families, communities, and society at large—a role often fulfilled by religion in other cultural traditions.

The nuanced, contextually grounded nature of traditional Chinese philosophy has often led to misunderstandings about the philosophical significance of its thought. Unlike the Western expectation of philosophy as a systematic metaphysics centered on a "single authoritative text," Chinese thought unfolds through sustained intertextual dialogue within a dynamic and evolving philosophical tradition. Take Confucianism: The significance of *the Analects* lies not in whether it meets Western expectations of "philosophy" as abstract theorization, but in how it inaugurated a generative framework—one that successive Confucians developed into a cohesive, systemic tradition centered on self-cultivation, social harmony, and virtuous governance.

While Chinese thought may not engage in metaphysical inquiry in the same manner as some Western traditions, it is nevertheless deeply rooted in metaphysical concepts that inform its ethical and moral dimensions. Unlike Western philosophy, which generally treats metaphysics and ethics as separate domains, Chinese thought sees them as intricately intertwined, so much so that any attempt to separate them risks an incomplete or distorted understanding of Chinese thought (Perkins, 2016). Concepts like the "Way of Heaven" (天道) and "heavenly principle" (天理) in Confucianism are not detached abstractions but normative foundations that guide ethical conduct, structure human relationships, and reinforce social harmony. Likewise, the concept of the "heart-mind" (心) transcends a mere psychological faculty; it serves as the ground of moral agency where virtues are cultivated and ethical choices enacted. Further supporting this view are enduring discussions of human nature, the role of emotions, and the ongoing process of self-cultivation, all of which attest to the richness, coherence, and distinctive character of Chinese approaches to moral philosophy.

Confucianism's dual mission, namely, the integrative pursuit of moral cultivation and philosophical discourse, exemplifies this characteristic (Liu, 2014) and reinforces the central argument that moral cultivation should be viewed as a comprehensive philosophical system encompassing both metaphysical inquiry and the pursuit of moral development. It is through the practice of moral cultivation, guided by the framework of Heaven-humanity unity, that we can appreciate the full scope of Chinese thought, witnessing how individual transformation seamlessly expands into a vision of universal harmony and societal flourishing.

Delving deeper into this practice, a key distinction emerges between Chinese moral cultivation and Western ethics regarding their treatment of human emotions. While many Western traditions often portray reason and emotion as distinct—if not opposing—forces, with reason typically holding primacy, Chinese ethics adopts a more integrated view, valuing the dynamic interplay between moral principles, emotional responsiveness, and aesthetic sensibility. This emphasis on feelings is particularly evident in Confucian virtues such as humaneness and filial piety, which are rooted in natural affections toward family and friends. Similarly, qualities like empathy, loyalty, and respect are not treated as abstract obligations but as heartfelt expressions of a compassionate mind, essential to the authentic process of moral growth.

Another key difference involves the purpose of moral cultivation. Confucianism, for instance, adopts a socio-centric perspective, in contrast to the more individualistic orientation found in traditional Western ethics (Bockover, 2010). Whereas Aristotle's framework emphasizes personal virtue and the individual's fulfillment within the polis, a dominant strand of ancient Chinese philosophy—particularly Confucianism—prioritizes the cultivation of moral character not merely as a path to personal flourishing, but as a foundation for building a well-ordered society grounded in harmonious relationships and ethical governance. Moral cultivation thus becomes a collective endeavor, aimed at addressing social unrest and promoting the ideal of good governance for "All under Heaven." This shared aspiration deeply informs Chinese cultural values and everyday conduct, making moral cultivation a cornerstone for understanding ancient Chinese civilization.

Chinese philosophical traditions ground moral cultivation in enduring metaphysical frameworks that presuppose a coherent, purposive cosmic order. This belief inspired a transformative ethical pursuit: aligning human behavior with the rhythms of Heaven and Earth to achieve social harmony. While modern sensibilities may question the pursuit of a singular "ultimate truth," the profound sociocultural influence of this paradigm on Chinese society remains undeniable. Dismissing these philosophies as mere historical relics overlooks their unique historical context and enduring contributions to Chinese civilization's exceptional continuity, as well as their profound influence on Chinese society today. In an age increasingly preoccupied with discord, the emphasis on relational harmony within this intellectual heritage offers more than historical curiosity—it calls for critical engagement to address modernity's discontents.

Accordingly, comprehending Chinese moral cultivation demands a holistic and interdisciplinary research paradigm. As a dynamic and interconnected discourse, moral cultivation spans diverse yet complementary schools of thought and is deeply embedded in Chinese society, shaped by, and in turn shaping, political institutions, educational systems, artistic traditions, and historical development. Fully grasping the nuances of this tradition requires conceptual integration across disciplines. Such a paradigm helps illuminate the structural logic of Chinese intellectual life and guards against the distortions that arise when reductive analytical frameworks are imposed on a culture defined by profound interconnection. This emphasis on systemic understanding is not unique to Eastern thought. Western thinkers such as Max Weber and John Dewey likewise employed holistic methodologies to explore the philosophical underpinnings of civilization, illustrating how transcultural approaches can yield deeper insights into complex moral and cultural systems.

1.3 Fundamental Questions of Chinese Civilization

Through the lens of moral cultivation, this book offers a comprehensive exploration of Chinese philosophy and civilization, seeking to answer fundamental questions: What are its metaphysical foundations and ethical values? How are these virtues cultivated? And what constitutes the essence of Chinese identity—its enduring ethos, national character, cognitive patterns, and the institutional structures that have sustained social cohesion for millennia? In addition to these core inquiries, the book examines related themes such as China's secular orientation and civilizational resilience. It then critically assesses structural problems, cultural constraints, the role of hierarchy, social mobility, and the intricate relationship between Chinese cultural orientation and scientific development, tracing their shared philosophical roots.

Having examined these foundational questions, the book now addresses its broader and ambitious objectives: What role might revitalized traditional thought play in developing more ethically grounded democratic systems? How might the generative virtue—life-nurturing, renewal, and co-flourishing (生生之德)—inform global challenges in our contemporary era? What significance does the concept of the "Greater Self" (大我) hold for humanity's collective future? These inquiries ultimately converge on the defining question of our age: Can diverse civilizations achieve harmonious coexistence amid an increasingly interconnected yet contested world?

Admittedly, approaching complex phenomena like Chinese civilization through broad, overarching questions risks overgeneralization and may obscure its internal diversity. Yet, such an approach remains essential for counterbalancing the fragmentation that hyper-specialization can create, enabling us to discern the defining characteristics of Chinese civilization as an integrated whole. This calls for a holistic and transdisciplinary understanding of human history, one that bridges disciplines like philosophy, education, politics, cultural studies, and civilizational analysis. These expansive inquiries anchor individual meaning within collective cultural frameworks, transform historical wisdom into navigational tools for contemporary challenges, and ultimately reveal the profound interdependence shaping our global future.

To minimize the pitfalls of overgeneralization, the book consciously avoids normative evaluations—whether casting China's philosophical traditions as right or wrong, or superior or inferior. Instead, it situates Chinese moral values and concepts within their historical context, allowing readers to form their own interpretations. The analysis maintains critical balance, recognizing both the enduring relevance and inherent constraints of these ideas. It also avoids treating these conceptual frameworks as monolithic or static: Instead, it embraces diverse perspectives from various philosophers and schools within Chinese thought; by analyzing the evolution of the ideas over time, it reveals the dynamic development and nuances of China's moral-cultural ecosystem.

It is noteworthy that certain Western philosophical terms are used in this book as bridges for cross-cultural understanding. While the conceptual frameworks of Western and Chinese thought differ significantly, Chinese philosophy can be interpreted using Western philosophical tools and categories (Allinson, 1989). For example, Philip Perkins suggests that if the term "metaphysics" is defined broadly enough to encompass the diversity within European philosophical traditions, it can also be meaningfully applied to aspects of Chinese thought, thus facilitating a productive intercultural dialogue (Perkins, 2016). That said, such an approach requires careful discernment, with an awareness of the cultural nuances and contextual meanings these borrowed terms carry in both traditions.

Traditionally, two approaches are frequently used in both philosophical inquiry and scientific study. One involves a close, detailed examination of a specific theme, much like a frog observing its immediate surroundings. The other adopts a broader, panoramic perspective, like a bird surveying the landscape from above, particularly useful for engaging with foundational questions. This exploration will employ both methods, akin to a drone capable of soaring for the full terrain and descending for intricate details. By fluidly navigating between these perspectives, it can effectively grapple with fundamental questions while appreciating the nuances and richness of the details.

References

Allinson, R. E. (1989). *Understanding the Chinese mind: The philosophical roots*. Oxford University Press.

Barbalet, J., & Barbalet, J. M. (2017). *Confucianism and the Chinese self*. Palgrave Macmillan.

Bergsten, C. F., Freeman, C., Lardy, N. R., & Mitchell, D. J. (2008). *China's rise: Challenges and opportunities*. Peterson Institute.

Bockover, M. I. (2010). Confucianism and ethics in the western philosophical tradition I: Foundational concepts. *Philosophy Compass, 5*(4), 307–316.

Branson, B. (2020). The intertwining of philosophy and religion in the Western tradition. In B. Branson & C. Hendricks (Eds.), *Introduction to philosophy: Philosophy of religion* (pp. 9–21). Rebus Community Press.

Cai, Q. (2016). The unfolding of indoctrination and self-indoctrination in Wang Bi's commentary on Laozi. *Journal of Yunnan University: Social Science Edition, 15*(4), 68–74.

Chen, Y. (2019). Chinese and Western philosophy and its communication from the perspective of civilizationism. *Journal of Wuhan University, 4*, 64–74.

Chen, G. (2012). *The spirit of humanism in classical Daoism*. Chinese Book Press.

Confucius. (2016a). *Analects*. (J. Legge, Ed. & Trans.). In *Confucianism: The four books and five classics—collected works of Confucius*. Delphi Classics. (Original work published c. 551–c. 479 BCE).

Confucius. (2016b). *The commentaries on Changes*. (J. Legge, Ed. & Trans.). In *Confucianism: The four books and five classics—collected works of Confucius*. Delphi Classics. (Original work published c. 551–c. 479 BCE).

De Wulf, M. (1922/2008). *Philosophy and civilization in the middle ages*. Wipf and Stock Publishers.

Dewey, J. (1931). *Philosophy and civilization*. Minton, Balch & Co..

Durant, W. (2014). *The complete story of civilization*. Simon and Schuster.

Emerson, R. W. (1904). *The complete works of Ralph Waldo Emerson: Miscellanies* (Vol. 11).

Feng, Y. (1983). *History of Chinese philosophy*. Princeton University Press.

Foust, M. A. (2017). *Confucianism and American philosophy*. SUNY Press.

French, H. W. (2017). *Everything under the heavens: How the past helps shape China's push for global power*. Vintage.

Gibbon, E. (2001). History of the decline and fall of the Roman empire. *ebooksMall*.

Hegel, G.W.F. (2009). *Lectures on the history of philosophy 1825-6: Volume I: Introduction and oriental philosophy* (R. F. Brown, trans.). Oxford University Press. (Original work published 1837).

Hu, S. (2016). *The outlines of history of Chinese philosophy*. China Bookstore.

Huntington, S. P. (1993). The clash of civilizations? *Foreign Affairs, 72*(3), 22–49.

Huntington, S. P. (1996). *The clash of civilizations and the remaking of world order*. Simon & Schuster.

Jacques, M. (2009). *When China rules the world: The end of the western world and the birth of a new global order*. Penguin.

Kemmerer, L. (2009). The great unity: Daoism, nonhuman animals, and human ethics. *Journal for Critical Animal Studies, 7*(2), 63–83.

Kennedy, K. J., & Lee, J. C. K. (2020). Religion, modernities and education: Contexts for Asia's religious education. In *Religious education in Asia* (pp. 1–11). Routledge.

Kjellberg, P., & Ivanhoe, P. J. (Eds.). (1996). *Essays on skepticism, relativism, and ethics in the Zhuangzi*. SUNY Press.

Kohn, L. (2004). *Cosmos and community: The ethical dimension of Daoism*. Three Pines Press.

Lai, K. (2007). Ziran and Wuwei in the Daodejing: An ethical assessment. *Dao, 6*(4), 325–337.

Lai, K. (2017). *An introduction of Chinese philosophy*. Cambridge University Press.

Lao Tzu (2010). *Daodejing*. In R. T. Ames & D. L. Hall (Eds. & Trans.), *Dao de jing: A philosophical translation*. Ballantine books. (Original work published c. 6th cn. BCE).

Liu, H. (2014). *Research on Confucianism's thoughts of moral cultivation*. [doctoral dissertation, Lanzhou University].

Mencius. (2016). *Mencius*. In J. Legge (Ed. & Trans.), *Confucianism: The four books and five classics—collected works of Confucius*. Delphi Classics. (Original work published c. 4th–3rd century BCE).

Nelson, E. S. (2009). Responding with Dao: Early Daoist ethics and the environment. *Philosophy East and West*, 294–316.

Nobre, R. F. (2006). Culture and perspectivism in Nietzsche's and Weber's view. *Teoria & Sociedade, 2*(SE), 68–89.

Perkins, F. (2016). Metaphysics in Chinese philosophy. In E. N. Zalta (Ed.), *the Stanford Encyclopedia of philosophy (winter 2016 edition)*. https://plato.stanford.edu/archives/sum2019/entries/chinese-metaphysics/

Peters, M. A., & Meier, T. (2025). Civilizational collapse and the philosophy of post-apocalyptic survival: An introduction. In M. A. Peters & T. Meier (Eds.), *Civilizational collapse and the philosophy of post-apocalyptical survival* (pp. 1–24). Peter Lang.

Prior, W. J. (2007). Moral philosophy and moral cultivation. In B. Wilburn (Ed.), *Moral cultivation: Essays on the development of character and virtue* (pp. 49–67). Rowman & Littlefield.

Redmond, G., & Hon, T. K. (2014). *Teaching the I Ching (book of changes)*. Oxford University Press. https://academic.oup.com/book/8934/chapter-abstract/155250084?redirectedFrom=fulltext.

Russell, B. (2013). *History of western philosophy: Collectors edition*. Routledge.

Schweitzer, A. (1923). *The philosophy of civilization*. A. & C. Black.

Slote, M. (2016). Moral self-cultivation east and west: A critique. *Journal of Moral Education, 45*(2), 192–206.

Stone, L. (2018). Foreword: China is always China. In Z. You, A. G. Rud, & Y. Hu (Eds.), *The philosophy of Chinese moral education*. McMillan Palgrave.

Stroud, S. R. (2006). Constructing a Deweyan theory of moral cultivation. *Contemporary Pragmatism, 3*(2), 99–116.

Tao, C., & Guo, Q. (2012). The values of Confucian benevolence and the universality of the Confucian way of extending love. *Frontiers of Philosophy in China, 7*(1), 20–54.

Wang, H. (2015). A genealogical study of de: Poetical correspondence of sky, earth, and humankind in the early Chinese virtuous rule of benefaction. *Philosophy East & West, 65*(1), 81–124.
Weber, M. (2001). *The Protestant ethic and the spirit of capitalism* (S. Kalberg, Ed.; S. Kalberg, trans.). Routledge.
Wong, D. B. (2014). Cultivating the self in concert with others. *Dao companion to the Analects*, 171–197.
Xunzi. (2015). *Xunzi*. Beijing: China Bookstore. (Original work published c. 4th–3rd century BCE).
Zhang, S. (2016, February 19). *Aesthetic enlightenment. China Art Newspaper*.

Chapter 2
The Unity of Heaven and Humanity: On the Origin of Moral Cultivation

Ancient Chinese philosophy regards Heaven and Earth as cosmic exemplars, serving as the ultimate sources of moral guidance and societal order. Central to this paradigm is the notion of the Way of Heaven, a principle of cosmic regularity that undergirds virtue, shapes ethical norms, and harmonizes individual cultivation with the collective good (Brown, 2016). Unlike traditions that root morality in divine revelation, mainstream Chinese thought situates ethical authority within Heaven (tian)—conceived as a blend of celestial mandate and the patterned coherence of the natural world—emphasizing the alignment of human conduct with the inherent rhythms and structures of the cosmos rather than with divine edicts.

These ideas culminated in the framework of "the unity and harmony of Heaven and humanity (天人合一)," which holds that humanity and the cosmos are not separate but interconnected parts of a single, continuous whole, calling individuals to return to the innate virtue embedded in human nature. This holistic worldview articulates the imperative of situating the self within larger domains, whether natural order or sociopolitical sphere, thereby attaining a more expansive moral vision and attunement to the underlying principles of the cosmos. More than a philosophical abstraction, this belief lies at the heart of traditional Chinese thought, serving as both the foundation of moral cultivation and a key to understanding the enduring institutional coherence of Chinese civilization.

It is important to emphasize that the unity between Heaven and humanity is not exclusive to Confucianism, but a fundamental concern shared across all major schools of Chinese thought (Fang, 2003). It serves as both a foundational principle and an ultimate goal for Confucianism, Daoism, Mohism, Legalism, and Sinicized forms of Buddhism (Ding, 2015). This metaphysical framework has profoundly shaped the Chinese cultural ethos, influencing cognitive patterns, moral values, educational ideals, and aesthetic sensibilities—fostering a perspective that is holistic, relational, and oriented toward long-term considerations.

Z. You, Y. Hu, *Philosophy and Civilization: How the Idea of Moral Cultivation Shaped China*, East-West Dialogues in Educational Philosophy and Theory,
https://doi.org/10.1007/978-981-95-5660-1_2

2.1 Heaven-Humanity Relationship in Chinese Civilization

In Chinese thought, "tian (天)" or "Heaven" extends beyond just the physical sky to carry rich cultural meanings that span mythology, religion, transcendence, ethical values, and political legitimacy. In both philosophy and governance, "Heaven" is understood as the embodiment of cosmic will and natural order—expressed through the concept of "the Mandate of Heaven" (天命), which grants rulers legitimacy to rule, conditional upon their adherence to Heaven's ethical preference. At its heart lies the imperative for promoting virtuous leadership and a shared ethical aspiration through moral cultivation—a belief essential to grasping the foundations of Chinese civilization.

2.1.1 Cosmological and Ethical Implications of Heaven

While both the Chinese concept of "tian" and the Western notion of "heaven" evoke a sense of the divine, they differ markedly in meaning. Unlike Western idea of heaven as a separate realm governed by a higher power, "tian" (hereafter referred to as Heaven in this book) encompasses a wide range of implications including deity, sky, nature, principle, and the essence of the universe. It signifies the ultimate source of power shaping human destiny and embodies absolute virtue, or even morality itself. This nuanced and multifaceted conception forms a cornerstone of Chinese culture.

In the dawn of Chinese history, reverence for Heaven, alongside the worship of gods and spirits, had played a significant role in life. Through the practice of divination, Heaven revealed its will via oracle bones: pieces of ox scapulae and turtle plastrons that, when exposed to intense heat, developed cracks interpreted by diviners as ill omens or auspicious signs. Although such practice was eventually abandoned, belief in Heaven persisted. As people observed the regularity of celestial phenomena, they abstracted these patterns into image or symbolic representations, elevating them beyond mere fortune-telling to address broader ethical and political concerns. This emphasis on predictable order distinguished Heaven from the more capricious deities of earlier traditions, embodying a moral and purposeful force guiding the world (Perkins, 2015).

The ancient oracle script offers a fascinating glimpse into early Chinese conceptions of Heaven. The hieroglyphic character "tian" depicting a human figure beneath a square "天" signifies both Heaven's elevated position to humanity and humanity's intrinsic connection to it. During the Shang Dynasty (c. 1600 BCE to c. 1046 BCE), both Heaven and the deities within it were revered, though greater emphasis was placed on the gods. The Zhou Dynasty (c. 1046 BCE to 256 BCE) ushered in an important shift in Chinese thought. While preserving reverence for both, the Zhou reconceptualized Heaven as a supreme, inclusive, and impartial authority governing human affairs. This shift crystallized in the "Mandate of Heaven," a cosmic doctrine that tied dynastic legitimacy and the ruler's fate directly to their "de" (moral virtue)—positioning them as stewards of order, peace, and righteousness for their subjects. No longer merely a physical or spiritual presence, Heaven now embodied an ethical imperative, irrevocably linking political power to ethical accountability.

Multiple viewpoints exist regarding the essence of Heaven. Modern scholar Feng Youlan identifies five key interpretations of Heaven in Chinese classics: the material Heaven, the Heaven of lordship, the Heaven of destiny, the Heaven of nature, and the Heaven of righteousness (Feng, 2001). Among these, Confucianism's focus on the Heaven of righteousness and Daoism's emphasis on the Heaven of nature stand out for their rich philosophical implications. For many Chinese thinkers, Heaven represents either the ultimate source of moral order or the supreme principle in itself.

The concept of Heaven evolved throughout history. While the early Zhou Dynasty still emphasized Heaven's religious connotations, later Zhou philosophers largely reframed it as the intrinsic source of virtue or a natural generative force. Building upon this, scholars of the Song and Ming dynasties (960–1644 CE) further deepened its metaphysical dimensions, developing increasingly sophisticated ontological frameworks. Zhang Zai introduced the concept of "ultimate void" (太虚), a boundless wellspring of qi (vital energy); Zhou Dunyi proposed the idea of "the boundless" (无极, or non-polarity); the Cheng Brothers and Zhu Xi formulated "the heavenly principle" (天理), while Lu Jiuyuan and Wang Yangming identified the cosmic principle as internal, referring to it simply as "the heart," which encompasses the universe. With these philosophizing efforts in Neo-Confucianism, the concept of Heaven completely sheds its anthropomorphic, divine implications to become an abstract metaphysical-ethical idea. The following chapter will discuss the nuanced implications of these concepts for understanding moral cultivation.

Much like God in European culture, Heaven stands as the supreme moral arbiter. But unlike the Judeo-Christian God who issues decrees and demands obedience, Heaven in Chinese philosophy silently embodies the principles of harmony, balance, authority, kindness, and righteousness. To defy its natural-moral laws is to invite chaos; to align with them is to unlock the deepest wisdom governing life's various domains: from statecraft and warfare to medicine, human relationships, and the cultivation of virtue. Accordingly, those who grasped Heaven's Way were revered as sages or "true men," their insights steering empires and shaping the moral compass of generations.

The ideas of Heaven and Heaven's Way permeate the Chinese consciousness. Even among the nonreligious, few would deny its enduring significance. Heaven inspires awe and reverence not only for its perceived role in shaping destiny but also for embodying the supreme wisdom and impartiality that sustain all things. This reverence helps explain why ancient Chinese cosmology, while involving sophisticated astronomical observation and calendar making, was primarily approached within a ritualistic framework. Sky gazers observed the Heavens not merely to chart celestial movements or measure time, but more importantly, to interpret the heavenly mandate—the cosmic signs believed to confer legitimacy upon rulers and guide the course of the empire.

2.1.2 The Harmonious Unity of Heaven and Humanity

Though distinct in their method and emphasis, Confucianism and Daoism converge in their foundational pursuit: self-cultivation through aligning the human path with the Way of Heaven, ultimately achieving the harmony of Heaven and humanity. Daoism emphasizes alignment with the Dao—the spontaneous, natural rhythm of the universe—advocating wuwei (noninterference) to attain inner tranquility and manifest one's inherent virtue. Confucianism, while similarly acknowledging Heaven's transcendent authority, prioritizes its ethical dimension, framing moral refinement and social responsibility as the path to cosmic and human unity.

The harmony of Heaven and humanity is deeply rooted in the cosmic triad of Heaven, Earth, and Humankind. As articulated in *the Commentaries on the Book of Changes*, "They exhibited the way of heaven, calling yin and yang; the way of earth, calling the weak and the strong; and the way of men, under the names of humaneness and righteousness" (Appendix 5 Chapter II. 4). This tripartite harmony reveals an inherent correspondence between cosmic patterns and moral norms, framing ethical conduct as an earthly manifestation of celestial order. Here, Heaven is not merely a backdrop but the architect of social and natural harmony, weaving the human realm into its moral fabric. To act justly is to align with the universe itself; to deviate is to rupture the sacred symmetry binding all existence.

While the unity of Heaven and humanity may blur the boundaries between subject and object, potentially discouraging the detached observation crucial for scientific inquiry, it presents an alternative framework that helps alleviate the tensions inherent in ontologies centered exclusively on God, humans, or nature within moral philosophy. Theocentric worldviews, for instance, often suppressed individual autonomy; anthropocentric models risk inflating the authority of reason, inviting human hubris and an illusory sense of control; and naturalistic ontologies may drift toward nihilism, eroding meaning and fueling the existential disquiet of modernity. In contrast, the vision of unity between Heaven and humanity offers a more integrated and relational worldview—one that may help relieve the psychological and societal pressures generated by reductive, single-axis ontological models.

2.1.2.1 Generative Virtue

In contrast to the micro-perspective that fixates on nature's cruelty, traditional Chinese culture adopts a macro vision, centering on its life-sustaining essence. Ancient Chinese viewed Heaven and Earth as generating forces, embodying the generative virtue (sheng-sheng zhi de, 生生之德) that manifests in life-nurturing, renewal, and mutual flourishing (Confucius, 2016b, Xici II). The first "sheng" signifies life, vitality, birth, and growth, the generative force that nurtures all existence. The repetition of sheng suggests perpetual renewal of life, a dynamic process weaving all beings into a web of harmonious interdependence. This worldview reveals a cosmos rooted not in brutality, but in benevolent creativity—an enduring commitment to fostering life in all its forms. The significance of the universe being life-generative in Chinese culture is that it transforms a cosmological observation into a powerful ethical framework, guiding human behavior towards fostering well-being, promoting growth, and living harmoniously within an interconnected and ever-unfolding cosmos.

This deep ethical and cosmological commitment to generative life permeates various schools of Chinese philosophical thought. In Daoism, it manifests as the creative power of the Dao—a life-sustaining force that nourishes the natural world and fosters harmony in human affairs. Confucianism views it as the vital pulse of the cosmos, guiding all living beings toward growth, moral development, and peaceful coexistence. Even Legalism, often perceived as antithetical to "sheng-sheng" due to its punitive methods and capacity for destruction, can arguably be seen as contributing to the broader cycle of renewal—like a typhoon that, though uprooting trees, clears the ground for future growth. This reflects nature's cyclical rhythm: harsh, perhaps, yet ultimately regenerative. All these traditions underscore a continuous process of generation, transformation, and renewal, both in individual lives and in the broader social order.

The Chinese philosophical emphasis on generative life shares notable parallels with Aristotle's concept of eudaimonia, often translated as "flourishing." Both traditions underscore the importance of leading an ethical life characterized by excellence and fulfillment through the realization of one's potential and the cultivation of virtues, supported by engagement with others in the broader world. Yet, a fundamental distinction lies in their underlying principles: Whereas eudaimonia centers on individual excellence and personal virtue as the path to flourishing, the Chinese notion of mutual flourishing places greater emphasis on interconnectedness and interdependence—not only as a context for moral development, but as a constitutive part of virtue itself.

Confucianism, a philosophy rooted in ethical living and social harmony, places mutual flourishing at the heart of its virtues, particularly humaneness and ritual propriety. As Confucian Dai Zhen insightfully explains, "By observing the generative virtue as life-nurturing, renewing, and co-flourishing, one can understand the meaning of humaneness; observing the inherent patterns of the world, one can comprehend ritual propriety" (Dai, 1724–1777). Mutual flourishing embraces compassion to others and the creation of conditions that support their growth and success. It calls for a generous and inclusive big-picture perspective that fosters the prosperity of all living beings by maintaining balance through moderation and consciously avoiding extremes or absolutes. After all, to seek an absolute is to risk inviting its inevitable opposite, for absolute brightness implies the presence of absolute darkness. The world thrives on the interplay of difference and diversity, which provide the opportunities and resilience needed to navigate life's uncertainties.

Humans are thus urged to align themselves with celestial principles, supporting one another's growth to restore balance among individuals and between Heaven and humanity. This ideal transcends the bounds of a mere belief system, functioning as an educational and ethical framework that also informs social and political life, revealing the deeper meaning of human existence. It embodies a wisdom that places the collective good and the long-term flourishing of all above the pursuit of short-term personal gain. Through a selfless and wholehearted embrace of the larger community and social order, individuals attune themselves to the cosmic rhythm—fostering a world of mutual flourishing and lasting harmony.

2.1.2.2 Empathic Resonance

Achieving harmony with Heaven requires "gan-tong" (感通)—an empathic, spiritually attuned perception that transcends mere observation and analysis. This interactive-sensory attunement allows the self to perceive its intrinsic bond with the world, where human and natural rhythms engage in mutual resonance. Such a heightened awareness allows individuals to intuit the underlying patterns, principles, and truths of the universe, guiding ethical conduct in alignment with the cosmic flow. The hexagram "Xian" (䷞) in *the Book of Changes*, depicting a mountain crowned by a lake, echoes this idea. It illustrates how water nourishes the mountain while also alluding to a romantic connection between a young man and woman—symbolizing the subtle chemistry through which humans sense, respond to, and harmonize with one another.

The hexagram "Xian" illustrates a distinctly Chinese emphasis on holistic, subtle, and intuitive perception, particularly in discerning moral relationships between individuals and in the interconnectedness of humanity and nature. It portrays the harmonious interplay of Yin and Yang, the feminine and masculine forces that generate all life. Through this dynamic, Xian affirms an intuitive attunement to the harmony of Heaven and Earth, nurtured through embracing complementary opposites, recognizing the interdependence of all existence, and honoring the ceaseless cycles of transformation and renewal.

This sensitivity is the wellspring of humaneness, from which compassion and reciprocity emerge, not as imposed duties, but as natural outgrowths of our interconnected existence. Within the heart, intuition complements reason, offering a holistic grasp of the world's impermanence and the subtle interdependent realities that reason alone cannot fully apprehend. From this intuitive awareness arises love, the deepest force in the cosmos. Only through spontaneous, selfless care—free from the constraints of ego—can we attain the impartial resonance that aligns human life with the ethical order of Heaven.

2.1.2.3 The Heaven's Way and Human Immortality

Across cultures, the concept of the Heavens has profoundly shaped human understanding. From the vaulted ceilings of Christian cathedrals to the celestial pathways charted by Chinese sages, the relationship between humanity and the divine has long captivated the human imagination. In the West, particularly within Christianity, God is often conceived as an architect gazing upon His creation from afar. This perceived divide has inspired efforts to bridge the divine-human gap through studying divine revelation, interpreting the world as a sacred text, and seeking communion with the divine, often with the promise of immortality in the afterlife. Such pursuits had, in turn, fueled intellectual and scientific endeavors, as humanity sought to uncover the workings of divine creation.

In contrast to many Western perspectives, Eastern philosophies like Confucianism offer a different narrative. Heaven, though exalted, is not wholly separate from humanity; its principles echo within the human heart, and the ethical path mirrors the celestial order. This belief served as a moral compass, guiding the pursuit of virtue and harmonious life. Consequently, much of ancient Chinese philosophy focuses on exploring the intricacies of the Heaven-human relationship and contemplating ethics through concepts such as the Mandate of Heaven, the Way of Heaven, and the heavenly principle.

Interestingly, the Way of Heaven embodies the ultimate ideal of immortality within the indigenous Chinese this-worldly perspective, which lacks a definitive framework for postmortem soul immortality, leaving the ultimate question of life after death largely unresolved. For many ancient Chinese, immortality, if attainable, lies in attuning oneself to earthly existence and achieving harmony between Heaven and humanity. This belief system invites a profound exploration of virtuous conduct, whether ethical or spontaneous, in navigating life's challenges and fulfilling its intrinsic value. In Classical Daoism, immortality is attained through harmonizing with Dao, the eternal natural order. In Confucianism, it is found in aligning one's actions with the cosmic order, leaving behind a moral legacy, and contributing to the flourishing of the world. Such a legacy, honored and remembered by future generations, becomes a form of enduring presence—an earthly immortality.[1]

2.1.3 *Moral Cultivation as Geo-Cultural Expression of the Heavenly Way*

It is essential to acknowledge that philosophical thought and social norms seldom emerge from abstract speculation alone; rather, they are deeply influenced by intricate interplay among geography, climate, economic conditions, and social organization. This section explores how agricultural patterns, geo-cultural milieus, and shifting familial and societal structures jointly shaped the conceptions of Heaven and the broader paradigm of moral cultivation.

[1] As Shusun Bao declares, true immortality (legacy) comes in three forms: virtue, contribution, and lasting words. This statement is recorded in the chapter of 24th year of Duke Xiang, *the Chronicle of Zuo*.

2.1.3.1 Agrarian Cosmology: Tilling and Heaven

To fully appreciate the role of Heaven in ancient China, it must be understood within the context of a unique and advanced agrarian civilization. Like other early riverine agrarian civilizations such as Mesopotamia, Egypt, and the Indus valley, ancient China flourished along fertile river plains. However, unlike these three, China benefited from arguably more favorable geographic and climatic conditions. Mesopotamia and Egypt, situated in arid regions, relied heavily on irrigations and were hemmed in by deserts and mountains, somewhat limiting agricultural flexibility and territorial expansion. The Indus Valley, while agriculturally rich, grappled with unstable river patterns due to erratic monsoons and relatively limited access to external resource networks.

In contrast, China's more temperate climate and expansive arable lands supported greater agricultural productivity, territorial expansion, and political endurance, which deeply informed its cosmological and moral worldview. Though not entirely isolated, China's geography—including surrounding seas, deserts, and plateaus—offered a degree of natural protection. Its chief external pressures came from nomadic tribes to the north, whereas its northwestern frontiers functioned as a key conduit for cultural and commercial exchange. This combination of vast land, favorable climate, trade routes, and relative security enabled intensive agriculture and the formation of large, multiethnic, kinship-based communities along the Yellow and Yangtze River basins and their tributaries. Such geographic breadth and ecological diversity provided fertile ground, both literally and figuratively, for the development of overarching cosmological concepts like "Heaven."

Furthermore, sustaining such a large-scale agricultural civilization necessitated a highly organized society, a context that profoundly shaped conceptions of morality and Heaven. Land cultivation involved labor-intensive tasks requiring coordinated communal effort to clear forests, construct reservoirs and flood control systems, and till the soil. As early as 3300 BCE, the Liangzhu culture demonstrated this level of organization through the construction of city walls and sophisticated irrigation systems designed to support expanding agriculture and a growing population. Within this densely agrarian community, values such as harmony, ancestor veneration and lineage, ritual, and mutual assistance took root, reinforcing a strong social fabric grounded in family and clan ties. This patriarchal kinship system, with the father as the central authority and lineage traced through the male line, formed the sociocultural foundation upon which traditional Chinese moral cultivation was built.

Heaven, essential for agricultural life, was profoundly connected to rituals, which served as the bedrock of ethical life in ancient China. From the earliest times, successful farming heavily relied on natural rainfall and precise knowledge of seasonal patterns (Wang, 2016). This connection to the Heavens thus was not merely a matter of religious reverence, but a vital concern for survival, as celestial time was, in effect, farming time—critical to the well-being of clans and the stability of the state. Consequently, rulers had a sacred duty to observe the Heavens, a practice that conferred both practical authority and immense prestige. According to *the Book of Documents,* a key responsibility of ancient kings was to send emissaries to study celestial movements and establish a calendar to guide agricultural activities (Confucius, 2016c). Archaeological discoveries from the prehistoric "Taosi" site supports this connection, revealing a structure that likely functioned both as a celestial observatory and ceremonial center. This dual-purpose space enabled the tracking of the sun's movements, the measurement of seasonal shifts, and the determination of optimal planting times, while also serving as a setting for rituals tied to the agricultural cycle.

This emphasis on celestial observation in China carries profound philosophical significance, highlighting the intrinsic interconnectedness between Heaven and humanity. Unlike classical Western traditions, which often attribute the first principle or self-causality to a transcendent God, Chinese thought tends to regard Heaven as the fundamental nature of existence itself (Perkins, 2015). In this perspective, humans are not passive observers but active participants in dynamic cosmic process, where the phenomenal world and the underlying noumenal order are intimately interwoven.

While the astronomical calendar provided guidance on the timing of agricultural seasons, it was the accumulated wisdom of elders that refined and adapted farming practices to local conditions. Their accumulated experience rendered them invaluable advisors, respected for their practical wisdom rather than seen as familial burdens. The reverence for elders, reinforced by the patriarchal social structure, laid the foundation for ancestor veneration, anchoring an ethical order rooted in agrarian life and aligned with the Way of Heaven. Rituals of Heaven worship and ancestor veneration often coexisted, and at times even merged, reinforcing both cosmic and familial values. This kinship-based hierarchy fostered familial ties and collective cooperation essential for agricultural survival, with Heaven-based ethics functioning as the social glue that bound families and clans together. Within this intricate social fabric, individuals were expected to cultivate filial devotion and communal virtue, which served as ethical foundations for navigating life's challenges.

Chinese social norms sought to optimize the organization of a vast population and ensure the efficient use of limited resources—an imperative for sustaining a densely inhabited agrarian society. Shared beliefs in "Heaven" and "celestial time" helped bind together diverse families, tribes, and regions, fostering a strong sense of common destiny and interconnectedness that transcended tribal boundaries. Despite recurring conflicts and wars, this spiritual and cultural unity laid the normative foundation for the formation of allied clans, which gradually evolved into states and, ultimately, a unified country. Within this grand harmony under Heaven, moral norms were not merely a source of social cohesion, but the fertile soil from which one of the world's enduring civilizations emerged and flourished.

In this cultural context, managing complex and intimate human relationships became a central priority, with an emphasis on both hierarchy and harmony. Virtues such as filial piety and ritual propriety upheld social distinctions and fostered reverence, whereas humaneness and temperance cultivated empathy, mitigated conflict, and discouraged self-aggrandizement. Humility and respect further reinforced social cohesion, enabling the reconciliation of competing interests and promoting effective cooperation. Thus, moral cultivation in ancient China went beyond individual refinement; it represented a collective investment in social interdependence and prosperity, ultimately supporting the stability and well-being of the entire nation.

2.1.3.2 Topo-Ethical Formation: Social and Geo-Cultural Dimensions

Beyond agriculture, geo-cultural and political factors also profoundly influenced Chinese moral cultivation. While recognizing the inherent limitations of historical reconstruction, the analysis highlights the complex interplay between geography, societal structures, and philosophical thought in shaping moral ideals in ancient China.

China's unique geographical features are likely related to its worldview and philosophical foundations. Its vast and cohesive landscape, coupled with interconnected river transportation systems, may have fostered a holistic outlook that values unity and interconnectedness. This outlook could have contributed to the development of cosmology like "all things in one" and the emphasis on moral cultivation, where social order and harmony take precedence. The close-knit nature of communities in such an environment likely blurred the boundaries between personal rights and responsibilities, leading to a greater focus collective well-being. In contrast, ancient Greece's fragmented coastline, numerous islands, and rugged terrain—along with its migratory origins and tribal diversity—may have contributed to the rise of independent city-states and the development of an analytical philosophy with an individual-oriented worldview (Wang, 2012).

This emphasis on collective values is manifest in Chinese moral precepts, which prioritize filial piety, societal obligations, stability, and social harmony over the prioritization of individual liberties. Filial piety, for instance, mandates reverence and obedience toward one's parents and ancestors, reinforcing a hierarchical and duty-bound social order. This collectivist and hierarchical tendency stands in contrast to the ethos of certain ancient Greek city-states, such as Athens, where engagement in maritime trade and commercial activities fostered a spirit of individual agency, freedom of expression, and a stronger emphasis on social equality among citizens. The autonomous nature of social relations, combined with decentralized political structures and commercially driven environments in the Greek polities, often necessitated the use of contractual agreements and formalized legal systems to regulate interpersonal and civic affairs.

In densely populated China, maintaining harmony demanded the observance of rites—norms that cultivated self-restraint and the disciplined fulfillment of role-specific duties. By discouraging transgression and excess, ritual propriety helped prevent conflict, sustain order, and optimize resource distribution for a large population. Chinese mainstream philosophies, primarily Confucianism and, in a different vein, Daoism, advanced a humanistic vision prioritizing human welfare, survival, and prosperity. The "Mandate of Heaven," therefore, was not just a cosmological principle but a moral imperative: It demanded social stability and earthly flourishing, while ethical wisdom enabled the mediation of competing interests and the preservation of societal equilibrium.

These geo-cultural and social factors help illuminate why Confucianism was chosen as the official ideology in China, as its focus on moral cultivation and social order closely aligned with the needs of a vast agrarian empire. The factors also explain the complementary role of Daoism, which counterbalanced Confucian rigor with its advocacy for simplicity, reduced desires, and the cultivation of spontaneity. In a society rooted in close-knit kinship, a governance model centered on ethical principles and moral development, tempered by a naturalistic path to inner peace, proved more effective than one based solely on legal codes and contractual obligations. This context accounts for why traditional Chinese morality prioritized values such as humaneness, righteousness, harmony, self-restraint, spontaneity, and humility—virtues that mitigated conflict and reinforced social cohesion.

Geo-cultural factors help explain the prominence of celestial rites in ancient China, distinguishing it from the deity-centered religions of other early civilizations. Whereas many ancient civilizations developed organized religions centered on a specific god or on pantheons of deities, indigenous China's belief system, while also including gods, mainly evolved around the veneration of Heaven—an all-inclusive cosmic force representing ultimate authority and moral order. This reverence for Heaven gave rise to a corresponding system of rites aimed not only at worshiping but also at moral cultivation, reflected in enduring cultural practices such as ancestor worship and the honoring of sages who embodied virtues in harmony with the celestial order.

The relatively subdued role of deities in ancient Chinese spirituality may be partly attributed to the region's expansive and ecologically diverse geography. The vast terrain allowed clans significant mobility to resettle following natural calamities, potentially reducing psychological reliance on specific deities and redirecting spiritual focus to ancestral wisdom. Notably, many Chinese gods were originally deified historical figures or ancestral spirits, reflecting this cultural prioritization of human experience over divine intervention. This dynamic also contributed to the historical subordination of religious authority to political power. As clans consolidated into larger tribes and eventually centralized states, their parochial deities were systematically integrated into the more universal concept of Heaven, the normative symbol of political legitimacy. In this way, Heaven and ancestor worship emerged as a shared cultural framework of ancient Chinese (Shi, 2018). State rituals honoring legendary progenitors like the Yan Emperor and Yellow Emperor, enshrined as common ancestors of the Han Chinese, epitomize this worldview, where political unity and cultural continuity were sacralized through shared genealogical mythology.

Ancestor worship was, in fact, regarded as a central affair of state, on par with matters of warfare. The solemnity and ceremonial weight of these practices served to reinforce national unity and shared cultural convictions. Oracle bone inscriptions reveal that ancestor veneration already occupied a prominent role in ritual life of the Shang. The Zhou dynasty further institutionalized this tradition by developing a comprehensive system of rites and music, which functioned as tools of both political governance and moral education. This system emphasized the importance of lineage, reinforcing social cohesion through ancestral worship, state sacrifices, funerary customs, and marriage rituals.

Rooted in filial piety toward parents and ancestors in the Heavens, these rituals assumed a quasi-religious character. This emphasis on filial devotion helped cultivate the Confucian virtue of humaneness, which finds its roots in the natural affections shared between parents and children, as well as among siblings. Consequently, the system of rites and music evolved as both an expression of reverence for heavenly order and a foundational method for moral cultivation.

2.2 Heaven's Revelation and the Path of Moral Cultivation

In contrast to many religions focused on the afterlife, the Chinese concept of "celestial revelation" emphasizes the present life and worldly affairs. This notion actively shaped social customs and cultural narratives, serving as a guiding principle for good governance and moral development. It provided cosmic laws for transforming disorder into an ordered state, embodying the ideal harmony between Heaven and humanity. Even Chan Buddhism, though rooted in transcendence, assimilated this ethos of worldly engagement. As the Sixth Patriarch Hui Neng proclaimed: The Buddha-Dharma manifests in the mundane; it does not reside in seclusion (Huinen, 2022).

2.2.1 Rituals for Heaven-Humanity Reunion

Intriguingly, a Chinese myth, reminiscent of the Western concept of a lost paradise, provides a mythological basis for the concept of "unity between Heaven and humanity," reflecting an ancient Chinese aspiration to restore primordial harmony. According to this legend, there was once a time when cosmos and the terrestrial realm were connected and deities and humans coexisted, until a prehistoric emperor ordered the dismantling of the ladder connecting Heaven and Earth—a tale known as the "separation of Heaven and Earth" (Confucius, 2016c). This narrative may reflect early rulers' attempts to curtail the power of diviners who claimed to mediate divine will, thereby subordinating religious authority to royal power. The perceived loss of unity gave rise to rites, often featuring sacrifices and elaborate ceremonial performances conducted by rulers to symbolically bridge the celestial and human realms (Yu, 2014).

The profound interconnection between Heaven and humanity gave rise to the belief that enlightened sages could interpret celestial patterns and discern the destiny of the state. This insight was codified in *the Classic of Changes*, an ancient divinatory text composed of hexagrams that distilled natural and cosmic patterns into a coherent framework for understanding transformation. As one of China's oldest and most revered texts, *the Changes* served not merely as a tool for divination but as a philosophical lexicon, revealing developmental trajectories and potential future states through the interplay of dynamic lines and trigrams. This text became a foundational source for Chinese philosophy, informing both Confucianism—with its emphasis on active virtues such as moral responsibility and the fulfillment of social roles—and Daoism, which drew upon its passive virtue, aligning with the natural flow of the Dao through action in noncoercive action. Together, these interpretations demonstrate how *the Changes* transcended its oracular origins to shape enduring paradigms of Chinese cosmology, ethics, and metaphysics.

The Confucian *Commentaries on the Changes* reinterpreted the Heaven-Earth paradigm as a model for human relationships. The seemingly opposite yet harmonious interplay between these cosmic forces was mirrored in the ideal roles governing family and society: father and son, husband and wife, and sovereign and minister. By grounding these relationships in cosmic harmony, Confucian thought elevated ritual propriety and righteous conduct, rendering them practical conduits for moral cultivation. Consequently, what was previously the domain of diviners and sages—communion with Heaven through esoteric practices—was transformed into a moral pursuit open to all through ethical behavior and ritual observance. This shift marked a redefinition of the Heaven-humanity relationship, evolving from a system based on divination into a philosophical framework that profoundly shaped Chinese ethics, politics, medicine, literature, and the arts.

In effect, an intrinsic connection existed between divination and the origins of Confucianism. The earliest Confucians (儒) were considered skilled ritual specialists, orchestrating ceremonies that integrated music and rites for deities, ancestral worship, and funerals. During rituals, they employed sacred objects like jade and bronze vessels as mediums for communicating with the divine. Given the close association between ritual practice and political authority, Confucians in the late Zhou Dynasty gradually distanced themselves from the role of the diviners and redefined themselves as scholar-officials, engaging in both governance and education. Confucius and his disciples embodied this transformation. As Shi (士), low-ranking aristocrats, or even commoners trained in various cultural and administrative arts, they leveraged ritual knowledge and moral cultivation to promote political ideals and serve the state.

Bronze tripod cauldrons (鼎), employed for both culinary and ritual purposes, came to symbolize prestige, political authority, and moral legitimacy, embodying balance, fidelity, and justice. The consumption of meat prepared in these vessels was an exclusive privilege of the elite, serving as a tangible manifestation of their elevated status. The "Rites of Zhou" codified this hierarchy further, stipulating the precise number of tripods permitted in rituals and burials according to aristocratic rank. Through such regulations, bronze cauldrons functioned as material embodiments of the Zhou social order, reinforcing stratification through ritual practice. Likewise, jade artifacts were more than ornamental; they served as sacred symbols of status and moral refinement. The ancient Chinese believed that jade's smooth and luminous texture embodied the core virtues of a noble person—humaneness, righteousness, propriety, wisdom, and trustworthiness. Accordingly, an ideal gentleman, or junzi (君子), wore jade as a symbol of both his high social status and his cultivated inner character.

Much of ancient Chinese architecture was designed to reflect the essence of ritual. Recent archaeological discoveries, dating back 5000 years, offer fascinating glimpses into the earliest ritual spaces. In the Hongshan culture (Inner Mongolia), altars and temples were arranged along a central axis, encircled by stone burial mounds. Similarly, in the Liangzhu culture (Zhejiang), ritual architecture occupied the central area, encircled by elevated burial mounds (Wu, 1995). Mirroring the cosmos, perceived as a realm of perfect order, the ancient Chinese practice of emphasizing centrality and axial alignment symbolized both authority and impartiality. Over time, it became a powerful expression of political supremacy and the legitimacy of a hierarchical, yet ethically grounded, social order.

Reverence for Heaven formed the ethical basis for ritual's pivotal role in moral cultivation. Through the proper performance and observance of such reverence-based ritual, both rulers and individuals aligned themselves with the cosmic order. The Mandate of Heaven (天命), therefore, was not limited to sovereigns; it extended to every individual, each entrusted with a unique destiny to secure their livelihood, establish social standing, and fulfill ethical responsibilities. This pursuit of personal fulfillment sought to harmonize material well-being with spiritual growth, framing self-cultivation as the essential pathway to apprehending one's destiny while honoring familial and societal duties.

2.2.2 Heaven as the Wellspring of Moral Cultivation

Heaven has perennially functioned as the wellspring of moral cultivation within the triadic harmony of Heaven, Earth, and humanity. In this cosmological framework, perfected human virtue—embodied by the sages—attains resonance with the moral majesty of Heaven and Earth. These sage-paragons, through their attunement to celestial principles and natural rhythms, manifest the pinnacle of ethical and spiritual enlightenment.

The classic text *Commentaries on the Changes* eloquently captures this ideal: "The great man is he who is in harmony, in his attributes, with Heaven and Earth; in his brightness, with the sun and moon; in his orderly procedure, with the four seasons; and in his relation· to what is fortunate and what is calamitous, in harmony with the spirit-like operations (of Providence)" (Confucius, 2016b, KHIEN, 34). This state of alignment is known as the unity of Heaven and humanity in virtue (天人合德), reflecting the fundamentally ethical nature of the world. While Heaven orchestrates the cycle of seasons, offering the balance of warmth and cold, Earth coordinates myriad resources, nurturing a fertile foundation for the prosperity of life, an inspiration for the development of human virtues. Note that such "change" in ancient China does not imply linear progress but rather a cyclical pattern of generation and regeneration. The enduring virtue of Heaven and Earth lies in their ceaseless nurturing and transformative power that sustains all living things.

Chinese culture deeply associates growth with goodness and destruction with evil. Ethical principles stem from Heaven's inherent virtue: its selfless, generative care for all living beings, urging individuals to actively cultivate their innate moral potential in the cosmic spirit of mutual flourishing. Conversely, violations of moral norms not only harm others but also disrupt the harmony of the cosmos. As integral parts of nature, humans express their highest virtue through participation in the creative and nurturing cycle, a process embodied in "humaneness"—or benevolence, as practiced within human society. Ultimately, humaneness enables all beings to flourish through balanced and reciprocal growth, harmonizing outward conduct with inner compass to realize ethical excellence and spiritual integration within the cosmic order. In this ethos, the paths of Heaven, Earth, and humanity converge, and the individual's pursuit of Heaven's Way becomes a transformative journey of moral self-cultivation.

The conception of Heaven carries profound ethical implications for human unity and collective development. Inclusive by nature, Heaven's boundless canopy symbolized a universal order that transcended tribal divisions and geographical constraints, uniting communities under a shared cosmic vision. Though regional distinctions endured, all peoples shared the same celestial expanse, drawing sustenance from its blessings and synchronizing their lives with its cyclical rhythms. This collective consciousness crystallized in the ideal of All under Heaven (天下), which promoted cultural integration, mutual responsibility, and the cultivation of virtue as the basis for universal harmony.

This ethical consensus is exemplified by Chinese traditions of aiding fallen tribes or states and restoring broken noble lineages during times of hardship. The story of Yu the Great illustrates this principle vividly. In prehistoric China, when a great flood devastated the land, Yu, a leader of allied tribes, undertook an immense flood-control effort, aiding afflicted clans and helping them recover their land or cultivate new territories. His unwavering dedication to the survival and prosperity of all people during this crisis established his legacy as a paragon of virtue. His humaneness, demonstrated through altruistic action rather than mere pronouncements, earned him the revered title of sage-king, an enlightened ruler attuned to the Way of Heaven and a timeless model for those aspiring to moral self-cultivation.

The belief in a virtuous cosmic force, often referred to as "the spirit of Heaven and Earth" or the Dao, permeates Chinese philosophical thought, uniting its major traditions through a shared emphasis on altruistic harmony. For instance, Confucianism's emphasis on the Way of Heaven embraces kindness, interdependence, and mutual flourishing in a selfless aspiration toward all beings. This altruistic principle finds a parallel in Lao Tzu (2010)'s concept of the Dao, which creates and nurtures all things without expectation of reward, embodying impartiality and humility. A similar inspiration, drawn from the perceived impartiality of Heaven and Earth, led Mozi of Mohism to advocate for universal love (兼爱), urging equal concern for all people. Ultimately, the realization of the Way of Heaven or the Dao within the human realm are realized through cultivation of expansive love.

Of course, not all philosophers endorse this celestial-human unity. Xunzi, for instance, propounds a separation between Heaven and humanity, conceiving of Heaven as an impersonal natural system rather than a moral arbiter. He contends that human nature's innate self-interest necessitated external cultivation through ritual and law to correct harmful tendencies and enable ethical conduct. Regarding humanity's relationship with nature, Xunzi (1997) emphasized the importance of understanding and utilizing the laws of Heaven for human benefit, rather than passively conforming to them. This perspective contrasts with Daoist ideals of effortless harmony, yet it embodies a utilitarian strand in Chinese thought—one that affirms human agency and the capacity to actively shape the world. More importantly, it exposes a fundamental dialectic in Chinese philosophy: the perpetual negotiation between transcendent moral ideals and the pragmatic concerns for feeding a growing population or defending against external invasion.

As a highly developed agrarian civilization, China perpetually confronted the fundamental challenge of sustaining a vast and densely populated society, which necessitated systematic approaches to natural resource management that balanced immediate survival needs with long-term civilizational development. During periods of intensified demographic pressure, these imperatives became particularly acute, driving technological and organizational innovations—from advanced irrigation systems to precision land management techniques. This enduring civilizational priority on resource optimization illuminates China's historical predisposition toward large-scale infrastructural solutions, a tradition that continues to shape its developmental trajectory.

While a tension may exist between this results-oriented approach and the idealistic pursuit, a more nuanced perspective reveals their complementarity. Virtues cultivated through the concept of Heaven fostered social cohesion and reduced conflict, thereby establishing the necessary preconditions for effective governance and resource management. In this sense, moral cultivation not only preserved transcendent values but also supported the pragmatic objectives of societal stability and collective flourishing.

2.2.3 Heaven's Mandate and Moral Cultivation

China developed a distinctive system that harmonized royal power and divine influence, contrasting with the rivalries between kings and priests characterized many other ancient civilizations. This synthesis was institutionalized through the emperor's dual identity as both sovereign ruler and "Son of Heaven"—the paramount mediator between human and cosmic realms. As the ritual architect of cosmic order, the emperor conducted state sacrifices to maintain Heaven-Earth harmony while administering virtuous governance to ensure social stability. Confucian philosophy systematized this structure by formalizing the Mandate of Heaven doctrine, which framed ethical rulership and moral self-cultivation as prerequisites for maintaining celestial sanction and dynastic legitimacy.

2.2.3.1 Evolution of the Idea of Heaven's Mandate

Throughout much of ancient China, political legitimacy was rooted in the Mandate of Heaven, a cosmological principle that conferred authority based on virtuous governance. This sacred pact between Heaven and sovereign was neither permanent nor unconditional—its withdrawal or bestowal served as the ultimate sanction for dynastic change, becoming the dominant paradigm through which Chinese historiography interpreted regime transitions and political upheavals.

The ethical significance of this notion emerged during the tumultuous transition from the Shang to the Zhou Dynasty. The Shang, China's second dynasty, venerated a vast pantheon of capricious deities believed to determine everything from individual fates to the destiny of the entire kingdom. To appease these deities and retain their divine favor, Shang rulers performed elaborate ceremonies and gruesome rituals, including extensive human sacrifices, primarily of war captives and slaves. Archaeological excavations at Anyang, the Shang capital, have uncovered thousands of skulls and skeletal remains bearing witness to this dark practice. For the Shang kings, maintaining the favor of their ancestral spirits and the High God was considered paramount to securing the Mandate and securing their continued reign.

However, the seemingly invincible Shang Kingdom was abruptly overthrown circa 1046 BCE by an alliance of states led by the Zhou, aided by a revolt of Shang slaves who joined the campaign against their oppressive rulers. In the wake of this decisive victory, the Zhou faced a daunting challenge: how to establish their political legitimacy as the new sovereign power. How could a relatively small tributary state justify seizing authority from the once-mighty Shang? More importantly, how could they persuade the people that the Mandate of Heaven had shifted to them—and ensure that they could uphold it in the long term?

To address these pressing concerns following the death of King Wu, the Duke of Zhou, a foundational figure in the early Zhou Dynasty, redefined the Mandate of Heaven. He proclaimed that the mandate was not granted arbitrarily, but earned through moral virtue. This made the Mandate conditional, favoring rulers who exemplified righteousness and ethical conduct. In doing so, he reimagined kingship as a moral responsibility rather than merely a divine entitlement. No longer were brute force or noble lineage sufficient; only a virtuous ruler could claim Heaven's approval and the right to govern. Through this reinterpretation, the Duke of Zhou not only legitimized the Zhou's rise to power but also inaugurated a political philosophy in which morality, not just might, became the true foundation of legitimate rule.

To maintain the Mandate of Heaven, the Duke of Zhou instituted a governance model centered on virtuous rulership. This paradigm transformation made moral leadership, characterized by benevolent care for the populace, a defining legacy of Zhou political philosophy. In accordance with this ethical vision, the Zhou opposed human sacrifice, asserting that Heaven's will, as the supreme moral force, valued human welfare and dignity. The philosophical reorientation simultaneously elevated Heaven itself as the ultimate object of worship—no longer merely a celestial power, but the embodiment of moral authority. This also led to the veneration of sages, individuals of profound virtue who lived in accordance with Heaven's principles.

This profound transition in ancient Chinese political and social thought marked a shift from superstition-driven practices toward a more rationally articulated and ethically grounded framework. The primary celestial duty of kings and emperors evolved from appeasing deities and practicing divination to performing sacrificial rites to Heaven and Earth and reporting their virtuous governance. Meanwhile, sorcerers were gradually replaced by official historians, who, while continuing to observe celestial phenomena, made their principal task documenting historical events, particularly the words and actions of rulers. As a result, ancient China developed a unique tradition of using historical recordkeeping as a source of reference, admonition, and moral cultivation with implications for society of their time and future generations (Ng & Wang, 2013).

2.2.3.2 Family, State, and the Development of Kinship-Based Morality

The Zhou Dynasty's moral philosophy arose not merely from political exigency after their rise to power, but as an organic outgrowth of their intricate patriarchal clan system, embedded in a rigid feudal hierarchy. This sociopolitical foundation became institutionalized as kinship networks expanded into state governance, particularly through the principle of primogeniture: The eldest son of the principal consort inherited the throne, while junior sons were systematically integrated into the bureaucracy through conferred noble titles, effectively transposing familial hierarchy onto state administration.

As the new suzerain of ancient China, the Zhou kings perfected its consanguineous political order by enfeoffing relatives and loyal ministers as territorial lords. These nobles, conferred ranks like dukes and marquises, extended Zhou influence by establishing semiautonomous vassal states to the kingdom's expanding frontiers. Each fiefdom replicated the royal succession model, enforcing strict primogeniture that privileged the primary wife's eldest son with inheritance, while relegating younger sons to subordinate ministerial positions. Across generations, cadet branches experienced gradual status attrition until their descendants merged with the common populace. This pyramidical kinship governance enabled the fledgling Zhou dynasty to administer its expansive, ethnically diverse territories while maintaining systemic stability. Consequently, the king evolved into the realm's supreme patriarchal symbol, weaving the state into a unified whole through interlocking blood ties and feudal obligations.

The Zhou derived its ethical foundations from this societal structure. Elders, esteemed for their accumulated wisdom, assumed responsibility for guiding younger generations, who reciprocated with filial deference. This institutionalized synergy between domestic and governing hierarchies further gives rise to the cardinal virtues of filial piety and loyalty, effectively merging moral cultivation with state administration. Consequently, the Zhou polity privileged a kinship-based ethical system over formal legal codification: the former being suited to relational governance and the latter to impersonal, transactional rules. This choice established China's earliest paradigm of "rule by virtue" rather than rule of law. To perpetuate this system, the Zhou developed an elaborate system of rites and music, which simultaneously reinforced sociopolitical stratification and inculcated the moral dispositions required to maintain it.

Yet the kinship-based moral framework was inadequate for administering China's expansive and ethnically diverse territories. While effective in fostering solidarity within kinship-based groups, this familial paradigm struggled to accommodate outsiders and ethnic diversity. To transcend this limitation, the Zhou emphasized the concept of "All under Heaven" to broaden the scope of the morality of Zhou, bringing in inclusivity, diversity, and a more universal vision. This expanded embrace contributed to the development of an ethical continuum: the self, family, state, and All under Heaven—a framework that further solidified the Zhou's commitment to moral development as a foundation for political unity and cultural integration.

2.2.3.3 All Under Heaven as a Moral Responsibility

The worldview of "All under Heaven" envisioned the Heaven as a dome arching over a square, flat earth bordered by the Four Seas. This framework encompassed all regions within and surrounding China's perceived boundaries, fostering a strong sense of unity and shared cultural identity. It laid the ideological groundwork for the notion of "great unification," emphasizing the inherent oneness and indivisibility of the Chinese realm. The Zhou institutionalized this concept through an extensive kinship network: Most regional lords and officials could trace genealogical connections to the royal house, whether through consanguinity or affinity. These ties operationalized the "state-family continuum," where domestic structures mirrored governance hierarchies and the polity functioned as an amplified kinship unit. This reciprocal framework proved instrumental not only in territorial expansion but also in establishing the shared normative foundation.

That said, unifying a sprawling kingdom fragmented by powerful clans necessitated a vision extending beyond mere familial loyalty. Traditional Chinese society was organized around extended kinship networks bound by bloodlines and shared surnames. While these clans provided protection, support, and resource distribution to their members, they also competed intensely with one another, threatening broader social cohesion. Aware of these divisions, Zhou leaders advanced the moral and political ideal of "All under Heaven"—a unifying framework emphasizing hierarchy, inclusivity, and social harmony. This concept sought to reconcile the complex web of interclan or interlocal relationships, offering a higher collective identity that transcended narrow family or regional loyalties and promoted a shared sense of purpose across the entire realm.

Originally a geographic concept, "All under Heaven" had been transformed by the Zhou into a powerful symbol of political legitimacy, moral guidance, and universal human concern. Unlike the Shang's clan-based deities tied to specific lineages, the Zhou—ruling over a much broader and more diverse territory—required an inclusive and unifying spiritual authority. Hence, they proposed a universal Heaven, which transcended tribal affiliations and included all within its celestial order. The shift, centered on the concept of All under Heaven, recast the Zhou from a territorial state into a world unified by shared values and a common destiny, transforming its primary tribal and political identity into a culturally cohesive community (Xu, 1994). This approach made the Western Zhou Dynasty a highly influential period in Chinese cultural history. By integrating celestial rituals with earthly governance, the Zhou imbued Heaven with ethical implications and established an inclusive ideological foundation that would shape the trajectory of Chinese civilization.

The concept of "All under Heaven" inherently calls for the cultivation of "de" (moral virtue), a universal ethic encompassing both personal character and collective responsibility. Grounded in this moral framework, individuals with an "All-under-Heaven" ideal extended their care and concern beyond kinship ties and territorial borders, embodying an inclusive vision of human solidarity. The Duke of Zhou institutionalized this ethic by linking morality to the Mandate of Heaven, positioning "de" as the supreme guiding principle governing the entire realm. To cultivate virtue across society, he developed a comprehensive system of rites and music, including rituals for sacrificial, marriage, funeral, and court ceremonies, all designed to instill virtue across society, integrating rulers, vassals, ministers, lower-ranking nobles—"shi" (士)—and commoners into a unified ethical community (Wang, 1997).

Within the framework of All under Heaven, the Zhou's Heaven transcended mere divine justification and came to embody the collective will of the people. Drawing lessons from the Shang, whose disregard for their subjects contributed to their downfall, the Zhou argued that Heaven's favor is aligned with the people's desires. As King Wu proclaimed, "Heaven sees according as my people see; Heaven hears according as my people hear" (Confucius, 2016c, The Oath of Tai). Similarly, Chancellor Guan Zhong (2009) of the vassal state Qi asserted that the rulers should regard people as their Heaven. While the "people" in this context primarily referred to the aristocratic class and the broader population, rather than individual citizens with voting rights in the modern sense, these pronouncements redefined the Mandate of Heaven as a reflection of popular approval, thereby establishing virtuous government as a central political imperative. From this foundation arose the Zhou's emphasis on virtuous leadership and moral cultivation. A ruler's legitimacy now depended on revering Heaven, honoring ancestors, and, crucially, caring for the people—for a leader who lost Heaven's trust, as reflected in the suffering of the populace, risked forfeiting the Mandate.

2.3 Chinese Moral Cultivation in the Heaven-Human Framework

Moral cultivation in the Chinese tradition represents a unique synthesis of transcendent philosophy and embodied social practice, a living discipline permeating all aspects of existence. For millennia, this pursuit has been deliberately advanced on a national scale by China's ruling and intellectual elites. *The Book of Rites* (2016d) poetically articulates this ethos, comparing ethical refinement the careful tending of a field: "they fashioned the rules of ceremony to plough it. They set forth the principles of righteousness with which to plant it. They instituted the lessons of the school to weed it. They made love the fundamental subject by which to gather all its fruits, and they employed the training in music to give repose" (LÎ YUN, Section 4.8). This agricultural metaphor, central to Confucian thought, conveys the belief that all individuals possess the potential for virtue—if cultivated with care, discipline, and harmony.

2.3.1 Moral Cultivation as a Humanistic Ethos

Chinese moral cultivation is a human-centered, fundamentally individual, and social endeavor grounded in the cosmological paradigm of Heaven-human harmony. Eschewing solitary self-perfection, it emphasizes the dialectical relationship between personal moral agency and structured communal cultivation—a dynamic institutionalized when Confucianism attained state orthodoxy. This sociopolitical institutionalization thoroughly infused moral development with governance imperatives, cultural reproduction, normative socialization, and pedagogic systems, making ethical formation inseparable from social context and essential to civilizational continuity.

The moral ecology of Chinese society arises from a dynamic constellation of mutually reinforcing systems. Political structures institutionalize ethical governance through structural frameworks, while philosophical-ethical traditions codify behavioral norms and evaluative standards. Rites and ceremonies foster reverence for the divine and ancestral, bolstering collective identity; pedagogical systems, in tandem, cultivate virtues such as humaneness, integrity, and social responsibility.

Vernacular culture from folk customs to popular entertainments further embeds moral formation, championing filial piety, righteousness, trustworthiness, and loyalty. In counterpoise, Daoism offers a naturalistic reprieve that alleviates the tension inherent in strict ethical obligations, easing the rigors of ethical duty with room for autonomy and spontaneity. Together, these strands weave a subtle yet profound moral milieu, molding conduct across a continuum from gentle persuasion and affirmation to communal censure and institutional penalty.

That said, self-cultivation remains central to Chinese moral cultivation, a principle Confucius (2016a) enshrined in his dictum that authentic virtue must germinate from within (12.1). While external structures provide a supportive environment, the transformative labor of character formation remains an individual's sovereign responsibility. Values are internalized through lived experience, woven into the rhythms of daily life from family relationships to public service. Through the tripartite discipline of the scholarly learning, introspective refinement, and practical embodiment, practitioners progressively deepen their moral consciousness and nurture virtuous dispositions. This lifelong journey of self-perfection draws its impetus not from transactional calculus, but by a Confucian commitment to promoting humaneness and a desire to contribute meaningfully to a flourishing society.

This process is inherently holistic: Confucian self-cultivation aims at profound transformation through the pursuit of moral excellence, spiritual liberation, aesthetic refinement, and existential fulfillment, ultimately culminating in universal compassion and enlightened wisdom. It begins with reflection on interpersonal relationships and extends outward in ever-expanding concentric circles of care, until achieving the sage's panoramic vision of impartial benevolence. In an increasingly interconnected world, this process offers a shared foundation for navigating complex relationships, reminding us that the path to becoming better humans begins not in distant places, but within oneself and with those nearby.

Although moral cultivation is sometimes classified as religious due to its spiritual dimensions and belief in Heaven, this label is only partially valid. It never developed into a fully institutionalized religion, lacking key features such as devotion to an omnipotent deity, belief in the afterlife, personal salvation, or divine judgment. Confucius (2016a), for instance, while revering deities, maintains a distance from theological speculation, emphasizing practical ethics instead (6.22). Thus, despite its spiritual dimensions, Confucian moral cultivation remains fundamentally distinct from conventional religion.

Both Confucian and Classical Daoist thought operate primarily within the parameters of rational discourse and metaphysical contemplation, deliberately eschewing anthropomorphic divinity in favor of ethical systems (as in Confucianism) and natural virtue (as in Daoism). Rather than seeking divine salvation, their focus lies in transcending the limitations of finite human life through the cultivation of enduring moral values. In this sense, while fulfilling a religious function by offering meaning and ethical guidance, Chinese moral cultivation—unlike many religions that worship a transcendent God—venerates sagely exemplars: perfected individuals who embody cosmic principles and direct others toward awakening through harmonious alignment with the Dao or the Heavenly order.

2.3.2 Rites and Music in Moral Cultivation

From a philosophical-cultural perspective, both rites and music were rooted in the ancient Chinese endeavor to imitate and synchronize with the cosmic patterns of Heaven and Earth. Music, in particular, embodied the "unity of Heaven and humanity," institutionalized through the correspondence between the Twelve Musical

Pitches and the Twelve Solar Terms. This created a unified system that wove music, calendrics, and cosmology into a coherent whole (Dai, 2013). Ritual practice likewise transposed the cosmic order of sincerity and harmonious hierarchy onto the social sphere. Mimicking heavenly and natural frameworks, rites served as a fundamental conduit for cosmic connection, standing alongside music and the calendar as definitive expressions of China's pursuit of unity. Together, they anchored moral cultivation in the harmony between Heaven and humanity.

The intertwined practices of rites and music were among the earliest institutionalized forms of moral cultivation in ancient China. These traditions evolved from prehistoric shamanistic ceremonies and ancestral worship music into a sophisticated ethical-political system during the Zhou dynasty. The Duke of Zhou institutionalized this transformation by rationalizing earlier mystical practices into a coherent framework of rituals, musical forms, and social norms aimed to cultivate key virtues such as orderly observance of social hierarchy, compassion for the people, self-discipline, deference to elders and superiors, and reverence for morally exemplary figures.

2.3.2.1 The Role of Rites

The Zhou ritual system marked a decisive departure from Shang religious practices, transforming rites from supernatural propitiation into a mechanism for social rationalization and relational harmony. Central to this perspective, as outlined in *the Book of Rites,* is the principle of cosmic hierarchy. Just as Heaven presides over Earth, so too must human society embody this natural order through clearly delineated role relationships. Rites thus became performative manifestations of cosmological patterns, providing both structural framework and behavioral norms for moral life. This conceptualization reached its philosophical apogee with Song dynasty Neo-Confucian scholar Zhang Zai's proposition that rites express the Principle in the Heaven (Zhang, 1978), thereby completing the metaphysical grounding of Confucian ethics.

Specifically, rites embody core Confucian values such as hierarchical social order, deference, cultivated refinement, sacred reverence, and humane benevolence that constitute the bedrock of moral formation. While historically rooted in ancestral and spiritual veneration, these rites underwent a profound secularization, evolving into an elaborate system of social grammar that regulated interpersonal dynamics. They delineated hierarchical relationships, distinguishing between status (higher and lower), gender (male and female), age (old and young), and relational proximity, while emphasizing reciprocal exchanges, respect, and propriety in greeting and conduct. Their prescriptions extended beyond mere behavior to encompass linguistic patterns, bodily deportment, and even affective displays—each calibrated to one's social position to preserve interpersonal and systemic harmony. Consequently, ritual performance emerged as a potent pedagogical technology, simultaneously inculcating values and buttressing sociopolitical structures. This transformation marked China's civilizational shift from a shamanistic culture of supernatural mediation to a ritual civilization grounded in moral cultivation.

The Rites of Zhou are notable for their prescriptive nature. They detailed every facet of court and aristocratic life from attire and hand gestures to sacrificial practices, all meticulously calibrated to the individual's social rank and role. In worship, for example, only the king of Zhou could offer sacrifices to Heaven and Earth. Vassals honored mountains and rivers, ministers paid homage to the five local deities, and lower-ranking aristocrats worshipped their ancestors. Any transgression was deemed a serious violation. These ritual codes served not only as religious observances but also as mechanisms of political governance, delineating power, responsibilities, and privileges, and reinforcing hierarchical order. While mutual respect for these roles was essential to maintaining social harmony, compliance was further ensured through sanctions for breaches of ritual propriety.

Yet, the essence of the rites transcends mere hierarchical formalism; it operates as a cultural system embedded with ethical principles aimed at cultivating self-discipline and communal harmony. Through mutual respect, rites facilitate smooth social interactions and regulates desires, preventing transgressions such as usurping the power of superiors or encroaching upon the interests of subordinates—sources of social discord. These structured symbolic performances employ calculated temporal pacing and deferred gratification to engender four cardinal dispositions: reverence, restraint, elegance, and discursive subtlety, which temper excessive desire and nurture humaneness. Confucianism has long employed ritual propriety as a technology of desire management. Texts such as the Duke of Zhou's "Admonition of Drinking" and inscriptions on the "Prohibition of Wine" bronze vessel exemplify this approach, extolling temperance in alcohol consumption as a virtue of self-discipline and effective leadership—a principle central to the very concept of rites.

Unwavering observance of ritual propriety fosters profound moral gravitas, instilling in the nobility both the dignified composure to fulfill the obligations of their station and the spiritual fortitude to face mortality with equanimity. Through comprehensive ceremonial practice spanning mundane etiquette to state rituals, these disciplined performances gradually transform external formalities into internalized virtues, forging what Confucians termed "ritualized disposition." While this emphasis on ritual bears some resemblance to medieval European chivalry—particularly in their shared valuation of honor, decorum, and moral courage—it diverges in fundamental ways. Chivalry often centers on martial valor and the defense of the vulnerable, whereas the Chinese system of rites places greater emphasis on the preservation of social order, reciprocity, and harmony.

The scope of influence, too, diverges fundamentally. Although rites in the Zhou—much like Western counterpart—were initially reserved for the nobility, later classical Confucians and Neo-Confucians extended their applicability to all social classes. They reinterpreted ritual as a vehicle for universal moral cultivation, essential not only for shaping the character of elites but also for guiding the ethical development of commoners. This conceptual broadening allowed ritual principles to permeate all strata of Chinese society, ultimately making propriety and self-cultivation foundational aspects of mainstream cultural identity.

2.3.2.2 The Role of Music

In ancient China, music constituted an active ritual component rather than mere accompaniment—a dynamic synthesis of choreographed movement, chanting poetic verse, and instrumental harmony. It initially served as a medium for expressing emotions, facilitating communication with deities and ancestral spirits, and mediating the Heaven-human relationship. Over time, this sacred "ritual music" evolved into "elegant music," better suited to express a gentleman's ethical aspirations: celebrating sage-kings' virtuous governance, refining individual moral character, harmonizing familial and social relations, and modeling benevolent statecraft.

While rituals emphasize social hierarchy and distinctions, music serves as a force of unity, bonding diverse individuals and alleviating tension. As recorded in *the Book of Rites*, rites define Heaven-Earth order, while music harmonizes their relationship (Confucius, 2016d). Grand ceremonial performances—featuring synchronized group dances accompanied by the resonant tones of bronze ritual bells and stone chimes—played a central role in major rituals, cultivating solemnity, shared purpose, and collective identity. Archaeological finds from Taosi site (ca. 2450–1900 BCE), including drums, chimes, and bells, attest that rites and music emerged over four millennia ago as instruments of cosmic worship and tribal cohesion, heralding the dawn of an enduring cultural tradition.

Music played a unique role in moral cultivation by orchestrating emotional refinement that gently aligns individual dispositions with societal expectations while elevating interpersonal harmony to an art form. This exemplifies Chinese moral education's distinctive paradigm: the strategic channeling of aesthetic experience and affective resonance to achieve profound ethical internalization. Through its melodic alchemy, music cultivates cardinal virtues including reverential awe, tranquility, balanced moderation, filial devotion, and communal solidarity, attuning personal sentiments to normative ideals. This synergy between structured ritual and affective artistry forms a sophisticated system for moral development—one that artfully weaves individual hearts into social fabric through the golden threads of shared aesthetic-ethical sensibility.

From a broad perspective, moral cultivation through rites and music transcends mere instrumental function, offering a timeless path toward universal values. This process operates beyond ceremonial observance; it elevates personal emotion to a transcendent plane, encouraging individuals to prioritize the collective good and act in concert with their community. The Neo-Confucian conception of "heavenly principle" provides the metaphysical foundation for understanding the ethical significance of rites and music. While "Principle" constitutes the ontological ground of moral reality, rites, and music function as its phenomenology—the embodied means through which abstract principle becomes socially instantiated and culturally sustained. In this dialectic, ritual-music practice simultaneously legitimizes cosmic order while actualizing its transformative potential in human affairs.

2.3.3 Heaven-Human Framework Across the Three Teachings

Moral cultivation, the pursuit of harmony between individual, society, and the cosmos, has long been a central concern of Chinese philosophy. Confucianism established the dominant paradigm, framing individual ethical development as the conscious embodiment of cosmic harmony through ritualized social relations. Classical Daoism presented a complementary vision, advocating spontaneous alignment with nature's inherent patterns as the path to authentic harmony. When Confucian metaphysics later proved insufficient to address existential and transcendent concerns, Buddhism infused the tradition with deeper spiritual insight and broadened its universal perspective. This intellectual synthesis reached its zenith in Song-Ming Neo-Confucianism, which integrated these diverse influences into a cohesive and enduring philosophical edifice.

Even before the development of elaborate metaphysical systems, the relationship between the celestial realm and humanity was central to the cultivation of virtue for early Confucian masters like Confucius and Mencius. While Confucius (2016a) focused primarily on human affairs, he expressed deep reverence for Heaven, praising sage King Yao for aligning with Heaven and attributing his own moral integrity to Heaven's influence. Mencius (2016) similarly upheld a cosmic view of morality, asserting that "all things are already complete in us. There is no greater delight than to be conscious of sincerity on self-examination" (13A:4). He further elaborated on the process of nurturing these inborn virtues through self-reflection and moral effort.

"He who has exhausted all his mental constitution knows his nature. Knowing his nature, he knows Heaven. To preserve one's mental constitution, and nourish one's nature, is the way to serve Heaven. When neither a premature death nor long life causes a man any double-mindedness, but he waits in the cultivation of his personal character for whatever issue—this is the way in which he establishes his Heaven-ordained being" (13A:1).

Mencius' approach beautifully epitomizes Confucian self-cultivation, focusing on aligning life path with Heaven's Way through cultivating inherent moral disposition. Like Confucius, Mencius holds that humaneness is endowed by Heaven and urges individuals to consciously cultivate this innate goodness in their pursuit of the highest ethical ideal. This foundational Confucian belief in humanity's innate moral potential—and the lifelong responsibility to cultivate it through conscious effort and reflection—is eloquently articulated in *The Doctrine of the Mean*: "What Heaven has conferred is called The Nature; an accordance with this nature is called The Path of duty; the regulation [following] of this path is called Instruction [moral cultivation]" (Zisi, 2016).

Challenging Hegel's dismissal of Confucianism as merely a compendium of moral teachings, the Heaven-human relationship unveils its profound metaphysical dimension, wherein moral cultivation serves as humanity's conduit for cosmic alignment and participation. Yet classical Confucianism's Heaven-centered ethics, while positing a transcendent source of values, remained underdeveloped ontologically. This philosophical limitation persisted until the rise of Neo-Confucianism that completed Confucianism's metaphysical transformation by abstracting the ultimate source of virtues as the Principle (理) or the heart (心). This evolution was influenced by a synthesis of cosmic-human ideas from Daoism's dialectical principles and ontology, Chan Buddhism's perspectives on nature and the heart, and the reframing of Confucianism's own Heaven-humanity framework.

Chinese Buddhism, particularly Chan (禅) tradition, developed a profound metaphysical system characterized by its non-dual ontology and soteriology of "ordinary mind as the Way." Chan Buddhists emphasize an in-world cultivation, believing that "Buddha-nature" fully manifests in present-moment awareness, making enlightenment attainable within mundane activities—a stark contrast to ascetic detachment models in other Buddhist schools. While Chan's this-worldly orientation parallels Confucianism's embodied cultivation, its doctrine of universal interdependence introduced transformative dimensions into Chinese ethics, providing a strong impetus for compassion-centered self-cultivation. The idea of Buddha-nature further enriches the Confucian understanding of human nature, adding universality and a spiritual dimension that transforms Confucian self-cultivation into a journey that moves beyond mere societal norms to attune with ultimate reality.

The Daoist concept of the Dao, as the primordial source of all existence and spontaneous creativity, significantly expanded the cosmological dimensions of Confucian Heaven-human harmony. While early Chinese thought recognized celestial-terrestrial correlations, it was Chuang Tzu (2013) who vividly articulates the philosophy of cosmic unity, declaring: "Heaven and Earth were born at the same time I was, and the ten thousand things are one with me" (p. 13). Such a unity of Heaven and man calls for cultivating an authentic self liberated from social constructs, grounded in the ontological equality of all beings, and attuned to spiritual freedom through unmediated communion with nature. This harmony between self and nature complements the Confucian emphasis on a socially embedded and relational self, providing a naturalistic grounding for Confucian moral norms and informing the later Neo-Confucian conception of Principle as a metaphysical representation of Heaven.

Lao Tzu (2010) affirms the Heaven-humanity framework by situating ethical cultivation within the cosmic rhythms of the Dao. He views Heaven as encompassing both nature and ethics, thus grounding moral development in a natural realm. This perspective encourages the cultivation of virtues like simplicity, humility, and spontaneous order. The idea finds an echo with Confucius (2016a) who, at times, embraces this naturalistic way by asking rhetorical questions: "Does Heaven speak? The four seasons pursue their courses, and all things are continually being produced, but does Heaven say anything?" (17.19) This Daoist-Confucian synthesis profoundly shaped the moral praxis of later Confucian thinkers, who cultivated a dynamic equilibrium between unwavering principle and situational flexibility. They recognized the value of pausing, stepping back, and waiting for the right moment to act in challenging circumstances, infusing their approach to statecraft with resilience and a spirit of inclusivity.

The syncretic intellectual lineage ultimately culminated in Neo-Confucianism, which incorporated Buddhist and Daoist ideas into a renewed Confucian framework. In doing so, it reconceptualized Heaven from a quasi-personal cosmic force into either an abstract Principle that is both immanent and transcendent in structuring reality, or the inherent moral heart-mind embodying profound moral intuition and ethical agency. This shift grounded moral cultivation in a more sophisticated metaphysical system, where ethical practice was no longer merely a matter of social propriety but a holistic alignment with the transcendent principle. By placing human agency at the heart of moral perfection, Neo-Confucianism emphasized the individual's active role in transcending selfish desires and harmonizing their intentions with the greater pattern of existence—the Principle (理). Consequently, it not only deepened the philosophical foundations of moral cultivation but also significantly expanded its scope, uniting personal virtue, social duty, and cosmic purpose into a unified ethical vision.

References

Brown, J. R. (2016). Revelation in Confucianism. In B. M. Mezei, F. A. Murphy, & K. Oakes (Eds.), *The Oxford handbook of divine revelation*. Oxford University Press.

Chuang Tzu. (2013). *The complete works of Zhuangzi*. (B. Watson, Trans.). Columbia University Press.

Confucius. (2016a). *Analects*. In J. Legge (Ed. & Trans.), *Confucianism: The four books and five classics—Collected works of Confucius*. Delphi Classics.

Confucius. (2016b). *Commentaries on Changes*. In J. Legge (Ed. & Trans.), *Confucianism: The four books and five classics*. Delphi Classics.

Confucius. (2016c). *The book of documents*. In J. Legge (Ed. & Trans.), *Confucianism: The four books and five classics—Collected works of Confucius*. Delphi Classics (Original work published c. 551–c. 479 BCE).

Confucius. (2016d). *The book of rites*. In J. Legge (Ed. & Trans.), *Confucianism: The four books and five classics*. Delphi Classics.

Dai, N. (2013). Commenting on ancient Chinese concept of "world harmony" from the perspective of music. *Chinese Musicology, 3*, 11–18.

Dai, Z. (1724–1777). *Yuan Shan*. https://ctext.org/wiki.pl?if=gb&chapter=259154

Ding, W. (2015). Formation and evolvement of the concept of "unity of man and nature". *Tangdu Journal, 31*(6), 1–18.

Fang, K. (2003). The unity of heaven & man and the ecological wisdom in ancient China. *Social Science Front, 4*, 207–217.

Feng, Y. (2001). *The new history of Chinese philosophy*. People's Press.

Guan, Z. (2009). *Guan Tzu*. Zhonghua Book Company.

Hui-nen. (2022). *The sixth patriarchal sutra*. Wunan Book.

Lao Tzu. (2010). Daodejing. In R. T. Ames & D. L. Hall (Eds. & Trans.), *Dao de jing: A philosophical translation*. Ballantine Books.

Mencius. (2016). *Mencius*. In J. Legge (Ed. & Trans.), *Confucianism: The four books and five classics*. Delphi Classics.

Ng, O.-C., & Wang, Q. J. (2013). Characteristics of ancient Chinese historiography in comparative perspective. *Historiography Bimonthly, 4*, 37–48.

Perkins, F. (2015). Metaphysics in Chinese philosophy. In *Stanford encyclopedia of philosophy*. https://plato.stanford.edu/entries/chinese-metaphysics/

Shi, Z. (2018). *The Hubris*. Guangxi Normal University Press.

Wang, G. (1997). Theory of Shang and Zhou systems. In J. Fu (Ed.), *The collections of Wang Guowei*. China Social Sciences Press.
Wang, J. (2016). The characteristics of Chinese civilization and its formation process—A comparison of eastern and western civilizations. *West Archaeology, 2*, 13–22.
Wang, K. (2012, February 13). The development of Chinese philosophy. *Guang Ming Daily*.
Wu, R. (1995). An exploration of several issues on the origin of Chinese civilization. *Huaxia Archaeology, 2*, 55–60.
Xu, Z. (1994). *History of the Western Zhou*. Life-Reading-New Knowledge.
Xunzi. (1997). *Xunzi*. Liaoning Education Press (Original work published c. 310–c. 238 BCE).
Yu, Y. (2014). *On the relationship of heaven and man: An exploration of the origin of ancient Chinese thought*. Linking Publishing Company.
Zhang, Z. (1978). *Collections of Zhang Zai*. Zhonghua Book Company.
Zisi. (2016). The doctrine of the mean. In J. Legge (Ed. & Trans.), *Confucianism: The four books and five classics—Collected works of Confucius*. Delphi Classics.

Chapter 3
Metaphysical Foundations of Moral Cultivation

The architecture of a civilization's moral order rests upon a deeper, often unspoken, metaphysical substratum—a set of foundational assumptions about the nature of existence, consciousness, substance, and the self. These are not merely abstract intellectual constructs but constitute the essential grounds that render moral cultivation both necessary and possible. Within this framework, convictions about divine order, natural law, the cosmic-human relationship, and human nature provide the foundation upon which core values and ethical principles are built. Therefore, to fully comprehend the specific practices of moral cultivation, one must first excavate these deepest ontological and epistemological premises—the fundamental truths that ground a civilization's highest virtues and justify the translation of its moral ideals into lived experience.

In his influential work *The Philosophy of Civilization*, Albert Schweitzer (1923) argues that the well-being and resilience of a society rest on an optimistic and ethical worldview—one that ultimately determines whether a civilization flourishes or declines. This insight suggests that civilizational longevity is closely tied to its life-affirming moral vision. Ancient China, with its emphasis on virtue and ethical living, exemplifies the principle, providing a profound and enduring ethical worldview that laid the conceptual foundation for moral cultivation within a resilient Chinese civilization.

Grounded in the Heaven-humanity framework, this chapter explores a broad metaphysical worldview underlying Chinese moral cultivation, arguing that the Dao, change (易), nature (性), the Principle (理), and the heart are intricately interwoven, each playing a vital role in promoting ethical development. Together, these elements form the bedrock of moral cultivation, unfolding as a harmonious synthesis of metaphysical insight, existential reflection, ethical principles, and the practice-oriented epistemology of "gongfu" (工夫). In this context, "metaphysics" refers to a long-standing philosophical tradition that underpins the Chinese worldview. It explores the origins, intrinsic nature, modes of transformation, and governing

Z. You, Y. Hu, *Philosophy and Civilization: How the Idea of Moral Cultivation Shaped China*, East-West Dialogues in Educational Philosophy and Theory,
https://doi.org/10.1007/978-981-95-5660-1_3

principles of ultimate reality—a domain surprisingly understudied in academic discourse (Li & Perkins, 2014).

In fact, defining metaphysics and elucidating its relationship with worldviews is a notoriously challenging task. Metaphysics, also known as the first philosophy, is regarded as the foundation of philosophy, and as Aristotle (2014) put it, a "wisdom to deal with the first causes and the principles of things" or "being qua being" (p. 1553). Or it is, as modern scholars term it, a "study of ultimate reality" (Van Inwagen, 2014) or "a set of views about the nature of the world taken as a whole" (Barseghyan et al., 2018). It engages with transcendent concepts such as "forms," "God," and the "noumenal" (Li & Perkins, 2014), grappling with questions about existence, being, becoming, and reality.

Other contemporary scholars offer less esoteric descriptions of the term. Van Inwagen (2018), for instance, cuts through the thicket of terminology, proposing three fundamental inquiries that define metaphysics: What constitutes the world? Why does it exist? And where do we fit into it? These questions suggest that metaphysics is closely tied to people's worldviews. Barseghyan et al. (2018) offer a clear definition, stating that worldview is "a community's unique constellation of metaphysical components, and it characterizes how they understand the general features of the world taken as a whole." Similarly, Cobern (1996) defines worldviews as encompassing ultimate categories, suggesting that its cognition requires delving into both epistemology and metaphysics. Hence, exploring the terrain of metaphysics becomes a key to unlocking the hidden dimensions of a civilization's worldview.

While traditional Western and Chinese metaphysics both occupy central roles in their respective philosophical traditions, they center on different domains. Western metaphysics primarily investigates the ultimate nature of reality, emphasizing the "mechanics" of causation (metaphysics of causation) with "moral metaphysics" as an important subfield. In contrast, Chinese metaphysics is largely oriented toward constructing a philosophical foundation for ethical life (Yu, 2016), placing a "metaphysics of morals" at the heart of its framework for guiding behavior.

Even the concept of "moral metaphysics" takes different forms across cultures. In Western philosophy, moral metaphysics often frames moral truths as either rooted in universal human sentiments (as in Hume) or grounded in rational universals (as in Kant), with Kant prioritizing the formal validity of the moral law over the situated, developmental cultivation of virtue.[1]

Conversely, mainstream Chinese thought integrates moral inquiry with both universal significance and particular social contexts. It moves beyond the mere justification of moral values, engaging instead in dynamic, context-sensitive reflection that guides the cultivation and flourishing of virtue within a holistic framework—both cosmological and humanistic. This distinctive emphasis on moral cultivation warrants sustained scholarly attention, as it deepens our understanding of both the ethical structure of the universe and the evolving moral realization of humanity.

[1]Admittedly, there are also traditions that emphasize virtue and cultivation (e.g., Aristotelian ethics) within Western philosophy. However, they are not the dominant trends within Western moral metaphysics.

A fundamental discrepancy between traditional Chinese and Western metaphysics centers on the nature of their respective cosmologies. Whereas Aristotle envisions the cosmos as driven by an "eternal unmoved mover," in Chinese thought, ultimate reality is not just transcendent, but also immanent—present within and permeating all existence, intimately interwoven with the world and characterized by continuous transformation. With its emphasis on the present world, social life, and "becoming" over "being," Chinese philosophy stands apart from many strands of Greek thought, which pursues ultimate truths in existence, form, and attributes—an orientation that fostered the rise of analytical philosophy and systematic science.

This Chinese emphasis is exemplified by philosophers within both Confucianism and Daoism who tend to prioritize "becoming virtuous" over "being true," emphasizing transformation and self-actualization through a progression from undesired to ideal states. This dynamic worldview affirms the capacity of human agency, both individual and collective, as the catalyst for creating a better world. This focus explains why moral cultivation occupies such a central position in Chinese philosophy, as the idea of cultivating virtues aligns with the metaphysical ideal of transformative harmony.

3.1 Ancient Chinese Cosmology and Worldview

Metaphysics serves as the fundamental ground of moral philosophy, establishing the ontological parameters that shape our understanding of reality, existential meaning, and the structures of knowledge—each of which, in turn, exerts a formative influence on ethical systems. Because ontological commitments often carry inherent ethical implications, both reflecting and guiding one's aspirational path, "it would be a mistake to divorce the general consideration of value from ontology, by isolating it in some 'value theory'" (Earle, 1972, p.182). This constitutive relationship between being and values is evident in classical Chinese thought, where cosmological principles like the Dao and qi are never merely descriptive, but inherently normative, simultaneously explaining the structure of reality and prescribing the contours of the good life.

Ancient Chinese metaphysics is predicated on the principle of universal interdependence, a vision of cosmic harmony that simultaneously informs and is informed by its ethical system. The idea can be traced back to the rhythms of agricultural life, where nature's reciprocity and unity are observed in phenomena such as plants responding to sunlight, insects pollinating flowers, and the cyclical alternation of the seasons. French Sinologist Marcel Granet (1975) characterizes this philosophical cosmology as a worldview that emphasizes continuity, dynamism, relationship, and wholeness, rather than a philosophy that values stasis, isolation, and subject-object dichotomy. Similarly, Chen Lai (2013) describes Chinese cosmology as organic holism, proceeding from the idea that "everything in the universe is interdependent and interconnected, and that each thing reveals its existence and value in relation to the other." Understanding this holistic worldview is essential for grasping the core tenets of Chinese philosophy and the underlying dynamics of Chinese society.

3.1.1 Metaphysical Worldviews in the Book of Changes

The genesis of Chinese cosmological and ethical thought is found in its most primordial expressions in "*I Ching*" or *the Book of Changes* (hereafter, *Changes*), a text whose divinatory facade belies its profound philosophical depth. Often reduced to its function as an oracular manual for personal and state prognostication, *Changes* operates as a foundational metaphysical guide to virtuous living. Though the concept of the unity of Heaven and humanity is not explicitly articulated, the text and its later commentaries embrace a triadic cosmology of Heaven, Earth, and humanity, which would undergird all subsequent Chinese philosophical traditions. It serves as the seminal source for key concepts such as Lao Tzu's Dao and Confucius's Heavenly Way. This intellectual continuity is particularly evident in the *Ten Wings*, a set of interpretive commentaries traditionally attributed to Confucius. Together, *Changes* and its commentaries chart the pathways of human conduct through the observation and interpretation of celestial and natural patterns.

3.1.1.1 Change as Generative Virtue

Changes portrays a cosmos in perpetual flux and renewal, molded by the dynamic interplay of Heaven and Earth, where novelty continually emerges and regenerates, echoing Heraclitus' dictum that that the only constant is change. Consequently, the cryptic symbols recorded in *Changes* are, in fact, abstractions and simulations of the transformative processes in the cosmos. This cosmology establishes the foundation for individuals' worldviews, moral values, and their pursuit of moral cultivation.

First, *Changes* presents a holistic worldview in which all phenomena exist as interconnected parts of an organic whole, engaged in a ceaseless, dynamic interplay. Within this framework, nothing is in isolation—each element reflects the entirety of the cosmos while simultaneously contributing to its dynamic balance through its relationship with all other elements.

Central to this framework are the complementary forces of yang (the active, expansive force) and yin (the passive, contractive force), which organize reality into interdependent pairs such as Heaven and Earth, warmth and cold, ascent and descent, superiority and inferiority. These oppositions are not absolute but remain in continual fluidity, each containing the seed of its opposite: Yin harbors the potential for yang, just as yang encloses the nascent essence of yin. Intertwined like the sides of a coin, yin and yang coexist and mutually transform, generating the universe's boundless diversity.

The yin-yang transformation is grounded in qi, a vital life force or energy that permeates the cosmos. While yin and yang represent the two fundamental modes or attributes that qi assumes in the processes of movement and differentiation, qi serves as the material substrate that enables the existence and mutual transformation of yin and yang. Their continuous dynamic interplay gives rise to the full range of entities and phenomena, a process structured by the five agents (五行): Fire, Water, Wood, Metal, and Soil—the fundamental phases of change, with the interactions between any two of these agents producing either generative or restraining effects.[2] These dynamics, reflecting the movement of qi, drive cycles of transformation that either maintain or disrupt cosmic equilibrium. Together, such frameworks transcend theory to function as intellectual tools that guide reasoning and analysis: Yin-Yang fosters holistic and dialectical thinking, whereas the Five Agents cultivate relational and systems thinking, giving rise to a mode of thought characterized by ceaseless generation.

Ancient Chinese metaphysics views worldly change as cyclical, not linear. Nothing is permanent, with all things in a perpetual cycle of waxing and waning between opposing forces. When a system's balance is disrupted, a new equilibrium is reestablished through subsequent adjustments. These ceaseless cycles of creation and transformation reflect the nature of the Dao, the cosmic pulse of existence, where all things emerge through the interplay of being and nonbeing, the dynamic transformation of yin and yang, and the eternal interaction between Heaven and Earth. Beneath apparent complexity lies an ordered cosmos operating through discernible patterns. Tradition holds that *the Changes*, a text compiled by ancient sages, reveals the cosmos' governing principles through symbolic representations of celestial and natural phenomena—encoded as hexagrams to illuminate the divine will.

Specifically, this system is coded by eight trigrams and 64 hexagrams, each represented by a glyph composed of three or six horizontal lines. Every line is either solid "–" (symbolizing yang) or broken "--" (symbolizing yin). By combining these lines in various configurations, this symbolic system captures the essence of all phenomena and their transformative dynamics. The underlying idea is that all changes in the world can distill into fundamental, simple factors. By understanding these elements and the patterns of change, one can discern the course of events and anticipate their elusive consequences (Hu, 2018).

Rich in ethical implications, "living" (sheng) emerges as a dynamic force grounded in the world of change and becoming (Ames, 2024): not created ex nihilo, but nurtured into existence through the interplay of cosmic forces. This worldview sees morality as inherent in the procreative processes, exemplified by nature's unceasing growth and vitality. The term "procreation" rather than "creation" is used here because, according to *Changes*, Heaven and Earth nurture all things through the interaction of yin and yang, similar to the union between male and female. Through the alternation of yang and yin, all entities coexist, flourish, and refresh. Thus, growth and prosperity are viewed as the very nature of existence (Perkins, 2015), from which ancient Chinese derived their ethical principles.

The Commentaries on Changes encapsulate the dynamism of nature as the great generative virtue (生生之德) entailing three interconnected dimensions: the imperative of individual growth, the benevolence of collective development, and the ceaseless renewal of life and society as a whole.[3] This embodies the ethos of coexistence, as demonstrated in the Mandate of Heaven or the endowed human disposition (Wang, 2011a). In the endless circle of life and death, all things are interdependent, nourishing

[2] The idea of five agents was incorporated into the system of *Changes* in the Han Dynasty.

[3] See Xi Ci I, 28–29. "The daily renovation which it produces is what is meant by 'the abundance of its virtue.'" "[Ceaseless] production and reproduction is what is called (the process of) change."

others even in their passing, ensuring the symbiosis and continuity of all beings. From this perspective, those who disrupt this delicate equilibrium and exploit resources with insatiable greed, ultimately invite their own downfall, devoured by the very depletion they instigate. Life, then, is the beating heart of the cosmos, symbolizing growth, benevolence, and the intricate web of interdependence.

Ancient Chinese thought viewed humans and nature as intrinsically interconnected, deriving ethical guidance from the cosmic patterns (Adler, 2012). This generative virtue, rooted in nature, becomes a foundational source of value in Lao Tzu's Dao and Confucius's ideal of humaneness—each oriented toward the betterment of humanity. In both traditions, individual growth entails uplifting others, fostering cooperation, and cultivating a symbiotic harmony that encompasses all beings. Consequently, the Way of Heaven instills an altruistic imperative: to care for the common good. This reflects the essence of virtue (de), as "de" in Chinese implies a process of "acquiring" through the heart's alignment with the Dao or Heaven.

Even Legalism, a philosophy often seen as antithetical to moral cultivation, can trace its intellectual roots to *Changes*. The idea of change, for example, provides a theoretical foundation for reform and transformation, supporting societal renewal and resilience. While late-stage Legalism explicitly sidelines moral cultivation, its emphasis on dismantling entrenched power structures, particularly the monopolies of special interests, can indirectly create conditions favorable to moral development. This implies that, under certain circumstances, Legalism may function as an unexpected ally to moral cultivation.

3.1.1.2 Imagistic Thinking and Its Ethical Implications

Changes presents a distinctive mode of thought grounded in symbolic imagery (象) and analogy, connecting the natural and human realms. While the essence of the world may not be described directly, it can be apprehended through images, which convey deep meaning. Following the tradition, both Confucius and Lao Tzu emphasize imagistic thinking. Lao Tzu, for instance, holds that images precede and engender reality; in his view, the world first emerges through elusive, inchoate forms—images—from which tangible things (物) subsequently arise (Lao Tzu, 2010). Thus, images encapsulate the inner essence of phenomena, while entities or events are their external manifestations, generated through the dynamic interplay of yin and yang. In the human sphere, Confucius's concept of "Name" (名) serves to delineate the proper and authentic identity of human behavior, requiring a true correspondence between name and reality—or, more deeply, between the perceptible forms and the underlying essence of the world—to achieve full realization. This alignment, grounded in sincerity (诚), becomes the foundational ethical principle for individual and cosmic harmony.

Ancient Chinese perceptions of the world were initially recorded through imagery. Natural phenomena—sky, Earth, and all that lies between—were observed and rendered as symbolic patterns of change imbued with meaning. These images went beyond visual representation; they served as encoded messages, keys to unlocking the underlying principles that govern both the natural world and human affairs. This imagistic thinking embodies the power to communicate layered and intuitive meanings, often richer than those captured by abstract symbols, and aligns with the holistic mode of thinking central to Chinese culture. Imagery offers a more resonant expression of human experience and emotion, where abstract concepts might fall short. Through the imaginative transformation and synthesis of these archetypal images, individuals come to an intuitive, integrated understanding of the world's harmony and interdependence, absorbing ethical insight while transcending the limitations of linear rationality.

Imagistic thinking is a common thread in Confucianism, Daoism, and Buddhism, where ultimate truths are frequently conveyed through nonverbal means. Its most vivid expression is found in the diagram of Supreme Ultimate (taijitu), where pictures and symbols are used to depict the cosmic genesis and operating principles as continuous unfolding of existence through dynamic interactions. Another example arises from a Chan Buddhist anecdote: Siddhartha, during a sermon, held up a flower. His disciples remained perplexed, except for Mahākāśyapa, who broke into a radiant smile, revealing his enlightenment and demonstrating how nonverbal expression can transcend language, effectively communicating profound wisdom and emotions.

Imagistic thinking facilitates the understanding of the ethical implications embedded in *Changes*, which uses trigrams and hexagrams to symbolically map the cosmos' unfolding order (Hon, 2019). The trigram of "qián" (☰) with three solid bars represents Heaven; the trigram of "kūn" (☷) with three broken lines signifies Earth; the trigram of "gèn" (☶) with one solid line above two broken lines symbolizes mountain. By pairing any two of the eight trigrams in various combinations, a matrix of 64 hexagrams, arranged in an eight by eight format, is formed. Each hexagram carries a specific meaning. For instance, the hexagram of "qiān" (humility) "䷎" is made up of two stacked trigrams with "kūn" atop "gèn." The imagery of a lofty mountain concealed beneath the earth suggests that people, no matter how noble or talented, should be humble in social interactions. In this view, one important purpose of *Changes* is to guide human behaviors by unveiling the inherent harmony and ethical principles found in nature.

This holistic imagery-based approach contrasts sharply with the principles of analytic philosophy, epitomized by Wittgenstein's early dictum, "the limits of my language mean the limits of my world" (Wittgenstein, 1922, p.74), which posits language as both the framework and boundary of intelligible reality. Here lies a defining divergence between certain prominent strands of Eastern and Western philosophical thought: Where one privileges intuitive resonance and synthesis, the other champions epistemic precision and logical rigor—each with its own intellectual virtues and constraints. Imagistic thinking excels at conveying interconnected, experiential wisdom, yet its subjective nature can obscure objective clarity. Analytic philosophy, conversely, advances scientific and logical reasoning through linguistic exactitude, but often at the cost of fragmenting the fluid complexity of lived experience. Language itself—while a powerful instrument of articulation—inevitably filters, constrains, and reshapes what it seeks to explore and express. The tension between these two modes of knowing reveals not a hierarchy, but a reciprocity, each illuminating what the other leaves in shadow.

3.1.1.3 Triadic Harmony: Heaven, Earth, and Humanity

Changes presents a holistic worldview by portraying a harmonious trinity of Heaven, Earth, and humanity— each operating under its respective Dao: the Dao of Heaven, the Dao of Earth, and the Dao of Humanity. Together, these realms inspire individuals to align with natural principles in the cultivation of an ethical society. Morality ("de") can be understood as the shared language of this cosmic trinity, translating the rhythms of the universe into human virtue. For instance, *Changes* depicts natural progression as a sequence of stages—Yuan (primal), Heng (prosperous), Li (beneficial), and Zhen (steadfast),—later interpreted as the cardinal virtues of humaneness, righteousness, propriety, and sagacity. Sages, accordingly, are those who have mastered this moral-cosmic language, aligning their character with the cycles of cosmic transformation (Confucius, 2016c).

The view that the world is inherently ethical lies at the heart of early Chinese philosophy. For the authors of *Changes* and its *Commentaries*, nature is not just a silent backdrop; it is tightly woven with moral lessons. They deciphered this cosmic code, drawing parallels between celestial order and human values, or conversely, actively ascribing deep ethical significance to natural phenomena (Bi, 2001). As evidence, the *Commentaries* are filled with proverbs for moral cultivation through emulating nature's attributes.

Read the following beautiful lines: The movement of Heaven is strong and unceasing, and thus, the gentleman strives for constant self-improvement and perseverance; the Earth is vast and yielding, symbolizing the virtues of generosity, compassion, and the ability to bear and support all things. Mountains, slowly adorned with forests over time, symbolize the ongoing process of self-cultivation for gentlemen and the need to transform social customs (Confucius, 2016c). All these suggest the importance of daily renewal in cultivating virtues. Just as the Heavens and Earth ceaselessly nurture and sustain life, moral development should be a continuous, life-generating process.

3.1.2 Metaphysics in Daoism, Confucianism, and Buddhism

Despite sharing metaphysical roots in *Changes*, Confucian and Daoist interpretations diverge significantly. Confucianism emphasizes the text's affirmative aspects, interpreting it as a summon to deliberate self-cultivation and social betterment. Daoism, conversely, finds solace in *Changes*' quieter messages that underscore spontaneity, where flourishing emerges from nature's unfolding.

Accordingly, the two philosophies developed distinct yet complementary metaphysical frameworks for moral cultivation: Confucianism upholds the ideal of the unity of Heaven and humanity, framing virtue as the individual's conscious pursuit of harmony with both the cosmic and social order. Daoism, in contrast, grounds its ethics of wuwei in natural virtue, achieved by aligning with the spontaneous flow of the Dao. By cultivating detachment, individuals transcend desires and societal pressures, engaging with the world effortlessly and with equanimity. Where Confucianism provides structured moral rigor, Daoism offers fluidity, ensuring virtue remains dynamic and authentic rather than rigid or contrived. Together, they form a balanced philosophy of self-realization—one grounded in active moral striving and the other in intuitive attunement.

The introduction of Buddhism from ancient India also profoundly reshaped the metaphysical landscape of moral cultivation in China, prompting Daoism and Confucianism to develop more sophisticated ontological and epistemological frameworks. This encounter fostered a unique ethical syncretism: Buddhists absorbed the ideas of the Dao and harmony; Confucians adopted Buddhist meditative techniques to enrich self-cultivation; and Daoists integrated concepts such as compassion and karma into their moral vision. The resulting fusion of the three teachings—Confucianism, Daoism, and Buddhism—reveals both their shared concerns and philosophical divergences regarding the metaphysical foundations of virtue. Their respective reflections on "Heaven," "Dao," "nature," "principle," "qi" (vital energy), "heart," and "enlightenment" collectively enriched Chinese understandings of existence and morality, leaving a profound legacy on both individual and societal ethical development.

3.1.2.1 Dao and Moral Cultivation

The concept of the Dao in Daoism, literally "the Way" or "path," stands as a cornerstone in the metaphysics of Chinese philosophy. Unlike "Heaven," which remains intertwined with our world and is often seen as morally responsive or interventionist, the Dao is formless, boundless, ineffable, and eternal, transcending the physical realm as the ultimate ground of reality. It resembles the Kantian noumenon, the thing-in-itself that eludes human perception, and parallels the Brahman of Hinduism, the ungraspable source of all being (Chaudhuri, 1954). In this sense, the Dao operates at a higher order of transcendence than Heaven, serving as the supreme metaphysical principle in Chinese philosophy: immanent in its workings yet eternally beyond full articulation.

Yet unlike its detached Western counterparts, the Dao, both transcendent and immanent, is not utterly an aloof observer. It breathes within every leaf, manifests in every storm, and binds all existence in an indivisible unity. Though the Dao itself eludes direct grasp, its resonance can be sensed in each heartbeat, every act of compassion, and every moment of genuine harmony with the surrounding world. Neither is the Dao an unmoving ultimate. It exists in a perpetual state of flux, continually transitioning between nonbeing (无) and being (有), as all things under Heaven spring from being (the manifested world), which in turn springs from nonbeing (the undifferentiated state) (Lao Tzu, 2010). Thus, if we want to use a term to encapsulate the primordial nature of the Dao, perhaps it is the Boundless (wuji, 无极), denoting not a state of nothing, but an original state brimming with inexhaustible creativity and potential, and a generative source transcending the duality of being and non-being.

The Dao's movement from nonbeing to being represents the fundamental process of cosmic genesis and transformation, as captured in Lao Tzu's famous saying: "Dao engenders one, one two, two three, and three, the myriad things" (Lao Tzu, 2010, chap. 42). Heaven and Earth exemplify this life-giving force, which forms a cornerstone of ancient Chinese ethics—sustaining life and fostering mutual flourishing. While both Daoists and Confucians recognize the Dao as the ultimate source of moral cultivation, their interpretations diverge significantly. Daoists view the Dao as the underlying principle of nature, emphasizing alignment with its spontaneous flow. Confucians, by contrast, regard it as the foundation of morality, building a detailed ethical framework grounded in the Dao's generative virtue.

As the Dao's dynamic creation first reveals images before manifesting things or events (Lao Tzu, 2010), the patterns and principles discernible in the cosmos can be understood as expressions of the underlying Dao. The Dao's influence is ubiquitous, evident in the unfolding of natural processes and the authentic expression of human potential. This notion of aligning with the natural disposition inherently carries normative implications for ethical ideals, favoring virtues that arise naturally rather than through rigid imposition (Lai, 2007). This spontaneous nature, along with its pervasive presence, highlights its role as more than just a metaphysical abstraction, but also a belief system central to individual and collective moral development.

The concept of "oneness of substance and function (体用)" or "unity of essence and manifestation" illuminates the workings of the Dao. Here, substance refers to the underlying essence, while function pertains to the manifested reality or power. These two aspects are inseparable: Dao represents the substance, while virtue serves as its function or power in the world. When actualized in human life, Dao takes the form of virtue, embodying the principle of ceaseless creation and nurturing (Chen, 1984). In this sense, Dao serves as the wellspring of existence and flourishing, while virtue manifests as its guiding principle in ordering and sustaining the world (Chan, 1963), hence the "oneness of substance and function."

It is essential to recognize that Lao Tzu's purpose in composing *DaoDeJing* is not solely to expound the ultimate truth, but also to lay the philosophical groundwork for his unique understanding of virtue. The very structure of the text, divided into sections on Dao and de, underscores its dual aim: to present virtue (de) as an active potency of attunement to the Dao, while affirming that a genuine understanding of the Dao is impossible without embodying de. Certainly, Lao Tzu's concept of virtue stands in contrast to Confucian norms, as it is rooted, not in rigid codes or elaborate norms, but in natural ethics. It promotes simplicity, frugality, humility, and, above all, noncoercive action, in harmony with authentic human nature and the essence of the Dao. Confucian norms represent a moral decline precisely because they are artificial constructs—well-intentioned, yet ultimately futile or even detrimental efforts to remedy humanity's estrangement from the Dao.

Lao Tzu's ethics can be better understood with his famous quote: "Returning is how Dao moves, and weakening is how it functions" (Lao Tzu, 2010, Chap. 40). Much like the moon's phases, all things experience cycles of peak, inevitable decline, and subsequent renewal. This natural rhythm highlights the interconnectedness of opposites. The existence of all things is anchored in relation to their opposites, with each entity carrying within it the seed of its counterpart. This delicate interplay underscores the importance of inclusivity and a broad perspective—only by acknowledging and accepting the full spectrum of existence can one truly align with the Dao. Thus, rather than adhering to rigid moral codes and coercive norms, Lao Tzu advocates for a more flexible and adaptable approach to ethics, where the seemingly "weak" qualities, such as humility and wuwei, are regarded as the supreme virtue. By embracing these seemingly "weak" qualities, one can actually be strong, able to navigate worldly challenges with ease and resourcefulness, and to live a more spontaneous and fulfilling life.

The concept of wuwei is central to Daoist self-cultivation. Wuwei does not signify doing nothing but rather noncoercive action—engaging with the world in accordance with its natural flow, without imposing rigid plans or forcing outcomes. For Daoism, the issue with Confucianism lies in its overreliance on external norms and goals, which can suppress the spontaneous unfolding of human nature. When external pressures eclipse the innate dispositions, individuals lose touch with their genuine aspirations, breeding both personal dissonance and societal conflicts. In contrast, noncoercive action invites a return to natural rhythm: moving through the world with attentive calm, embracing humility, and avoiding futile contention. By shedding artifice and complexity, one rediscovers simplicity and genuine compassion. In this state of inner alignment, authentic virtue arises—not as a prescribed norm, but as a spontaneous expression of one's true nature in harmony with the cosmic order.

It is noteworthy that the concept of the Dao serves as a unifying metaphysical thread across Chinese philosophical traditions, often regarded as the ultimate standard and highest truth, though its interpretation and application vary significantly among schools. Daoism emphasizes the Dao of nature, Confucianism the Dao of Heaven, and Mohism the Dao of former kings. Han Feizi, representing Legalism, likewise defines law as the embodiment of the Dao, the ultimate authority on right and wrong (Han, 1999). Even Chinese Buddhists adopted the term Dao to translate key Buddhist ideas, facilitating the integration of their doctrines into Chinese cultural and philosophical contexts.

3.1.2.2 Dao in Confucian Metaphysics

The concept of Dao is fundamental to Confucianism, as it enriches and deepens the philosophical foundation of "Heaven." This development finds its clearest expression in the idea of "the Heaven's Dao," which reconceived Heaven as both natural law and moral imperative—a fundamental moral-cosmic order that reinforces the normative authority and legitimacy of Confucian doctrine. This shift marked a pivotal moment in the evolution of Confucian metaphysics: Heaven, while still the source of moral authority, came to be understood through the lens of the Dao—as the immanent principle of cosmic creativity and moral coherence. This reinterpretation grounded Confucian ethical and political principles in a broader cosmic order and refined the very concept of Heaven itself. By unifying Dao, Heaven, and morality, Confucianism constructed a coherent metaphysical system that harmonizes the cosmic and human realms, affirming the universality of its moral vision.

This philosophical synthesis reached its mature expression through the works of Confucius, Mencius, and later Confucian scholars, who systematically transformed the earlier focus on Heaven into a more sophisticated Dao of Heaven. Central to this development was the imperative to harmonize the Dao of humanity with the Dao of Heaven—the operational realization of Heaven-human unity. During the Song dynasty, Neo-Confucian philosophers abstracted this system further to develop the concept of the "Righteousness of Heaven," which culminated in the doctrines of the "heavenly principle" and the "heart" as the metaphysical and ethical essence of ultimate reality. This conceptual evolution redefined Heaven as a transcendent moral order, wherein Principle became the inherent structure of both nature and ethics, operating with the same inevitability as physical laws.

Yet even as Confucianism incorporates the concept of Dao, its interpretation differs significantly from Daoist thought, emphasizing its normative dimension rather than its natural attributes. In *Commentaries on Changes*, Dao is defined as the dynamic interplay between yin and yang, through which virtues grow (Confucius, 2016c). This perspective sees virtues as blossoms rooted in the cosmic rhythms, legitimizing both social hierarchies while fostering harmonious relationships. In the framework, Dao, morality, and human nature are inseparably intertwined in the pursuit of ethical living, with Dao serving as ontological and normative foundation—a cosmic architecture that generates and sustains all ethical principles. This synthesis finds its institutional expression in the Confucian Orthodoxy (道统), conceived as the lineage and system through which this refined understanding of Dao is transmitted across generations. Neo-Confucianism, aptly named the Study of Dao, carries this tradition forward, further expanding its ethical scope and deepening its metaphysical foundations.

For Confucians, the world is a moral cosmos in which values and ethical order are embedded within both human relationships and the rhythms of nature, with natural phenomena often seen as expressions of an underlying rational principle. Since the Dao embodies both the universe's generative force and its guiding wisdom, the pursuit of the Dao entails attuning oneself to its ethical order to realize harmony and holistic flourishing. This emphasis on harmony and moral practice distinguishes Confucianism from many Western traditions. Whereas Western philosophies often emphasize "seeking the truth," Confucianism centers on "seeking the Dao (the Way)." As Zhang Dainian (1982) argues that "seeking the Dao is seeking the truth, and at the same time seeking the good" (p. 7), highlighting an integration of truth and goodness. Moreover, Confucianism goes beyond merely "learning the Way" to "fulfilling the Way," which lay the foundation for Confucian moral cultivation—a lifelong journey of aligning thought, word, and action with the Dao.

A key contribution of the Dao for moral cultivation lies in its universal nature. As the source of all existence, the Dao flows with equal grace toward every speck of dust and every beating heart. This universality holds particular significance within Confucian ethics. Whereas certain Confucian virtues, grounded in familial affection and kinship ties, may incline individuals toward partiality, the Dao serves as a moral counterbalance—reminding practitioners to uphold integrity, impartiality, and a broader ethical concern in all human relationships. The tension between particularistic consideration and broader moral obligations is poignantly captured in the *Book of Rites*, which states: "when the Grand course [Dao] was pursued, a public and common spirit ruled all under the sky" (Confucius, 2016b, LÎ Yu). This canonical reference suggests how the Confucian Dao introduces a transcendent ethical dimension that both encompasses and supersedes relational particularism.

Moreover, the Daoist principles of spontaneity and noncoercive action function as important correctives to the potential rigidity of Confucian ethical prescriptions, introducing a necessary fluidity and responsiveness into the process of moral cultivation. As ontologically grounded ethical concepts, spontaneity and noncoercive action foster individual authenticity by countering external imposition, thereby tempering the constraints of social norms (Lai, 2007).

This mediating role finds its clearest expression in Neo-Daoism, which negotiates the inherent tension between Confucian social codes and human yearning for spiritual autonomy, reinterpreting the Dao not merely as spontaneous natural flow but as the dialectical alternation of nonbeing (无) and being (有)—an interplay between ontological foundations and value structures. In this framework, moving beyond an externally imposed "being" toward embracing "nonbeing" liberates inner freedom, heightens self-awareness, and enables the dynamic unfolding of one's potential.

The Neo-Daoist perspective significantly enhances human agency by grounding Confucian ethical action in a deeper awareness of one's place within the cosmic pattern. While upholding core Confucian values, Neo-Daoists introduced a strong sense of autonomy, harmonizing the pursuit of personal fulfillment and spiritual liberation with societal obligations. Wang Bi, a leading Neo-Daoist thinker, advocates for a moral cultivation rooted in nonbeing, a state of spontaneity that counterbalances rigid societal norms and rituals. Guo Xiang (2011) takes it further, proposing that both individuality and moral rules are needed, as ethical codes are the "traces" or outward manifestations of spontaneity. This led to a more dynamic model of self-cultivation that emphasizes inner transformation and subjective consciousness. Such a philosophical shift would later leave a profound imprint on Neo-Confucian thought, particularly in its conception of Principle that is simultaneously immanent in human nature and pervasive throughout the cosmos.

3.1.2.3 Buddha Nature and Moral Cultivation

The introduction of Buddhism to China, too, played a significant role in transforming Chinese metaphysical landscape (Li & Perkins, 2014). It offered new perspectives on the ultimate questions such as the nature of existence, the causes of suffering, and the path to liberation, addressing metaphysical gaps that classical

Confucianism either did not develop or deliberately avoided. Given the complexity of Buddhist doctrines, this chapter will focus on how Buddhist worldviews intersect with the pursuit of moral cultivation.

Buddhism perceives the world as fundamentally empty (空) and impermanent (无常). Here, emptiness does not signify nihilistic nothingness, but rather the absence of inherent, independent existence. With no phenomenon possessing a fixed essence, all things exist in a state of ceaseless interdependence and flux, rendering emptiness and impermanence inseparable. This dynamic world is governed by causality: everything arises from a web of causes and conditions, and nothing exists in isolation. Like waves in the ocean, all phenomena are shaped by their context and constantly evolving. Whether spiritual or material, every entity emerges from specific causal conditions and ceases to exist when those conditions dissolve.

This principle, known as dependent origination, reflects a reality governed by impermanence, a fundamental source of suffering rooted in attachment and craving for transient things. The illusion of permanence traps beings in an endless cycle of pursuit and disillusionment, as all cherished objects and achievements inevitably dissolve. Birth, aging, sickness, and death are the most visceral manifestations of this ephemerality. Further compounding this suffering is the law of karma, which binds present actions to future consequences, perpetuating the cycle of rebirth. In this way, human suffering becomes unceasing, sustained by ignorance and the relentless machinery of cause and effect.

The doctrine of karma, or ethical causation, holds that intentions and actions produce corresponding consequences, influencing both present existence and future rebirths. The karmic quality of an act depends primarily on the intention behind it—even outwardly benevolent deeds can bear negative consequences if rooted in selfishness or malice, while truly virtuous actions, such as selfless kindness and compassion, foster favorable rebirths. This framework emphasizes personal accountability, encouraging ethical conduct through the cultivation of wholesome deeds and the avoidance of harmful ones, with the aim of attaining ultimate liberation from the karmic cycle of suffering.

While acknowledging the impermanence of the physical world, Buddhism upholds the enduring truth of the Dharma, the Buddha's teachings. These teachings reveal the interconnectedness and transient nature of existence, guiding individuals toward nirvana—a state of eternal peace and bliss. Notably, the Buddha is not a deity, but an enlightened human being who transcended individual limitations to offer a path to enlightenment to all beings. Thus, the goal of Buddhist self-cultivation involves the transformation from ignorance to enlightenment and from the state of ego-centeredness to the state of nonself (anātman).

Buddhism in China developed primarily through the Mahāyāna ("Great Vehicle") tradition, which exerted a dominant influence. In contrast to Theravāda's focus on individual enlightenment, Mahāyāna emphasizes a universal Buddha-nature, which holds that enlightenment is universally accessible and redefines the ultimate liberation as a collective pursuit, not merely an individual one.

Chan Buddhists, for instance, hold that Buddha-nature inherently resides within the heart—the very core of our being and the wellspring of moral and spiritual awareness, where ethical insight, compassion, and awakened understanding converge. Like a dormant seed awaiting awakening, this latent potential unfolds through a dedicated path to enlightenment: ethical conduct (the five precepts), mental discipline (meditation), and the cultivation of wisdom (prajña). Through sustained Dharma practice, individuals nurture this innate potential, gradually dissolving delusion to attain a direct, experiential understanding of reality, culminating in the full actualization of their intrinsic Buddha-nature.

This awakening is a profound realization of the non-duality of self and others. As one realizes their own Buddhahood, the illusion of a separate self begins to unravel. Coupled with the recognition of universal suffering, this gives rise to an inexhaustible compassion that naturally compels the awakened to devote themselves to the liberation of all sentient beings.

The conviction that all sentient beings possess Buddha-nature lies at the heart of Buddhist ethics, fostering a profound sense of interdependence, grounding moral responsibility in the shared destiny of life. Thus, relieving others' suffering becomes more than mere kindness—it is an indispensable expression of one's own journey toward Buddhahood. Such compassion naturally gives rise to the Bodhisattva ideal, where the vow to guide all beings to awakening takes precedence over individual transcendence.[4]

These Buddhist metaphysical ideas of the heart-mind and Buddha-nature did not enter a philosophical vacuum in China; they profoundly echoed and enriched a Chinese tradition that, since Confucius, had already grappled with questions of human nature and the mind's moral capacities. Mencius, for example, advanced his theory of innate moral knowledge (良知), an inborn ethical sensibility that gives rise to the four cardinal virtues: compassion, shame, modesty and deference, and discernment between right and wrong. However, while Mencius invoked Heaven as the ultimate moral authority, his thought remained essentially anthropocentric—rooted in human morality and social ethics—rather than grounded in an abstract metaphysical principle that transcends the social realm to attain universal and enduring significance.

Buddhism addressed this philosophical incompleteness by introducing the concepts of a universal heart-mind and Buddha-nature. Chan Buddhism, in particular, engaged in deep dialogue with indigenous Chinese conceptions of mind and human nature, elevating them to a transcendent and ultimate level. By probing the nature of reality and existential questions, it asserts that liberation arises from rediscovering the universal heart-mind and Buddha-nature, which granted the terms "heart-mind" and "nature" with unprecedented metaphysical sophistication. These conceptual innovations were subsequently appropriated and transformed by Confucian thinkers, laying the groundwork for Neo-Confucianism's effort to establish a comprehensive metaphysical framework for ethics, where ethical order and universal principle

[4]This strong sense of interconnectedness and altruism may be why Buddhism was so widely embraced in ancient China, as its ethical core resonates deeply with indigenous Chinese culture emphasizing interdependence.

converge as one and where moral significance became both immanent within human nature and pervasive throughout the cosmos.

Furthermore, Daoism and Buddhism have profoundly broadened Confucian worldview by introducing complementary perspectives that lend conceptual flexibility and create space for metaphysical inquiry. Where Confucianism champions disciplined self-cultivation, Daoism embraces natural spontaneity, and Buddhism advocates mindful nonattachment. Together, these traditions constitute the three pillars of Chinese thought, forming an organic philosophical ecosystem in which Daoist fluidity and Buddhist transcendence temper the exacting demands of Confucian moral rigor and soften the relentless pursuit of social achievement with wisdom and inner tranquility—one that harmonizes social accountability with spiritual freedom and existential–cosmic awareness.

Throughout history, Confucian literati have often integrated Daoist and Buddhist ideas into their own worldviews to justify and promote moral cultivation. This cross-pollination is significant because strict adherence to a single system of thought can limit perspective. By embracing diverse ideas, Confucian frameworks demonstrates a remarkable ability to remain dynamic and evolve over time, adapting to new contexts and challenges.

3.2 Harmonious Universalism in Moral Cultivation

Chinese moral cultivation is deeply grounded in a distinctive tradition of harmonious universalism, a philosophical and ethical framework that emphasizes expansive ethical relationships, the interconnectedness of all beings, and the cultivation of harmony across diverse cultures, beliefs, and systems. Through its emphasis on relational virtuosity and cosmic resonance, it fosters an inclusive yet coherent vision of moral flourishing that bridges human relationships, ecological balance, and metaphysical unity.

Unlike Western universalism, which prioritizes abstract principles and individual rights, Chinese universalism manifests through practical ethics and the continuous refinement of one's character within a communal and cosmic order. This perspective, shaped by centuries of dialogue among Confucianism, Daoism, and Buddhism, has developed a uniquely Chinese understanding of universality. The resulting holistic worldview, grounded in shared beliefs about Heaven, human nature, and the heart, cultivates an expansive yet integrated vision of ethical life—a vision inspiring a profound commitment to moral cultivation while embracing diverse paths toward ethical growth and spiritual fulfillment.

3.2.1 *The Logic of Chinese Moral Universalism*

Examining the Chinese approach to universal values necessitates engaging with competing theories of universalism. Moral universalism is the meta-ethical position that certain moral principles hold universally, applying to all individuals regardless of culture or background. Critics, however, argue that this approach can be overly rigid, potentially overlooking cultural particularities and concealing ethnocentric biases. Ethical relativism, conversely, maintains that morality is entirely context-dependent, though this position struggles to account for intercultural moral consensus (Richardson & Williams, 2009). A mediating perspective—soft or pluralistic universalism—proposes that while certain fundamental values (like reciprocity and compassion) possess universal validity, their manifestations remain culturally nuanced. This framework not only reconciles shared ethical foundations with diverse expressions but also reveals how seemingly distinct value systems can mutually inform and enhance one another, whether operating at global or local scales (Pohl, 2002).

The universality of traditional Chinese philosophy has long been a subject of debate. Confucianism, for instance, espouses universal values such as harmony and ritual propriety, yet its strong emphasis on particularistic relationships, especially familial bonds, raises questions about its compatibility with universalist reasoning and egalitarian love (Wang, 2015). This tension is further compounded by Confucianism's simultaneous commitment to transcendent moral truths and to the preservation of cultural distinctiveness and autonomy (Zhang, 2009), creating a unique synthesis of cosmopolitan ideals and rooted tradition.

While Chinese philosophy may not conform to a Western model of universalism, dismissing it as purely particular overlooks its broader perspective. Many Chinese metaphysical concepts, such as Heaven, human nature, and golden mean, carry universal significance and can resonate across diverse cultures. In addition, Chinese ethics offers unique contributions to the global discourse on universal values. Confucian virtues like humaneness, which promotes kindness, loyalty, and reciprocity, embody values with global relevance; Daoist notions of Dao, noncoercive action, and spontaneity have gained international appeal for their potential to alleviate modern anxieties and pressures, promoting inner peace and harmony for all individuals. These concepts and ideas, while marked by distinct national characteristics, still possess a universality that speaks to fundamental aspects of the human condition.

Among these universal contributions, a significant one lies within the Neo-Confucian concept of the heavenly principle (li), a higher order infused with moral attributes that govern the cosmos (Liu, 2017). Blakeley (1998) provides a clear summary of how this Principle informs Zhu Xi's universalist thinking, highlighting the centrality of Principle in his cosmology and ethics, the course of moral development as the recovery of Principle, the ideal of impartiality in moral cultivation, and the concept of differentiated love as a practical application of universal principle and human nature. The last point suggests that this universality is not absolute, since it must accommodate particularity, as illustrated by Neo-Confucian dictum that the Principle is one, but its manifestations are many (Li & Xiang, 2020). Whereas the heavenly principle implies an overarching guiding principle for all, it simultaneously allows for individual differentiation, recognizing diverse roles and responsibilities. This subtle tension between universal order and individual particularity is the defining characteristic of the Neo-Confucian universality.

Similarly, the concept of the "heart-mind"—a notion embraced by Confucianism, Daoism, and Buddhism—presents a rich framework for moral development that encompasses both universal and particularistic dimensions. Universally, the heart-mind, with its innate capacity for empathy and care, signifies a shared human foundation for ethical reflection across cultures. At the same time, it is uniquely shaped by individual experience and cultural context, revealing its particularistic character. This dual nature underscores the importance of self-awareness and introspection, rendering moral cultivation a profoundly personal journey that resonates with universal ethical aspirations.

While Chinese philosophy enriches the shared pool of universal values, its universality is expressed through particularism, fostering a tolerance for diverse ideas across cultures. In this sense, Chinese philosophy somewhat aligns with soft or pluralistic universalism—a paradigm that avoids rigidity and pure rationalism.[5] As a form of universalism, it seeks principles applicable to everyone. But unlike rigid, one-size-fits-all approaches, it posits that this common ground can be found amidst diverse perspectives.

Notably, this "softness" suggests an openness to varied understandings and expressions of universal values, acknowledging that they may manifest differently across cultures. The term "pluralistic" further emphasizes that the world is not monolithic, but that consensus can be reached from differing perspectives, preserving the richness of human experience. In our increasingly interconnected world, this perspective promotes inclusivity and a broad-minded approach to addressing complex ethical challenges.

This pluralistic universalism, however, should not be conflated with relativism, which rejects universal truths altogether. Instead, it resonates with the Rig Veda's assertion that "truth is one; sages call it by various names" (Griffith, 2013, 1:164:46). This ethos acknowledges the universality of core values, such as kindness and respect, while honoring the diverse ways these principles are expressed across cultures. Moreover, the Chinese philosophical emphasis on interconnectedness enriches pluralistic universalism by shifting the focus from individual autonomy to relational harmony. It underscores the role of humaneness, compassion, and harmony in bridging differences, fostering an "ethos of interrelatedness that views all people as siblings under Heaven (Confucius, 2016a). Such a perspective nurtures a profound

[5] The traditional Chinese universalism is less about absolutism but more a kind of soft universalism that tends to seek "common ground beneath the variety of opinions and mores" due to similar human nature (Rosenstand, 2017, pp. 119–120) in Rosenstand (2017). The moral of the story: An introduction to ethics (eighth ed.). McGraw-Hill Companies. (41).

responsibility for the whole of existence, encouraging moral cultivation that transcends the self to embrace the interdependence of all beings.

Building on this understanding, it is harmonious universalism, more than pluralism, that best expresses the spirit of Chinese universality. While pluralistic universalism recognizes diversity, it often stops short of integration, a core imperative in Chinese thought. Harmonious universalism, by contrast, actively synthesizes diverse ethical traditions into a cohesive vision that upholds both social harmony and cosmic equilibrium. Beyond merely balancing universal norms with cultural particularities, China has pursued a dynamic unity rooted in the interplay of Confucian, Daoist, and Buddhist wisdom. Such a framework not only grounds ethical dialogue but also enables mutual transformation—offering a vision of universalism that is truly integrative, vibrant, and enduring. It cultivates a culturally inclusive universality (Roetz, 2009), one that accommodates diverse traditions while advancing a shared goal of promoting life-nurturing, renewal, and co-flourishing.

This moderate and adaptive stance, grounded in humanistic philosophy instead of absolute truths or religious doctrine, is often praised for its flexibility and capacity for tolerance. Yet, this model has its limits: its very commitment to a "culturally inclusive universality"—while accommodating diverse traditions—has also been critiqued for tacitly privileging its own foundational assumptions, thereby undermining claims to true universality in practice. Furthermore, unlike more rigid systems, its reliance on context-sensitive principles can sometimes struggle to provide definitive guidance when adjudicating irreconcilable moral differences across vastly distinct cultural or belief systems. Even so, as a framework aspiring to foster life-generative coexistence amid global diversity, it remains a compelling, if imperfect, model for shared flourishing.

3.2.2 Universal Moral Cultivation Across the Three Teachings

For centuries, Confucianism, Daoism, and Buddhism have formed the three cornerstones of Chinese philosophy and culture, with Confucianism assuming a particularly prominent role in moral cultivation. As both a path to personal fulfillment and a guiding framework for social and political life, it upholds the universal ideal of humaneness. This ideal resonates with Lao Tzu's pursuit of omnipresent Dao and echoes Mahāyāna Buddhism's vow to liberate all sentient beings, contributing to the enduring synthesis of the Three Teachings.

3.2.2.1 Holistic Cosmology

Chinese moral cultivation is built upon a holistic, unified cosmic framework—where Heaven, Earth, and humanity exist in inclusiveness, interdependence, and impartiality. As *the Book of Rites* notes, "Heaven envelops everything impartially; earth supports and contains everything impartially; the sun and moon shine on everything impartially" (2016b, KHUNG-DZE HSIEN KU). Such all-encompassing virtue creates the conditions for all beings to flourish according to their nature, fostering a profound sense of universal responsibility.

This holistic paradigm centers on three fundamental principles: the Dao (or Supreme Ultimate) as the generative source of all existence, whose essence permeates every being; the ceaseless dynamism of yin and yang, which structures and interconnects all phenomena; and an ethical framework that prioritizes collective flourishing and mutual interdependence, reflecting the worldview that "events never occur in isolation, but emerge within a meaningful cosmic totality" (Nisbett, 2005, p. 27). Traditional Chinese philosophy embodies this interconnectedness par excellence—its worldviews, political theories, cultivation practices, and pedagogies forming an integrated system of thought. Consequently, only a holistic approach that situates these elements within their broader context, while carefully discerning the nuances among different philosophical traditions, can yield an authentic understanding of Chinese philosophy.

This worldview profoundly shaped Chinese personhood, not as isolated entities, but as integral parts of interconnected networks. Under Confucian tutelage, identity emerged through social embeddedness: individuals found meaning by discerning their roles within concentric circles of obligation. These structures—from family to community to state—functioned as reciprocal systems, offering security and resources while demanding loyalty and service. As civilizational horizons expanded, this relational ethic evolved into a framework of universal responsibility that transcended mere local loyalty. Concurrently, the principle of equitable benefit-sharing gained traction, acknowledging that while perfect material equality might be unattainable, all members deserved participation in collective prosperity. The ultimate aspiration was to cultivate universal harmony and mutual flourishing across All under Heaven.

Built upon the holistic worldview, Confucian moral cultivation prioritizes the nurturing of virtuous relationships, fulfilling one's designated roles and responsibilities within the broader frameworks. In this tradition, personal accomplishments and aspirations, while valued, are always considered in relation to the collective needs of the family or community. The very act of cultivating virtue, given the constraints of shared resources, often requires tempering individual desires to support the well-being and growth of others. Thus, moral cultivation is not merely a form of self-perfection but a commitment to upholding collective flourishing.

3.2.2.2 Moral Cultivation in the Vision of All Under Heaven

The Chinese moral cultivation envisions a transformative process where refined personal character became the foundation for state prosperity and universal harmony. While the concept of All under Heaven may seem outdated in modern cosmology, its enduring significance lies in articulating a visionary humanistic ideal: the conviction that all people "within the four seas,"" irrespective of origin or status, share an essential humanity and exist in webs of reciprocal obligation.

"All under Heaven," pivotal to Confucian moral cultivation, embraces inclusivity over exclusivity, embodying a universal spirit that encompasses all people and entities. While Confucian ethics originate within the intimate circle of familial relationships and clan bonds, it gradually extends outward, transcending narrow nepotism and cliquishness to embrace unrelated individuals and a broader sense of community. Metaphysically, this conceptual framework intricately merges the realms of Heaven and humanity, embedding inclusivity and universality at the heart of moral cultivation. By attributing supreme authority to Heaven, it instills in individuals the values of broad-mindedness and altruism. At its highest level, it calls on people to transcend distinctions among people, states, and even species, recognizing their interconnectedness within the vast web of existence and fostering harmony and peace throughout the world.

This concept of universal moral cultivation was systematically developed by Northern Song Confucian scholars: Cheng and Cheng (1981) argued that individuals embodying humaneness perceive the fundamental interconnectedness of all existence, while Zhang Zai's famous dictum—"All people are my siblings; all things are my companions" (Zhang, 1978)—epitomized this ethical worldview. This philosophy of shared cosmic kinship and inclusive destiny served as a powerful unifying force, facilitating both cultural assimilation and territorial consolidation throughout imperial China.

Next, the notions of human nature (性) and the heart (心) serve as bridges between Heaven and humanity, facilitating universal moral cultivation. This connection is corroborated by the unearthed Guodian bamboo slips, which explicitly state that [human] nature is derived from Heaven's Mandate (Liu, 2025). While scholars often root virtue in a transcendent heavenly source, they also acknowledge its intrinsic grounding in human nature, rendering it an inherent aspect of being human. Thus, virtue is both transcendent in its celestial origin and immanent in humanity.

Accordingly, the universal moral cultivation in Confucianism rests on the belief that all humans possess an endowed nature and an innate moral heart-mind, enabling individuals—regardless of social status, cultural background, or level of education—to connect through the shared pursuit of virtue. Conversely, one might argue that morality is a human projection onto the universe, highlighting human agency's centrality in moral development. By imbuing the cosmos with moral significance, Confucianism achieves a profound ethical transformation—one that not only deepens the philosophical foundation of moral cultivation but also facilitates the dissemination of ethical principles across a vast land and through successive generations.

The shared goal of moral development in Chinese philosophy does not negate the presence of diverse voices and pathways. Daoist spontaneity, Mohism's impartial care, and Buddhism's enlightenment and compassion offer distinct yet complementary pathways alongside Confucian ideals, collectively enriching the Chinese ethical landscape. This dynamic interplay of diversity and universality can be comprehended from a broader perspective. In ancient China, virtue or "de" was a foundational belief, originally referring to the patterns of Heaven or nature. It emphasizes the flourishing of life, balance within diversity, and the promotion of peace and social stability—shared aspirations across various philosophical traditions. While each school emphasizes different aspects of moral cultivation, they all affirm its significance for individual fulfillment and social harmony.

Daoism and Buddhism played a pivotal role in promoting a universal yet diverse spirit of moral cultivation. Chuang Tzu (2013), for instance, propose the idea of equality of all things. This equality, however, does not imply uniformity; rather, it dissolves rigid ontological boundaries between "things" and "self" and, more importantly, transcends the fixed dichotomies of right and wrong (Yang, 2015). Daoist thinkers, while upholding All under Heaven, emphasize spontaneity as essential to aligning with the Dao. They recognize the intrinsic uniqueness and interdependence of all beings, cultivating an attitude of receptivity and a deep sense of harmony amid differences. All these ideas have profoundly influenced Confucian thought, enriching the universality and inclusiveness of Confucian moral cultivation.

In effect, the pragmatic Confucian culture, with its emphasis on effort and achievement, inevitably generated pressures that required balancing mechanisms. Daoism and Buddhism fulfilled this vital role. Daoism, with its celebration of natural spontaneity, served as a liberating counterweight to Confucian discipline, while Buddhism, through its teachings on impermanence and emptiness, provided an even more profound release from the anxieties of worldly striving. Together, these traditions softened the rigidities of Confucian ambition, creating a dynamic cultural equilibrium.

Buddhist thought profoundly enriched the universal ethos of Chinese culture. The doctrine of dependent origination illuminated the fundamental impermanence and interdependence of all existence, inspiring an ethic of all-encompassing compassion. When combined with the Buddhist teaching of nonself, this worldview dissolved rigid ego-boundaries and discriminatory tendencies, fostering a truly inclusive moral vision. Most transformative is the Mahāyāna ideal of universal salvation, which boldly challenged conventional Chinese hierarchies by asserting that all sentient beings equally possess the capacity for enlightenment. Collectively, these principles cultivated a spirit of universal altruism, motivating individuals to extend care and moral responsibility toward all living beings.

The evolution of Chan Buddhism exemplifies the dynamic interplay and cross-pollination between Confucianism, Daoism, and Buddhism in ancient China. Emerging from its mystical Buddhist roots, Chan evolved into a simpler, more accessible form, emphasizing the inherent Buddha-nature within each individual's heart rather than reliance on esoteric scriptures. It appears to have been influenced by Chuang Tzu's belief in the pervasive Dao, present in every aspect of existence, and Confucius' assertion that the Dao is not distant from human experience. These influences illustrate how Chan Buddhism actively integrated elements of indigenous Chinese philosophy, forming a distinctive synthesis that reflects and reinforces the universalist spirit of Chinese culture.

Chan Buddhism's distinctive contribution to universal moral cultivation lies in its radical democratization of spiritual attainment, making enlightenment accessible across all social strata and educational backgrounds. By affirming the immanence of Buddha-nature in all beings, Chan empowered individuals to attain liberation through direct awakening to their innate wisdom. This paradigm of self-realization, centered on immediate, intuitive insight rather than textual study, exerted profound influence on Neo-Confucianism's School of Mind, particularly in shaping its doctrines of ethical enlightenment. In this Chan-inspired framework, moral cultivation becomes an introspective journey: Rather than conforming to external norms, the ethical agent discovers an inexhaustible wellspring of moral understanding within the heart-mind, transforming religious enlightenment into a paradigm of ethical self-discovery and actualization.

3.3 Metaphysical Reconstruction and the Establishment of an Ethical Cosmos

Indigenous Chinese culture is predominantly secular, prioritizing practical human affairs—social harmony, ethical conduct, and worldly flourishing—over metaphysical speculation about ultimate reality or divinity. While this pragmatic focus fostered a rich tradition of situational ethics and relational wisdom, it also constrained the development of a robust moral universalism—an ethical framework grounded in principles transcending specific cultural or historical contexts. This limitation became particularly evident with the introduction of Buddhism, whose sophisticated cosmology and soteriological vision offered compelling answers to existential questions that Chinese thought had largely left unaddressed, thereby attracting widespread intellectual and popular appeal.

Faced with intellectual and popular challenges, Confucianism underwent a profound metamorphosis during the Song Dynasty (960–1279 CE). Drawing inspiration from both Daoism and Buddhism, Neo-Confucians expanded their focus beyond practical ethics and ritual propriety to engage deeply with cosmology and metaphysics, including reinterpretations of cosmic genesis depicted in *the Changes*. This intellectual revolution not only endowed Confucian ethics with new metaphysical foundations but also sacralized moral cultivation by grounding it in the very fabric of the cosmos, thereby significantly enhancing both its philosophical rigor and its spiritual appeal.

Zhou Dunyi (1017–1073 CE), the architect of Neo-Confucian cosmology, established the Confucian framework of cosmic origins. He integrated the Daoist concept of the Boundless (无极) with the Confucian notion of the "Supreme Ultimate" (太极, also referred to as the Supreme Polarity), positioning both as foundational principles of the universe. In Zhou's view, the Boundless—functionally similar to the Dao—is the primordial ground of reality itself: not an absence of existence, but a pre-cosmic reservoir of undifferentiated being and non-being, brimming with infinite potential.

From this state arises the Supreme Ultimate, representing the first movement from undifferentiated potentiality to dynamic actuality. As the primary source of cosmic differentiation, it gives rise to the fundamental polarities of yin and yang, whose ceaseless interaction produces the infinite complexity and diversity of existence (Zhou, 1936). Philosophically conceived, the Supreme Ultimate marks the critical ontological threshold where nonbeing becomes being through the activation of a cosmic creative principle. It imbues the undifferentiated void with generative potency, transforming absolute potentiality into ordered manifestation.

In Neo-Confucian thought, Dao embraces both the Boundless and the Supreme Ultimate, reflecting the dynamic process by which "nonbeing" gives rise to "being." This framework compellingly justifies Neo-Confucianism's self-designation as "the Study of Dao." From this perspective, the pursuit of personal cultivation and the establishment of social order are not merely ethical pursuits but are intrinsically tied to the fundamental structure of the universe, highlighting the ontological consistency between "Dao" and "Principle." Consequently, virtue in Neo-Confucianism transcends social convention, attaining a deeper, metaphysical significance.

Zhu Xi (1130–1200 CE), a leading figure in the School of Principle, further refined the Neo-Confucian cosmological model. He contends that the Boundless and the Supreme Ultimate are not sequential states, but rather different "names" or complementary aspects of a single ultimate reality: The Boundless signifies the transcendent, unchanging source—an inexhaustible wellspring of potential—while the Supreme Ultimate embodies its dynamic, generative aspect, the principle or process through which the Boundless manifests. Zhu Xi emphasizes the term Supreme Ultimate, distinguishing it from the Daoist concept of the Boundless which remains primarily transcendent and apophatic. For Zhu Xi, the Supreme Ultimate is a distinctly Confucian notion that integrates ontological foundation with normative paradigm. As a primordial and resourceful state that generates all things, the Supreme Ultimate functions as a creative power without requiring a creator behind the scenes (Song, 2018). It encapsulates the universal ethical principles of generativity, renewal, and shared flourishing, manifesting the highest good in Confucian ethics.

Zhu Xi's reinterpretation carries profound philosophical significance, which systematically mediates between the transcendent Dao and concrete human praxis, particularly in moral cultivation. For Neo-Confucians, the Supreme Ultimate operates dialectically as both the ontological foundation of generative moral value and the teleological aim of ethical practice—whereby cultivation becomes the process of actualizing and manifesting this supreme principle in daily life. By aligning thought and deeds with the essence of the Supreme Ultimate, characterized by dynamic equilibrium and the harmonization of opposites, individuals attain equilibrium within themselves, with others, and in their engagement with the wider world. This state of harmony is also referred to as following the Way (Dao) or Heaven, alternative expressions of the Supreme Ultimate. Ultimately, this conceptual framework proves indispensable not only for comprehending Neo-Confucian metaphysics, but also for grasping fundamental aspects of the Chinese ethos, illuminating the normative foundations underlying social behavior and ethical reasoning.

The concept of heavenly principle (天理) lies at the heart of Neo-Confucian thought, carrying profound ontological and ethical significance. Rooted in the belief that Heaven embodies the highest virtues, Neo-Confucians abstracted the idea into heavenly principle—variously understood as principle, order, pattern, or reason. While bearing some resemblance to the Western notion of reason, the heavenly principle is imbued with far deeper ethical significance. It signifies the fundamental law or underlying pattern governing both nature and human society, suggesting a profound harmony between natural laws and human ethics. In this framework, the ethical principles that guide human society are not merely social constructs but are seamlessly aligned with, and endorsed by, the very structure of the cosmos, emphasizing the interconnectedness of all existence.

The heavenly principle, hereafter referred to as "Principle," can be understood as a Neo-Confucian interpretation of the Dao or the Supreme Ultimate, carrying profound ethical implications that affirm moral cultivation. Unlike Plato's abstract Forms, which exist in a detached, immutable realm, Principle functions as both the ultimate reality underlying existence and a comprehensive matrix encompassing key Confucian virtues such as humaneness, righteousness, ritual propriety, and wisdom that shape ethical practice. Zhu Xi (2013), for instance, equates Principle with the Way of Heaven and identifies the Supreme Ultimate with Principle, thereby solidifying Principle's role as the overarching metaphysical framework and normative order that governs all aspects of existence. While the Dao encompasses ultimate reality, Principle articulates its normative dimension, and the Supreme Ultimate drives its generative unfolding.

A defining feature of Principle is its capacity to bridge the seemingly disparate realms of universal morality and individual experiences. This duality is vividly captured in Zhu Xi's adaptation of a Chan Buddhist metaphor: Imagine the moon, singular in the night sky, yet reflected in myriad forms across rivers, lakes, and ponds. Just as the moon remains one, Principle embodies a singular truth with universal significance, yet it is also manifested within each individual and situation. This suggests that Principle can be grasped through the careful examination of all phenomena in the world, an intellectual and introspective process involving reading, observation, inquiry, reflection, and moral practice.

Next, Principle is an inclusive concept that extends beyond a self-centric or human-centered perspective. While morality primarily concerns values and norms governing human relationships, Principle encompasses all living beings and even the natural world—an all-encompassing quality reminiscent of Dao. Drawing on Principle, Neo-Confucians established a moral framework rooted in inclusivity, impartiality, and universality. This counteracts biases and favoritism, upholding an objective ethical standard that transcends personal partialities.

Due to its rich metaphysical and ethical implications, Neo-Confucians tended to use Principle in place of the more primordial concept of the "Way of Heaven" when articulating the unity of Heaven and humanity. More importantly, it allows Confucianism to confidently integrate insights from Daoism and Buddhism. As Zhu Xi (1986) aptly states, "there is no two different Dao in the universe…and there is only one single Principle" (Vol. 126). This concept propels China's philosophical inquiry toward a rationalized understanding of the world, yet remains grounded in humanistic and pragmatic moral principles. By permeating every corner of existence, Principle gives moral meaning to the entire universe and ultimately sanctifies the pursuit of moral cultivation.

3.3.1 Principle and Desire

A central Neo-Confucian teaching maintains that to uphold Principle, one must overcome selfish desires (人欲). While acknowledging basic human needs such as food and sex as natural and legitimate, they criticize excessive cravings for luxury, sensual indulgence, or fame. Zhu Xi (1986) illustrates this distinction with a vivid analogy: "Eating three modest meals a day accords with Principle, but demanding lavish banquets daily represents desire" (p. 389). In this context, "desire" refers to the insatiable pursuit of excess and indulgence, whereas Principle represents the fulfillment of essential, balanced needs in harmony with one's moral nature.

Confucian scholars, along with Daoists and Buddhists, strongly oppose unbridled desires. This call for temperance may reflect the practical imperatives of a densely populated agrarian society like China, where unchecked indulgence by the elite risked overexploitation and social unrest. From this perspective, Neo-Confucianism advocates for a balanced life and ethical rigor grounded in collective good, emphasizing self-discipline and vigilance against excesses such as extravagance and sensual indulgence.

This ethical orientation has deep historical roots. As early as the Pre-Qin era, Confucians vigorously debated the tension between righteousness (义) and personal gain (利), consistently affirming the primacy of righteousness. Neo-Confucians deepened this discourse by examining the tension between Principle and desire. They relentlessly pursue self-restraint, advocating the deliberate mastery of selfish impulses as essential to preserving Principle and upholding a broader ethical vision that prioritizes societal flourishing and universal order.

Cheng Yi (1033–1107 CE) proposes self-restraint through heart-mind cultivation, positing a dualistic framework of human psychology: the heart of Dao, which embodies our capacity to apprehend Principle, and the human-heart, which contains primal instincts and desires for luxury. These constitute an existential dichotomy—where the human-heart naturally tends toward selfish gratification, the Dao-heart, as the repository of Principle, inherently aligns with moral universality. Neo-Confucian self-cultivation thus emerges as an ontological project: Through disciplined restraint of the human-heart's cravings, one actualizes Principle latent within the Dao-heart.

As the paramount law governing nature and human society, Principle embodies universality and impartiality that can enhance traditional Confucian virtues. While these family-based virtues foster loyalty and righteousness within familial and social circles, they are vulnerable to being undermined by favoritism and nepotism—forms of "private desire" capable of corrupting even the most virtuous. Thus, the true significance of Principle, and the heart-mind that cultivates or recovers it, lies in its ability to transform initially limited and hierarchical affection into a universal and impartial compassion. Upholding Principle, then, reflects a commitment to maintaining a public heart devoted to collective welfare and fairness.

3.3.2 *The Generative Debate: Primacy of Qi or Li?*

Neo-Confucians complement Principle with the vital concept of qi (气), the dynamic, substantive energy that constitutes the very fabric of existence. While etymologically rooted in notions of "air" and "breath," qi operates metaphysically as the animating force that vitalizes both the cosmos and human life. This primal substance exists in varying states of clarity and turbidity, directly shaping human temperament and moral capacity. As the medium through which Principle manifests its formative patterns in the phenomenal world, qi occupies a crucial position in Neo-Confucian ethics—its cultivation and refinement becoming essential to moral self-perfection and cosmic harmony.

China boasts a long tradition of cultivating qi for moral development. Mencius (2016), for instance, describes qi as passion-nature, claiming "[I am] skillful in nourishing my vast, flowing passion-nature." And "it is exceedingly great, and exceedingly strong. Being nourished by rectitude, and sustaining no injury, it fills up all between Heaven and Earth" (6A:2). For Mencius, qi is not merely physical matter or energy, but a vital, spirited force infused with a sense of righteousness and nobility, unfolding through the cultivation of a steady moral compass. Conversely, neglecting this cultivation results in stagnation and the flagging of one's moral energy.

Neo-Confucian thinker Zhang Zai (1020–1077 CE) revolutionizes the concept of qi, presenting it as the vital force that animates the universe. He positions qi, rather than Dao or the Supreme Ultimate, at the very heart of cosmic genesis. Based on qi, he introduces the concept of the Ultimate Void (太虚), which is not a simple emptiness, but a brimming reservoir of undifferentiated qi, a boundless potentiality to be realized. There is the Ultimate Void where qi is dispersed, and there emerges the physical world when qi converges (Zhang, 1978). Principle comes out of qi's movements of convergence and divergence, revealing an underlying order—a set of rules governing its movement. This, for Zhang, is Principle, the cosmic law embedded within the very fabric of existence. It is not something separate from qi, but an intrinsic aspect of its nature.

Humans, as an essential part of this world, are composed of qi as well. Like all things, they possess both the nature of the Ultimate Void and a physical nature. The former, constituted by a refined qi, embodies the essence of Heaven and Earth, housing our inherent potential for virtue in alignment with Principle. The latter, formed from turbid qi and shaped by acquired habits, encompasses not only goodness but also human desires such as greed, self-centeredness, and narrow-mindedness, which obscure the virtue within us. Hence, Zhang Zai advances the doctrine of transforming one's physical nature to reclaim the innate nature endowed by Heaven, offering a rationale for the pursuit of moral cultivation.

Whereas Zhang Zai conceives qi as the primordial substrate that sustains and gives rise to Principle (li), Zhu Xi inverts this metaphysical relationship by positioning Principle as the transcendent ground from which qi emanates. In Zhu Xi's framework, Principle constitutes the formless ultimate reality, while qi operates as its dynamic, differentiated manifestation. Although Principle remains inherently good, human beings inherit varying admixtures of qi—from the most refined to the turbid. This ontological condition renders moral cultivation fundamentally introspective: one must discern and actualize Principle while systematically purging qi's distorting influences—particularly partiality and selfish desire. Through this disciplined refinement of qi, the practitioner progressively recovers their original nature, realigning with the cosmic harmony of Heaven and Earth (Zhu, 2013).

Grounded in their distinct ontological assumptions, Zhu Xi and Zhang Zai propose differing approaches to moral cultivation. Zhu Xi's Principle-centered ontology gives rise to a more inward-looking and academic form of self-cultivation, prioritizing "inner sage"—the pursuit of moral self-perfection through introspection, reading, inquiry, and self-reflection. In contrast, Zhang Zai's qi-based metaphysics results in a more pragmatic approach that underscores learning through service to the state. This aligns with the Confucian ideal of "outer king"—the application of moral principles to influence others and contribute to societal betterment. Yet, despite their different focus, both approaches reflect core ideas in Confucian moral cultivation, illustrating the richness and diversity within the tradition.

3.3.3 The Heart-Mind as Embodied Principle

The distinctive role of the heart-mind (心) in Confucian moral cultivation traces its origins to Mencius' declaration that "he who has exhausted all his mental constitution [the heart] knows his nature. Knowing his nature, he knows Heaven" (2016, 7A:1). Mencius positions the heart-mind as both the seat of innate moral sprouts and the conduit for cosmic connection, advocating the recovery of one's "original heart" and nourishing it with moral qi. This foundational framework is later expanded by Neo-Confucians, who, drawing inspiration from Daoism and Chan Buddhism, develop a more comprehensive understanding of the heart-mind, significantly enriching its metaphysical dimensions. This effort transformed the heart-mind from primarily an ethical faculty into a cosmological interface where human nature, moral principle, and cosmic vitality dynamically intersect.

Shao Yong (1012–1077 CE) occupies a unique position in Neo-Confucianism for his systematic integration of Daoist cosmology with Confucian ethics, particularly through his seminal distinction between the "Study of Innateness" and the "Study of Acquirement." The former represents a metaphysical inquiry into the primordial patterns of *the Changes*—numerical and cosmological principles that closely align with his Daoist sensibilities. The latter represents the Confucian path of moral cultivation, concerned with realizing human nature and fulfilling ethical destiny (性命). Unlike Kant's rigid dichotomy between phenomena and noumena, Shao's framework presents these as complementary aspects of a continuous reality—what Neo-Confucians would later describe as the inseparable relationship between "substance" (体) and "function" (用). The Study of Innateness provides the cosmological foundation for virtue, while the Study of Acquirement offers the practical means for its embodiment in human life.

Shao Yong's (2016) synthesis of Daoist metaphysics and Confucian ethics rests on his privileging of the heart-mind's dynamic function. This inner realm of the heart, housing a spark of cosmic spirit, serves as the ontological foundation of human nature. By cultivating this inner spark, individuals align themselves with cosmic patterns, fostering a harmonious alignment between Heaven and humanity in virtue. It is in this light that he refers to the Study of Innateness as "the law of the heart" and the Study of Acquirement as "the trace of the heart" (Shao, 2016). The path of self-cultivation, then, involves returning to the ontological heart-mind, dissolving the dichotomy between cosmology and human affairs, and elevating moral cultivation to a central metaphysical concern.

Unlike Shao Yong, the Cheng-Zhu Learning treats the heart-mind more ambiguously, viewing it as a transcendent faculty that may embody the Principle. Zhu Xi, for example, views the heart-mind as a battleground for the Principle and desire. He categorizes the heart into two opposing aspects: the heart of Dao, which embodies Principle, and the human heart, which harbors desires. Moreover, Zhu Xi contends that Principle is not confined to the heart of Dao but also permeates the external world as the universal law governing all existence. Thus, the pursuit of Principle involves the interplay between internal cultivation and external investigation. Through careful observation of the natural world and human society, individuals can discern the underlying order of the cosmos. Concurrently, by restraining the unruly desires of the human heart and practicing virtues in daily life, they can restore their heart of Dao and deepen their understanding of Principle.

Even Cheng Hao (1032–1085 CE), who seeks to establish an equivalence between the heart and Principle, concedes that the two are not identical in the realm of reality. For Cheng Hao, the key lies in nurturing intrinsic [human] nature, which links the heart to the Principle. He maintains that Principle constitutes the essence of human nature and can be apprehended through the clarity of the original heart. That said, the heart remains subordinate to these higher ontological realities of Principle and nature.

The full ontological elevation of the heart-mind culminated with the emergence of the School of Mind, which profoundly reshaped Neo-Confucian conceptions of moral agency. Lu Jiuyuan (1139–1193 CE), the founder of the School of Mind, rejects Zhu Xi's bifurcated heart-mind theory, positing instead a singular original heart (本心) that is ontologically identical with Principle itself. This revolutionary formulation transformed the heart from a mere receptacle of cosmic order into its very embodiment—what Lu (1980) famously expresses as "the universe is my heart, and my heart is the universe" (p.273). This process allows Lu to finalize the metaphysical framework of the School of Mind, emphasizing the initiative and autonomy of the self in the task of self-cultivation. Consequently, the responsibility of moral development shifts from being divinely ordained to residing squarely with each individual.

Wang Yangming (1472–1529 CE) takes the concept of the heart-mind to a step further. His famous pronouncements, "there is nothing outside the heart-mind" and "there is no Principle beyond the heart-mind," and "Principle is the pattern or organization of the heart" (Wang, 2011b, p. 308), suggest that the heart is the ultimate source of Principle. That said, Wang's ideas do not negate the external world, but highlight the significance of the heart, particularly innate moral knowledge, in understanding and transforming reality. It is the heart-mind that imparts meaning to everything, reversing the conventional perspective that the external world assigns meaning to the heart. In this regard, Wang's concept of the heart shares certain parallels to Kant's notion of a priori synthetic judgment, as both highlight the role of innate knowledge and the mind in shaping understanding. Yet distinctions emerge, as Wang places a greater emphasis on moral significance, while Kant centers on the structuring of sensory experience and knowledge.

The ontological transition from Principle to the heart carries profound implications for moral self-cultivation. When virtue is anchored in an external Principle as the substance of the world, it risks devolving into rigid doctrines and oppressive conformity. In contrast, elevating the heart-mind as the primary source of moral insight allows for an authentic and dynamic moral framework, where virtue and vice are not fixed categories but fluid expressions of one's inner sincerity and ethical awareness. As Wang (2011b)'s seminal formulation declares: "The original substance of the heart is neither good nor evil; notions of good and evil emerge only when thoughts are activated" (p. 1976). By transcending dualities, the heart-mind attains an ultimate significance akin to the Dao or the Boundless, making enlightenment through introspection and self-cultivation possible. It becomes the nexus where the Dao, the Way of Heaven, and the Principle converge, endowing individuals with enhanced autonomy, moral flexibility, self-awareness, and a heightened capacity for ethical inquiry. Through this transformation, the concept of the self in Chinese thought reaches its fullest articulation.

Wang's doctrine of innate [ethical] knowledge (良知) further deepens the subjectivity of the heart. While rooted in Mencius' conception of innate knowledge and capacity, Wang's formulation transcends these ethical foundations, elevating innate knowledge to the ontological ground of the original heart-mind. Wang (2011b) characterizes this primordial awareness as "the luminous clarity of heavenly principle itself—the numinous consciousness that generates and orders all existence: it fashions Heaven and Earth, ordains spiritual and secular powers" (p. 61). Through this transformation, Wang's system ultimately inverts the Cheng-Zhu paradigm: the heart-mind no longer serves as a vessel for apprehending Principle, but rather becomes the dynamic wellspring from which all moral and cosmic order emanates.

Wang's philosophy of heart-thing unity fundamentally reorients Confucian self-cultivation as a dynamic process of extending innate knowledge (致良知) while unifying cognition with praxis. The heart functions as the central orchestrator, actively shaping external events and imparting meaning to them. His evocative metaphor of the flowering tree within a mountain rock captures this interdependence: the blossoms' chromatic splendor only achieves actualization until someone turns their attention to it—until the heart unlocks its vibrant hues (Wang, 2011b, pp. 107–108). Likewise, when confronted with ethical quandaries in life, individuals should first consult the heart's innate moral compass, which contains a priori ethical knowledge, and then verifies and refines this knowledge in application. Through this reciprocal cultivation, Wang's system affirms not only the heart's sovereign moral authority and the world's indispensable role as the proving ground of virtue, but also the imperative to extend knowledge toward transforming the world.

The conception of the heart-mind in Lu Jiuyuan and Wang Yangming bears some imprint of Chan Buddhist metaphysics, particularly in their adaptation of the Buddha-nature paradigm to Confucian ethics. Like Chan masters guiding disciples towards a direct apprehension of universal Buddhahood within individual consciousness, they reconceptualize the heart as an ethical microcosm of the universe, teeming with potential and endowed with the capacity for self-directed action. In this view, the heart is less an organ than a locus of choice, empowering individuals to actively develop their own path of moral cultivation. While their ultimate goal differs from Chan Buddhism—cultivating sages and virtuous individuals rather than seeking Buddhahood—Lu and Wang share Chan Buddhism's emphasis on sudden awakening: an epiphany-like, transformative moment that illuminates profound truths and unlocks the innate goodness residing deep within the heart.

The fundamental divergence between Zhu Xi's Principle-centered metaphysics and Wang Yangming's heart-centered ontology is most evident in their respective approaches to apprehending the Principle. Zhu Xi's method emphasizes an outward-focused approach to understanding Principle, advocating careful study of external phenomena and classical texts as a gradual path to wisdom. In contrast, Wang Yangming prioritizes inward reflection, arguing that true knowledge of Principle arises through intuitive introspection of the heart-mind and its innate moral awareness. Of course, neither wholly disregards the other's emphasis. Zhu Xi too acknowledges the importance of inner cultivation, while Wang Yangming's innate knowledge naturally extends outward, incorporating external experiences and feedback. This dynamic interplay creates a harmonious loop that unites knowing and action in daily life.

3.4 Conclusions

Despite the diversity of their schools, ancient Chinese thinkers were bound by a shared yearning: to let the harmony of Heaven and Earth find its reflection in the realm of human affairs. Gazing upon the cosmic order—majestic, balanced, and enduring—they sought to weave its patterns into the governance of society, nurturing peace, virtue, and prosperity. Thus, the laws of Heaven and the principles of humanity meet in a single, transcendent purpose, surpassing the boundaries of doctrine.

Accordingly, some contemporary scholars argue that Chinese metaphysics is essentially the metaphysics of ethics, centered on the cultivation of a virtuous life (Yu & Xu, 2009). As a pragmatic culture, Chinese thought emphasizes the well-being of this life with the purpose of achieving harmony and flourishing in the present world. This pragmatic focus is reflected in their metaphysical-worldview. Ancient Chinese philosophers were less concerned with engaging in abstract reasoning to arrive at the ultimate answer; instead, they studied metaphysics driven by ethical concerns for human society (Li & Perkins, 2014), encouraging individuals to consciously develop characters in accordance with the celestial principle.

This ethical imperative lies at the heart of Confucian philosophy, where the pursuit of harmony operates on multiple dimensions. The cardinal virtue of humaneness crystallizes celestial equilibrium in human relations, urging humans to treat each other with empathy and kindness and tempering self-interest with grace. Unchecked greed, after all, disrupts the societal balance, much like a discordant note in a symphony. Similarly, the Confucian doctrine of the Mean mirrors the state of the Supreme Ultimate—a perfect state where the qi of yin and yang blends, interacts with, and finds equilibrium. This principle extends beyond individuals, encompassing peaceful coexistence between all beings, a harmonious relationship between humans and nature, and balance within society.

Beneath the surface of China's three philosophical teachings lies a profound undercurrent: the belief in a universal spirit guiding moral cultivation. Concepts like Dao, Heaven, the Principle, nature/Buddha nature, and the heart, though expressed in various ways, resonate across individuals and eras. Rather than rigidly imposing universal values or absolute norms, these concepts promote tolerance and inclusivity, reminding us that under the vast expanse, all groups can find their place in this shared journey toward flourishing and harmony.

With this worldview, individuals became active participants in a grand ethical drama, driven by the desire to harmonize with the cosmic virtues of Heaven and Earth, ultimately achieving ethical and spiritual enlightenment. In this sense, mainstream traditional Chinese thought can be seen as an embroidery woven with the threads of cosmology, ontology, and epistemology dyed in ethical hues—a manifestation of ethical cosmology, ethical ontology, and ethical epistemology. Every branch of knowledge, from the study of the universe to the pursuit of inner knowledge, ultimately serve as a path toward moral cultivation. At its core, this journey signifies a process of transformation, a quest to shed the layers of acquired selfish habit and reclaim the innate moral potential to embrace all.

References

Adler, J. (2012). The great virtue of heaven and earth: Deep ecology in the Yijing. In J. Miller (Ed.), *Religious diversity and ecological sustainability in China*. Routledge.

Ames, R. T. (2024). *Living Chinese philosophy: Zoetology as first philosophy*. SUNY Press.

Aristotle, J. B. (2014). *The complete works of Aristotle*. Princeton University Press.

Barseghyan, H., Overgaard, N., & Rupik, G. (2018). *Introduction to history and philosophy of science*. Open Library.

Bi, T. (2001). The ethical thought of the unity of heaven and man in changes and the moral tradition of the Chinese people. *Journal of Henan Institute of Education, 20*(1), 5–9.

Blakeley, D. N. (1998). Neo-Confucianism and universalism. *Dialogue and Universalism, 8*(11/12), 169–183.

Chan, W. (1963). *The way of Lao Tzu*. The Library of Liberal Arts.

Chaudhuri, H. (1954). The concept of Brahman in Hindu philosophy. *Philosophy East and West, 4*(1), 47–66.

Chen, G. (1984). *Annotation and comments of DaoDeJing*. China Bookstore.

Chen, L. (2013). The philosophical foundation of Chinese civilization. *Social Science in Chinese Colleges and Universities, 1*, 37–50.

Cheng, H., & Cheng, Y. (1981). *Collections of the Cheng brothers*. Zhonghua Book Company.

Chuang Tzu. (2013). *The complete works of Zhuangzi (B. Watson, Trans.)*. Columbia University Press.

Cobern, W. W. (1996). Worldview theory and conceptual change in science education. *Science Education, 80*(5), 579–610.

Confucius. (2016a). *Analects*. In J. Legge (Ed. & Trans.), *Confucianism: The Four Books and Five Classics*. Delphi Classics.

Confucius. (2016b). *Book of rites*. In J. Legge (Ed. & Trans.), *Confucianism: The Four Books and Five Classics*. Delphi Classics.

Confucius. (2016c). *Commentaries on Changes*. In J. Legge (Ed. & Trans.), *Confucianism: The Four Books and Five Classics*. Delphi Classics.

Earle, W. A. (1972). *The autobiographical consciousness*. Quadrangle Books.

Granet, M. (1975). *The religion of the Chinese people*. (M. Freedman, Trans.). Blackwell.

Griffith, R. T. (2013). *The rig veda* (Vol. 1). Library of Alexandria.

Guo, X. (2011). *Annotation of the Zhuangzi*. Zhonghua Book Company.

Han, F. (1999). *Hanfeizi*. Gansu Nationality Publishing House.

Hon, T. K. (2019). Chinese philosophy of change (Yijing). In E. N. Zalta (Ed.), *The Stanford encyclopedia of philosophy*.

Hu, S. (2018). *Outline of the history of Chinese philosophy*. Beijing Book CO. INC.

Lai, K. (2007). Ziran and Wuwei in the Daodejing: An ethical assessment. *Dao, 6*(4), 325–337.

Li, C., & Perkins, F. (2014). Chinese metaphysics as a fruitful subject of study. *Journal of East-West Thought, 4*, 71–86.

Li, J., & Xiang, S. (2020). Zhu Xi: His life, his works, and the evolving formation of his philosophy. In *Dao companion to ZHU Xi's philosophy* (pp. 15–46). Springer.

Liu, J. (2017). *Neo-Confucianism: Metaphysics, mind, and morality*. John Wiley & Sons.

Liu, Z. (2025). *Annotations on Guo Dian Chu Jian*. New China Press.

Lao Tzu. (2010). Daodejing. In R. T. Ames & D. L. Hall (Eds.), *Dao de jing: A philosophical translation* (R. T. Ames & D. L. Hall, Trans.). Ballantine Books.

Lu, J. (1980). *The collection of Lu Jiuyuan*. Zhonghua Book Company.

Mencius. (2016). *Mencius*. In J. Legge (Ed. & Trans.), *Confucianism: The Four Books and Five Classics*. Delphi Classics.

Nisbett, R. (2005). *The geography of thought: How Asians and westerners think differently... and why*. Nicholas Brealey Publishing.

Perkins, F. (2015). Metaphysics in Chinese philosophy. *Stanford Encyclopedia of Philosophy*. Retrieved from https://plato.stanford.edu/entries/chinese-metaphysics/

Pohl, K. H. (2002). Chinese and Western values: Reflections on a cross-cultural dialogue on a universal ethics. In *Komparative Ethik: Das gute Leben zwischen den Kulturen*. Chora.

Richardson, H. S., & Williams, M. S. (Eds.). (2009). *Moral universalism and pluralism* (Vol. 49). NYU Press.

Roetz, H. (2009). Tradition, universality, and the time paradigm of Zhou philosophy. *Journal of Chinese Philosophy, 36*(3), 359–375.

Rosenstand, N. (2017). *The moral of the story: An introduction to ethics* (8th ed.). McGraw-Hill Companies.

Schweitzer, A. (1923). *The philosophy of civilization*. A. & C. Black.

Shao, Y. (2016). *The collective book of Shao Yong*. Shanghai Classics Publishing House.

Song, B. (2018). *A study of comparative philosophy of religion on" Creatio ex Nihilo" and" Sheng Sheng (Birth Birth, 生生)"*. [Doctoral dissertation, Boston University].

Van Inwagen, P. (2014). *Existence: Essays in ontology*. Cambridge University Press.

Van Inwagen, P. (2018). *Metaphysics*. Routledge.
Wang, K. (2011a). The Taiji explanation of good medical behavior and its management. In *2011 proceedings of the Tsinghua international conference on healthcare management* (p. 472). Tsinghua University Press.
Wang, Y. (2011b). *Collected works of Wang Yangming*. Shanghai Ancient Books Publishing House.
Wang, C. (2015). Confucianism and citizenship. *Theorizing Chinese Citizenship*, 49–81.
Wittgenstein, L. (1922). *Tractatus logico-philosophicus*. Harcort, Brace & Company, INC.
Yang, G. (2015). Interpretation of the Treatise on Qiwu. *Journal of East China Normal University, 47*(3), 1–25.
Yu, J. (2016). Moral naturalism in stoicism and Daoism. *Philosophical Inquiry, 40*(1/2), 95–112.
Yu, W., & Xu, J. (2009). Morality and nature: The essential difference between the Dao of Chinese philosophy and metaphysics in Western philosophy. *Frontiers ofPhilosophy in China, 4*(3), 360–369.
Zhang, D. (1982). *Outline of Chinese philosophy*. China Social Science Press.
Zhang, X. (2009). The philosophical feature of Confucianism and its position in inter-cultural dialogue: Universalism or non-universalism? *Frontiers of Philosophy in China, 4*(4), 483–492.
Zhang, Z. (1978). *Collections of Zhang Zai*. Zhonghua Book Company.
Zhou, D. (1936). *The collections of Zhou Lianxi*. Shanghai Ancient Works Publishing House.
Zhu, Xi. (1986). *Analects of Zhu Xi* (Edited by Li, J.). Zhonghua Book Company.
Zhu Xi. (2013). *Collected commentaries on the Analects of Confucius*. Beijing: China Society Press.

Chapter 4
The Art of Moral Self-cultivation

In traditional Chinese philosophy, where metaphysics envisions an intrinsic unity between Heaven and humanity, self-cultivation is more than mere personal betterment—it is the process by which individuals attune their inner selves, the microcosm, to the broader macrocosm of society and nature. This emphasis on moral development is no accident; it embodies a profound cultural conviction in communal harmony and interdependence. Whereas selfishness and indifference sow conflict and disorder, virtues such as humaneness, righteousness, deference, compassion, and humility bind the collective, creating a dynamic equilibrium where personal cultivation and societal flourishing reinforce one another.

4.1 Philosophical Frameworks of Moral Self-cultivation

This chapter examines the foundational frameworks of moral self-cultivation that support shared flourishing and harmonious coexistence. While grounded primarily in Confucian moral philosophy, it also incorporates key insights from Daoist and Buddhist traditions, offering a more holistic understanding of ethical development in the Chinese philosophical context.

4.1.1 Human Nature as the Ground of Self-cultivation

Human nature is a starting point of Chinese ethical thought. This innate disposition—shaping our instinctive reactions to the world—not only necessitates moral cultivation but also charts its course, illuminating our inherent potential for virtue. As a universal characteristic, it establishes common ground for inclusive moral

Z. You, Y. Hu, *Philosophy and Civilization: How the Idea of Moral Cultivation Shaped China*, East-West Dialogues in Educational Philosophy and Theory,
https://doi.org/10.1007/978-981-95-5660-1_4

education and meaningful intercultural ethical dialogue. A thorough examination of human nature's ethical dimensions thus serves as an essential prerequisite for comprehending the transformative path of self-cultivation.

Chinese philosophers have unraveled diverse interpretations of human nature's moral inclinations: are we born with an innate compass pointing toward virtue, toward evil, or toward spontaneous naturalness? Mencius (2016) articulates a notably optimistic view, positing an inherent goodness in human nature. His framework identifies four foundational moral emotions within the heart-mind: compassion, a sense of shame and moral aversion, deference and respect, and discernment of right and wrong. These affective responses constitute the germinal roots of virtue—developing into humaneness, righteousness, propriety, and wisdom, respectively, through proper cultivation (2A: 6). Mencius maintains that through conscientiously nurturing these innate moral sprouts, individuals can actualize their ethical potential and thereby foster social harmony.[1]

Xunzi (1997), by contrast, conceives human nature a wild and untamed field, rich with potential, yet overrun by the thorns of selfish desire and entangling vines of greed, threatening to choke the delicate shoots of virtue. For Xunzi, moral development is not about nurturing preexisting seeds, but rather about a transformative process of weeding and reforming. Only through the disciplined application of ritual and social norms, Xunzi argues, can these unruly impulses be pruned and redirected, gradually transforming chaotic wilderness into orderly gardens of humaneness and righteousness.

Building on both Mencius and Xunzi, Han Confucian Dong Zhongshu presents a sophisticated model of human nature. He likens it to the dual nature of Heaven, such as light and darkness, arguing that humans possess both inherent good and evil. This is elaborated in his three-tiered system of human nature: the rare sage who manifests innate virtue, the morally ambivalent majority whose nature mingles good and evil, and the irredeemably wicked few (Dong, n.d.). While acknowledging the existence of moral darkness within the middle tier, he emphasizes their innate goodness and capacity for transformation through proper cultivation. His system provides both a philosophical justification and practical blueprint for the widespread promotion of moral cultivation during the Han dynasties.

It is noteworthy that both Daoist and Buddhist philosophies offer distinctive yet complementary conceptions of human nature that expand upon mainstream Confucian thought. Where Confucianism emphasizes cultivated moral potential, Daoism celebrates spontaneous "self-so-ness" as the authentic human nature—innate, uncontrived, and as pure as that of a newborn. Chinese Mahayana Buddhism introduces another perspective through its doctrine of universal Buddha-nature. This concept remarkably parallels Mencius' theory of innate moral knowledge, as both traditions posit an inherent capacity for spiritual-moral development of all. These intersecting yet distinct visions of human nature—Confucian, Daoist, and Buddhist—collectively justified rich and diverse self-cultivation practices, each offering a unique pathway while mutually enriching the others.

[1] Scholar Yan Pen argues that Mencius' focus on human nature and heart shifted philosophy from Heaven's external transcendence to the individual's immanent transcendence.

4.1.2 Visions of Love and Compassion

Throughout history, a vast majority of world philosophies and religions uphold love as a fundamental principle, not only as an affective bond among family and friends, but also as a unifying force that promotes ethical behavior, social cohesion, and spiritual fulfillment on a broader scale. Chinese philosophy contributes vital insights to this global discourse. Inspired by the cosmic harmony of Heaven and Earth, many Chinese philosophers perceive the world as a dynamic interplay of forces—inherently life-generative and necessitating love and compassion. Within Chinese philosophical traditions, this universal essence takes on distinct yet interconnected expressions.

Confucian humaneness, rooted in family bonds, fosters a deep sense of care that extends beyond kin to embrace all of humanity. Daoism upholds the virtue of compassion, mirroring the spontaneous generosity and selflessness inherent in the Dao, while Buddhism broadens this into a universal compassion, extending kindness and empathy to all sentient beings. In these schools, love is not merely a fundamental principle but the essence and goal of self-cultivation. Also noteworthy is that love in Chinese culture, as in many others, does not signify softness, but rather wisdom and courage to stand up for what is just and right, especially in trying times.

4.1.2.1 Confucian Humaneness

The Confucian virtue of "ren," often translated as "co-humanity" or "humaneness" or "benevolence," embodies the earthly manifestation of the heavenly way. The hieroglyphic character of humaneness "仁" is particularly revealing. First appearing in the Western Zhou Dynasty, it combines the character for "person" with the number "two," signifying "other-directedness" —the principle of loving and caring for others. When fortified by "courage" and illuminated by the "wisdom" to distinguish right from wrong, humaneness becomes the integrative virtue of the Junzi, harmonizing emotion, action, and reason; it represents a love that is both discerning and steadfast: compassionate without indulgence, and principled without rigidity.

Essence of Humaneness

Humaneness is the highest Confucian virtue, representing the ideal state of human flourishing and moral excellence. At once a distinct ethical attribute and an all-encompassing moral paradigm, it forms the conceptual core of Confucian ethics, integrating all other virtues. It serves not only as the foundation upon which other virtues such as righteousness and ritual propriety are built, but also as the ultimate goal toward which they aspire (Shun, 2002). At its core lies empathy, an innate capacity to understand and respond to others' needs as we would our own, thereby deepening human connection and cultivating a compassionate, harmonious society.

This relationship-centered virtue expands outward in concentric circles—beginning with innate affection for immediate family, such as the love between parent and child, bonds among siblings, and loyalty within the extended kin group—before gradually extending to those beyond familial ties. Such a layered approach recognizes varying degrees of attachment based on relational proximity and corresponding responsibilities, giving rise to the notion of "differentiated love" or "gradated love." This characteristic distinguishes "ren" from ethical frameworks like Christian universal love, which emphasizes an equal love for all beings.

However, the love rooted in family affection—yet extending beyond it—should not be dismissed as inferior, as it reflects the Confucian ideal that moral agents should express care in contextually appropriate and relationally sensitive ways (Huang, 2005). While the Confucian love emphasizes blood ties and acknowledges differentiation, it also encompasses compassion and altruism capable of transcending familial bonds. When properly cultivated, this family-based love becomes a natural foundation for broader moral concern, offering a practical path to social harmony. Confucian scholars illustrate this through the innate empathetic concern one feels upon seeing a child about to fall into a well—an instinctive, altruistic response to a stranger's plight, which reveals the true essence of humaneness.

This perspective reflects Confucianism's vision of a harmonious society, one grounded not in strict equality but in a hierarchical order regulated and tempered by humaneness, considerateness, and ritual propriety. Yet if left unchecked, this approach risks fostering nepotism or cronyism by prioritizing close-knit relationships, ultimately undermining the very social harmony and fairness Confucianism aims to uphold. Thus, while natural partiality has its place, it must be balanced by a commitment to impartiality and justice in the public sphere.

Confucians addressed concerns about favoritism by extending humaneness beyond filial affection to cultivate a broader sense of compassion and responsibility. This expanded ideal, often termed "expansive humaneness," differentiates this higher ideal of "humanness" from "small humaneness," illuminating its true spirit of inclusivity and public-mindedness. While Confucianism primarily emphasizes ethical human relationships and social harmony, its ultimate ideal is to cultivate an all-encompassing care for the world. This aspiration is reflected in the words of Confucius's disciple Zi Xia, who declared, "All within the four seas are brothers" (2016, 12.5), and in the Book of Rites (Confucius, 2016b), which states that "When the Grand course was pursued, a public and common spirit ruled all under the sky" (Li Yun).

This inclusive and universal spirit is well summarized by Tang dynasty scholar Han Yu (2022), who states, "All-encompassing love is called humaneness. Practicing humaneness and acting appropriately is called righteousness. Moving forward in accordance with humaneness and righteousness is called the Dao, and achieving self-fulfillment without relying on external supervision is true virtue" (vol 11, misc. 1.4). Han's formulation encapsulates the shift of Confucian virtue from differentiated affections to a more inclusive love for all humanity. Neo-Confucian thinkers further deepen this vision, advocating an even broader inclusivity. They assert that people of humaneness treat "all things in the world as oneness," emphasizing a moral philosophy that prioritizes righteousness and the public good over favoritism and personal gain.

Next, humaneness, as the overarching Confucian virtue, radiates outward as a constellation of interdependent virtues—each facet reflecting a unique dimension of this profound moral love. Filial piety, righteousness, ritual propriety, faithfulness, reciprocity, wisdom, and credibility all emerge from this fundamental virtue, forming an integrated framework for ethical conduct. There exists a substance-utility relationship: While humaneness represents the ultimate ideal and inner driving force, its full realization in the world depends on the practice of these secondary virtues, which, in turn, contribute to the continual expansion and influence of humaneness in society. Consider righteousness: Whereas humaneness embodies the highest form of goodness, righteousness ensures that one's actions remain motivated by and aligned with this profound moral love. At its highest expression, righteousness flowers into humaneness, fulfilling its deepest moral purpose. This transformative alchemy reveals how discrete virtues interweave in the cultivation of character—each step in this lifelong journey bringing us nearer to embodying humaneness in thought, action, and the very fabric of society.

Confucianism identifies humaneness as the indispensable virtue of leadership and the foundation of virtuous governance, where the welfare of the people holds paramount importance. This love for others thus becomes the fundamental criterion for assessing both moral worth and political capability. Leaders who embody humaneness earn respect and legitimacy, while those deficient in it forfeit such claims. For Confucian scholars, therefore, the cultivation of humaneness constitutes a dual imperative—essential for personal moral development and indispensable for effective statesmanship.

Filial Piety as Humaneness

Confucianism views filial piety—the reverent devotion to parents and ancestors—as both the seed and the concrete expression of humaneness (ren), as well as a vital path of moral cultivation that begins within the family. Rooted in a child's natural response to parental love and care, filial piety serves as the most fundamental and intuitive starting point for developing moral sensibility, which is then extended outward to create a harmonious and ethical society. Emotionally, it fosters humaneness by nurturing familial affection that naturally radiates outward as benevolent care for others; practically, it instills virtues essential for maintaining harmony from household to empire. By cultivating reverence, responsibility, and loyal reciprocity, filial piety orders relationships through layered yet harmonious hierarchies—transforming family and state into an ethically grounded unity.

For Confucians, filial piety reflects the moral structure of Heaven. A revered Confucian text, *the Sutra of Filial Piety*, metaphorically equates Heaven to a fatherly figure. Just as Heaven nurtures life and harmonizes existence, fathers assume the roles of providers, educators, and guides for the family. Thus, a child's filial sentiment embodies deference for the cosmic order, manifested through honoring parents, supporting them in old age, conducting solemn funerals, and commemorating ancestors. Confucians recognize the profound transformative power of filial piety in moral cultivation. As Confucius' disciple Zengzi states "Be circumspect in funerary services and continue sacrifices to the distant ancestors, and the virtue of the common people will flourish" (Confucius, 2016a, 1.9).

Filial piety cultivates a profound sense of dual responsibility—to both family and state. Ancient China thrived on a unique "familial-state paradigm" that highlighted the structural and functional homology between domestic and political spheres. Families served not merely as society's basic unit, but as the moral template for state governance. Chinese conceived the family as a miniature state and the state as an expanded family, creating a continuum of familial-state obligations.[2] Consequently, exemplary fulfillment of one's filial duties was seen as essential preparation for loyal service to the sovereign and the broader polity. This intrinsic linkage between familial ethics and political order underpinned Confucianism's enduring hegemony as China's governing philosophy. Its seamless alignment with the family–state order not only reinforced the moral legitimacy of imperial rule but also entrenched Confucianism as the prevailing framework for cultural and political life.

Ultimately, the manifestation of filial piety lies in its political and social implications, where familial virtues transform into public virtues. At this juncture, the principles of filial piety and fraternal love intersect with the concepts of political loyalty and moral righteousness: Just as a son's reverence for his father becomes a subject's loyalty to the ruler, so too does brotherly affection translate into righteous conduct among peers. Confucius (2016a) affirms this connection, stating, "They are few who, being filial and fraternal, are fond of offending against their superiors" (1.2). While modern scholars may question the exact mechanisms of this virtue transference, its historical significance remains incontrovertible. The filial-loyalty paradigm emerged as both a cornerstone of Confucian moral cultivation and a fundamental principle of statecraft, serving for centuries as a stabilizing force in Chinese society and governance.

As an important expression of humaneness, filial piety functioned as a foundational ethical benchmark by which all individuals were morally assessed. The imperial government, for instance, institutionalized filial devotion as a critical criterion for official recruitment and evaluation, while ordinary people who failed to uphold its standards often faced severe social sanction. Even emperors were obliged to perform filial piety, at least ceremonially, to legitimize their rule and model virtuous governance. The "filial governance" paradigm became instrumental in maintaining China's sociopolitical harmony, its influence permeating all aspects of traditional life. This principle's cultural hegemony was so complete that it compelled even

[2] For a comprehensive understanding of the concept of the "culture of family and state," see You, Z., Rud, A., Hu, Y. (2018) *The Philosophy of Moral Education: A History. Palgrave Macmillan*, p. 16.

Buddhism—a tradition initially predicated on monastic renunciation of familial ties—to assimilate filial piety as a central doctrine in its Sinicized form.

Ritual Propriety as Humaneness

Ritual propriety is more than a set of external rules or formalities; it is an essential vehicle for the expression and cultivation of humaneness. Originating in religious ceremonies honoring deities and ancestors, Confucian rituals evolved into a comprehensive system of social etiquette that structured and mediated human relations across ranks and roles, with the aims of fostering civility and trust. Though hierarchical in structure, its graded order serves an integrative function—harmonizing social interactions through clearly defined roles and responsibilities, ensuring that neither superiors nor subordinates encroach upon each other's rightful interests. By consciously observing ritual propriety, individuals align themselves with the moral order of society, cultivating virtues such as benevolence, reciprocity, and equilibrium. In this way, ritual propriety serves both as the social grammar and as a mirror of the ethical patterns that govern the universe, made manifest within the human community.

Ritual propriety played an important role in the cultivation of humaneness. Through daily observance, it transforms the abstract idea of humaneness into actionable respect, empathy into appropriate conduct, and goodwill into specific duties, eventually internalizing these virtues. Whether expressed through familial rites, social customs, or reverence for elders, rituals are rooted in a profound respect and concern for human value and well-being. Through these acts, individuals developed the capacity to show respect and express concerns within structured social relationships. For example, family rituals—like honoring ancestors or expressing filial piety—are not just formalities but opportunities to reflect on one's personal obligations, family role, and broader societal responsibilities. This transformative pedagogy cultivated both individual virtue and collective moral consciousness, ultimately contributing to a more harmonious and cohesive social order.

Confucian ritual propriety emphasizes self-discipline and rule-abiding, thereby fostering key other-oriented dimensions of humaneness such as moderation, collaboration, humility, and compassion. Through this practice of self-regulation, individuals temper excessive self-interest, creating the moral space necessary for others to flourish—an ethic that underpins social harmony and stability. Confucius' response to his disciple Yan Hui's question on humaneness beautifully captures this idea: "To subdue one's self and return to propriety, is perfect virtue [humaneness]. If a man can for one day subdue himself and return to propriety, all under Heaven will ascribe perfect virtue [humaneness] to him" (Confucius, 2016a, 12.1). The act of self-restraint, he elaborates, involves refraining from sights, sounds, words, and deeds that violate propriety. This restriction may seem austere or close-minded, yet its original purpose was to emphasize the imperative of curbing insatiable cravings that can hinder the cultivation of humaneness.

While ritual propriety provides the structural framework for moral development, it is humaneness that breathes life into these rituals and animates their ethical essence. Ritual propriety without "ren" risks becoming a hollow, rigid set of formalities, devoid of genuine ethical substance. In the worst cases, it can even devolve into an instrument of social coercion rather than moral cultivation. History offers examples of such misuses, notably in the "doctrine of rites" (礼教) during certain periods of Chinese history. This system, designed to enforce strict social hierarchies, was criticized—particularly in the early modern era—for suppressing individual rights, freedom, and creativity. Yet, a return to the original vision of classical Confucianism reveals a more nuanced and balanced understanding of ritual propriety. When infused with humaneness, it is not a mechanism of control but a means of moral cultivation—one that ensures harmony between inner sincerity and outward expression, fostering both personal ethical integrity and social well-being.

Reciprocity and Faithfulness as Humaneness

Reciprocity (恕) lies at the heart of humaneness. More than just a simple exchange, "reciprocity" embodies deep considerateness and empathy—treating others as we would wish to be treated and extending forgiveness when needed. Confucius (2016a) succinctly captures this idea when asked for a single guiding principle for becoming humane: "Is not reciprocity such a word? What you do not want done to yourself, do not do to others" (15.23). The "negative golden rule" translates humaneness into daily practice by demanding active consideration of others' perspectives and welfare and by encouraging individuals to hold themselves to a higher standard than they do others. Through this mechanism, moral development becomes an inward journey of transformation rather than mere compliance with external norms.

Faithfulness, encompassing loyalty, sincerity, and steadfast commitment in both personal and political relationships, forms a dialectical pair with reciprocity, collectively known as "faithfulness-reciprocity (忠恕)." This complementary duality represents the operational core of humaneness, where authentic devotion to one's duties harmonizes with empathetic consideration for others. In the Confucian political framework, faithfulness holds particular significance in the relationship between monarch and minister, where ministers are expected to wholeheartedly dedicate themselves to supporting the monarch by offering forthright counsel and by assisting in virtuous governance.

Yet, faithfulness to sovereignty is not unconditional in classical Confucianism: It does not endorse blind obedience but rather demands a reciprocal relationship. Just as a monarch should treat his ministers with ritual propriety, ministers should respond with loyalty and dedicated service (Confucius, 2016a). Xunzi (1997) carries this idea further, asserting that adherence to the Dao, the supreme virtue, takes precedence over allegiance to the monarch. In his view, when a ruler's directives contradict the Dao, ethical obligation to the greater good outweighs loyalty. This principle reflects a core Confucian belief: Ethical decisions should be guided not by the ruler's whims but by the well-being of all people under Heaven.

As a fundamental expression of humaneness, faithfulness-reciprocity carries universal significance. By fostering empathy and concern for others' welfare with sincerity and dedication, it serves as a guiding principle for advancing both personal integrity and societal harmony. The ethical guideline extends beyond individual relationships to encompass all beings, promoting respect, reliability, and mutual kindness. Especially pertinent in today's interconnected yet often distrustful world, this principle provides the much-needed ethical and emotional anchor for bridging divides and enabling meaningful intercultural dialogue.

Risks of Instrumentalizing Virtues

Confucian philosophers, like many thinkers across world traditions, articulated their foundational virtue and its associated virtues in idealized terms. Yet, a critical tension persists between these elevated ideals and the complexities of lived experience. For while these philosophical visions envision a world of harmony and ethical perfection, they must continually grapple with the messy, imperfect evolution of human societies—and the challenge of preserving their integrity within it.

These dynamics were often intensified by the pragmatic cultural context of ancient China, where virtue served not only as a personal ideal but also as a guiding principle for governance and social order. While Confucian virtues such as filial piety, loyalty, and ritual propriety were intended to cultivate ethical relationships and promote social harmony—embodying values that still resonate across time and cultures—their norms concerning gender distinction and hierarchical seniority carried inherent implications of inequality. When rigidly applied, these ideals could reinforce vertical power structures such as ruler over subject, father over child, and husband over wife.

While such structures helped preserve social stability, they also posed risks. When ideals of order and deference were overly emphasized, they could legitimize authority in ways that constrained individual autonomy, particularly for women and those of lower social status. At times, these norms were wielded as instruments of control—whether in patriarchal family settings where elders dictated the lives of the young, or in state systems that prioritized conformity over moral agency. In such cases, the ethical framework, originally intended to cultivate virtue, risked being reduced to a mere tool of coercion.

For example, excessive emphasis on ritual formalism could reduce moral practice to superficial compliance—prioritizing outward observance while neglecting the inner cultivation of humaneness. In such cases, the empathetic core of Confucian ethics was vulnerable to being overshadowed by performative norms that prioritized obedience over sincerity. Confucius himself warned against such distortions, advocating the golden mean as a balanced embodiment of virtue (Analects 6.29). This paradox reveals a deeper tension: Even the noblest principles, when rigidly applied or excessively formalized, can betray their original purpose and diminish the very humaneness they were designed to foster.

From a cultural-historical perspective, the potential for instrumentalization of Confucian virtues lies in the very nature of Confucianism itself: it was conceived as both an ethical system and a political framework aimed at promoting social harmony and state stability. Thus, dismissing Confucian moral cultivation for not being "ethics for its own sake" is a misconception, since its sociopolitical application was intrinsic to its original design. Yet beyond its functional role in governance, Confucian virtue ethics—when genuinely rooted in humaneness—profoundly shaped the moral consciousness of Chinese society, fostering a tradition of ethical life that transcended mere statecraft.

4.1.2.2 Impartial Care, Daoist Compassion, and Buddhist Compassion

Beyond Confucian humaneness, ancient Chinese culture also features diverse expressions of love, including Mohist impartial care, Daoist spontaneous compassion (慈), and Buddhist compassion (慈悲). These diverse yet interconnected conceptions of love expanded Chinese philosophical framework, each offering distinct contributions to the moral and spiritual traditions of Chinese civilization.

Mohism presents a radical departure in the mainstream Chinese philosophy (e.g., Confucian's graded love) through its doctrine of impartial care. Mozi envisions Heaven as an unbiased moral authority, whose will mandates universal righteousness and mutual benefit. Thus, following the example of Heaven, he calls for equal moral concern toward every individual, irrespective of social hierarchy or familial ties. By encouraging people to transcend selfish desires and biases, impartial care fosters empathy, collective moral duty, and active engagement in shared beneficence. Ultimately, Mohist ethics reframes moral philosophy around absolute equity and impartiality, offering a pragmatic solution to social discord while envisioning a society built on mutual prosperity.

Not merely an abstract ideal, impartial care is a call to altruistic action. Mozi promoted the cultivation of paragons of virtue called "Jian Shi," individuals who embody impartial love and possess the practical skills to implement it in society. The world will be a happy place if everybody can practice impartial love and benefit each other. However, his vision was met with significant resistance. Mencius (2016) saw impartial love as a destabilizing force, likening it to the unrestrained behavior of wild beasts. Lao Tzu (2013), while acknowledging the moral nobility of Mozi's vision, questions its feasibility, suggesting that human nature's inherent self-interest would hinder its full realization. Despite these critiques, Mohism left an enduring mark on Chinese thought. Even after its decline, its advocacy for universal fraternity continued to shape philosophical discourse, fostering ideals of inclusivity and a chivalrous spirit within Chinese society.

In Classical Daoism, spontaneous compassion shines as a central virtue, especially in the teachings of Lao Tzu. For him, the virtue of compassion embodies the very essence of the Dao, the natural order features Heaven, Earth, and the wisdom of sages. This compassion manifests in three key ways. First, it arises effortlessly and naturally, like water flowing to sustain all things. Second, it expresses itself as selfless love—given quietly, without expectation of acknowledgment or reciprocation. Third, it embraces all existence impartially, mirroring Heaven's nurturing of the myriad creatures without discrimination. Transcending human-centered morality, Daoist compassion extends universally to all beings, reflecting the Dao's inclusive generosity.

Daoist compassion fundamentally differs from Confucian humaneness in its spontaneous emergence and boundless scope. Lao Tzu critiques Confucian ideals of humaneness and righteousness as artificial constructs that, when externally imposed, encourage partiality and performative behavior rather than authentic virtue. Thus, Daoist compassion is better termed as "spontaneous compassion," where moral action flows effortlessly from one's alignment with the natural order. This effortless attunement enables compassion to manifest without egoic intention yet with perfect efficacy, nurturing holistic harmony. By transcending Confucian hierarchical relationships, spontaneous compassion attains a truly cosmic dimension, offering an altruistic ethic that embraces all beings alike.

This all-encompassing and undiscriminating nature is well illustrated by Lao Tzu's (2010) words: "The heavens and the earth are not partial to institutionalized morality [humaneness] …[and] take things and treat them all as straw dogs" (Chap. 5), underscoring nature's impartiality in treating all with equal consideration. The ethos aligns with Heaven's Way in promoting equilibrium—using abundance to nourish scarcity and balance excess—contrasting with the human tendency to exacerbate inequalities, enriching those who already have plenty while depriving those in need (Chap. 77). Lao Tzu envisions sages embodying this altruistic, compassionate wisdom, possessing both courage and discernment to harmonize competing interests and care for the well-being of All under Heaven.

Like Daoism, Buddhism brought to China its own distinct expression of compassion—karuṇā—a deep awareness of universal suffering and a heartfelt desire to alleviate it for all sentient beings while guiding them toward enlightenment. The path is illuminated by a profound wisdom rooted in a sophisticated spiritual pursuit, which cuts through illusion to reveal the impermanent and interdependent nature of all things—often expressed through the concept of emptiness. Recognizing the evanescent existence fosters a profound empathy for shared suffering, inspiring Buddhists to transcend ego-attachment and devote themselves to the great mission of universal liberation.

Buddhist compassion serves as a powerful catalyst for both religious and moral self-cultivation. In Mahāyāna Buddhism, it becomes the ethical, emotional, and spiritual drive of the Buddhists, propelling them toward enlightenment while anchoring them in an unwavering commitment to the well-being of others (Shogo, 2015). Aspirants are urged to cultivate this boundless love, actively lending a hand to fellow travelers on their own journeys. Bodhisattvas, in particular, take a profound vow to delay their own liberation, choosing instead to remain in the world to guide others toward it. This unwavering commitment to selflessness and all-encompassing empathy exemplifies Buddhist compassion in its highest form.

Buddhist compassion profoundly enriched Chinese altruism, adding to it greater depth and inclusivity. Both Daoist and Buddhist compassion are altruistic virtue expecting nothing in return. Yet, unlike the celestial scope of Daoist compassion, often associated with nature or sagacious leaders, Buddhist compassion is accessible to all, rooted in the conviction that every being, regardless of circumstance, holds the potential for Buddhahood. This understanding is rooted in the principle of interdependence, which reveals that each individual is part of a greater whole within an ever-changing reality. Consequently, Buddhist compassion ignites a noble aspiration, transcending personal salvation to embrace the liberation of all. This compassion enhances the Confucian vision of "All under Heaven" by introducing a deeper sense of selflessness and impartiality.

For instance, Neo-Confucianism actively integrated Buddhist altruistic sentiment to broaden its ethical horizon. Inspired by this universal compassion, Neo-Confucians redefined humaneness with deeper care and a wider cosmological scope. This enriched perspective strengthened the altruistic dimension of Confucianism, extending moral cultivation to all beings—sentient and non-sentient alike—guided by the compassionate heart inherent in humanity.

4.1.3 Moral Perfection Through Equilibrium and Harmony

The notion of achieving equilibrium-harmony (致中和) is the foundational principle of Confucian moral cultivation, serving both as a methodology and its ultimate ideal. As *the Doctrine of the Mean* eloquently states, when equilibrium and harmony extend across the cosmos, all things in Heaven and Earth assume their rightful places and reach their fullest potential (Zisi, 2016). These interdependent principles operate dialectically: Equilibrium establishes the groundwork for harmony by fostering internal balance and moral integrity, while harmony ensures that balance transcends mere superficial appeasement, leading to genuine ethical flourishing. Both concepts stress the importance of moderation, the avoidance of extremes, and the cultivation of virtuous behavior to maintain peace and unity.

Equilibrium can be understood as a direct result of practicing the Golden Mean, not merely denoting a middle position but embodying an artful balance of moderation and proportion—one that continuously adapts to life's complexities. Traditional Chinese culture strongly opposes extremes, viewing them as sources of volatility and discord. For Confucianism, moral rightness is never absolute but always contextual, for exceeding a proper measure is just as problematic as falling short (Confucius, 2016a, 11.15). The ideal approach is to discern the most appropriate point between opposing forces, maintaining a dynamic equilibrium that serves as the key to attaining the optimal state in all aspects of life, from the cosmos to personal conduct.

The Confucian Mean serves as a methodological guide for moral cultivation, offering a steady ethical compass rooted in moderation and appropriateness. It enables individuals to explore the essence of moral excellence and the means to achieve it. Going to extreme undermines morality—even Confucian virtues, when pushed too far, can stray from their intended purpose. As the esteemed Ming general

Qi Jiguang (2021) notes, "The misuse of trust leads to obsession, the misuse of humaneness leads to indulgence, the misuse of courage leads to brutality, and the misuse of strictness leads to harshness. None of these extremes are appropriate" (vol. 14). This insight reminds us that even the golden rules must stay in the appropriate position to remain truly virtuous.

The ultimate purpose of pursuing equilibrium is to achieve harmony, a foundational ideal of Chinese culture. Harmony embodies a holistic state of balance, order, and coordination among diverse individuals, elements, or forces. It transcends conflict through embracing unity, cooperation, peaceful joy, mutual respect, and shared benefit, advocating for dynamic equilibrium where differences complement rather than oppose one another. Grounded in the principle of universal interdependence, harmony is vital to the flourishing of both individuals and society, bearing profound ethical and universal significance.

Harmony is a central goal of Confucian moral cultivation. It manifests across a continuum: internal, interpersonal, familial, social and political, international, humanity's relationship with nature, and, ultimately, the grand harmony of the cosmos (Li, 2006). True harmony arises when each person fulfills their role, finds their rightful place and rhythm, and cares for others, and all elements resonate in balanced accord within the greater composition of existence.

While Confucian harmony emphasizes order and structure, it should not be misconstrued as enforced uniformity that suppresses diverse voices. Its true beauty lies in embracing differences and integrating varied perspectives. True harmony nurtures mutual understanding by reconciling conflicting needs, fostering relationships built on dynamic balance and mutual respect. This reconciliation requires an adaptive and creative approach that prioritizes the common good while respecting individual concerns, emphasizing mutual support and interdependence (Li, 2013). Harmony is essential for the stability and flourishing of ancient Chinese society, encouraging collaboration among various groups and enabling communities to pool their strengths to overcome challenges, innovate, and thrive.

Together, equilibrium and harmony foster both inner tranquility and universal peace. As stated in *Doctrine of Mean*, equilibrium is defined as the state of mind before emotions arise, while harmony is the state when emotions are expressed in their due measure (Zisi, 2016). Whereas equilibrium assumes the role of an inner compass for peaceful mind and emotional neutrality, harmony works as the expression with ethical and social purpose, embodying the balanced interaction necessary for cosmic order. Together, they embody humanity's innate moral nature aligned with the heavenly principle, actualized through the cultivation of propriety, the rectification of the heart, the pursuit of sincerity, and the refinement of virtue. Ultimately, the Confucian ideal—the harmony between Heaven and humanity—epitomizes the highest fulfillment of self-cultivation.

Harmony is not solely a Confucian ideal but a shared aspiration across various Chinese schools such as Daoism, Mohism, and Buddhism. Taking Daoism, for example, the purpose of "wuwei" is to achieve a balanced and harmonious existence. While Confucian harmony seeks equilibrium through emphasizing social order and adherence to propriety, Daoist harmony flourishes by embracing the spontaneous flow of the Dao and respecting the individuality and uniqueness of all things. For Lao Tzu and Chuang Tzu, this means finding balance and tranquility by aligning with the diversity, flexibility, and rhythm found in nature, rather than imposing rigid structures.

Daoist harmony transcends mere human-nature emulation, emerging instead as a triune system of interdependent realms: natural, human, and social. Natural harmony calls for spontaneity, maintaining a noninterfering and reverent attitude to nature's ebb and flow. Human harmony embodies wuwei—a release from artificial desires to cultivate serene, authentic relationships. Social harmony envisions modest, autonomous communities that honor simplicity, shun excess, and distribute resources with fairness. These dimensions coalesce into an indivisible whole, orienting both personal conduct and collective life toward the Dao—the primordial harmony that births and sustains all being.

4.1.4 Righteousness Across the Public-Private Divide

Righteousness signifies the commitment to doing what is right, aimed at fostering a cohesive society. It embodies principled conduct aligned with moral duty, where actions and decisions prioritize collective welfare over personal advantage. This foundational virtue operates in dynamic harmony with humaneness, the spiritual core of Confucian ethics. While humaneness evokes empathy and benevolence, righteousness channels these feelings into concrete ethical action, directing compassionate intentions toward socially responsible ends. The principle of righteousness, with its complex implications, exemplifies how the Chinese navigated the sometimes conflicting demands of both individual needs and public duty.

4.1.4.1 Self-interest and Public Righteousness

In Confucian moral discourse, public righteousness (公义) is often contrasted with personal gain (私利), framing a core ethical dichotomy. Albeit righteousness encompasses personal moral commitments like loyalty and gratitude, its supreme expression manifests as public dedication and service. Classical Confucian discourse consistently privileges this other and public orientation as morally superior to the pursuit of private or factional benefit.

The tension between righteousness and [narrow] self-interest is a central ethical concern in moral cultivation, as Confucius (2016a) noted that "the gentleman is conversant with righteousness, and the small person is conversant with gain" (4.16). This concern is highly justifiable within a patriarchal system, where blood ties and filial piety carry significant weight, often giving rise to favoritism and conflicts between private and public obligations. The intertwining of family and state, exemplified in relationships such as father and son or monarch and minister, further complicates the proper distribution of power and resources within a hierarchical system. To address this issue, Confucianism advocates placing public righteousness above personal gain, ensuring that moral integrity governs both individual behavior and societal order.

At its core, the debate reflects the conflict between the public and private spheres. For Confucianism, the "public" realm encompasses the collective and long-term interests of the state and the broader social order, often aligned with the principle of righteousness. The "private" sphere, by contrast, refers to narrow personal, familial, and small-group interests that, when driven by self-interest rather than ethical obligation, conflict with the public needs. Originally, the idea of righteousness was associated with the nobility who held moral authority. Their broader perspective, responsibility for the collective good, and access to resources positioned them to mediate between public and private interests. Over time, this principle evolved, suggesting that anyone who prioritizes the public good—regardless of social status—can embody the virtue of righteousness.

Confucians regard the unrestrained pursuit of personal interest as a root of conflict and social unrest, thus elevating public righteousness as a necessary counterbalance—a normative framework to curb selfish profit-seeking. That said, classic Confucianism does not deny the pursuit of personal advantage, as Confucius (2016a) declares his readiness even to serve as a carriage driver to obtain it (7.12). However, he emphasizes that wealth and advancement should be sought in accordance with righteousness, stating, "Riches and honors acquired by unrighteousness are to me as a floating cloud" (7.16). Neo-Confucianism take a more stringent stance, viewing these two as mutually exclusive: The pursuit of personal profit precludes the pursuit of righteousness, and vice versa (Cheng & Cheng, 1981). Overall, a junzi is expected to consciously regulate personal desires, uphold a steadfast commitment to righteousness, and act to prevent harm or exploitation—thereby contributing to the well-being of the broader community.

Pre-Qin Daoism presents a radical departure from Confucian ethics by rejecting both righteousness and self-interest as artificial constructs that distort humanity's spontaneous virtue (Xu & Zhu, 2003). For Lao Tzu, the relentless profit-seeking alienates people from their true nature, fomenting conflict and unsettling their hearts. In this context, personal desires can become sources of trouble, jeopardizing well-being and even life itself. Lao Tzu (2010) also criticizes Confucian righteousness as merely a clumsy remedy that rulers impose to correct deviations from the Dao (Chap. 38). The more it is emphasized, the further it strays from the Dao. Consequently, he advocates for a return to an original state of simplicity, where virtue emerges spontaneously rather than through imposed rules. This requires rulers to neither seek personal gain nor govern by manipulating people's desires. Instead, they should adopt an exemplary and noninterfering approach, allowing individuals to develop freely according to their inherent potential and naturally embrace virtue.

Mohism, grounded in impartial care and mutual benefit, proposes a synthesis of righteousness and interest. Mozi (2009) regards righteousness as inseparable from collective benefit, arguing that true virtue cannot exist without yielding tangible advantages for others. Unlike self-centered notions of interest, Mozi's concept of benefit is inherently other-regarding, making ethical conduct a mechanism for universal flourishing. Within this framework, the principle of righteousness must translate into actions that contribute to the welfare of the broader community. Mozi's pragmatic orientation further distinguishes Mohism from traditions that emphasize moral intentions over tangible outcomes. For him, the righteousness of an action lies not solely in its intent, but in its actual social impact, reinforcing a results-driven vision of ethics.

4.1.4.2 The Spectrum of Righteousness: Greater and Lesser Forms

While the distinction between righteousness and self-interest is significant, framing them as a strict dichotomy risks oversimplifying the nuanced ethical landscape of ancient China. Righteousness itself is multifaceted, varying in degree and significance. Confucian thought recognizes this complexity, acknowledging that the ethical weight of righteousness depends heavily on the specific contexts. Resolving such dilemmas requires careful consideration of circumstances, prioritizing and harmonizing competing obligations, an approach reflected in the dynamic interplay between greater and lesser righteousness. Though seldom made explicit, the dynamic between greater and lesser righteousness can be inferred from the underlying logic embedded in Confucianism's dispersed ethical discourses.

Lesser righteousness, also known as private righteousness, emphasizes fulfilling personal obligations within one's immediate social circles. It manifests in actions such as fulfilling filial duties, honoring promises, doing favor for specific individuals, upholding the interests of relatives and friends, and maintaining local allegiances, all of which strengthen social bonds. It is considered righteousness because it aligns with certain moral principles and involves acts of altruism within specific groups. However, their narrower focus can sometimes conflict with broader principles, leading to their classification as "lesser righteousness." In such cases, it may be influenced by private interests or even overlap with them.

Greater righteousness, or public righteousness, is a virtue that transcends narrow self-interest, upholding the common good, fairness, and broader social obligations. The key distinction between greater and lesser righteousness lies in their scope: The former prioritizes the well-being of the greater community, while the latter is confined to the interests of family or smaller groups. Nonetheless, lesser righteousness remains essential in the Chinese context, for it helps reinforce the moral fabric of foundational social structures and can lay the groundwork for a broader moral vision: Greater righteousness does not arise in a vacuum but grows from, and can coexist with, lesser righteousness. As individuals expand their moral horizons and embrace broader concerns, they can elevate lesser righteousness into greater righteousness. Confucianism illustrates this ethical progression: The loyalty one shows to family serves as a foundation for broader allegiances, such as loyalty to the state, reflecting the dynamic interplay between personal and public righteousness.

Yet, while honoring lesser righteousness is essential for maintaining social cohesion, an overemphasis on personal obligation can create partiality and injustice, potentially harming a broader community or undermining long-term societal needs. A narrow focus on close-knit ties may become a source of unrighteousness:

Defending the interests of a small circle without considering the greater good can compromise the rights of those outside it and the well-being of the wider community. The challenge in Confucian ethics lies in striking a balance between these two forms of righteousness or determining which to prioritize in a given context. Recognizing that favors for one group may come at the expense of others, Confucian virtue rests not in blind adherence to personal obligations but in upholding greater good. True virtue, then, is not merely about weaving personal threads but about knitting the grand tapestry of humanity.

Overall, Confucian moral cultivation calls for giving precedence to greater righteousness over lesser righteousness. Upholding greater righteousness requires individuals to consider the well-being of broader communities and coordinate their actions for the long-term common good. When this public imperative clashes with personal obligations to family and friends, mainstream Chinese ethics prioritizes greater righteousness, viewing it as essential to ensuring social fairness and justice, which ultimately safeguard the benefit of both society and individuals. This inspires altruistic actions such as advocating for the vulnerable, combating social injustice, and sacrificing personal interest or even one's own life for the [greater] righteousness (Mencius, 2016, 6A:10).

Despite the ambiguous dividing line, it is important to distinguish between lesser righteousness and personal gain: Whereas the former is driven by genuine concern for those bound by social ties, the latter is a calculated pursuit of self-interest. Yet, this dichotomy is not absolute. When misapplied, even seemingly selfless acts of lesser righteousness can harbor ulterior motives, like bolstering reputation for future advantage, raising questions about their true ethical nature. This complexity is particularly salient in the Chinese context, where guanxi's intimate web often blurs public and private interests, cloaking corruption as righteous duty.

Such entanglement often brings greater righteousness and lesser righteousness into tension: While fulfilling immediate obligations—such as those to family and close relations—is important, an exclusive focus on them can narrow moral perspective, overlook broader societal needs, and even perpetuate inequality and injustice. Conversely, overemphasizing greater righteousness at the expense of personal bonds may erode the ethical fabric of Chinese society, which is deeply rooted in familial and communal relationships. In Confucian thought, greater righteousness draws its moral strength from the lesser righteousness cultivated within the family; when individuals' rightful interests and entitlements are ignored, it loses its ethical grounding and risks degenerating into an empty grand narrative—or worse, a form of dangerous fanaticism or a vehicle for personal ambition disguised as moral cause. In such cases, the pursuit of "righteousness" can devolve into coercion, exclusion, or even persecution, betraying the very values it claims to defend.

The key lies in maintaining a delicate balance between competing ethical demands, while preserving both the wisdom of a broad perspective and the embrace of a caring mind. Lesser righteousness provides the foundation for cultivating deeper moral responsibilities, while greater righteousness extends these principles beyond the personal sphere to advance social justice and the public good. Creative approaches can often meet both needs and keep them in balance. Yet when an either-or choice arises and public resources or collective welfare are at stake, greater righteousness often takes precedence—not as a rejection of lesser duties, but as their logical culmination: the highest expression of the same moral principles, extended to broader horizons.

4.1.5 Humility as the Subtle Workings of Virtue

Humility is a profound moral disposition—a conscious restraint of ego and avoidance of arrogance that keeps one open to self-improvement. It manifests through three dimensions: self-forgetting in service to others, attributing achievements to collective effort, and constant self-examination to overcome complacency. Chinese ethics place a strong emphasis on humility, which goes beyond a personal virtue to serve as an ethical framework that guides learning, human relationships, and leadership. This emphasis on humility draws inspiration from the cosmic order that is beneficial for growth, where Heaven exemplifies humbleness with the moon's waning after waxing, and Earth imparts humbleness through water's natural tendency to flow downward (Confucius, 2016c, Tuan Zhuan A). Embracing humility yields positive consequences by preventing envy and resentment, whereas arrogance, greed, and self-conceit invite trouble and sow discord.

Both Confucianism and Daoism embrace humility, though with nuanced interpretations. In Confucianism, humility first manifests as modesty, which acknowledges one's own limits and emphasizes learning from others' strengths. It also entails courteous social etiquettes and a considerate and other-oriented self, counterbalancing excessive self-concern. This, in turn, fosters harmony, puts others at ease, and encourages collaboration (McLeod, 2020). A key example is the practice of courteous yielding (让), which entails graciously stepping back to let others take opportunities, share in honors, or assume prominence.

Courteous yielding encompasses both attitude and action. The attitude involves a sincere recognition of others' abilities and worth, while the actions prioritize others' needs and concerns, fostering cooperation and preventing conflict (McLeod, 2020). The underlying idea is to create space for others' growth, promoting mutual flourishing and contributing to a more harmonious society. Confucian humility is a graceful expression of goodwill, but it is not entirely unconditional. It carries an expectation of reciprocation, not as a demand, but as a natural consequence of genuine human interaction. This act of yielding is not a sign of weakness, but a testament to the Confucian gentleman's moral strength—steadfast in principle, yet discerning in guarding against exploitation.

In comparison, Daoist humility adopts an even less assertive stance, emphasizing not just yielding but also staying low, ultimately leading to non-contention. Although Lao Tzu does not explicitly use the term humility, his teachings are infused with ideas of modesty, self-effacement, and conflict avoidance in human relationships. Lao Tzu (2010) embodies this through his three treasures: compassion, frugality, and a reluctance to seek preeminence. The notion of staying low and inconspicuous reflects the Dao's humble nature, paradoxically allowing practitioners to "become chief among all things" (chap. 67). This characteristic is vividly illustrated by valleys and water. Valleys, deep and unfilled, symbolize inclusivity and open-mindedness. Water, seemingly soft and yielding, permeates and nourishes all things, embodying the Dao's highest virtues: beneficence, humility, and generosity. This nonassertive approach fosters harmony and exemplifies a leadership style rooted in humility.

Bottom line, humility is a highly valued virtue in ancient Chinese moral cultivation with hidden strength. In a large, densely populated agrarian society, it plays a crucial role in minimizing conflict and fostering harmonious relationships. Humility encourages respect, courteous yielding, and the tempering of personal ambition for the sake of self-cultivation and social cohesion, endowing it with universal resonance. While deeply rooted in Chinese tradition, humility is a virtue embraced by many cultures, making it ever relevant in today's world—particularly in promoting intercultural dialogue and collaboration.

4.1.6 Naturalistic Frameworks for Moral Development

Daoism contributes to moral cultivation through its naturalistic framework that offers an alternative to the structured virtue ethics of Confucianism. While Daoism is not typically classified as a strictly "moralist" philosophy, its central concept of the Dao inherently encompasses ethical principles and ways of living. These principles function as channels, not instruments of control, through which the Dao's vitality unfolds in the world, giving rise to its own naturally grounded ethical preference. That is why, on occasion, Daoism is referred to as Dao-Moralism.

Lao Tzu (2010), through his distinction between superior (profound) virtue and inferior virtue, articulates a naturalistic framework for moral development that stands distinct from Confucian conceptions of virtue. Within this framework, true moral development is not a human-constructed system based on external norms, but an organic process of rediscovering and expressing spontaneous virtue innate to all beings (Chap. 38). Developing superior virtue, therefore, involves preserving or returning to one's natural state of spontaneity and authenticity: "It gives things life yet does not manage them. It assists them yet makes no claim upon them; rears them yet does not lord it over them" (Chap. 51). Following the Dao, this highest virtue reflects an altruism that benefits all things while remaining humble and unobtrusive—an effortless grace that neither claims nor intrudes. This naturalistic approach, accordingly, helps to temper the rigidity of moral structures, resist ethical instrumentalization, and enhance the generative power of authentic moral cultivation.

This naturalistic framework of moral cultivation operates on the principle of noncoercive action. Contrary to common misconception, Lao Tzu's wuwei (noncoercive action) is not passivity but effortless action, or acting through nonaction (Loy, 1985). For him, the problem with Confucian moral cultivation lies in its excessive intellectualization, deliberate striving, and attachment to outcome, which can ironically lead to anxiety, manipulation, and even hypocrisy. The ethical implications are profound: Rather than striving to mold people according to rigid virtues or external expectations, the Daoist way allows virtue to arise naturally—much like water flowing downhill or a tree growing toward the light. This cultivation leads not to domination but to subtle influence, not to heroic virtue but to quiet efficacy. Ultimately, the Daoist framework offers a countermodel to, and at times a complement of, Confucian moral cultivation—one that emphasizes balance over perfection, presence over performance, and spontaneous harmony over hierarchical control. In this way, it serves as a vital corrective and a harmonious counterpart to more effort-driven ethical systems, inviting a rethinking of what it truly means to live virtuously and in harmony with the world.

Non-coercive action offers profound guidance for self-cultivation in navigating life's complexities. Nonaction, at its core, does not mean doing or owning nothing, but rather ensuring that nothing owns you. It involves acting with intention while maintaining a mindset of detachment from specific outcomes. Rather than enforcing it, it allows things to unfold naturally or responds in alignment with larger currents of change. This mindful approach minimizes internal struggles and external conflicts, helping individuals prioritize what truly matters over fleeting desires or societal pressures. By cultivating nonaction, individuals can foster inner peace, build resilience against frustration, and free themselves from the relentless pursuit of external validation.

To attain the naturalistic virtues, Lao Tzu advises people to guard against excessive desires. Unrestrained craving for success, status, and material wealth disrupts one's natural balance, giving rise to arrogance, hatred, tension, and conflict. As he warns, "The five colors blind the eye, the hard riding of the hunt addles both heart and mind; property hard to come by subverts proper conduct, the five flavors destroy the palate, and the five notes impair the ear." These external stimuli, Lao Tzu (2010) suggests, overwhelm the natural senses and divert attention from inner peace. To counter these tendencies, he champions the virtue of frugality, which "display[s] a genuineness like raw silk and embrace a simplicity like unworked wood, lessen[s] your concern for yourself and reduce your desires" (Chap. 12). The ultimate goal is to liberate individuals from the fetters of worldly desire, attaining visionary wisdom and spiritual freedom.

Consistent with this emphasis on natural and unobstructed cultivation, Lao Tzu (2010) advocates for a subtle, spontaneous "silent teaching." Sages, in his view, are not rigid instructors, but individuals who embody the Dao through their actions. Rather than relying on verbal pronouncements or imposed rules, they lead by example, guiding others through their tacit, virtuous conduct. In the absence of external coercion, people naturally follow their leaders' good example and undergo self-transformation in accordance with their own nature. This allows them to remain genuine and sincere, aligning with the powerful yet silent flow of the Dao.

Beyond being an independent path of self-cultivation, the Daoist natural framework has helped to prevent Confucian moral cultivation from becoming overly dogmatic, externally driven, or psychologically burdensome. Daoism reconsiders the very source of virtue, suggesting that a deeper, unconditioned goodness resides within individuals and that moral action should arise spontaneously, not through rigid ritual mastery. It reframes ethical development as a process of uncovering one's innate potential rather than internalizing external norms. Moreover, it expands the scope of harmony, redefining it not as a duty-bound, hierarchical order, but as a dynamic, non-coercive flow aligned with the Dao—a vision that encompasses social balance, ecological attunement, and a profound sense of belonging within the interconnected cosmos.

4.2 Approaches to Moral Self-cultivation

Self-cultivation in Chinese thought is a distinctive and holistic pursuit—not merely an intellectual endeavor, but an embodied process that weaves together moral learning, critical reflection, lived experience, and deep introspection. While ancient philosophers like Lao Tzu, Confucius, and Mozi laid the groundwork by debating the nature and content of virtue itself, later Chinese philosophers shifted their emphasis towards the cultivation of virtue and its metaphysical justifications. This focus is particularly salient in Neo-Confucianism, which drew upon the classics, adapted methods of other schools, and innovated sophisticated frameworks to chart the path of self-cultivation.

4.2.1 Settling Oneself and Fulfilling One's Mission

Moral cultivation in ancient China fundamentally sought to guide individuals in securing their rightful place within the world, while actualizing their higher moral purpose or destiny (安身立命). The concept is rooted in Mencius' (2016) teachings: "When neither a premature death nor long life causes a person any inner conflict, but they patiently cultivate their personal character, accepting whatever outcome may come; — this is how they establish their Heaven-ordained existence" (7A:1).

"Settling down" involves cultivating personal security and family stability by ensuring financial well-being, health, and meaningful relationships. A mindful and balanced approach to these areas fosters inner peace and resilience, enabling individuals to navigate life's challenges with greater equanimity. The concept of the life mission or purpose (ming, 命) goes beyond predestination. While acknowledging fate's role such as lifespan and fortune, it emphasizes consciously fulfilling ethical responsibilities and making meaningful contributions to the world.

In Confucianism, the concept of "ming" signifies a divine ordinance with ethical implications. Confucius (2016a), for instance, highlights the role of "ming" in promoting humaneness, asserting that it is impossible to become a Junzi without recognizing the ordinances of Heaven. In this context, "ming" represents a gentleman's duty to uphold moral principles. This perspective suggests that individuals should pursue moral excellence, regardless of their lifespan or challenges. This moral pursuit offers a measure of solace in addressing life's uncertainties, guiding individuals through setbacks and unfulfilled aspirations. It encourages reflection on life's purpose while fostering Confucian virtues within families and society, which instill a sense of belonging, direction, and resilience. As Mencius (2016) eloquently states, "A scholar, though poor [in distress or despair], does not let go his righteousness; though prosperous, he does not leave his own path" (7A:9), exemplifying how moral cultivation provides purpose and inner strength amid life's fluctuations.

This aspiration finds its fullest expression in Neo-Confucian scholar Zhang Zai (n.d.), whose resolute commitment to cultivating the moral heart-mind for Heaven and Earth serves as a guiding principle for ethical self-cultivation. While Heaven and Earth manifest their inherent principles, such as life-nurturing, renewing, and co-flourishing, their ethical significance is actualized through human recognition, enactment, and embodiment. "Establishing the heart-mind," accordingly, signifies humanity's moral subjectivity within the cosmos, highlighting the importance of ethical principles for both individuals and this world. This, in turn, inspires people to undertake their own moral responsibility in fulfilling the mission of life, providing individuals and society with a stable value system.

The idea of "settling down" and fulfilling one's celestially bestowed mission aligns with the concept of immanent transcendence introduced by modern scholar Mou Zongsan (2003), who posits that transcendence can be achieved through Confucian moral practice. He argues that the ultimate reality, often associated with Heaven, is not separate from daily human experience but immanent—manifesting through and within the mundane. In other words, it is a reality that is everywhere and beyond everywhere, all at once. This perspective clarifies why individuals possess an innate capacity to cultivate moral and spiritual qualities that embody the principle of Heaven, positioning moral self-cultivation as an internal and relational process, which primarily reflects immanent rather than external transcendence.

While Confucianism does not promise salvation in the same way as Abrahamic religions, it offers a unique path to transcendence—one rooted in self-cultivation and ethical living, fostering social harmony and personal fulfillment in this life. As Mencius emphasizes, humans possess an innate goodness, enabling them to lead a moral life and fulfill their heavenly mandate. Notably, this Confucian immanent transcendence remains inclusive and compatible with other belief systems, as following the Confucian path of moral perfection does not preclude adherence to other religious or political ideologies.

4.2.2 Inner Sage-Outer King: Ideal and Practice

The Confucian ideal of "inner sage-outer king" (内圣外王) envisions moral cultivation as a seamless unity of self-perfection and world-transformation, as well as knowledge and action. Like Plato's philosopher-king, it upholds the harmony between inner moral refinement (inner sage/sagehood) and external governance (outer king/kingliness). At its core, this principle dissolves the artificial divide between private virtue and public responsibility. The cultivated, sage-like mind—refined through study, reflection, and ritual—becomes the wellspring for kingly conduct in family, community, and state. Here, Confucianism makes its boldest claim: that Confucians' true self-cultivation is never solipsistic, but always social; that the microcosm of the virtuous heart must ultimately reshape the macrocosm of the world.

While the term "inner sage-outer king" appears in both Confucianism and Daoism, their interpretations differ significantly. Daoism emphasizes aligning with the natural order, cultivating the Dao within oneself, and contributing to world harmony through noninterference. Confucianism, by contrast, centers on the cultivation of the "sage-king"—a ruler who not only inspires through moral example but also leads through active governance, guiding the people and transforming society. As Confucius (2016a) observes, a virtuous leader influences others through his character, much like the North Star, which remains fixed while all other stars revolve around it (2.1). This analogy underscores the necessity of self-cultivation, especially for those in authority, to assume leadership. Accordingly, only junzi and sages, individuals with true virtue, are fit to govern, thereby realizing the Confucian Kingly Way (王道) and establishing a harmonious world.

The Confucian "Eight Entries" outline a dynamic blueprint for self-cultivation, emphasizing continuous improvement and comprehensive development. The first five entries—investigating things through careful observation and reflection, achieving knowledge, being sincere, rectifying one's heart—focus on inner transformation, forming the foundation of the "inner sage." The remaining entries—family regulated in harmony, kingdom well-governed by benevolent leadership, and All under Heaven in peace—extend this cultivation outward, embodying the duty of the "outer king." Crucially, these dimensions are not sequential steps but concurrent practices: Like roots and branches of the same tree, inner sagehood nourishes outer kingliness, while engagement with the world deepens self-understanding. The "Eight Entries" thus depict a holistic process in which personal moral growth and societal contribution reinforce each other, fostering both individual fulfillment and collective harmony.

The ideal of Inner Sage and Outer King embodies the Confucian synthesis of moral excellence and social responsibility, uniting virtue with action in an indivisible whole. For Confucians, genuine virtue is never confined to introspection; it must be realized through concrete deeds. The Outer King represents this outward expression, where moral principles animate one's conduct across all spheres, from personal relationships to governance and the creation of a just society. Meanwhile, the Inner Sage serves as the moral compass, ensuring that external actions remain aligned with ethical truth. The two dimensions form a dynamic reciprocity: Noral clarity guides worldly engagement, while lived experience refines inner virtue. This unity reaches its most explicit formulation in Wang Yangming's doctrine of the unity of knowledge and action, which asserts that understanding and practice are fundamentally one and the same.

Different Confucian scholars may emphasize different aspect of the "inner sage" and "outer king" ideals. Mencius, who upholds humanity's innate goodness, prioritizes cultivating humaneness—the essence of "inner sage." In contrast, Xunzi focuses on the "outer king," advocating for social order through established rituals and effective governance. These differing perspectives shape two distinct, though not always mutually exclusive, major currents in Confucian thought: one centered on self-cultivation as the foundation for personal virtue and social harmony and the other emphasizing the practical role of moral development in stabilizing and enriching the state.

4.2.3 Practical Learning for Worldly Service

As a development of the Confucian ideal of outer king, Practical Learning (实学) represents a distinct form of self-cultivation that emphasizes learning for the purpose of doing and concrete application. It emerged as a challenge to, yet also a complement for, the dominant Song-Ming Neo-Confucian Learning of the Principle (理学), which prioritizes recovering innate knowledge, rigorous self-discipline, and achieving inner moral perfection through metaphysical inquiry. While Learning of the Principle left a profound impact on Chinese intellectual history, the lasting significance of Practical Learning lies in its focus on real-world relevance—grounding moral ideals in practice and balancing philosophical idealism with pragmatic concerns.

Far from being purely theoretical, Confucianism, as understood by scholars of Practical Learning, is a philosophy of action centered on the application of virtue. Statecraft is not merely administrative skill but an extension of achieved self-cultivation, where personal virtue serves to benefit the world. Influential thinkers such as Xunzi (pre-Qin), Wang Chong (Eastern Han), Chen Liang (Southern Song), and Huang Zhongxi (Ming-Qing) champion this pragmatic approach. This idea echoes Mohist ethics, which prioritize practical utility and maintain that true righteousness is found in actions that produce concrete benefits for the greater good.

Throughout Chinese history, pragmatism has been a vital current within the river of Confucian thought by venturing beyond theoretical ideals to engage with daily life and national concerns. It had contributed to the development of the School of Practical Learning for the World (经世致用) during the Ming-Qing Dynasties, which emphasizes applying philosophical learning to safeguard the country. This humanistic pragmatism also played a crucial role in addressing the national crisis in the early modern China, demonstrating Confucianism's enduring adaptability in times of great challenges.

The merits of Practical Learning, nonetheless, have been a subject of debate throughout history. Zhu Xi, for instance, regarded desires as obstacles to moral progress, warning that a pragmatic orientation might inflame self-interest at the expense of righteousness. In response, Chen Liang of the Utilitarian School argued that desire and righteousness are not inherently incompatible. He maintains that virtue is grounded in meeting human needs and achieving practical goals, arguing that righteousness without real-world application loses its relevance. Notably, Practical Learning does not abandon the pursuit of virtues. Instead, it proposes a more integrated and realistic approach, where individuals can pursue both righteousness and practical benefits. For these scholars, the Dao—the path to harmony—is not separate from utility and desire but realized through them.

Practical Learning is an indispensable dimension of Confucianism. While the pursuit of the inner sage offers a moral compass, practical learning anchors these ideals in real-world application. By addressing the inner-sage approach's limited engagement with concrete social challenges, Practical Learning extended the reach of Confucianism through action and problem-solving, exemplifying how Chinese culture integrates moral idealism with pragmatic spirit.

4.2.4 *Moral Cultivation as Gongfu*

While often associated with martial arts today, the term "gongfu (功夫)" is originally a philosophical term referring to the ongoing process of self-cultivation through sustained effort, self-discipline, and practice, aimed at personal refinement and mastery. "Gongfu" plays a crucial role in Confucian moral cultivation. While the "Way of Heaven" provides the cosmic framework and the "theory of heart and nature" offers an ontological legitimacy, the theory of gongfu serves as a Chinese epistemology (Cheng & Zou, 2000), which encourages Confucians to cultivate virtue through engaging with classical texts, embodying filial piety and ritual propriety, and committing to state service. This continuous effort bridges what is within (inner sage) and what is without (outer king), making Confucianism a praxis philosophy that reveals ontological truth through the daily effort of acquiring and practicing virtues.

Gongfu theory differs from its Western counterparts in emphasizing self-cultivation over abstract theorization. While Western epistemology, particularly in classical Greek philosophy, often seeks to construct abstract knowledge systems using logic and analytical language, gongfu theory prioritizes embodying moral truth—aligning one's actions with the Heaven's Way or the heavenly principle. This approach entails not only understanding the cosmic order but also internalizing and manifesting it in daily experience. For example, the principle of "knowing through the investigation of things" encourages active engagement with the world, serving as a path to actualizing ethical truth and fulfilling the heavenly mandate.

Gongfu represents a transformative process of moral and spiritual cultivation, bridging the gap between ethical ideals and lived reality. Like all great traditions of self-cultivation, it is an ongoing journey toward moral excellence. Yet unlike many rigid doctrinal systems, gongfu does not prescribe a fixed procedure; instead, it allows moral agents to exercise innovation and autonomy in forging their own paths. This flexibility is exemplified by Zhu Xi's emphasis on exhaustive self-examination and intellectual inquiry, as well as Wang Yangming's advocacy for intuitive enlightenment and the unity of knowledge and action.

In Confucianism, metaphysics and gongfu are not separate domains but two dimensions of a single pursuit—the art of cultivating oneself to full humanity through learning. While Confucian philosophers engage in profound metaphysical inquiries, their discussions ultimately circle back to the essential task of self-cultivation. Metaphysics provides the why—the cosmic framework that gives meaning to human virtue; gongfu embodies the how—the concrete practices that transform lofty ideals into lived experience. In this sense, the philosophy of Confucian moral cultivation is essentially a philosophy of gongfu. Neo-Confucianism, the torchbearer of this tradition, summarizes and further develops various methods for gongfu practice, including fostering sincerity, maintaining inner tranquility, moderating desires, cultivating the heart and qi, engaging in investigative learning, and extending innate knowledge. These approaches, though distinct, converge on a shared goal: to illuminate the moral significance permeating both self and world, and to attune humanity to the celestial rhythm. Here, metaphysics descends from abstraction, becoming breath, gesture, and deed—the daily proof of cosmic harmony in human life.

While gongfu finds its most systematic expression in Confucianism, its spirit animates China's entire philosophical landscape. In Daoism, gongfu involves harmonizing with the Dao through practices such as meditation, cultivating spontaneity, detachment, and inner tranquility. In Buddhism, gongfu is a path toward Nirvana, transcending worldly attachments in pursuit of ultimate liberation. Compared to the Confucian one, which remains deeply engaged with human affairs, gongfu in these two schools seem to be less attached to the worldly concern. Yet, these paths are not entirely separate. Threads from both Daoism and Buddhism can enrich and broaden the Confucian texture of self-cultivation with more spontaneous and universal perspectives. This cross-pollination between traditions underscores the multifaceted nature of "gongfu" and its capacity to guide individuals on diverse journeys of self-transformation.

4.2.4.1 Attaining Sincerity

Being sincere (诚) literally means staying true and authentic to oneself and others. In Confucianism, sincerity is not merely a virtue but an ontological principle—the very heartbeat of existence. This concept originates from the faithfulness of Heaven and Earth, which usher in the four seasons in an unceasing cycle. Likewise, sincerity in Confucian thought signifies genuine honesty, integrity, credibility, and dedication, signifying human commitment to what is true and virtuous. Just as sincerity in nature nurtures all things, sincerity in humanity serves as a core dimension of human nature, manifesting as humaneness and earnestness in moral cultivation.

Sincerity embodies humanity's highest aspiration—to align human conduct with the celestial order. As articulated *in the Doctrine of Mean*, "sincerity is the way of Heaven; the attainment of sincerity is the way of humanity" (Zisi, 2016, No.21). This principle calls for harmonizing one's inner compass with the pursuit of the greater good, leading to authenticity in thought, word, and deed in accordance with virtue. Encompassing the courage of conviction, the foundation of integrity, and the wellspring of trust, sincerity fulfills its ultimate purpose: transforming the self while weaving the fabric of harmonious community. It is how finite humans participate in Heaven's infinite generative power.

Sincerity serves as the cornerstone of moral self-cultivation, requiring continuous self-reflection and self-regulation. It calls for individuals to confront their own strengths and shortcomings with unflinching authenticity, acknowledge the imperative for personal betterment, and commit to cultivating virtue. Through earnest dedication to virtue, individuals cultivate consistency between their inner character and outward conducts. It permeates the entire arc of human development, serving as both the starting point and the ultimate fulfillment of moral life. Without sincerity, all efforts risk becoming hollow performances—devoid of genuine transformation, susceptible to self-deception, and reduced to the mere appearance of virtue.

In Confucian thought, true self-understanding requires the exercise of sincerity—examining one's own actions with a sense of shame, a discerning awareness of right and wrong, and a clear conscience. The concept of shen-du (慎独)—prudent vigilance in solitude—epitomizes this moral commitment, underscoring personal accountability, disciplined self-governance, and unwavering fidelity to ethical principles even in the absence of external scrutiny. Such commitment cultivates harmony between inner conviction and outward action, reflecting a profound devotion to personal integrity and to the well-being of the community.

4.2.4.2 Moderating Desires and Practicing Meditation

Confucian self-cultivation emphasizes the practice of self-restraint, where moderation tames unbridled desires. Confucius (2016a) articulates this by teaching that to attain humaneness, one must exercise self-control, regulate desires, and return to the path of propriety (12.1). In this process, ritual propriety transcends mere suppression, functioning instead as a framework for harmoniously regulating desires in accordance with moral principles and societal norms. By moderating excessive impulses, individuals not only avoid conflict but also cultivate commitment to ethical standards. It empowers individuals to transcend the confines of personal cravings and rediscover their intrinsic moral nature.

This cultivated self-restraint carries profound implications for societal harmony. While desire can drive human progress—fueling innovation, competition, and wealth creation— unchecked desires can result in conflict and social unrest as people vie for advantage. In ancient China, where a densely populated agrarian society faced limited resources, moderation was especially underscored. Chinese ethics regarded excessive desires as a root cause of societal disorder, advocating restraint to preserve social balance. By curbing extravagance and luxury, the more fortunate could help ensure the survival of less privileged families, contributing to a more stable and equitable society. In this context, self-restraint was not mere asceticism but a conscious choice to place communal well-being ahead of individual indulgence.

Overall, Confucianism presents a nuanced view of desire. Classical Confucians take a relatively moderate stance. Confucius (2016a) himself is not an ascetic. He acknowledges the pursuit of wealth as acceptable, provided it remains within ethical boundaries (7.6). What he opposes are excess and the indulgence of greed, both of which can corrupt moral conduct. For Confucius, people should exercise temperance, keeping desires in check to prevent them from becoming monstrous forces that disrupt social order. Neo-Confucianism takes a stricter approach, upholding the slogan of "extinguishing human desires to preserve cosmic principle." Over more than a thousand years of development, Confucianism has greatly enhanced its philosophical depth and absolutism, yet this evolution may have inadvertently reduced its tolerance and adaptability.

That said, even within Neo-Confucianism, the treatment of desire is not entirely absolutist. Zhu Xi (1986), for instance, holds basic human needs aligning with the heavenly principle but views excessive desires as disruptive. To clarify this distinction, Neo-Confucians articulate a duality between the public and private spheres: The public sphere, characterized by a concern for the collective good, is aligned with Principle; the private sphere, rooted in self-interest and excessive desire, is viewed as potentially harmful and thus requires vigilant regulation or even elimination. Since unchecked desires can obstruct an individual's pursuit of Principle, identifying and curbing them became a central, ongoing task in Neo-Confucian self-cultivation.

Traditionally, Confucian ritual propriety serves a vital function in guiding and moderating desires, thereby cultivating both personal restraint and social harmony. Through these proprieties, individuals learn to regulate their emotions, prioritize duty over impulse, and derive fulfillment from ethical living. By channeling desires into established norms and refining them through humaneness, ritual propriety ensures that personal aspirations align with ethical principles. Neo-Confucians further advocate using Principle, the highly abstracted ritual propriety, to restrain excessive desires, emphasizing that individual desires should not override social justice. This moral imperative reinforces the primacy of collective well-being in Chinese society, where social order and communal harmony often take precedence over individual gratification.

Quiet sitting, or sitting meditation, is another important technique in self-cultivation. This meditation involves sitting in a relaxed, upright posture while focusing on one's breath and mind to enhance moral awareness and cultivate inner peace. Originally developed for medical or spiritual purposes, Confucians repurposed it as a method for tempering desires and attaining moral insight. Unlike religious meditation, which often aims for transcendence or communion with the divine, Confucian meditation emphasizes ethical introspection and philosophical reflection. Its goal is to illuminate innate goodness and universal principles, fostering a mental tranquility conducive to ethical growth and moral awakening.

Daoist meditation, by contrast, focuses more on spiritual development and the cultivation of spontaneous virtues. It seeks the harmony between Heaven and humanity through inner stillness and alignment with the natural flow. Lao Tzu (2010), for example, advocates for a path of utmost emptiness and tranquility (Chap. 16), seeking to shed the shackles of desires and to sense the rhythm of the Dao. Chuang Tzu (2013) expands on these ideas, introducing "fasting the heart-mind" (心斋), a practice of cleansing the mind of distracting thoughts and worldly concerns to achieve profound quietude and insights. He further advances "sitting to forget" (坐忘), a meditative state in which one dissolves into stillness, relinquishing both self-awareness and external preoccupations. These techniques allow Daoist practitioners to rise above the pull of desires, cultivating a serene and open awareness that harmonizes with the Dao—the silent, omnipresent rhythm underlying existence.

Both Buddhism and Daoism offer meditative techniques that deeply influenced Neo-Confucianism. Buddhist meditation trains the mind in concentration and deep quietude, cultivating awareness and insight. Its ultimate aim is to dissolve clinging to the idea of a permanent self; freeing one from desires, delusions, and ego attachments; and leading to enlightenment—a direct, nonconceptual realization of core Buddhist truths. Daoist meditation, by contrast, seeks a return to their uncorrupted original self by shedding artificial desires and rediscovering spontaneity, a concept exemplified by Lao Tzu's ideal of the newborn's unblemished soul. Neo-Confucians critically absorbed elements from both traditions, drawing from the Buddhist concept of sudden enlightenment and the Daoist notion of the original heart-mind, while ultimately prioritizing the development of Confucian virtues to deepen their understanding of the heavenly principle and refine their approach to self-cultivation.

4.2.4.3 Nurturing the Heart and Cultivating Qi

In classical Confucianism, the heart is not merely a physical organ but the cognitive-affective center with the capacity to discern and respond to virtue. It is also the locus of self-determination, enabling individuals to make conscious ethical choices, cultivate inner peace, and ultimately attain genuine freedom and happiness. Confucius illustrates this ideal when he remarks that by his seventies, he could follow his heart's desires without straying from the path of moral rectitude (2016a, 2.2).

Mencius (2016) introduces the concept of nurturing the heart (养心) as a vital aspect of self-cultivation. While all people are born with moral predispositions of compassion, shame, humility, and a sense of right and wrong within the heart-mind, it is often obscured or stifled by worldly influences. Thus, nurturing the heart is about uncovering and cultivating the goodness that is already within you, allowing it to grow from a small sprout into a full-fledged moral character that aligns with the Way of Heaven.

The Neo-Confucian School of Mind reoriented the discourse on self-cultivation by centering on the innate moral capacities of the heart-mind, diverging from the School of Principle's reliance on external principles. This shift powerfully affirmed the moral agent's subjectivity, prioritizing self-awareness and the inner capacity for ethical judgment. Wang Yangming (1992) illustrates this idea with the image of a vibrant flower becoming real only when perceived by the heart-mind (pp.107–108), suggesting that meaning is not imposed by the world but granted by the metaphysical heart itself. Since the heart houses the world's essence and significance, it becomes central in self-cultivation. In this view, virtue is not primarily instilled from external sources but arises from nurturing the heart's innate potential for goodness. This transformation opens the door to liberate the individual from rigid dogma, promoting a more autonomous and introspective path to moral understanding.

Moreover, Mencius (2016) complements his doctrine of nurturing heart-mind with the practice of cultivating qi (养气), the vital energy of moral righteousness. He envisions the cosmos as permeated by a dynamic, ethically charged qi that expands and flourishes through virtuous conduct. Individuals are encouraged to daily accumulate this "flood-like qi," an immense and vigorous moral energy capable of filling the space between Heaven and Earth (2A:2). Through disciplined practice of righteous actions and mindful self-examination, one cultivates this noble qi, replenishing innate reservoir and guarding against the erosion of one's virtuous nature. As this righteous energy grows within, it not only perfects individual character but also nourishes the universal flow of cosmic justice.

The interplay between nurturing the heart and cultivating qi works synergistically to advance moral development. Nurturing the heart is the inner work of fostering, nourishing, and enriching moral awareness, laying the fertile groundwork for the seed of virtue to take root and flourish. Practices such as meditation, introspection, reflection, and engagement with the arts all contribute to refining the inner moral qualities. Building upon this foundation, cultivating qi extends outward: it fortifies moral resolve, broadens ethical vision, and empowers individuals with the courage and integrity to resist injustice and fulfill the Dao's mission in humanity. Together, these complementary practices shape the junzi—a person of composure, virtue, and resilience—who moves in harmony with the rhythm of the cosmos.

Departing from the Confucian focus on recovering the moral heart through cultivation within social norms, Daoism emphasizes cultivating the heart-mind by freeing it from external rules, clearing mental clutter, and attuning it to the natural order. Lao Tzu (2013) illustrates it by distinguishing between two kinds of heart-mind: "the acquired heart" and "the permanent heart." The acquired heart is preoccupied with worldly concerns—gain and loss, right and wrong—whereas the permanent heart represents a deeper, unconditioned state of inspiration, intuition, and spontaneity, which helps liberate the heart-mind from the constraints of rigid rules and external norms. This process involves shedding the shackles of (or forgetting) the "acquired heart" and returning to the "permanent heart," thereby attaining true freedom of mind. Cultivating the permanent heart empowers fragile human beings to achieve spiritual and moral autonomy in the face of a vast universe, a chaotic world, relentless history, and the inevitable cycle of life and death (Zheng, 2003).

4.2.4.4 Engaging in Inquiry and Study vs. Honoring Innate Virtue

Honoring virtuous nature and engaging in inquiry and study are two fundamental avenues of Confucian moral cultivation, as stated in *the Doctrine of the Mean* that "Junzi honors his virtuous nature (尊德性), and maintains constant inquiry and study (道问学)" (Zisi, 2016). In classical Confucianism, the two approaches are not isolated pursuits but mutually reinforcing paths. While the cultivation of one's innate moral potential fosters an intuitive grasp of Confucian ethical truth, inquiry into knowledge sharpens and strengthens gentlemanly virtues. Together, they ensure a well-rounded and integrated path to moral development and shape the fully realized Confucian gentleman.

Neo-Confucians, however, engaged in a debate over which approach is the key to understanding the moral truth, with the School of Principle emphasizing inquiry and study, while the School of Mind emphasized honoring virtuous nature. This divergence culminated in a famous debate between Zhu Xi and Lu Jiuyuan. Zhu Xi envisioned attaining ultimate truth through accumulating insights: systematically investigating the world and studying classical texts to eventually construct a comprehensive understanding of the heavenly principle. Lu Jiuyuan, however, dismissed Zhu Xi's gradual approach as fragmented and ineffective, advocating instead for a direct inward turn to grasp one's innate moral knowledge holistically and instantly. Unlike Zhu, who believed that Principle exists in all parts of the universe, Lu contended that Principle resides within the heart, awaiting awakening through self-exploration and intuitive realization.

These differing approaches to learning can be also traced to the famous axiom: "When we have intelligence resulting from sincerity, it is called nature, and when we have sincerity resulting from intelligence, it is ascribed to instruction" (Zisi, 2016, No.21). The Lu-Wang School endorses "sincerity to intelligence" approach that highlights intuitive understanding, asserting when individuals directly comprehend the moral essence in the heart, they can obtain all ethical knowledge immediately. In contrast, the Cheng-Zhu School embraces the "intelligence to sincerity" path, which champions external inquiry and in-depth learning, advocating for knowledge built up through careful reading, observation, and thoughtful reflection. Such an approach emphasizes aligning thoughts, words, and actions with ethical principles, ultimately leading to the realization of Principle and the attainment of sagehood. This illustrates the path from acquired knowledge to a sincere moral state.

This emphasis on inquiry into the external world has raised interesting discussion on its potential impact on ancient Chinese scientific inquiry. Zhu Xi, for instance, advocated for the meticulous investigation of things, a method that fostered a spirit of close observation. Yet, unlike Western scientific traditions that developed primarily as empirical disciplines, Zhu's approach remained fundamentally rooted in moral metaphysics. His investigative method ultimately served a different telos: not the accumulation of factual knowledge per se, but the revelation of Principle as manifested in all things—a process whose true completion lay in moral self-cultivation and the realization of Confucian social harmony.

It is worth noting that, despite its strong advocacy on external inquiry, the School of Principle does not disregard the role of the heart in attaining holistic moral insight. Cheng Yi, for instance, argues that Principle is inherent in human nature, which manifests within individuals as the heart-mind (Cheng & Cheng, 1981). In this sense, the Principle governing the external world also exists within people's heart, and moral self-cultivation involves harmonizing these internal and external dimensions.

4.2.4.5 Pursuing Moral Enlightenment

In opposition to the School of Principle's external orientation, the School of Mind locates the pursuit of truth mainly within the heart-mind. This inward investigation gives rise to a distinctive mode of moral cultivation known as enlightenment. Similar to the Western concepts of eureka or epiphany, enlightenment is a unique learning process marked by a profound mental awakening or cognitive leap. This approach emphasizes direct intuitive realization—the instantaneous recognition that moral truth is never separate from the self, but merely awaiting rediscovery within. This breakthrough, allegedly, enables individuals to grasp the cosmic and moral truth all at once, wherein all secondary moral principles are understood instantly, signifying a transformative journey from "sincerity" to "intelligence."

Yet, achieving this state of enlightenment demands sustained spiritual discipline. The School of Mind advocates daily cultivation through experiential perception, thought-provoking dialogue, intuitive reflection, and the unity of knowledge and action. Practitioners engage in contemplative methods such as quiet-sitting meditation and the extension of innate moral knowledge to create the conditions for breakthrough. Though rarely attained, successful practice can bring about a profound moral-metaphysical transformation, culminating in a sublime integration of ethical clarity, existential peace, and spiritual fulfillment. In this heightened state of consciousness, moral principles are no longer perceived as external norms but as the very fabric of one's being.

Moral enlightenment entails a profound, often ineffable, realization of fundamental truths. Rather than relying heavily on reason or logic, this state of mind is primarily attained through intuition and inspiration. In both Confucianism and Buddhism, truth is often transmitted heart-to-heart, from master to disciple, beyond the confines of language. Confucius, for example, excels at using subtle and responsive pedagogical methods to guide his students from confusion to clarity, often through moments of sudden insight and illumination.

Even Zhu Xi, despite his emphasis on external inquiry, acknowledges the importance of intuitive resonance in moral learning. Echoing—but not fully adopting—the Chan Buddhist idea of "heart-to-heart transmission," he maintains that later generations could grasp the sages' ethical spirit by reading the classics with a sincere and open heart-mind. Being enlightened signifies a qualitative transformation in the inner cognition of the moral subject, accompanied by a spiritual awakening and consummation. This profound experience defies verbal expression—attempting to describe it is like trying to convey the scent of a rose through touch; the essence remains tantalizingly beyond words.

Daoism, likewise, offers profound insights to the idea of enlightenment. Since the Dao transcends reasoned comprehension, grasping its true nature requires moving beyond sensory experiences and analytical cognition—such as logic and analysis—and instead perceiving it from a higher, more holistic perspective accessed through intuition. This process requires letting go of preconceived notions and judgments, allowing the Dao to reveal itself through inner attunement and intuitive experience. This idea is embodied in the Daoist concept of "Xuan-Lan," or the "mysterious mirror" (Lao Tzu, 2010, Chap. 10), which likens one's inner consciousness to a perfectly clear mirror that reflects the world with calm and impartial clarity. By "scrubbing and cleansing" this mirror, one purifies the heart, allowing the Dao—the natural order of all things—to reveal itself to an open and receptive mind.

This idea also resonates with Confucian moral cultivation, where obtaining the [Confucian] Dao, often referred to as the heavenly principle, is the ultimate goal. While the specific understandings of the Dao and virtue vary, both traditions emphasize self-cultivation through the intuitive heart, highlighting a parallel path of inner transformation that leads to enlightenment.

Why, then, is enlightenment so crucial to Confucian moral cultivation? While emphasizing step-by-step learning, Chinese moral development ultimately aspires to a profound understanding of the Dao—or Principle—and its role in guiding and nurturing virtues. However, grasping the Dao's essence—rooted in the elusive unity of Heaven and humanity—cannot be fully apprehended through intellectual reasoning alone. Here, holistic intuition becomes indispensable, offering a profound and immediate grasp of the metaphysical foundations of ethical life. Within this paradigm, enlightenment constitutes an intuitive epistemic breakthrough that moves beyond analytical cognition to attain an experientially integrated and existentially transformative apprehension of moral and metaphysical truth.

4.3 Transcendental Realms of Moral Self-cultivation

The Chinese tradition of self-cultivation reveals its profound transformative power when approached holistically—not as mere intellectual training, but as spiritual alchemy that culminates in transcendent enlightenment. This ultimate state is often described as a "realm (境界)," where individuals transcend analytical constraints and reach a higher plane of spiritual freedom marked by an integrated experience of profound satisfaction, intuitive insight, moral ecstasy, and emotional fulfillment. For Confucians, it represents the consummation of moral development in the pursuit of gentleman-hood and sage-hood. For Daoist scholars, it signifies a state of spiritual freedom characterized by inner peace, serenity, and happiness attained by returning to the pure and spontaneous flow of nature.

4.3.1 Realm of Virtuous Joy

At the heart of this moral landscape lies the realm of virtuous joy. Here, the junzi, who embodies virtue and uplifts society through moral influence and ethical leadership, aspires to sagehood—a state of supreme virtue and perfect harmony with the world. Confucius (2016c) describes the sage as one who "acts according to the exigency of circumstances, without being carried away by their current; he rejoices in Heaven, and knows its ordinations; and hence he has no anxieties" (Xici, A.4.3).

This joy, this freedom from anxiety, is the hallmark of a sage. It is a life lived in perfect attunement with the Dao, the cosmic order, where every action flows seamlessly with harmonious purpose.

The pursuit of virtuous happiness has long served as a profound motivator across cultures and traditions. For many, true happiness does not come from material gains, but from cultivating inner peace, a serenity rooted in moral self-cultivation. Even without religious solace, this internal compass can still guide individuals toward virtuous life and provide a profound reward: the deep satisfaction of living ethically, meaningfully, and with purpose.

Confucianism exemplifies this moral pursuit, suggesting that a peaceful and contented mind arises from a clear conscience and a deep understanding of one's role in life. While recognizing fate's unpredictability, Confucians concentrate on what they can shape—their choices, virtues, and attitudes—thereby crafting meaning amid life's uncertainties. This outlook fosters equanimity in facing both fortune and adversity. As Confucius (2016a) observes, "the superior man is satisfied and composed; the mean man is always full of distress" (7.36), burdened by endless worries. This contrast conveys a deeper moral truth about joy: through disciplined self-cultivation, individuals dissolve the mental obstructions of greed and guilt, attaining inner alignment that lets joy arise spontaneously, like sunlight through dispersing clouds.

The Analects records Confucius (2016a) praising his dedicated student, Yan Hui, for finding joy even in poverty. Yan Hui's happiness stems not from material possessions but from his pursuit of virtuous ideals, a concept termed "the [virtuous] joy of Confucius-Yan" (6.9). Mencius (2016) further reinforces the idea, stating, "[since] all things are already complete in us, there is no greater delight than to be conscious of sincerity on self-examination" (7A:4). This moral happiness, born from righteous living, brings a profound sense of comfort, joy, well-being, and contentment. Furthermore, such a joy transcends mere personal fulfillment; it arises when individuals perceive a deepened awareness of the interconnectedness between humanity and the cosmos—a recognition of the unity of all beings and a quiet pride in one's moral integrity. This understanding, where truth, goodness, and beauty converge, evokes an ecstatic aesthetic experience from the heart.

The experience of joy finds varied expressions in other philosophical traditions. Chuang Tzu of Daoism, who introduces the idea of harmonious unity between Heaven and man, encourages the pursuit of great joy not through rigid moral codes, but by liberating the mind and embracing the Dao's natural flow. He distinguishes between two forms of happiness: human joy, found in harmonious relationships, and heavenly joy—the result of aligning with the Dao's cosmic rhythm (Chuang Tzu, 2013, p. 99). In contrast to Confucianism's emphasis on structured ethics, Chuang Tzu's vision of cosmic joy embraces spontaneous and effortless harmony with the world. At its core, this approach seeks to dissolve social distinctions, pressures, and constraints that hinder individual spiritual freedom, allowing people to fully realize their true nature.

Buddhism also offers a path to profound delight known as Dharma joy, which arises when the meditative mind is synchronized with Buddhist teachings, dissolving the illusion of a fixed, separate self and awakening to the reality of interconnectedness. This radiant state transcends the negative emotions of craving, hatred, and ignorance, fostering a deep realization of oneness—the recognition of all beings' interdependence and an altruistic commitment to their liberation. Dharma joy brings a profound sense of fulfillment, like a drop of water returning to the vast ocean, or a leaf reconnecting with the land. It is the experience of finitude dissolving into the infinite, evoking a deep and abiding sense of peace and happiness.

While this Buddhist bliss carries religious connotations, it parallels core themes found in the previously discussed philosophies. Considered collectively, the virtuous and spiritual joy expressed in these diverse traditions reflects a fundamental aspect of human nature—a deep yearning for unity with the whole and the transcendence of the self's limitations. It is a homecoming, a return to the essence where the mind can shed its burdens of pain and worldly concerns. In this state, one spiritually enters the infinite, where the true nature of existence reveals itself—not as something graspable through reason or knowledge, but as a profound experience realized through ethical living.

4.3.2 Realm of Expansive Humaneness

The notion of cosmic unity, wherein all beings are interconnected, is deeply rooted in Chinese philosophy, predating the Qin Dynasty. Philosophers like Chuang Tzu famously proclaims "all things are one with me," while Mencius asserts, "all things are already complete in me." This perspective underscores our intrinsic connection to the world and inspires an ethic of compassion or humaneness extending beyond humans to encompass the entirety of existence. This unification is not merely an intellectual understanding but a deeply felt, existential connection, fostering boundless compassion and an abiding sense of universal belonging.

In Confucianism, the ideal of expansive humaneness represents the highest realm of moral self-cultivation: a unifying force that harmonizes all people and all things under Heaven. Pre-Qin Confucians center humaneness on interpersonal relationships, whereas Neo-Confucians significantly broaden its scope to include the entire cosmos, moving beyond anthropocentrism. They conceive of a broader ethical vision in which humaneness nurtures and embraces all beings, both sentient and non-sentient. Cheng Hao, for example, proclaims that a truly humane person regards all things as one body (Cheng & Cheng, 1981, p. 14), while Zhang Zai (1978) envisions "all people as brothers and sisters, and all things as companions" (p. 62). This holistic ethic transcends prescriptive morality, reimaging humaneness as a cosmic principle that permeates all existence and becomes apprehensible through human consciousness. In this view, consciousness is not merely the bearer of moral insight but the medium through which the universe itself is rendered ethically alive.

Neo-Confucianism's vision of "cosmic unity" finds its fullest expression in Wang Yangming's redefining the heart not merely as the seat of humaneness, but as the very ontological foundation of existence itself. The heart-mind transcends individual subjectivity, embodying a universal and immanent principle that binds all beings into an indivisible whole, where humaneness becomes the dynamic, generative force of the cosmos. This enables Wang Yangming (1992) to idealize "the expansive (enlightened) person, who perceives all things in Heaven and Earth as one, and sees the world as a unified family" (p. 373). Here, "expansive" denotes not dominance or material power, but an awakened consciousness—a heart-mind so attuned to the cosmic principle that it dissolves the illusion of separateness. This state of awareness reveals the profound spiritual dimension of humanity: to realize one's identity with the totality of existence is to fulfill the highest Confucian imperative.

From a contemporary standpoint, these ideas embody the spirit of Confucian humanism, a philosophy that, at its core, transcends parochial concerns to embrace a universal model of humaneness. It marks a metaphysical leap extending ethical concern beyond family and state to include all under Heaven, where the concept of the "greater self" arises. This represents an expansive ethical consciousness that dissolves boundaries, fostering a deep sense of responsibility for all existence—not as an abstract, impersonal universalism, but as one that still cherishes every individual. In its highest form, humaneness dissolves the dichotomy between self and world, rendering moral cultivation an active participation in the eternal cosmic generation of life.

References

Cheng, H., & Cheng, Y. (1981). *Collections of the Cheng brothers*. Zhonghua Book Company.

Cheng, M., & Zou, L. (2000). The Confucian way of thinking on equilibrium and harmony. *Confucius Studies, 3*, 23–32.

Chuang Tzu. (2013). *The complete works of Zhuangzi* (B. Watson, Trans.). Columbia University Press.

Confucius. (2016a). *Analects*. In J. Legge (Ed. & Trans.), *Confucianism: The Four Books and Five Classics*. Delphi Classics.

Confucius. (2016b). *Book of rites*. In J. Legge (Ed. & Trans.), *Confucianism: The Four Books and Five Classics*. Delphi Classics.

Confucius. (2016c). Commentaries of changes. In J. Legge (Ed. & Trans.), *Confucianism: The Four Books and Five Classics*. Delphi Classics.

Dong, Z. (n.d.). *The luxuriant dew of the spring and autumn annals*. Chapter shen cha ming hao. Retrieved from https://ctext.org/chun-qiu-fan-lu/shen-cha-ming-hao/zhs

Han, Y. (2022). Inquiry into the essence of the Dao. In *The collections of Han Yu*. Unity Press.

Huang, Y. (2005). Confucian love and global ethics: How the Cheng brothers would help respond to Christian criticisms. *Asian Philosophy, 15*(1), 35–60.

Lao Tzu (2010). Daodejing. In R. T. Ames & D. L. Hall (Eds.), *Dao de jing: A philosophical translation* (R. T. Ames & D. L. Hall, Trans.). Ballantine Books.

Li, C. (2006). The Confucian ideal of harmony. *Philosophy East & West, 56*(4), 583–603.

Li, C. (2013). *The Confucian philosophy of harmony*. Routledge.

Loy, D. (1985). Wei-wu-wei: Nondual action. *Philosophy East and West, 35*(1), 73–86.

McLeod, M. (2020). *[Incomplete reference - please provide title and source]*.

Mencius. (2016). *Mencius*. In J. Legge (Ed. & Trans.), Confucianism: The Four Books and Five Classics. Delphi Classics.

Mou, Z. (2003). *Mou Zongsan's complete works*. Lianjing.

Mozi. (2009). *Translation of Mozi*. Guizhou People's Press.

Qi, J. (2021). *Ji Xiao Xin Shu*. People's Physical Education Press.
Shogo, W. (2015). Compassion and pity in Mahayana sutras. *Journal of International Philosophy, 4*, 267–272.
Shun, K. L. (2002). Ren and li in the analects. In B. V. Norden (Ed.), *Confucius and the analects: New essays* (pp. 53–72). Oxford University Press.
Wang, Y. (1992). *The complete works of Wang Yangming*. Shanghai Ancient Books Publishing House.
Xu, Y., & Zhu, Y. G. (2003). The pre-Qin Taoist concept of righteousness and profit. *Journal of Jinan University, 13*(5), 29–32.
Xunzi. (1997). *Xunzi*. Liaoning Education Press. Chapter music instruction.
Zhang, Z. (1978). *Zheng Meng*. China Bookstore.
Zhang, Z. (n.d.). *Analects of Zhangzi, No.111*. https://ctext.org/wiki.pl?if=gb&chapter=214776&remap=gb
Zheng, K. (2003). A study of Daoism's theory of mindfulness. *Philosophical Studies, 8*, 80–86.
Zhu Xi. (1986). *Analects of Zhu Xi*. China Bookstore.
Zisi. (2016). The Doctrine of the Mean. In J. Legge (Ed.), *Confucianism: The Four Books and Five Classics* (J. Legge, Trans.). Delphi Classics.

Part II
Philosophical Interpretation and Comparison

Chapter 5
Between Freedom and Belonging: Selfhood, Agency, Rights, and Equality

The rich metaphysical and ethical frameworks of Chinese philosophy, though examined in preceding chapters, demand fresh engagement through modern lenses. Their arcane terminology and culturally situated conceptual frameworks pose significant interpretive challenges—especially for readers unversed in China's intellectual traditions. It is precisely to mediate this divide that the current chapter offers a critical reconstruction of traditional moral cultivation through the prism of modern philosophical priorities: the nature of selfhood, moral autonomy, individual rights, and social equality.

While central to modern discourse, concepts such as the self, dignity, free will, rights, and individual autonomy are seldom, if ever, explicitly conceived in classical Chinese thought. For example, Confucian and Daoist traditions affirm the intrinsic worth of the self and the dignity of human life, yet they do not systematically theorize these concepts, nor do they directly address free will or individual rights in the manner of modern liberal philosophy. That said, these ideas are not absent, but instead manifest in latent forms, embedded within Chinese cultural contexts and philosophical discourses. This approach underscores the need for contemporary reinterpretation—not only to gain a more nuanced understanding of Chinese philosophy but also to broaden the scope of global ethical discourse, offering distinctive and profoundly relevant perspectives on enduring human concerns.

5.1 The Idea of the Self

The timeless question "Who am I?" has resonated across cultures and centuries, capturing the complexity of selfhood—a dynamic interplay of cognition, emotion, social identity, and the moral dialectic between self-interest and compassion. From mental states to moral judgment, the self is the lens through which we experience

Z. You, Y. Hu, *Philosophy and Civilization: How the Idea of Moral Cultivation Shaped China*, East-West Dialogues in Educational Philosophy and Theory,
https://doi.org/10.1007/978-981-95-5660-1_5

the world and contemplate our place in it. It is the source of our individuality—the essence that makes us, us. Historically, the intuition of an essential self has repeatedly appeared in spiritual traditions worldwide, from the immortal atman of Hindu thought to the divine pneuma in Stoic philosophy, reflecting a widespread human tendency to perceive a transcendent dimension within everyday existence.

The exploration of the self in Western philosophy traces back to Socrates and the classical Greek period. Socrates, as portrayed by Plato, emphasized the soul as the seat of moral self-knowledge. Plato and Aristotle refined the idea, identifying reason or intellect as the defining aspect of the soul and the true self. Fast forward to Kant. He expanded the concept, viewing the self not only as the rational unity that organizes thoughts and perceptions, but also as a beacon of freedom and autonomy, guided by universal moral principles (Kant, 2002). This rationally autonomous self, closely tied to free will and individual responsibility, highlights introspection and critical inquiry, thereby profoundly influencing the development of modern natural and social sciences.

In contrast to the relatively individual-centered notion of the self in the West, Chinese moral cultivation embraces a more expansive and relational perspective. Rooted in the concept of the unity of Heaven and humanity, the self is not viewed as an isolated entity but as intrinsically embedded within a dynamic web of relationships—familial, social, and cosmic. Whereas Western epistemology often draws a sharp distinction between the knowing subject and the external object, Chinese thought emphasizes the fundamental interconnectedness of the individual with the world, embodying an ontological unity of subject and object, or, analogously, human and Heaven.

Grounded in this worldview, the ethics of moral cultivation in China focuses not on what "I," as an individual, am looking for, but on what "I" ought to do as a member of a larger community; it is a philosophy rooted less in independence and more in interdependence. In classical Chinese thought, the self is inherently relational, formed through reciprocal roles within familial and social networks. Often conceptualized in sociological terms as guanxi, this structure emphasizes virtues that promote interpersonal harmony and collective responsibility over individual autonomy.

5.1.1 Individual Self and Free Will

Exploring the concept of the self provides valuable insights into the cultural and social diversity (Rasmussen, 2008). Contemporary scholarship typically identifies three fundamental dimensions of selfhood: the individual self, constituted by unique attributes, goals, and personal agency; the relational self, formed through interpersonal connections and role-based identities; and the collective self, derived from membership in larger social groups (Brewer & Gardner, 1996).

While all individuals incorporate these aspects to varying degrees, cultural frameworks significantly influence their respective salience and normative prioritization. For example, many Western cultures foreground the autonomous individual self, celebrating personal freedom, self-actualization, and distinctive achievement, with relational and collective identities occupying subsidiary positions. Conversely, mainstream Chinese culture elevates the interdependent relational self as primary, situates the collective self as secondary, and conceptualizes individual identity as properly cultivated within the broader social context.

The concept of the "individual self" is deeply rooted in the principles of independence, free will, and autonomy. Within many Western intellectual traditions, the self is conceptualized as a self-contained being, endowed with the capacity of reason and moral agency. This focus on autonomy serves to protect individual freedoms, allowing for decision-making with minimal external interference (Bockover, 2010). While it is important to avoid overgeneralizing or stereotyping individuals or subcultures within any culture, mainstream Western culture's orientation toward individualism, in general, distinguishes it from the more relational or collectivistic tendencies found in many East Asian cultures. It is from these cultural contexts that the concepts of free will, rational thinking, and autonomy take on their most meaningful expression.

Rationality has been a central pillar of moral philosophy since antiquity. Classical thinkers like Plato and Aristotle positioned reason as the sovereign faculty of moral deliberation, enabling individuals to discern and consciously pursue virtuous action. In their frameworks, the rational soul exercises governance over disruptive passions and appetites, directing human beings toward eudaimonia—that state of flourishing achieved through the cultivation of moral excellence (Deci & Ryan, 2008). This tradition establishes reason not merely as an instrumental capacity, but as the essential foundation for ethical self-development.

The nexus between rationality and moral agency finds further expression in the concepts of free will and autonomy. Free will represents the human capacity to choose among genuine alternatives, with the normative expectation that these choices follow rational moral principles. Autonomy, more robustly conceived, denotes the self-governance of a reasoning agent—the ability to form intentions and make decisions based on internalized ethical frameworks rather than external coercion. It empowers individuals to function as self-determining authors of their ethical lives.

This unique ability to reason and make autonomous ethical choices elevates human beings beyond mere instruments, affirming their status as ends in themselves and making them deserving of inherent respect. (Waterman, 1981). For Immanuel Kant, self-cultivation focuses on achieving self-discipline rather than exerting control over others. Moral law, therefore, should not solely rely on societal norms or traditions, but must also reside within the individual, drawing upon both rational deliberation and the moral potential embedded in human nature (Chan, 2002).

In summary, foundational Western concepts such as free will, autonomy, and independence arise from philosophical commitments to rational moral agency and, later, to the principle of universal human equality, historically privileging individual sovereignty and clearly defined interpersonal boundaries. That said, contemporary Western thought has progressively incorporated more relational understandings of personhood. This is evident in "second-generation" rights theories that complement classical liberal individualism with collective social protections. Such frameworks, recognizing human interconnectedness, seek to address systemic inequities, including poverty, discrimination, and structural injustice, while maintaining respect for personal autonomy. For ultimately, the self, in its truest form, is not a solitary voyager, but a member of a collective, bound together by interdependence and cooperation.

5.1.2 Relational and Collective Self

Unlike the individualistic self-conception prevalent in the West, the Chinese notion of self is deeply embedded within its intertwined social networks, rendering it fundamentally relational and collective. While the Kantian tradition underscores individual rights and personal freedom, the moral compass of the relational self emphasizes fulfilling one's role within various relationships. Core Confucian virtues, like filial piety and faithfulness, exemplify this emphasis. Living ethically means honoring these roles, aligning with established moral codes, and contributing to broader social harmony. In such a community, the cultivation of virtue is both an individual and shared endeavor, one that is expected to influence others and be influenced in turn, thus reflecting the relational nature of moral development in Confucian thought.

The "collective self" represents a mode of identity formation wherein individuals derive their primary sense of being through membership in larger social units such as community, nation, or cultural group, often taking precedence over relationships with outsiders. This sense of belonging shapes one's identity, with personal rights and interests understood within the broader context of collective goals and communal well-being. While both the relational and collective selves are grounded in human relationships, they differ in scope: the former centers on interpersonal bonds, whereas the latter extends to intergroup connections. The collective self, in particular, transcends individual relationships to embrace a broader sense of community and social responsibility, providing a foundation for cultivating altruism and universal care based on social duties.

Within the Confucian culture, individuals are expected to fulfill their moral obligations within a community. The junzi, or exemplary person, embodies virtue by skillfully navigating complex social interactions and fulfilling duties across multiple spheres: family, society, and politics, with the goal of advancing collective well-being and communal prosperity. In this framework, Confucian virtues like humaneness and righteousness extend beyond personal virtue to become foundational social values. While not dismissing individual welfare, these virtues emphasize relational and collective harmony, often requiring the individual to subordinate personal desires to the needs of the family, community, and state.

Delving into these defining traits of the self reveals the unique moral landscape in Chinese society, where the self is shaped by strong familial ties and embedded within a web of social relationships. Within the family an individual often assumes multiple roles, caring simultaneously for children and aging parents. Fulfilling these responsibilities frequently takes precedence over personal ambitions, as the honoring of familial duties and social harmony are seen as foundational to living an ethical and meaningful life.

This dynamic does not necessarily reflect absolute altruism; rather, it operates as a mutually beneficial cycle in which individuals care for their parents with the expectation that their own children will one day do the same. Socially, people gravitate toward "in-groups" with shared interests and close ties, potentially creating tension or bias toward "out-groups" (Brewer, 2015). To mitigate this narrowness, broader identities are encouraged and cultivated, helping individuals transcend these divisions and unite both in-groups and out-groups. It allows individuals to view themselves as part of larger communities, from extended kinship networks to the state and ultimately All under Heaven.

At this expansive level, personal aspirations are entwined with broader responsibilities, requiring careful consideration in aligning individual goals with the greater good. This conception of the self reflects an interpersonal or group-oriented mindset, emphasizing the harmonious balance of interests between the individual, their family, and the wider community.

At times, it even advocates for subordinating individual interests for the collective good. In traditional Chinese culture, individuals are commended for their virtue when they willingly prioritize the greater group needs over their personal desires, or graciously yield to others to preserve social harmony. This framework gives rise to distinction between the "small self" and the "greater self." The former refers to individuals who prioritize their own interests, while the latter denotes those who, when necessary, elevate the needs of others or place the collective above their own, embodying a broader, long-term, and more altruistic moral vision.

A liberal critique might view Confucian prioritization of collective welfare as potentially restrictive, constraining individual autonomy through its emphasis on social obligations. This perspective rightly identifies tensions within Confucian role-ethics, yet risks mischaracterization if not situated within the Chinese holistic worldview, where individuals are seen as integral parts of a larger ecosystem and are expected to consider the interests and well-being of others. Pursuing shared goals and principles is regarded as essential for the long-term prosperity of society. Thus, cultivating moral behavior revolves around understanding and navigating one's "self" within these interconnected networks of relationships, where personal fulfillment is intricately tied to collective harmony.

Effective moral development fundamentally requires self-awareness, as ethical decision-making presupposes conscious understanding of one's values and motivations. Ancient Chinese philosophical traditions articulate this self-awareness through a distinctive synthesis of individual and collective consciousness, where self-cultivation is inseparable from the conscientious performance of social roles. Thus, the development of individual character is often achieved through reflecting on one's duties to family and society. In contrast, Western approaches tend to maintain a clearer distinction between self-consciousness and group-consciousness. Though both personal character and social responsibilities are valued in self-cultivation, they may not always be as closely integrated in moral reflection as they are in some Eastern cultures.

From a social perspective, the Western view of the self, with its emphasis on personal autonomy, can create a sense of horizontal equivalence, where individuals see themselves as fundamentally equal. Conversely, the Chinese concept of self, with its focus on social roles and hierarchies based on role differentiation, thrives on communal intimacy. It integrates individuals into a rich web of relationships, where individuals understand their position within larger structures and act in accordance with these roles (Barbalet & Barbalet, 2017).

Imagine two paths leading to the summit of self-understanding. The mainstream Western tradition, like a solitary peak shrouded in mist, prizes the individual journey, forging a unique identity through self-reliance and independent thought. This path fosters bold exploration and personal flourishing, yet it can also lead to isolation and self-absorption if the needs of community is overlooked. To the East, a different vista unfolds. Here, the self is not a lone, isolated peak, but a mountain range composed of family, community, and state. This path emphasizes collaboration and social harmony, though it may require some sacrifice of individual prominence for the sake of collective ascent.

Eastern philosophical traditions, particularly Confucianism, prioritize collective consciousness as the foundation of ethical life. Less emphasis is placed on "I" as individual self and more on "we"—each person's role within the social group. This path offers the strength of collaboration and shared wisdom, but it can also risk diminishing the individual voice.[1] Consequently, ancient Chinese self is more duty-oriented than rights-based, prioritizing communal obligations over individual entitlements. This outlook, emphasizing interdependence and obligations as members of family, state, and all under Heaven, contrasts with Western ideals of independence and civil liberties, resulting in a different understanding of social roles that focuses less on individual citizenship.

These contrasting paradigms—one emphasizing individual rights, the other centering on duty and social roles—each possess inherent strengths and limitations. Western traditions highlight autonomy, personal freedom, and self-determination, providing strong foundation for individual dignity and legal protection. Traditional Chinese thought, with its focus on relational identity and communal obligation, offers profound insights into social cohesion and moral responsibility. While the two may not fully align, each reminds us that human flourishing depends not only on the integrity of the individual but also on the health of the broader community.

Finally, it is worth noting that a collectivist conception of the self does not inherently guarantee altruism; without ethical guidance, it can instead give rise to selfish tendencies like parochial in-group favoritism and the suppression of individual moral agency. When grounded in ethical principles, all forms of selfhood—individual, relational, and collective—can foster altruism in distinct yet complementary

[1] Similar voice can be found in Zhang (2011). *Chinese and Western culture and self*. Beijing: People's Press.

ways. Individualism, for instance, can cultivate universal care and lead to self-chosen altruism as an autonomous moral choice. The relational self lays the groundwork for empathy, which can be extended to caring strangers. Collectivism, in turn, readily promotes pro-social behavior and altruism as a social duty, fostering deep care for a defined group or even All under Heaven.

5.2 Confucian Perspectives on Agency and Autonomy

The concepts of free will and individual autonomy are fundamental to moral agency in Western philosophical traditions. While Confucian thought does not privilege these notions with the same conceptual centrality, it would be philosophically reductive to regard them as wholly absent. Confucianism, as a philosophy centered on moral development, acknowledges the importance of free will and agency in a nuanced way, especially within the context of social relationships and obligations.

5.2.1 Confucian Conception of Agency and Free Will

Agency is often defined as the capacity of an agent to make autonomous choices, which is the practical expression of free will. When applied to Chinese philosophical traditions, this paradigm raises important questions about individual agency within Confucian role ethics. The apparent emphasis on conformity through ritual propriety and the absence of explicit "free will" terminology in classical texts initially suggest a more deterministic framework. So, does Confucian virtue allow individuals to captain their own ships in this "sea of morality," or are they simply passengers on a predetermined journey?

Kant might reject the idea of freedom constrained by social relationships, but Confucianism navigates these challenges in a more nuanced way, allowing for certain free will. While emphasizing virtues grounded in relationships, Confucianism also strongly advocates for self-cultivation, where the moral agent must consciously choose among various moral propositions. True, Confucianism offers guideposts for virtuous behavior, but the path to embodying these principles involves personal reflection and an inner struggle between what "is" and what "ought to be," as well as between righteousness and desire—this is the essence of Confucian agency. From this perspective, Confucian moral cultivation fosters a distinct form of freedom—one in which virtue arises from conscious choice and personal conviction, rather than from pragmatic considerations or fear of consequences (Carleo III, 2020).

Confucianism's aspiration (志), the striving for moral excellence, adds another dimension to the concept of free will. For Confucians, virtue does not come naturally, but must be actively pursued through effort. Beyond the influence of the social environment, individuals are expected to set ambitious goals in their pursuit of moral development. Mencius (2016), for instance, encourages people to become "the Great Man," the one who consciously upholds righteousness even in the face of adversity, no matter the cost. This active moral commitment is possible because Confucianism does not view the "Heaven's Way" as a denial of free will; rather, it places humans, Heaven, and Earth on equal footing, emphasizing humans' active role in shaping the destiny of this whole interconnected realm. Human beings are not passive followers but free agents with noble aspirations, choosing to pursue moral greatness. This aspiration and agency, though not identical to Western notions of free will, closely resemble it in that both involve the ability to act independently and shape one's own moral character.

Moreover, the influence of Daoism's concept of the spontaneous self on Confucian moral cultivation should not be underestimated. While not the dominant official ideology in ancient China, Daoism acts as both a counterculture and a complementary force to Confucianism. It introduces a more liberal and individualized notion of "self," which helps temper Confucianism's hierarchical and rule-bound structure. In effect, many Confucian scholars were drawn to Daoist ideas of spontaneity and a deeper connection with nature found in Daoist classics and literature. These ideas infused valuable flexibility, free spirit, and creativity into the otherwise prescriptive Confucian framework, softening the constraining effects of rigid norms on the Confucian self.

5.2.2 *Confucian Conception of Autonomy*

Autonomy, as the exercised manifestation of free will, lies at the core of moral agency—the human capacity for self-determined action. The Kantian tradition enshrines autonomy as rational self-legislation, positing individuals as sovereign authors of their ethical existence, unimpeded by heteronomous influences. Confucianism, by contrast, adopts a different approach. Rather than emphasizing individual moral legislation or free choice in the Western sense, it frames autonomy as relational self-cultivation, a process grounded in social harmony and the fulfillment of roles within an intricate web of relationships. While this relational focus enriches ethical life, it has also drawn criticism for potentially constraining individual autonomy.

Additionally, classical Confucian ethics, with its doctrine of Heaven's Mandate—a concept tied to destiny—raises concerns about its potential to suppress individual autonomy. This sense of predetermination also extends to the idea of human nature. Consider Mencius, who saw innate goodness in humanity. When coupled with the weight of social expectations such as reverence for sage exemplars and the demands of filial piety, the space for independent moral choice seems significantly constrained.

While understandable concerns exist regarding Confucian thought's limitations on individual autonomy, a deeper analysis unveils a sophisticated interplay between fate and free will. Even within its structured system of social roles and obligations, there remains space for self-determination, which is deeply informed by "mìng" (命), often translated as "destiny" but distinct from the fixed determinism of Greek moira. Mìng recognizes the limits imposed by circumstance, while affirming human agency in moral self-cultivation, preserving the autonomy to pursue a virtuous life.

Confucians explicitly reject passive fatalism; rather, they seek a dynamic equilibrium between the preordained and the malleable. They accept life's inevitabilities such as their lifespan or unforeseen misfortune, yet vigorously pursues moral refinement. This twofold orientation—serene acceptance of what cannot be changed, coupled with steadfast commitment to what can be improved—empowers individuals to shape both their personal development and their collective future. They cultivate character and seek to fulfill their heavenly mandate, not merely for personal success, but out of a commitment to virtue as an intrinsic good. This gives new meaning to the heavenly mandate which, initially associated with imperial rule, evolves to a broader moral imperative for all individuals to ethically fulfill their roles and contribute to the well-being of the greater good. History records numerous instances of individuals steadfastly adhering to their moral ideals, even when success appeared improbable and at significant personal sacrifice.

Next, Confucianism posits no direct causality between individual virtue and personal well-being. This understanding preserves the autonomy of self-cultivation, as being a good person does not guarantee happiness or worldly success. Without the promise of external reward, moral development becomes a sincere and voluntary commitment rather than a response to incentive or coercion.

That said, Confucianism does affirm a profound connection between morality and the collective flourishing. For Confucians, virtue, grounded in the harmony of Heaven and humanity, inherently serves to the common good, suggesting that the realization of cosmic virtue (the Dao) on Earth depends on human engagement and effort. Hence, every morally autonomous Confucian bears a critical duty: to cultivate "Dao" in this world through both self-improvement and outward action—nurturing their own virtue, inspiring others, and contributing to the overall welfare of humanity (Brindley, 2011). This altruistic pursuit, driven by conscious choice, enables individuals to achieve a "greatness" akin to that of Heaven and Earth. This book terms this mindset "the greater self," one transcending narrow perspectives to conscientiously prioritize the greater good—embodying the very essence of the Dao.

A close review of Confucian theories of human nature reveals substantial conceptual space for moral agency, explicitly resisting deterministic interpretations. The Mencian paradigm's seminal "sprout" metaphor, for instance, treats innate goodness as a potential rather than a guarantee, requiring conscious nurturing, disciplined cultivation, and volitional extension to be fully realized. In Confucianism, becoming virtuous requires personal effort, a sustained commitment to learning, and the deliberate choice to pursue good over evil. The path of self-cultivation is voluntary, not imposed; no one can be coerced into virtue against their will. In this context, the Confucian view of human nature functions as an internal source of ethical orientation, a role somewhat analogous to the Western notion of reason (Cheng, 2004), which offers a capacity rather than an assured outcome.

Another common critique about autonomy in Confucianism arises from its emphasis on a communal influence, particularly the guidance of revered sages. Such a concern, nevertheless, may overlook key cultural nuances. Ancient Chinese sages, though highly respected, did not impose rigid, one-size-fits-all moral prescriptions (Tan, 2005). Their teachings were often broad, open to interpretation, and incomplete, leaving room for individuals to adapt them to their individual circumstances and moral aspirations. This dynamic approach fostered diverse interpretations and a rich tradition of philosophical inquiry, sustaining enduring discussions of self-cultivation throughout Chinese intellectual history.

While inspiring, role models do not diminish individual moral agency (Brindley, 2011). Confucius himself affirmed that the pursuit of "humaneness" is a personal choice, not something externally imposed (2016, 12.1), signifying that individuals bear ultimate responsibility for their own moral development. That is why self-examination, critical debates, and reflection are cornerstones of self-cultivation. Such practices encourage learners to explore their distinct paths, interpret sages' teachings in light of their own experiences, and develop a moral journey that is both authentic and self-directed.

Furthermore, the concept of the heart-mind elevates autonomy in Confucian moral cultivation. The heart is not only the locus of thought but, more importantly, as the seat of the self and conscience responsible for navigating intricate human relationships, enabling individuals to contemplate ethical matters and make autonomous decisions. Neo-Confucian scholars further expand this concept, seeing the heart as the substance of the universe itself embracing Principle. By shifting emphasis from external authorities to an internal moral compass, this perspective significantly strengthens individual agency in ethical development.

Having said that, Confucian notion of freedom differs fundamentally from Western notions of "free will" and "free expression." In Confucianism, freedom is not defined by unfettered choice, but rather by the deliberate and devoted pursuit of becoming humane. The goal of moral excellence is prefixed, but the journey is uniquely personal. This approach differs from purely individualistic frameworks that prioritize freedom to choose one's own values. Confucian freedom operates within ethical boundaries defined by "humaneness" and the "Way of Heaven." It is not completely self-legislating, like Kant's rational morality, but rooted in a shared vision of collective good. Modern scholars describe this as a form of soft determinism or compatibilism (Hwang, 2013), which maintains that free will can coexist with a certain degree of determinism. This view reconciles individual agency with contextual influences, emphasizing that choices are exercised within the framework of communal norms and consensus-based goals.

At its core, Confucian thinkers conceive of the self as relational, shaped and refined through interactions with others, yet this perspective does not negate individuals' freedom and autonomy in their moral cultivation. Furthermore, while the pursuit of the relational self primarily aims at promoting the common good, it does not exclude self-interest, which is perceived as an integral part of the common good. This social embeddedness stands in clear contrast to the Western Enlightenment model; indeed, a central distinction between Confucianism and Kantian philosophy lies in their respective conceptions of the self in relation to the collective: Confucianism emphasizes relational self-awareness within interpersonal and social bonds, whereas Kantian philosophy emphasizes independent self-legislation through reason.

5.3 The Idea of Rights in Traditional Chinese Culture

The modern Western conception of "rights"—centered on inherent individual entitlements—finds no direct counterpart in traditional Chinese philosophy. This discrepancy raises a persistent question: Can Confucian ethics reconcile with notions of individual rights?

Unlike many Western traditions that prioritize individual rights, Confucianism focused more on communal well-being and personal obligations. As twentieth-century philosopher Liang Shuming (1993) observes, "the Chinese were only exposed to the concept of duty, not that of rights, as ethics stresses the importance of mutual respect rather than asserting one's personal claims" (p. 347). Henry Rosemont (2004) echoes this distinction, contrasting the community- and duty-centered Confucian ethics with the rights-centered Western ethics. So, while Westerners might raise the banner of individual rights, Confucians tend the garden of collective needs, believing that individual virtue blossoms most fully when rooted in the well-being of all.

Still, it would be an oversimplification to claim that Chinese society wholly disregarded individual rights. While the Western concept of inherent, inalienable individual rights was largely absent, Chinese society nonetheless offered protection and avenues of recourse against injustice—motivated not only by a commitment to social welfare but also by a concern for individual entitlements. Ancient China had its own mechanisms for safeguarding individual rights within a framework of social harmony and moral obligation. Rights were often conceptualized collectively, tied to one's familial and social roles and oriented toward the cultivation of virtue. For example, ritual propriety functioned not only as a code of conduct but also as a means of safeguarding the rights of all members within the social hierarchy, prohibiting transgressions by both superiors and subordinates. Alongside a morality-based legal system, this system partially served to protect people's rights against arbitrary state power.

While different social roles come with varying entitlements or privileges, all individuals are expected to prioritize the community's needs, a responsibility that, when upheld, serves to protect everyone's rights. In this framework, individual rights are not viewed as absolute but are balanced against the collective good. Since family and state play crucial roles in promoting social welfare, individual rights are sometimes considered subordinate to the needs of social harmony and stability. Actions that harm or exploit others are prohibited, as they undermine communal well-being. By placing the community's welfare first, individuals indirectly help safeguard both their own rights and those of others.

Take Confucianism, for instance: While it may not adopt a "rights-first" approach, it does encompass ideas about individual entitlements based on their roles and the duties towards others within a relational framework. The core belief is that all individuals possess equal moral worth and potential, which fosters a sense of rights intrinsically linked to human dignity (Chen, 2020; Henkin, 1998). Every person, regardless of their status or identity, is entitled to certain rights simply because they possess inherent value and fulfill certain role-based accountability. Thus, rather than isolating rights from duties, Confucianism integrates them, offering a nuanced understanding of individual rights embedded within a communal and ethical context.

A father, for example, was entrusted with the responsibility to raise and guide his children and, in turn, held the rightful expectation of receiving their care in old age. In this framework, rights and obligations were two sides of the same coin, grounded in their ethical significance (Sim, 2004). Confucianism, therefore, supports a particular notion of human rights—one that, while distinct from the Western emphasis on inalienable individual entitlements, affirms the legitimacy of personal rights within the moral fabric of family and community life (Rosemont, 2004).

The centrality of family in ancient Chinese society further complicates the idea of individual rights. In Confucian political ethics, loyalty to the state is deeply rooted in family ethics, particularly filial piety. This linkage creates a continuum between family and state, often positioning the family, rather than individuals, as the primary unit of political and economic agency. When resources such as land, noble titles, educational opportunities, and sometimes even official positions were allocated, it was often the family, including extended kinship networks or clans, that held primary authority and influence. As a result, individual rights were oftentimes tied to one's familial role, making it difficult to disentangle personal entitlements from the broader family-state relationship.

While understanding family roles is essential, a comprehensive interpretation of Confucian rights requires examining their application within the broader social and political context. Confucian virtues such as humaneness, righteousness, harmony, and faithfulness extend beyond the family to encompass the entire state and, ultimately, All under Heaven. This expansion is not only philosophically significant but also relevant to the contemporary notions of human rights. It calls upon individuals to transcend personal and familial interests or small-group concerns to consider the common good of all people, including those unrelated or marginalized. In this sense, Confucian virtues resonate with the foundational principles of human rights, which emphasize the protection of individual dignity within a broader commitment to social justice and collective well-being.

It should be noted that Confucian thinking often frames rights in political rather than purely individual terms. The philosophy, while acknowledging kingship as divinely sanctioned, holds that the continuity of this Mandate is conditional on the ruler's moral character. A ruler who acts immorally and cruelly (inhumanely) forfeits the Mandate of Heaven, granting the people, as a collective, the right to criticize or even depose him—an act known as executing the Dao on behalf of Heaven. Whereas Western traditions often emphasize individual rights as safeguards against state overreach, Confucianism envisions the people as a unified moral voice, possessing the ultimate authority to affirm or revoke political legitimacy.

In this context, Confucian scholars are as much academics as much active political players, entrusted with both the privilege and obligation to counsel rulers—even to the point of rectifying their mistakes. Unlike hereditary systems, Confucianism holds that public positions should be granted based on moral virtue and capability, irrespective of social status. Contrary to the stereotype of blind loyalty, Confucian scholar-officials maintained a degree of political autonomy to uphold ethical governance. It was both their right and duty to remonstrate when a ruler's actions deviated from righteousness or violated the principles of Confucian ritual propriety (Wong, 2004). This right to dissent is not equivalent to Western-style free speech, but it does emphasize that political rights are inseparable from moral responsibility. It is not just about power; it is about holding power accountable for the greater good.

Ultimately, both rights and power in traditional Chinese culture were grounded in virtue, as defined by one's social roles. In a collectivist society, individuals, from commoners to emperors and ministers, were expected to fulfill their roles within the family, community, or state to rightfully claim their entitlements. Rights and privileges were not merely inherited but had to be earned through moral cultivation and contributions to the common good. A failure in virtue often carried the risk of losing those privileges. While the hierarchical structure of traditional Chinese society is inherently unequal and restrictive, it fostered a shared ethical framework and a strong sense of collective responsibility, serving as a check against the abuse of power by those in authority.

5.4 Moral Cultivation and the Transcendence of the Self

The Chinese conception of "self" is distinguished by its richness and multidimensionality, with each philosophical tradition offering profound insights into its moral and spiritual cultivation. From Daoist self-forgetting to Buddhist non-self and Confucian greater self, all these concepts are anchored in cosmic principles, such as the unity of Heaven and humanity, the oneness between things and the self, or the doctrine of dependent arising. Collectively, these traditions orient individuals beyond egoistic concerns toward expansive ethical engagement. Within this framework, the Confucian conception of the "greater self" holds special significance. As both the cornerstone of traditional Chinese moral philosophy and a resonant paradigm for contemporary ethical discourse, this ideal continues to offer vital insights for addressing modern ethical challenges.

5.4.1 Daoist Self-forgetting

Classical Daoism is celebrated for its teachings of self-forgetting and no-self, both grounded in Lao Tzu's foundational principle of wuwei. Wuwei encourages effortless action in harmony with ziran—things as it is or spontaneous and unconditioned self, rather than imposing forceful or disruptive interventions (Lai, 2007). By relinquishing excessive desires and ego-driven pursuits, one develops self-forgetting, aligning with the natural order and attaining inner peace and authentic freedom.

Imagine transforming into a fluttering butterfly, wings dancing on the breeze, earthly burdens dissolving as you become one with nature's flow. This captures the essence of "self-forgetting" in Daoism, a concept beautifully illustrated in Chuang Tzu's famous dream story. It is not just about losing one's identity, but about finding deep serenity through spiritual unity with the natural world. While Chuang Tzu is sometimes viewed as a skeptic, his deeper aspiration lies in the "equalization of all things" (齐物), which is not a dull uniformity but a dynamic harmony where all beings, in their diversity, mutually transform and coexist (Chuang Tzu, 2013). Every grain of sand, every breath of air, contributes a distinct note to the symphony of existence.

How, then, can the self attain perfect harmony with all existence? Daoism teaches that through nonaction and self-forgetting, one dissolves dualities and boundaries, shedding the ego and returning to one's original nature. In this state of simplicity, individuals gradually attune to the dynamic harmony of the myriad things, uncovering a profound truth that everything, including oneself, vibrates with the rhythms of Dao.

For this, Chuang Tzu (2013) introduces a meditative practice known as "sitting and forgetting." This method unfolds in stages: first, quieting the mind; then, attaining a state of calm and openness; next, forgetting both the self and the surroundings; and finally, merging with all things. The key lies in forgetting what burdens and alienates us: To forget things is to free oneself from materialistic cravings. To forget virtue is to transcend the rigid confines of Confucian norms and relinquish formulaic moral judgments. To forget knowledge is to let go of preconceived notions and intellectual biases. And to forget oneself involves releasing attachment to form and overcoming self-preoccupation, thus aligning with the ultimate reality of the Dao (Chen, 2012). It is not about losing awareness, but about rediscovering freedom and peace by returning to our innate state of interdependence and harmony with all existence.

Through this practice of self-forgetting, the Daoist gradually cultivates the spiritual realization of no-self. By dissolving ego-boundaries and merging with the cosmic flow, one embodies the fundamental Daoist ideal—a state Chuang Tzu (2013) exalts when declaring "the perfect person has no self" (p. 3). This does not signify an annihilation of identity, but rather a profound liberation from the constraints of the ego: the weight of ambition, the illusion of self-importance, and the endless pursuit of worldly recognition. In letting go, one returns to their truest nature and becomes an integral part of the whole. Imagine a drop of water becoming one with the ocean, retaining its essence, yet merging with something far greater. This journey from "self" to "no-self" expands one's narrow perspective into boundless awareness—shifting from "me" to "us," from separation to seamless connection. No longer apart, the self flows with the rhythm of nature, obtaining both peace and a sense of eternity.

The Daoist ideas of self-forgetting and no-self exerted profound influence across Chinese philosophical traditions, particularly in self-cultivation. In Chan Buddhism, for example, "sitting meditation" embodies the essence of self-forgetting, helping practitioners transcend ego-driven thoughts and deepen their sense of interconnectedness. Confucianism, too, draws inspiration. While Confucian ethics emphasize the relational self, shaped by social roles and responsibilities, the Daoist path offers a release from these constraints. Through self-forgetting and no-self, Confucians can expand their moral vision, cultivating a broader, more inclusive compassion that reaches beyond familial ties to embrace All under Heaven.

5.4.2 *Buddhist Non-self*

Buddhist anatta (non-self) and Daoist no-self, though both reject the notion of a fixed, independent self, diverge in their interpretations of the nature of existence and the path to enlightenment. In Daoism, the self is not obliterated but reimagined as an inseparable part of the natural world, harmonizing with the Dao through spontaneity and self-forgetting, whereas the Buddhist view emphasizes sunyata (emptiness), viewing the permanent self as an illusion arising from karmic causes and conditions. According to the principle of dependent arising, nothing exists independently; all phenomena, including the self, are contingent and transient. Realizing the truth of non-self is essential for liberation from the cycle of suffering and rebirth, leading to enlightenment.

Buddhism teaches that the ego-self, driven by craving, aversion, and ignorance, keeps individuals trapped in a cycle of suffering. True liberation, the attainment of Buddhahood, requires dismantling this illusion of permanent self and realizing the ephemeral, interdependent nature of all things. The recognition of non-self, when paired with deep compassion for all beings, gives rise to an altruistic aspiration: a wholehearted commitment to alleviating the suffering of others. In Mahayana Buddhism, this ideal is embodied by the Bodhisattvas, who selflessly postpone their final enlightenment to guide others toward awakening—a demonstration of no-self not only in a religious but also in an ethical sense.

The Buddhist doctrine of non-self carries a transformative implication for Confucian conceptions of the self: It dissolves the rigid boundaries of individual identity, cultivating boundless openness to life. By revealing the profound interdependence of all existence, it awakens a compassion that transcends self-concern—embracing the suffering of every sentient being without exception. This Buddhist concept, alongside the Daoist "no-self," tremendously enhanced broad-mindedness and altruism in Chinese culture, influencing Confucian ideas of the "greater self" and "no-self," creating a unique synthesis in Chinese moral philosophy.

5.4.3 *Greater Self and No-self in Confucian Self-cultivation*

The Chinese philosophical framework of Heaven-humanity unity signifies not merely a metaphysical relationship between Heaven and humans, but more profoundly, an ideal of interconnectedness between the individual and the collective. This has inspired centuries of reflection on the concepts of the greater self and no-self—all in pursuit of a harmonious society where each being's flourishing contributes to, and is sustained by, the thriving of the whole.

Unlike Daoism, which emphasizes the dynamic interplay between nonbeing and being, and Buddhism, which delves deeply into the nature of nonbeing, Confucianism is primarily concerned with being—focusing on the cultivation of human flourishing within the manifest world and advocating for a stable and orderly cosmos. These differing ontological foundations shape their respective views of the self: Confucianism stresses the cultivation of the self and the ideal of the greater self, whereas Daoism promotes self-forgetting and the concept of no-self. Drawing from both traditions, Chan Buddhism introduces a three-tiered model of the self: the "small self," rooted in ego and desire; the "greater self," which arises from integrating the individual with the vast cosmos, fostering compassion and interconnectedness; and finally, "no-self," which transcends both by dissolving the illusion of a fixed, separate identity—not by negating existence, but by realizing its impermanence and relational nature (Shih, 1986). Notably, the concept of no-self is also embraced within Confucianism, especially in Neo-Confucianism, yet with different meaning.

Confucianism, with its emphasis on social harmony and role-commitment within a web of relationships—from close familial bonds to broader social networks—situates the self primarily within an interpersonal context, which forms the foundation of ethical living. Within this framework, the self is often linked to selfishness, and moral development requires overcoming self-centered impulses. Thus, eliminating "the self" in Confucian thought involves transcending egoism and prioritizing the collective good.

From a contemporary perspective, Confucian ethics maintains a cautious stance toward "the small self (小我)"—a limited, ego-centric orientation preoccupied with private advantage and parochial interests. In its place, the tradition elevates the ideal of the "greater self," an ethically cultivated identity that transcends narrow self-concern to embody the common good. This transformative vision perceives the self as an integral part of a larger cosmic and moral order and fosters an expansive consciousness that regards others as extensions of oneself, perceives the world as a single familial community, and resonates deeply with the collective joys and sorrows of All under Heaven. In this context, the principle of humaneness, when fully realized, converges with the notion of the greater self and even approaches the ideal of no-self—not as a denial of individuality, but as the embodiment of utter altruism: a self emptied of self-interest and fully attuned to the entirety of moral concern.

The Confucian conception of the "greater self" arises from the foundational principle of Heaven-human harmony, embodying a dynamic ethics of mutual care and collective moral responsibility. This vision finds its fullest manifestation in the vision of the Great Community (大同), an enlightened order where each member is nurtured according to their capacities and sustained according to their needs (Zisi, 2016). Mencius (2016) articulates this holistic ontology when declaring, "all things are already complete in me" (6A:4), suggesting a profound moral accountability toward the larger whole. Similarly, Neo-Confucian scholar Cheng Yi affirms, "The humane person perceives all things in Heaven and Earth as one body; there is nothing that is not himself" (Cheng & Cheng, 2000, vol.2A), indicating that ethical maturity dissolves boundaries between self and world. Collectively, these perspectives articulate the concept of the greater self as an expanded moral consciousness—one that evolves through engagement with the broader community, reconfigures self-worth through cultivating compassion, and embodies a sustained commitment to the collective flourishing and alignment with the cosmic order.

While the Confucian concept of the greater self shares similarities with the Daoist no-self—both advocating the merging of the self with all things—there are subtle yet significant differences. What Chuang Tzu envisions is a "no-self" through non-coercive action, a tranquil state where the self dissolves into the spontaneous flow of nature. Confucians, in contrast, conceive of "the greater self" or even "no-self" as an active moral journey, where the individual self expands through care for and meaningful engagement with others, grounded in a robust sense of agency and moral accountability.

Intriguingly, Confucian philosophy harmonizes two seemingly paradoxical yet profoundly consistent ideals of the greater self and the no-self. The greater self is marked by heightened moral awareness, a deepened social responsibility, and an expanded ethical vision, forming the groundwork for the ideal of the Confucian no-self, wherein personal desires are sublimated in service of communal flourishing and spiritual fulfillment. While the greater self still navigates a balance between individual and societal needs, the no-self fully centers on the collective good. This ideal is especially associated with virtuous leadership, as embodied by the sages, whose selfless devotion to the people reflects the highest moral calling.

Although the Confucian greater self already embodies supreme virtues and social responsibility, the pursuit of spiritual freedom often calls for a further step: the realization of no-self. By letting go of ego-centered perspectives and embracing a sense of interconnectedness with all beings, individuals can transcend the limitations of the individual self and align more fully with the cosmic order. This journey toward non-duality offers a form of spiritual liberation that reaches beyond moral precepts and prescribed social roles.

The Confucian concept of no-self has been enriched through incorporating ideas from Buddhism and Daoism (Chen, 1991). The idea finds illumination in Lao Tzu's (2013) renowned statement: "Heaven and Earth are not humane; they treat all things as straw dogs" (Chap. 5), reflecting the Dao's selfless impartiality and all-embracing nature. Buddhism echoes this sentiment, urging individuals to relinquish attachment and overcome the heart of discrimination by recognizing the illusory nature of a permanent self. Drawing on both traditions, Neo-Confucian thinker Cheng Hao explains that sages may appear unsympathetic or unattached because they care about everything (Cheng & Cheng, 1981). Therefore, no-self in Confucianism does not imply the absence of moral concern, but rather the transcendence of narrow affiliations and the cultivation of disinterested concern and universal regard.

The Confucian no-self is well illustrated in scholar Wang Yangming (2019)'s renowned statement: "The heart-mind's original substance is neither good nor evil" (Record of Qian Dehong). This potent declaration captures the unconditioned nature of the mind before it becomes clouded by dualistic thinking, desires, and external influences. The pristine state, embodying unobstructed wholeness and bearing profound ontological significance, represents the ultimate goal of Neo-Confucian self-cultivation. Freed from the distortions of labels, attachments, and rigid judgments, the heart remains impartial, unbiased, and universally inclusive. It is in this state of interior freedom that true wisdom arises—not from imposed norms, but from the boundless moral awareness that is inherently holistically intuitive and life-generative.

The idea of no-self, whether in Confucianism or Daoism, embodies an ethos of being public, selfless, and truly inclusive, extending concern beyond the individual to all beings and all things. This expansive vision is well illustrated by the story of the King of Chu, who, upon losing his prized bow, refused to search for it, stating, "The bow of Chu will be acquired by people of Chu." Confucius, hearing this, suggested dropping "Chu," instead stating, "The bow will be acquired by people," thereby expanding the inclusion beyond regional identity. Lao Tzu took the idea even further, arguing that even "people" should be dropped—mirroring the Dao's boundless nature and extending inclusivity to all existence, beyond human-centered distinctions (Lu, 2022).

It is noteworthy that the Confucian three-tiered conception of self—the small self, the greater self, and no self is not a linear progression but a dynamic coexistence within each individual. The small self, with its desires and attachments, is an inherent aspect of human nature, persisting even in those who seek enlightenment. What distinguishes a cultivated individual is the ability to employ the greater self's sense of moral responsibility or the no-self's spirit of universal compassion to navigate beyond egocentric impulses. In this light, the development of the greater self, rather than requiring the abandonment of one's own people or interests, emphasizes a balanced approach: one that harmonizes personal concerns with broader societal accountabilities and prioritizes the common good when circumstances demand it.

While the state of no-self is often associated with spiritual freedom and spontaneity, it does not necessarily constitute a higher moral stage than the greater self. Rather, the two states frequently coexist and function as complementary dimensions of ethical and spiritual development. Confucius' declaration, for instance: "At seventy, I could follow what my heart desires, without transgressing what is right" (Confucius, 2016, 2.4), embodies both the expansive moral care of the greater self and the spiritual freedom of no-self. Though still mindful of right and wrong, he achieves a state in which personal inclination flows effortlessly within an ethical framework, illustrating how the greater self and no-self together can enrich a life of virtue, wisdom, and inner freedom.

5.5 Ethics of Graded Equality and the Humility-Competition Dialectic

While not the central focus here, concepts such as equality, humility, and competition offer valuable insights into the complexity of Chinese ethics and the moral landscape it shapes. As with many other ideas in Chinese moral philosophy, these notions are best understood as dialectical counterparts, seemingly in conflict yet inherently dynamic and relational.

5.5.1 *Logic of Graded Equality: Mediating Inequality and Proportional Fairness*

While the modern Western conception of universal equality was foreign to ancient China's explicitly hierarchical order, the social logic it followed was not one of mere oppression but of a sophisticated graded equality within structured relationships. This system navigated a tension between entrenched social inequality and a deep commitment to proportional fairness. It recognized the intrinsic moral worth of all individuals yet distributed duties, rights, and privileges in proportion to virtue, social roles, abilities, and hierarchical positions. This framework enabled measured social mobility and meritocratic advancement not by dismantling hierarchy, but by harmonizing individual merit with collective stability. Within the hierarchical constraints, the system sought to reward talent and virtue, achieving a pragmatic balance between social order and personal opportunity.

Confucian society upheld a merit-based hierarchy in which authority was respected, but its privileges were conditioned on virtue and fulfilling one's role—creating a form of equality rooted in both merit and function. Within families, husbands and wives held distinct yet complementary responsibilities, not equal, yet both essential to the family's well-being (Nuyen, 2001). Likewise, elites enjoyed greater privileges but also shouldered heavier obligations, as resource distribution corresponded to their societal roles. Status was not merely inherited but earned through contributions to the collective good such that an individual's position and rewards were ideally commensurate with their role, virtue, and capabilities.

Thus, reducing Confucianism to a mere endorsement of inequality oversimplifies its complexities. While it did not champion absolute equality of outcomes, it embraced a more nuanced view where individuals of equal virtue deserved equal rights and privileges. Such a "proportional equality" reconciled the inequalities inherent in Confucian society with the principle of fairness, treating individuals according to their virtues and capabilities (Nuyen, 2001). This idea resonated with Aristotle's maxim on justice that equals should be treated equally and unequals unequally (Aristotle, 1984).

Consistent with this framework, imperial China offered, through most of its history, meaningful avenues for upward mobility based on merit—defined not only by military achievement but, more importantly, by moral virtue and cultivated talent. Compared to the rigid social hierarchies prevalent in many premodern societies, the Confucian vision of social mobility was remarkably progressive. By emphasizing personal cultivation over hereditary privilege, it offered a radical challenge to traditional hierarchies of birth and lineage. While aristocratic origins might provide initial advantages, true standing was ultimately determined by one's commitment to learning and ethical development. The Confucian ideal held that through devoted study and moral refinement, even individuals of modest beginnings could rise to become exemplars of wisdom and virtue. Conversely, those born to privilege who neglected their ethical cultivation risked degenerating into what Confucian texts deride as small persons.

Consequently, the traditional Chinese culture endorsed a form of equality of opportunity through moral cultivation, offering the possibility of ascending to elite positions and attaining economic, moral, and political rewards (Li, 2012). Although limited, this proportional equality introduced a sense of upward mobility, providing a degree of flexibility and dynamics within an otherwise highly rigid and steep social hierarchy. While proportional equality may seem unfair by modern standards, it was regarded as a just and equitable system in ancient China. It was believed that treating everyone identically, without regard for social roles and contributions, would lead to chaos and undermine social order.

The efficacy of this merit-based mobility system hinged upon ensuring equitable access to educational opportunities. Confucius himself champions the principle of teaching without discrimination, holding that wisdom should not be reserved for a privileged few but available to all who diligently seek it. Mencius and Xunzi affirm this view by asserting that even ordinary individuals possess the capacity to become sages. This emphasis on education reached its institutional peak with the establishment of the Imperial Exam system, which based official selection on merit and mastery of Confucian texts rather than hereditary privilege. It provided a concrete pathway for talented individuals from diverse backgrounds to attain power and influence, while promoting collective prosperity through virtuous and capable leadership.

5.5.2 Dialectic of Humility and Competition

Humility stands as a cardinal virtue in traditional Chinese society, encompassing reverence, courteous deference, intellectual receptivity, collective orientation, and a commitment to harmony. This multifaceted virtue, while deeply rooted in China's cultural fabric, is also shared across many world civilizations, sparking recent scholarly interest in comparative studies, particularly between Chinese and Western humility (Jackson & Park, 2023). As a result, humility emerges as a potent conceptual framework for fostering intercultural dialogue and bridging diverse ethical systems worldwide.

To fully grasp humility's role in traditional Chinese thought, it is essential to examine it in relation to seemingly opposing concepts such as competition. Contrary to the common misconception that ancient Chinese culture unilaterally valorized humility while dismissing competition, these two forces coexisted in a dynamic and complementary relationship. Neither Confucianism nor Daoism, despite their emphasis on humility, excluded constructive forms of competition. Indeed, China's extraordinary historical achievements and cultural resilience would be inconceivable without a resilient competitive spirit. This interplay reveals the need for a more nuanced analysis of how these ostensibly contradictory values were balanced and harmonized within the broader Chinese philosophical ecosystem.

Imagine a heart that bows not in defeat, but in deference. This, for the ancient Chinese, is the essence of humility. They saw it as a reflection of the natural world—the quiet care of Heaven and Earth that seeks no recognition, where towering mountains cradle valleys and vast oceans accommodate tiny streams. Humility, in this tradition, is a modest disposition, which does not consider oneself superior to others. It encompasses both a humble view of the self and genuine consideration for others, serving to mitigate potential conflicts and foster harmonious human relationships. Conversely, contending (争) or competing for personal gain was traditionally regarded as a dangerous pitfall, often giving rise to resentment, discord, and even warfare.

Although philosophically distinct, both Confucianism and Daoism elevate humility as an essential virtue and a wellspring of wisdom that tempers excessive competition. In the Confucian tradition, humility manifests as disciplined self-restraint aimed at cultivating a social and other-directed self to counter negative side of egoism, thus putting others at ease and bringing about communal harmony (McLeod, 2020). Confucian humility finds its most vivid expression in the virtue of "rang (让)," signifying the voluntary act of yielding to others with courtesy or relinquishing one's position in favor of others, thereby pacifying conflicts by giving others priority. From an epistemic perspective, it reflects a dual awareness: a recognition of one's own limitations and a respectful acknowledgment of others' abilities, value, and differential excellences (Hall & Ames, 1987). In this light, it represents a virtuous behavior intended to foster social cohesion and cooperation.

Daoism too advocates promoting ethical living through humility and simplicity. Compared to Confucian humility, which is consciously practiced through deference, respectful speech, and an awareness of one's place within the social hierarchy, Daoist humility is more receptive and natural, manifested not through a performance but a state of being, emphasizing the virtues of unassertiveness, self-effacement, and avoiding conflict in relationships. The humble posture, nonetheless, is not a sign of weakness, but an embodiment of noncoercive action, which paradoxically allows one to "become chief among all things" (Lao Tzu, 2010, chap. 67). This quiet power is exemplified by water, which effortlessly seeps through cracks and nourishes all (Chap. 8), seemingly weak yet ultimately invincible. Humility, far from shrinking away, becomes the source of boundless power.

That said, framing competition and humility as diametrical opposites fundamentally misrepresents their relationship in traditional Chinese thought. While excessive striving is discouraged, a healthy spirit of competitiveness is subtly embraced. Consider a martial arts competition, where mastery is pursued not only to defeat an opponent, but to refine oneself, promote mutual improvement, and show respect. In effect, the conceptions of humility and competition in both Confucianism and Daoism are not adversaries but complementary forces. True humility does not reject competition; it seeks to temper it, minimizing conflict while promoting cooperation, healthy competition, and humble leadership. This balance is cultivated through practices such as courteous yielding, reverence, and acting through non-action, all of which strengthen the bonds of a harmonious society.

A nuanced perspective is essential for understanding the dynamics of competition. While inherent drive for advantage can be productive, its outcomes vary widely depending on intensity: Competition can inspire innovation when low to moderate, but discourage it when excessive (Aghion et al., 2005), and foster hostility, anxiety, and tension (Kohn, 1992). To address this issue, Western scholars advocate for "healthy competition," a model that emphasizes excellence over domination, balancing personal ambition with mutual support and collective growth (Constantinou, 2014).

Likewise, competitions in ancient China broadly falls into two categories: those guided by ritual propriety and shared norms, and those driven by unrestrained opportunism. The former, resembling healthy competition, is celebrated in Confucian thought as the "competition of gentlemen": contests bound by rules, respect, and a shared commitment to moral and intellectual excellence. Confucius (2016) praises such noble rivalries, citing archery contests where honor and propriety take precedence over the outcome itself (3.7). This contrasts with the "contention of small persons," which abandons ethical standards in favor of ruthless tactics aimed at winning and personal gain, undermining both community and moral order.

Thus, contrary to the misconception that Confucianism opposes competition due to its emphasis on "rang," the philosophy actually endorses constructive competition within ethical bounds; courteous deference, in this context, does not mean withdrawing from competition altogether but serves to ensure that competition remains harmonious and fair (Jiang, 2009a, b). It calls for reframing competition as a collective endeavor, where individuals create space for others to grow alongside themselves, where competition would be played by the rules and moderated with courtesy, ultimately contributing to the common good. Importantly, "rang" is not an unconditional, one-sided concession: It involves a mutual willingness, where each party takes turns to make graceful accommodations or meet halfway as a gesture of kindness and respect. This spirit of reciprocity fosters collaboration, stability, and shared growth essential for collective prosperity.

Like Confucianism, Daoism promotes a harmonious competition based on "wuwei," where "one acts without coercion, and yet nothing is left undone" (Loy, 1985). This approach is conducive to long-term success for a couple of reasons: First, humility diffuses resentment and minimizes conflict. By letting go of ego-driven struggles, individuals redirect their energy toward broader objectives and mutual benefit. Second, the generosity embedded in humility fosters lasting alliances and goodwill, laying the groundwork for sustainable success. In this light, Lao Tzu's advice to "stay behind" and embrace wuwei is not a call to passive withdraw, but a strategic orientation, one that pursues far-reaching aims without being mired in short-sighted conflict. At its core, it is the art of winning the long game.

Accordingly, neither Confucianism nor Daoism categorically rejects competition per se. Both traditions differentiate between crude rivalry—driven by unchecked self-interest and the erosion of social harmony—and cultivated competition, which aligns personal achievement with the flourishing of the whole. Humility plays a crucial role in navigating this balance. It helps prevent destructive conflicts and guides the development of competitive strategies that are sustainable, reciprocal, and beneficial to all. Thus, humility and competition, while seemingly opposed, reveal a dialectical relationship, coexisting and even complementing one another.

The ancient Chinese approach to humility and competition offers valuable insights for today's fast-paced world. For modern Chinese, it is a reminder that the flame of competitiveness burns brightest when moderated by humility and kindness, leading to calmer minds, fewer conflicts, and stronger bonds. For the global community, it clarifies that humility in China does not imply surrendering competition or passively turning the other cheek; rather, it is about creating win-win scenarios without the sting of bitter rivalry. This spirit echoes the idea of "coopetition," where competition remains the engine, but collaboration ensures shared success,[2] fostering goodwill and foresight for peaceful coexistence in our increasingly interconnected yet tension-filled world.

References

Aghion, P., Bloom, N., Blundell, R., Griffith, R., & Howitt, P. (2005). Competition and innovation: An inverted-U relationship. *The Quarterly Journal of Economics, 120*(2), 701–728.

Aristotle. (1984). Nicomachean ethics. In J. Barnes (Ed.), *The complete works of Aristotle*. Princeton University Press.

Barbalet, J., & Barbalet, J. M. (2017). *Confucianism and the Chinese self*. Palgrave Macmillan.

Bockover, M. I. (2010). Confucianism and ethics in the Western philosophical tradition II: A comparative analysis of personhood. *Philosophy Compass, 5*(4), 317–325.

Brewer, M. B. (2015). Individual self, relational self, and collective self: Partners, opponents, or strangers? In *Individual self, relational self, collective self* (pp. 15–18). Psychology Press.

Brewer, M. B., & Gardner, W. (1996). Who is this "we"? Levels of collective identity and self representations. *Journal of Personality and Social Psychology, 71*, 83–93.

Brindley, E. (2011). Moral autonomy and individual sources of authority in the analects. *Journal of Chinese Philosophy, 38*(2), 257–273.

Carleo, R. A., III. (2020). Is free will Confucian? Li Zehou's Confucian revision of the Kantian will. *Philosophy East and West, 70*(1), 63–83.

Chan, J. (2002). Moral autonomy, civil liberties, and Confucianism. *Philosophy East and West*, 281–310.

Chen, L. (1991). *The realm of being and non-being—The spirit of Wang Yangming's philosophy*. Beijing University Press.

Chen, X. (2012). The "mutual forgetfulness" and "self-fitness"-on Zhuangzi's forgetfulness. *Philosophical Studies, 8*, 44–49.

Chen, X. (2020). Confucianism and cosmopolitanism. *Asian Philosophy, 30*(1), 40–56.

Cheng, C. Y. (2004). A theory of Confucian selfhood: Self-cultivation and free will in Confucian philosophy. In K. Shun & D. B. Wong (Eds.), *Confucian ethics: A comparative study of self, autonomy, and community* (pp. 124–142). Cambridge University Press.

Cheng, H., & Cheng, Y. (1981). *Collections of Cheng brothers*. Zhonghua Book Company.

Cheng, H., & Cheng, Y. (2000). *Posthumous papers of Cheng Brothers*. Shanghai Chinese Classics Publishing House.

[2] The concept is coined by Ray Noorda, the former CEO of Novell, in the 1990s.

Chuang Tzu. (2013). *The complete works of Zhuangzi* (B. Watson, Trans.). Columbia University Press.
Confucius. (2016). *Analects*. In J. Legge (Ed. & Trans.), *Confucianism: The Four Books and Five Classics*. Delphi Classics.
Constantinou, P. (2014). Promoting healthy competition using modified rules and sports from other cultures. *Strategies, 27*(4), 29–33.
Deci, E. L., & Ryan, R. M. (2008). Hedonia, eudaimonia, and Well-being: An introduction. *Journal of Happiness Studies, 9*(1), 1–11.
Hall, D. L., & Ames, R. T. (1987). *Thinking through Confucius*. SUNY Press.
Henkin, L. (1998). Epilogue: Confucianism, human rights, and cultural relativism. In Tu & de Barry (Eds.), *Confucianism and human rights* (pp. 308–314).
Hwang, K. S. (2013). Moral luck, self-cultivation, and responsibility: The Confucian conception of free will and determinism. *Philosophy East and West, 63*(1), 4–13.
Jackson, L., & Park, J. (2023). Humility in educational philosophy and theory. *Educational Philosophy and Theory, 55*(2), 153–157.
Jiang, G. (2009a). On rang—Also on modern application of Confucian rang. *Journal of Jiangsu Administration Institute, 6*, 11–16.
Jiang, K. (2009b). Training for competition: The origin and consequence of excessive competition in education. *Research in Educational Development, 30*(13), 76–81.
Kant, I. (2002). *Critique of practical reason*. Hackett Publishing.
Kohn, A. (1992). *No contest: The case against competition*. Houghton Mifflin Harcourt.
Lai, K. (2007). Ziran and Wuwei in the Daodejing: An ethical assessment. *Dao, 6*(4), 325–337.
Lao Tzu. (2010). *Daodejing*. In R. T. Ames & D. L. Hall (Eds. & Trans.), *Dao de jing: A philosophical translation*. Ballantine Books.
Li, C. (2012). Equality and inequality in Confucianism. *Dao, 11*(3), 295–313.
Liang, S. (1993). *The collection of Liang Shuming*. Qunyan Press.
Loy, D. (1985). Wei-wu-wei: Nondual action. *Philosophy East and West, 35*(1), 73–86.
Lu, B. (2022). *Lüshi chunqiu*. China Bookstore.
McLeod, A. (2020). Humility in early Confucianism. In *The Routledge handbook of philosophy of humility* (pp. 245–256). Routledge.
Mencius. (2016). *Mencius*. In J. Legge (Ed. & Trans.), *Confucianism: The Four Books and Five Classics*. Delphi Classics.
Nuyen, A. T. (2001). Confucianism and the idea of equality. *Asian Philosophy, 11*(2), 61–71.
Rasmussen, S. (2008). Personhood, self, difference, and dialogue (commentary on Chaudhary). *International Journal for Dialogical Science, 3*(1), 31–54.
Rosemont, H. (2004). Whose democracy? Which rights? A Confucian critique of modern liberalism. In K. L. Shun & D. Wang (Eds.), *Confucian ethics: A comparative study of self, autonomy, and community* (pp. 49–71). Cambridge University Press.
Shih, S. Y. (1986). *Zen*. Dongchu Publishing House.
Sim, M. (2004). A Confucian approach to human rights. *History of Philosophy Quarterly, 21*(4), 337–356.
Tan, S. H. (2005). Imagining Confucius: Paradigmatic character and virtue ethics. *Journal of Chinese Philosophy, 32*(3), 409.
Wang, Y. (2019). *Instructions for practical living, volume 2, record of Qian Dehong. Item 315*. Beijing United Publishing Company.
Waterman, A. S. (1981). Individualism and interdependence. *American Psychologist, 36*(7), 762.
Wong, D. B. (2004). Rights and community in Confucianism. In K. L. Shun & D. B. Wong (Eds.), *Confucian ethics: A comparative study of self, autonomy, and community* (pp. 31–46). Cambridge University Press.
Zhang, S. (2011). *Chinese and Western culture and self*. People's Press.
Zisi. (2016). The Doctrine of the Mean. In J. Legge (Ed.), *Confucianism: The Four Books and Five Classics—Collected works of Confucius* (J. Legge, Trans.). Delphi Classics.

Chapter 6
The Global Dialogue on Moral Cultivation: China, India, and the West

Few ideals have influenced human civilization more profoundly than moral cultivation. From the ancient wisdom traditions of China and India to the philosophical schools of the West, cultures across time and space have cultivated sophisticated and enduring visions of human refinement and transcendence. This chapter compares these three influential traditions, examining their distinct perspectives and shared insights into the nature and purpose of self-cultivation. Situating these ideas within their respective cultural contexts reveals how self-cultivation has shaped each civilization's intellectual and moral development.

These three traditions are selected for their distinctive yet complementary perspectives on self-cultivation, each illuminating different dimensions of human development through its unique philosophical framework. Despite their differences, a particularly revealing point of convergence emerges in their cosmological orientations: All view the self as intrinsically linked to a cosmic order or the greater community, which grounds their respective visions of moral development. Conversely, the divergences between these traditions can also be traced to the distinct logical approaches they employ in addressing the complex interplay between the cosmic and the human (Yu, 2002). This shared emphasis on the self-cosmic relationship—despite differing interpretations—holds significant potential to bridge cultural divides and open pathways toward a more integrated ethical progress, a theme further explored in the final chapter.

Prior to undertaking this cross-cultural analysis, several important methodological considerations warrant clarification. Given space constraints, a comprehensive survey of the philosophical landscapes is not feasible. Instead, the discussion will focus on moral cultivation, the central theme of this book, as it manifests across three influential cultural traditions. Next, the selected philosophers are intended as representative figures, not as exhaustive embodiments of the exhaustive intellectual diversity within each tradition. Finally, while juxtaposing these approaches offers insight into the values and methodologies underpinning each civilization's distinct

Z. You, Y. Hu, *Philosophy and Civilization: How the Idea of Moral Cultivation Shaped China*, East-West Dialogues in Educational Philosophy and Theory,
https://doi.org/10.1007/978-981-95-5660-1_6

moral framework, such discussions should be approached with caution and discernment, mindful of the internal complexity and variation of these traditions, and careful to avoid reductive generalizations.

6.1 Nondual Unity of Atman and Brahman

The expression "Atman is Brahman" encapsulates a fundamental principle of the ancient Indian worldview: the ultimate oneness of the individual soul (Atman) and the supreme cosmic consciousness (Brahman). It affirms that the Divine Self dwells within, and that through disciplined self-cultivation, the individual can awaken to this sacred truth, dissolving the illusion of separateness and attaining ultimate reunion with the universe itself. This insight profoundly shapes the Indian path of inner development, inspiring a transformative journey toward the realization of one's divinity and the attainment of spiritual liberation.

6.1.1 Identity of Individual Atman and Cosmic Brahman

Brahman, the eternal, infinite, and immutable essence, occupies a central place in Vedantic philosophy as the absolute ground of the universe and the supreme principle sustaining all existence. It is the wellspring of creation and the convergence point for all consciousness, transcending earthly limitations, categories, and the cycle of rebirth. This expansive, all-encompassing vision—central to many streams of Hindu thought—invites a universal embrace, reminding us of our inherent interconnectedness within a greater whole (Chaudhuri, 1954).

In many schools of Hindu philosophy, particularly Advaita Vedanta, the world and all its phenomena are viewed as manifestations of Brahman. "This universe comes forth from Brahman and will return to Brahman, verily, all is Brahman" (Swahananda, 2022, III 14.1). While sharing similarities with the concept of God as the absolute source of creation, Brahman, in some interpretations, differs from the anthropomorphic God of Abrahamic religions. Instead, it is often conceived of as an impersonal principle, similar in some ways to the Chinese Dao, both suggesting that the divine is immanent within nature. All things, therefore, possess and embody the qualities of Brahman, just as all things are said to embrace the Dao in Chinese thought.

Historically, the concept of Brahman underwent a profound evolution. Initially associated with the sacred power invoked through ritual sacrifice, it gradually developed, particularly in the Upanishads, into a philosophical principle representing the deepest metaphysical reality. Ultimately, this idea was internalized as the innermost, universal essence of the self, culminating in the powerful insight that "Atman is Brahman," a cornerstone of ancient Indian philosophy.

In Hindu thought, the soul is understood through the concepts of Atman and Brahman. Atman refers to the individual soul, the essential "spirit" or "self" that underlies each individual and is subject to the cycle of rebirth (samsara). This individual soul can be likened to a spark, distinct and dynamic, yet retaining its core identity. Brahman, by contrast, represents the cosmic soul, the vast, eternal source from which all existence emanates and to which it ultimately returns.

The fundamental teaching, "The individual soul is identical to the cosmic soul," underscores the intrinsic oneness of all beings. Each Atman, while exhibiting unique individual qualities, shares the same fundamental nature as Brahman. Within this non-dual framework, individual souls are not separate substances but differentiated expressions of the universal consciousness. Their apparent individuality is a provisional state, like a spark realizing its unity with the eternal fire from which it has always emerged.

From a contemporary perspective, Atman can be conceptualized as the true self, the pure consciousness within each person, transcending the ego—the illusory or false self. Brahman is understood as the universal self, the ultimate consciousness that permeates all existence. Though described differently, Atman and Brahman are ultimately one: as all living beings are expressions of Brahman, the pursuit of spiritual self-cultivation becomes an ontological necessity—a universal endeavor to return to one's true nature—realizing that the self has never been separate from Brahman. Yet, the practice requires a delicate balance: embracing the unique individuality of the "I" while recognizing the profound identity with the greater "Self" that encompasses all.

This spiritual quest reflects the foundational Hindu understanding of existence as inherently marked by suffering—birth, disease, aging, and death. Such suffering is rooted in the cyclical nature of existence, samsara, wherein the Atman, or individual soul, undergoes repeated rebirth, carrying the karmic weight of past actions. This results in a seemingly endless loop of pain and hardship. Liberation, or moksha, is the transcendence of this cycle, achieved by cultivating the true self through virtuous action and the pursuit of spiritual wisdom. The journey of self-discovery culminates in the profound realization of the fundamental oneness between the individual self and Brahman, the ultimate consciousness. This raises a profound philosophical question: How can a seemingly limited individual attain such an expansive state of being, merging with the all-encompassing reality and declaring, "I am consciousness"?

6.1.2 Path from Ignorance to Awakening

Hinduism identifies negative emotions as a major source of human suffering. Jealousy, greed, resentment, selfishness, and fear, along with the actions they provoke, obscure the true nature of the self, the Atman. These emotions form a veil of ignorance, leading individuals to misidentify with their transient bodies and egos, becoming entangled in fleeting pleasures and persistent anxieties rather than recognizing the eternal light within. Such delusions and desires lead to harmful or selfish actions, generating negative karma that perpetuates the suffering of samsara (reincarnation), the reason why ethical conduct is essential on the path to liberation. Accordingly, individuals remain bound to this cycle until they attain awakening by piercing the veil of ignorance and realizing that the Atman, the indwelling true self, is one with Brahman.

Ultimate enlightenment is pursued through multiple complementary paths. Sacred scriptures elucidate moral and metaphysical principles, karma highlights the ethical consequences of action, meditation cultivates mental equanimity, yoga harmonizes body and spirit, and ascetic discipline regulates desire—each contributing to the gradual inward journey of self-realization. Through this process, the Atman comes to apprehend its intrinsic unity with the cosmic order and the fundamental reality of Brahman. In this profound insight, the cycles of rebirth and suffering are progressively transcended. Moksha—the liberation from illusion and the cessation of reincarnation—represents the soul's ultimate fulfillment, a return to boundless, undifferentiated oneness.

The Hindu quest for liberation unfolds through a gradual transition from worldly concerns to an otherworldly journey, structured around life's four stages, or Ashramas: The student stage (Brahmacharya) focuses on acquiring knowledge under the guidance of a wise teacher; the householder stage (Grihastha) centers on building a family and fulfilling social responsibilities; the forest hermit stage (Vanaprastha) releases worldly attachments in pursuit of inner peace; and finally, the stage of wandering ascetic or renouncer (Sannyasa) strives to shed individual limitations and dedicates itself fully to attaining the ultimate liberation. These Ashramas align closely with the four aims of life, or Purushartha, including Dharma (piety, morality, and duties), Artha (wealth, health, and means of life), Kama (love, relationships, and emotions), and Moksha (liberation and self-realization) (Widgery, 1930). Together, the Ashramas and Purusharthas offer a holistic vision of life that weaves together the worldly and the spiritual, guiding the soul toward its final emancipation.

The path to the divine is paved with blossoming virtues. Throughout life's stages, particularly in the renunciate stage, individuals need to cultivate virtues that elevate the soul. Self-restraint serves as a bulwark against the tempests of desire; truthfulness becomes a mirror reflecting reality, dispelling illusions and sharpening discernment; unselfishness is a fragrant seed that blossoms into acts of generosity; noninjury is a gentle hand, seeking to harm no living creature; and kindness and compassion radiate like a luminous light, offering care and understanding to all. Among these, noninjury holds a central place in Hindu philosophy. By refraining from harm, practitioners acknowledge the sacred spark within every living being. To injure another is to injure a manifestation of the divine and, thus, a part of one's own self. This cultivation of nonviolence naturally fosters virtue, alleviates suffering, and guides the aspirant toward spiritual liberation.

Ultimately, the realization that "Atman is Brahman" evokes a boundless sense of unity, dissolving the illusion of separation and nurturing unconditional compassion for all life. True masters of Brahman, steadfast in their devotion, perceive the divine not only in those close to them but in every being, every breath, every flicker of existence—a vision that transcends self-interest, inspiring kindness, generosity, and universal care. This love for the all-encompassing Brahman radiates outward, embracing all creatures, all realms, and the vast, shimmering cosmos.

6.2 Philosophical Dialogue Between Chinese and Indian Metaphysics

From their dawn as cradles of ancient civilizations, China and India have bestowed upon the world profound cultural legacies and a history of enduring exchanges. For centuries, the Silk Road served not only as a conduit for trade but as a vibrant artery of thought, where philosophies intertwined, most notably in the journey of Buddhism from India to China. This centuries-long dialogue invites us to explore their distinct yet harmonious paths of moral self-cultivation, revealing both profound resonances and illuminating contrasts, each refining the other in the grand fresco of Eastern thought.

6.2.1 Shared Metaphysics of Cosmic-Human Unity

Despite their distinct cultural backgrounds, China and India share intriguing philosophical parallels, particularly between "harmony between Heaven and humanity" and India's "Atman is Brahman." Both traditions posit an intrinsic connection between a universal principle (Heaven or Brahman) and the individual (man or Atman), emphasizing the profound unity between the self and the greater whole. These parallel visions share a deeply holistic worldview—Hindu philosophy perceiving divinity as pulsating through all existence, while Chinese thought envisions an integrated and harmonious cosmos grounded in the generative Dao.

Chinese and Indian philosophies both derive from their metaphysical unity a profound ethical imperative: Recognizing this fundamental interconnectedness naturally gives rise to universal compassion. This understanding that "others" are not separate entities but extensions of the self, whose well-being and suffering are intrinsically linked to our own, leads both traditions to advocate spreading love and kindness to all beings. These metaphysical frameworks cultivate a disposition inclined toward nonviolence, grounded in ideals of harmony and noninjury. While historical realities were often more complex and at times cruel, this ethical orientation offers insight into the strong philosophical preference for peaceful coexistence observed across both Chinese and Indian traditions.

The convergence of worldviews naturally gives rise to parallel approaches to moral cultivation, with both traditions emphasizing a holistic understanding of transcendent reality beyond mere rational analysis. Understanding Brahman, for example, requires intuition and a purified heart-mind, cultivated through spiritual practices such as asceticism, yoga, and meditation. Similarly, both the Dao of Daoism and Principle of Confucianism call for holistic comprehension, attained through a heart free from desires and distractions. Many Chinese scholars stress purifying the heart-mind and engaging in meditative practices to perceive the harmony between nature and humanity, as well as within human relationships. Both traditions hold that such self-cultivation fosters transcendent wisdom and elevated virtue, ultimately leading to a liberated and blissful existence. This journey culminates in a return to the source of all being, whether envisioned as the Dao or Brahman.

6.2.2 Indian Transcendence vs. Chinese Immanence

Despite notable parallels, Chinese and Indian philosophies diverge in subtle yet significant ways in their orientations toward existence. China's "unity of Heaven and man" reflects a world-affirming vision—celebrating earthly life as the natural arena for cultivating virtue, where human flourishing aligns with cosmic order, fostering a positive and optimistic ethical outlook. In contrast, India's idea of "Atman is Brahman" charts a more introspective path, focusing more on inner realization as a means of transcending suffering and detaching from worldly entanglements, thus prioritizing spiritual pursuits over worldly concerns (Schweitzer, 1923). Accordingly, Chinese self-cultivation leans more toward this-worldly engagement, seeking to establish guidelines for social harmony and flourishing, whereas Indian self-cultivation gravitates toward other-worldliness, centering on individual religious liberation.

In Hindu philosophy, the highest aim of self-cultivation is the reunification of the individual soul (Atman) with the universal Absolute (Brahman). This metaphysical orientation directs consciousness beyond ephemeral worldly concerns toward the eternal and unchanging reality. It helps explain why Brahmins often renounce the worldly attachments to devote themselves wholly to spiritual realization. Consequently, the ultimate concern of life is not secular success, but the acquisition of the spiritual wisdom, leading to a return to the profound cosmic consciousness. This emphasis results in prioritizing spiritual pursuit over material achievement and valuing the soul over the body.

In contrast, the Chinese notion of the "unity of Heaven and man" places greater emphasis on the human dimension of this relationship. Here, Heaven is not a distant, transcendent realm but the immanent source of moral and natural order—a cosmic pattern to be mirrored in human conduct. This worldview gives rise to a pragmatic philosophy in which moral cultivation serves social harmony and political stability. As a result, ancient Chinese thought tends to integrate inner cultivation with outward engagement, focusing on the well-being of the present life rather than speculations about the afterlife. For example, Confucianism encourages individuals to refine their moral characters by emulating the virtues of Heaven, fulfilling familial and societal responsibilities, and actively contributing to the governance and betterment of society through ethical leadership. Even Daoism, while advocating detachment from excessive worldly desires, does not dismiss the value of earthly existence. Instead, it seeks peace and harmony through alignment with the natural order, advocating immersion in rather than escape from life.

Moreover, although both philosophies emphasize self-cultivation, their teleological orientations differ fundamentally. Hinduism's teaching that Atman is Brahman centers on realizing one's true nature—the individual spark recognizing its unity with the flame of Brahman. While the cultivation of virtues benefits worldly life, its highest purpose lies in transcendence: returning to cosmic consciousness. In this framework, virtues serve as essential steps toward oneness. For Confucianism, the telos is immanent ethical harmony; spiritual growth is an organic outcome of perfecting virtuous relationships to sustain societal stability. The harmonization of Heaven and humanity is directed less toward metaphysical unity and more toward nurturing virtuous relationships and sustaining societal stability through ethical living.

That said, it would be inaccurate to characterize Indian thought as wholly world-denying or Chinese philosophy as purely world-affirming. Both traditions encompass rich, multidimensional perspectives on human existence. While many Hindu traditions emphasize spiritual liberation, they also emphasize the fulfillment of Dharma—the righteous way of living that encompasses moral principles, social order, and individual responsibilities. Likewise, certain strands of ancient Chinese thought, particularly Chinese Buddhism, reflect otherworldly concerns. Concepts such as karma, rebirth, and enlightenment illustrate a focus that transcends immediate worldly existence.

Finally, while both traditions developed within hierarchical social structures—often rationalized as reflections of the natural or cosmic order—their underlying structures and philosophical justifications diverged significantly. In India, the profound non-dualistic insight of "Atman is Brahman" proclaims an ultimate spiritual equality, asserting that all being shares the same divine essence. Yet this insight remained largely metaphysical and soteriological, for it did not directly challenge the entrenched caste system, which was instead justified through doctrines of karma and dharma. It was with the rise of Buddhism and Jainism, both emphasizing the equal spiritual potential of all beings, that a philosophical tension with the prevailing social order began to surface.

Similarly, ancient Chinese philosophy, despite affirming the unity of Heaven and humanity, coexisted with hierarchical social structures—most notably reflected in Confucian teachings that emphasized social harmony within a stratified order. These social ranks, however, were not entirely rigid, as Confucianism encouraged social mobility through virtue and merit. It asserted that true worth lies in cultivated character, not birth, allowing individuals to ascend the social hierarchy through moral and intellectual development. Though limited, this meritocratic ideal was later institutionalized through the imperial examination system, which helped mitigate entrenched social divisions.

6.3 Bildung as the Model of Western Self-Cultivation

Given the expansive landscape of Western philosophies, this study centers on the distinctive tradition of Bildung—a German paradigm of self-formation that transcends conventional notions of education. It exemplifies a uniquely synthetic Western approach to self-cultivation—one that integrates intellectual growth with moral refinement, individual flowering with cultural participation, and theoretical contemplation with practical virtue.

Derived from the German word "Bildung," meaning "image," "education," "shaping," and "self-formation," the concept has a rich heritage rooted in both Hellenistic ideals of moral development and the theological traditions of spiritual cultivation (Siljander & Sutinen, 2012). This pursuit of self-cultivation flourished among ancient Greek philosophers. Plato, for instance, elevates the "Form of the Good" as both the highest object of knowledge and the key to true happiness. His allegory of the cave illustrates the journey of self-cultivation from ignorance to enlightenment, portraying education as the process of grasping "the Form"—the true nature of reality. For Plato, the enlightened individual bears a moral duty to guide others toward truth, despite the personal risks involved—a vision that echoes the life and mission of Socrates. This vision resonates with the ancient Chinese concept of self-cultivation, where personal moral advancement is inseparably linked to the broader commitment of uplifting others.

While sharing Plato's aspiration to eudaimonia through the pursuit of virtue, Aristotle diverges in several key ethical aspects. He emphasizes the actualization of individual potential through habitual action, reflection, and application of moral principles, challenging the Socratic notion that knowledge alone constitutes virtue. For Aristotle, ethical understanding is incomplete without practice; one must cultivate phronesis (practical wisdom) to navigate complex moral situations. These Greek ideas about soul development, the role of reason, reflection, practical application, and the pursuit of individual happiness and public duties profoundly influenced the later European conceptions of self-cultivation, including the German ideal of Bildung.

Many Hellenistic philosophers conceive of God not as a personal creator deity, but as an abstract principle or ultimate source of wisdom. Aristotle's formulation of God as the "Unmoved Mover" epitomizes this view—an eternal, immaterial intellect that actualizes all potentiality while remaining perfectly self-contained. This philosophical theology endured well into the medieval period. Christian scholastics like Thomas Aquinas synthesized Aristotle's framework with Christian doctrine, articulating God as the ultimate being and the foundation of natural law, employing logic and reason to argue for God's existence.

The early modern philosopher Baruch Spinoza espouses a pantheistic conception of God. Rejecting traditional theistic view of a personal creator, Spinoza equates God with nature itself—an infinite, necessary, and self-sustaining substance that encompasses all attributes and laws of the universe. Within this monistic framework, the distinction between creator and creation dissolves: individual beings are understood as finite modes or modifications of the one divine substance, unfolding with geometric necessity. The human mind, as the integral part of nature, can attain "an adequate knowledge of the eternal and infinite essence of God" (Spinoza, 2002, p. 24), insofar as it perceives things through the lens of reason and intuitive understanding. Consequently, individuals can achieve harmony with God and experience mental freedom by aligning their reason with the natural laws. These diverse conceptions of God, from the abstract prime mover to the immanent force of nature, contributed to the refinement of the "Bildung," informing evolving notions of self-cultivation and moral progress across various historical contexts.

In his *Critique of Practical Reason*, Immanuel Kant (2002) establishes God as a necessary postulate of pure practical reason, not an empirically demonstrable being, but an indispensable condition for the full realization of the moral law. In contrast to Spinoza's monistic identification of God with nature, Kant affirms a fundamental dualism: the phenomenal world, governed by causal determinism, and the noumenal realm, wherein free will resides. This distinction is crucial for Kant's moral framework, as it reconciles human freedom with the deterministic laws of nature. For Kant, genuine virtue cannot emerge within the causal chain of events; it must stem from the autonomous, self-legislating will of a moral agent. Absent this transcendental grounding, morality would collapse into mere epiphenomenal appearance—a mechanistic performance devoid of true obligation or moral worth.

While Kant posits the noumenal realm as the domain of freedom and autonomous will, his ethical philosophy remains grounded in practical reason as it operates within the phenomenal world. Though free will belongs to the noumenal, we cannot theoretically know it; yet its moral law manifests in experience as a "fact of reason"—an undeniable awareness of moral obligation. In this way, the autonomous will exerts influence in the phenomenal world through adherence to the categorical imperative. For Kant, moral action arises not from belief in an immortal soul or external reward, but from duty rooted in rational self-legislation. While he engages with metaphysical concepts like the "highest good," they serve a regulative rather than foundational role. Ultimately, Kant affirms that moral development emerges from the individual's reason, autonomy, and commitment to moral law—empowering the self to pursue ethical ideals through the exercise of free agency.

6.3.1 Genealogy of German Bildung

Bildung represents a profound Central and Northern European tradition that transcends conventional education, weaving together philosophical depth, cultural engagement, and personal transformation. Rooted in Platonic ideals yet distinctly modern in its aspirations, Bildung envisions learning as an integrative process in which knowledge becomes wisdom through lived experience and dialectical engagement of self and world, reason and emotion, and tradition and innovation. This inward odyssey unfolds as individuals, through reflective introspection guided primarily by reason, pursue personal growth and cultural maturation, while also attending to the refinement of feeling in support of moral and aesthetic development, deepening the individual's understanding of the world.

Bildung emphasizes self-education and personal development, aiming to cultivate and reveal one's "true nature" or "higher self" (Horlacher, 2004). This pursuit of individual flourishing is not isolated from society but deeply connected to the broader goal of realizing an ideal humanity (Masschelein & Ricken, 2003). Encompassing "a harmonious development of all human capacities" (Herdt, 2019, p. 32), Bildung cultivates key human qualities, including self-awareness, autonomy, reasoning, individuality, and accountability. This continuous process of self-renewal and critical engagement with established beliefs reflects Aristotle's ideal of "whole people" liberal education and the pursuit of eudaimonia—a form of flourishing that transcends fleeting benefits and instrumental utility.

Bildung is directly shaped by two interwoven threads: the theological and the pedagogical. The theological thread stretches back to fourteenth-century Christian mysticism, where individuals sought union with the divine through profound spiritual transformation. Central to this tradition is the belief that humans bear the image of God within their souls and can cultivate this divine likeness through moral and spiritual growth (Alves, 2019). While the German term Bildung—from Bild (image) and -ung (formation or cultivation)—does not originally denote a specifically Christ-like image, it carries spiritual undertones emphasizing the cultivation of human virtue and potential. The pedagogical thread emerged in the early Enlightenment with Anthony Ashley Cooper, the third Earl of Shaftesbury, whose concept of innere Bildung ("inner formation") emphasized aesthetic and moral refinement (Masschelein & Ricken, 2003). Translated into German as Bildung in the late eighteenth century, this concept retained some spiritual associations while evolving into a broader ideal of self-cultivation and social responsibility.

Over time, Bildung evolved beyond its early religious framework toward a more secular focus on human potential. For thinkers such as Johann Gottfried Herder, Wilhelm von Humboldt, Friedrich Schiller, and Georg Wilhelm Friedrich Hegel, Bildung came to represent the individual's inner journey of introspection, meaning-making, character development, and enlightenment (Stoll, 2020). Crucially, this inward focus is not self-serving but rather fulfills a higher purpose: the advancement of humanity. While personal moral development remains central, Bildung also encompasses a vision of a broader social transformation, where enlightened individuals, through their moral, emotional, and intellectual growth, collectively foster a more cultivated and responsible society, weaving together autonomy with accountable action (Nordenbo, 2002). This dual emphasis on education and public life underscores the inseparability of self-actualization and social responsibility in the pursuit of a meaningful and fulfilled life.

The fundamental tension between personal flourishing and communal responsibility has informed philosophical discourse since the Athenian agora. Within this enduring dialogue, the German tradition of Bildung presented a particularly nuanced resolution—one that neither subordinated the individual to the collective nor isolated self-cultivation from social engagement. As Wilhelm von Humboldt put it,

Bildung entailed "linking of the self to the world to achieve the most general, most animated, and most unrestrained interplay" (Von Humboldt, 2000, p. 58). This dynamic equilibrium is central to Bildung, as it deliberately avoids extremes that would compromise either individual or societal well-being. On the one hand, there is "alienation from the present self, the letting go of immediate desires and egotistic interests in order to allow for an immersion into the world," and on the other hand, there is "alienation from the world in order to return home to the self" (Schumann, 2019, p. 491).

Freedom of choice is the cornerstone of this balance, exemplified by von Humboldt's staunch defense of university autonomy (Nordenbo, 2002). Bildung involves the refinement and cultivation of the self, a process fundamentally driven by the exercise of free will. This capacity for self-governance allows individuals to pursue their unique development, strive for human perfection, and realize their unique potential. As such, Bildung stands in opposition to any attempts to restrict individuals to predetermined roles or to enforce conformity. By affirming the intrinsic worth of every individual, it maintains that genuine flourishing arises not through rigid adherence to societal expectations but through the freedom to grow and to express both oneself and societal concerns authentically.

While individual growth is essential, Bildung flourishes in a vibrant, diverse social environment that fosters introspection and mutual understanding. However autonomous an individual may be, true flourishing is not unattainable in solitude (Konrad, 2012). The ideal lies in actively engaging with the world, reflecting on it critically without being overwhelmed by its pressures. In this framework, rich social resources including education, art, culture, community, and even the challenges and conflicts inherent in human interaction serve as catalysts for personal development. The ultimate goal is to cultivate well-rounded, autonomous individuals who are deeply committed to the common good. Bildung, then, can be understood as the process by which individuals realize their fullest potential through meaningful engagement with their social and cultural contexts.

Beyond the dynamic between individual and society, Bildung also involves a dialectic between particularity and universality: Herder, for instance, endorsed a particularistic vision of Bildung, asserting that human flourishing arises from the harmonious coexistence of diverse cultures, reflecting his multiculturalist ideals (Herdt, 2019). In contrast, Hans-Georg Gadamer emphasized universality, warning that individuals who remain confined to the particular risk remaining uncultivated. While Bildung values difference, Gadamer (1992) argued that it must also foster the shared human capacities of empathy and understanding. This universality, he contended, is not an erasure of particulars but rather their refinement. True self-understanding emerges when individuals relate their unique experiences to the broader human condition.

Bildung occupies a central place in Hegel's philosophy, closely bound to his dialectical conception of the relationship between the particular and the universal. For Hegel, ethical development unfolds dialectically across the spheres of family, civil society, and the state: beginning with the immediate, affective bonds of the family; advancing through the competitive mediation of civil society, where individual interests clash and negotiate; and finally culminating in the rational ethical state, where personal freedom and collective welfare are harmonized through institutionalized rights and cultivated moral consciousness (Hegel, 2015). This progression enables individuals to move beyond their immediate particularity, embracing a shared ethical identity and a broader sense of communal responsibility. Thus, true Bildung is achieved—not as solitary self-cultivation, but as the conscious integration of the self into the universal fabric of ethical life.

Specifically, civil society functions as the arena where individuals engage in a dialectical exchange with one another. Through engagement with competing perspectives, they interrogate their own assumptions, expand their horizons, and cultivate mutual recognition. This process challenges prejudices and elevates self-awareness, ultimately preparing individuals for participation in the ethical state, where a universal self-consciousness is actualized.

This very movement, in which the self is transformed through its encounter with the other, constitutes the essence of Bildung. As subjects overcome their isolated subjectivity, they participate in the unfolding of the universal spirit, which does not suppress but rather embraces the richness of individuality. Thus, Bildung represents the spiritual ascent that harmonizes individuality and universality, enabling individuals to draw upon the collective wisdom of humanity while retaining their distinctiveness.

6.3.2 American Reinterpretations of Bildung

The influence of Bildung reached far beyond Western Europe, finding resonances in intellectual traditions across the Atlantic. While the term itself may not have been explicitly or extensively used in mainstream American philosophical discourse, its defining principles—self-cultivation, personal growth, and the harmonious development of the individual within society—echo throughout the works of thinkers like Ralph Waldo Emerson, John Dewey, and, in a more postmodern register, Richard Rorty. Each, in distinct ways, grappled with the interdependence of self-realization and communal life. Their emphasis on autonomy, reflective self-formation, and the ethical duties of citizenship mirrors key interpretations of Bildung, underscoring its enduring relevance to democratic education and civic culture.

6.3.2.1 Emerson's Transcendentalist Bildung

Ralph Waldo Emerson emerged as the defining intellectual voice of mid-nineteenth-century Transcendentalism. While rooted in American soil, his thought absorbs key elements of Bildung and other contemporary European philosophies, ultimately becoming a seminal influence for later thinkers ranging from Friedrich Nietzsche to John Dewey (Johansson & Schumann, 2019). At the heart of Emerson's vision lies his conviction of a divine essence inherent in every individual, a radiant inner truth that simultaneously unites humanity and deepens its bond with nature. This shared essence underpins his belief in humanity's boundless potential: the capacity to transcend material limitations and access a higher spiritual reality. For Emerson, the path to such transcendence lies not in reason alone, but in the cultivation of intuition, imagination, and introspection, thus affirming the centrality of individuality, initiative, and creative self-expression.

For Emerson, self-cultivation, which closely aligned with the concept of Bildung, is not just a noble pursuit; it is the very heartbeat of human existence (Brewton, 2003). The core of his philosophy is self-education fostering ongoing moral and intellectual perfectibility, a vision described by Stanley Cavell as Emersonian moral perfectionism (Cavell, 2018). Experience, not mere the accumulation of knowledge, spurs this ascent. As a modern scholar describes Emerson's journey, "growth consists of continuity of experience such that every new state of the self is but an intermediate step from the former toward constantly evolving new steps" (Kovalainen, 2012). This emphasis on "experience" accentuates education in the present moment and the dynamic interplay between individuals and their social environments, an idea that foreshadows John Dewey's later philosophy of experiential education.

While acknowledging the communal aspect of human development, Emerson also adopts a distinctly non-conformist approach to self-cultivation. He famously declares, "truly speaking, it is not instruction, but provocation, that I can receive from another soul" (Emerson, 1971, p. 80). For Emerson, self-cultivation thrives not through rote learning, but through personal experience and the dynamic exchange of ideas that inspire new insights. This perspective underpins his deep skepticism toward established dogma and societal conventions. Emerson champions an intellectual autonomy that learns from others while maintaining critical distance, coupled with a profound communion with nature as an antidote to institutional dogmatism. To preserve originality, he even cautions against conforming to one's own past experiences, urging individuals to embrace their boundless creative potential. Nature, the arts, and introspection, for Emerson, become essential resources for inspiring fresh perspectives and authentic expression.

Central to Emerson's philosophy of self-cultivation is its aim to foster a flourishing democratic society. He, like John Dewey, envisions democracy as sustained by autonomous, morally grounded individuals, driven by empathy, a commitment to peace, and a robust sense of civic responsibility. Emerson passionately champions both democracy and individualism, believing that a healthy democratic order depends on critically engaged and well-educated citizens. To reconcile the tension between individual autonomy and communal obligation, he posits a duty to pursue continuous self-renewal and to participate in dialogues that contribute to the revitalization of the democratic state. Emerson's philosophy thus converges into a vision that places the cultivation of democratic values at its core: his rejection of conformity, embrace of imaginative freedom, reverence for nature, commitment to public enlightenment, and the dialectic between the individual and community all contribute to the realization of this democratic ideal.

6.3.2.2 Dewey's Visions for Education and Democracy

Although Dewey does not explicitly adopt the term "Bildung," his philosophy engages a cognate ideal through his theories of continuous organic adjustment and environmental reconstruction (Bauer, 2003). For Dewey, growth arises when an organism—while pursuing its aims—both actively transforms and is transformed by its milieu (Dewey, 1985b). This dialectical process echoes the self-transformative and participatory essence of Bildung, with an emphasis on the organic, interconnected nature of individuals and their social environment. Dewey crystallizes this dynamic as "experience," a generative interplay that simultaneously cultivates individual agency and reshapes social institutions, all directed toward fostering more competent citizens and vibrant democratic communities.

John Dewey's philosophy forges a vital connection between self-cultivation and societal transformation. He conceives education not merely as a means of individual cultivation, but as the vital foundation for reinvigorating democratic life itself. While sharing with Bildung traditions an emphasis on critical inquiry, experiential reflection, and education's transformative power, Dewey's philosophy distinctively emphasizes social accountability and the pragmatic testing of ideas through active engagement with the world. His vision underscores the interdependence between the individual and society, championing experiential learning that empowers individuals to become active, engaged citizens, thereby facilitating democratic renewal and substantive social progress.

For Dewey, nurturing a robust democracy necessitates a fundamental rethinking of how we approach education. He critiques traditional schooling—with its emphasis on fixed knowledge, rote memorization, and didactic methods—for suppressing curiosity and initiative, regarding it as fundamentally antithetical to democratic ideals. Such schooling alienates children from meaningful lived experience, leaving them ill-equipped for the active participation, critical thinking, and lifelong learning essential to a self-renewing democratic society. True education, for Dewey, is not preparation for life but life itself: a dynamic interplay between self and world, grounded in social engagement and experiential learning. As he famously put it, "Society not only continues to exist by transmission, by communication, but it may fairly be said to exist in transmission, in communication" (Dewey, 1985a, p. 8).

In other words, democracy thrives on open dialogue, where knowledge is not merely dispensed but actively exchanged and co-created. This participatory model of learning, grounded in real-world experiences and problems, fosters public-mindedness and the skills essential for engaged citizenship. This is the vision of education that Dewey advocates for: a broader understanding of education that values the rich potential of informal learning and emphasizes the role of individual experience within society, integrating education with socialization (Bellmann & Su, 2016). Consider the experiences lived, connections forged, and the new ideas explored as children engage with their communities. This "learning by living," interweaving formal and inform education, offers a compelling alternative to rigid, institutionalized models of schooling.

Dewey's democratic educational model synthesizes multiple dimensions—student interests, experiential experimentation, collaborative inquiry, active problem-solving, and critical reflection—into an organic, unified approach to learning. This approach extends far beyond science education; it nurtures individual's moral cultivation, social growth, and identity formation through engagement with real-world problem-solving (Bauer, 2003). Children, especially, flourish in environments that encourage communication, dramatic rehearsal, reflection, and collaboration within a dynamic of process of mutual understanding. This empowers them to grow into well-rounded individuals and responsible, considerate citizens, illustrating the deep interconnection between personal growth and civic participation.

6.3.2.3 Richard Rorty's Edification: Postmodern Reimagining

Richard Rorty, known for his anti-essentialist stance, offers a distinctive take on self-cultivation, one that resonates, in spirit, with the ideals of Bildung while reconfiguring its meaning in a post-metaphysical context. Dismissing rationalist or universalist claims, Rorty argues that fixed doctrines constrain personal autonomy and inhibit receptivity to difference. In their place, he advocates for sentimental education, where exposure to the suffering of others cultivates sympathy and moral responsiveness. For Rorty, ethical progress springs not from detached reasoning but from this cultivated capacity for emotional attunement. This vision finds its apex in his ideal of a cosmopolitan human rights culture, built upon narratives of shared vulnerability and cross-cultural exchange. He terms this lifelong pursuit of moral and intellectual growth "edification," a continuous process of self-transformation driven by empathetic imagination and discursive engagement.

Rorty prefers the term "edification" to "Bildung" to express his vision of philosophy without epistemology (Rorty, 2009). Conceiving edification as a hermeneutically rooted cultural endeavor, he advocates replacing the systematic, truth-seeking Platonic philosophy with a focus on open, uninhibited human conversation—emphasizing a shift from self-discovery over self-creation. The older philosophical style, according to Rorty, hinders philosophy's transformative capacity: liberating individuals from social constraints, cultivating empathy and ethical awareness, and encouraging the authentic realization of individual potential. In this way, Rorty's edification philosophy offers a distinct path for personal development and critical social engagement, which marks a departure from conventional educational models.

For Rorty, edification aims "to help their readers, or society as a whole, break free from outworn vocabularies and attitudes" (Rorty, 2009, p. 360). He identifies two avenues to achieve this. The first, a hermeneutic passport, encourages exploring and conversing across diverse cultures, the self, and the vast spectrum of human experience, building bridges of understanding. This dynamic interplay of ideas sets the stage for the second avenue: poetic edification. This is where imagination takes flight, allowing us to envision new possibilities, craft exotic ideas, and paint a canvas of life beyond the familiar (Voparil, 2005).

Connecting with the "other" is not merely a cultural excursion; it is a transformative experience. When we enter genuine dialogue with the unfamiliar, our rigid frameworks fracture. Old languages of understanding crumble; inherited attitudes dissolve. This dialogue of cultures, this symphony of human experience, fosters compassionate connection, offers solace to suffering, and unleashes latent possibilities within. Such ideas reflect Rorty's idea of liberal democracy, where individuals serve as either agents of love or agents of justice in the pursuit of solidarity. Agents of love celebrate the uniqueness and diversity of other cultures, while the agents of justice, or the Guardians of universality, ensure that these cultures are understood and treated with equality and respect (Rorty, 1986, p. 206).

It is noteworthy that Rorty, like Confucius, advocates for sentimental education as a means of moral development. Both recognize the power of art and literature to stir the soul, cultivate empathy, and provoke ethical reflection. However, there are fundamental differences between their philosophies. As Rorty observes, "[I]n the Confucian tradition, as I understand it, a just public order is an end in itself. In the pragmatist tradition, it is a means to the development of individuals in their full uniqueness, a way of facilitating individual self-creation" (Huang, 2010, p. 291). This divergence is unsurprising, given Rorty's philosophy of edification seeks to dismantle fixed ideas, innate predispositions, norms, and transcendent truths—marking a clear departure from both the Platonic tradition and Confucian thought.

6.4 Comparison Between Chinese Moral Cultivation and Western Bildung

Imagine a young scholar in ancient China practicing his calligraphy, meticulously honing each stroke—not merely for its aesthetic beauty, but as a discipline of moral refinement for communal harmony. Now envision a university student in Europe poring over Goethe, engaging with texts as portals to self-discovery and universal truth. These two vignettes illuminate the fundamental philosophical divide between Eastern moral cultivation and Western Bildung. Though both traditions share the goal of developing virtuous, well-rounded individuals, their paths diverge radically in method, emphasis, and underlying worldview.

At the metaphysical level, these fascinating convergences and divergences between Chinese and Western thought stem from fundamentally different conceptions of the human-cosmos relationship. Mainstream Western thought privileges a subject-object dichotomy, framing humans as detached observers analyzing the world or the self as distinct entities. This contrasts sharply with the Chinese ideal of "unity of Heaven and humanity," which envisions the self as dynamically entangled with both social and natural worlds. That said, to categorize these traditions simplistically as "unity" or "separation" risks oversimplification. Chinese thought contains strands of analytical distinction, just as Western philosophy harbors currents of monistic holism. The true philosophical depth lies precisely in these interwoven paradoxes—in the subtle resonances and productive tensions that emerge when these worldviews are carefully juxtaposed.

Beneath their divergent expressions, Chinese moral cultivation, classical Bildung, and various Western philosophical traditions reveal a profound commonality: the human quest for moral perfection. Whether through Plato's Form of the Good, Christian communion with the divine, or Confucian harmony between humanity and cosmic order, each tradition articulates a path whereby the individual ascends toward a higher ideal. These transformative journeys, though culturally distinct, all entail spiritual awakening and ethical refinement, culminating in the rebirth of a more enlightened self. Such parallels speak to a universal yearning to surpass finite existence and touch enduring truth, however conceived across civilizations.

The discussions reveal a core principle that echoes across both Eastern and Western intellectual traditions: Many thinkers have posited the existence of a higher underlying reality—whether conceived as natural law, divine will, or cosmic principles—that precedes the universe and shapes our moral expectations. This transcendent order provides the ultimate ground for virtue and knowledge, which are intertwined within our innate capacities for reason, emotion, and the recognition of harmony. Understanding this framework allows individuals to translate its principles into lived virtue through moral cultivation and character development. While definitions of virtue may vary across cultures, the overarching aim remains consistent: Self-cultivation is often seen as a process of aligning oneself with this higher order. Crucially, this pursuit does not demand uniformity but permits diverse expressions of moral behavior, all contributing to a flourishing world. It is through this very dynamic that the connection between individual growth and a sense of belonging to a greater whole emerges as a recurring theme, suggesting that meaning and purpose often arise through commitment to shared existence.

The intrinsic link between goodness and happiness—living a fulfilling and meaningful life—forms a cornerstone of moral cultivation in both traditions. For instance, Socrates holds that knowledge of goodness and self-awareness, rather than other practical know-how, can elevate the soul and lead to true happiness. Similarly, Confucianism maintains that moral excellence, achieved through virtuous self-cultivation, leads to inner harmony and the serene happiness of a clear conscience. While both traditions employ reminders or external guidance as temporary scaffolding, they ultimately emphasize the individual's active pursuit of self-improvement—whether through Confucian ritual practice or Bildung's aesthetic education—as the path to genuine goodness and a profoundly satisfying life.

The metaphor of growth permeates both Eastern and Western intellectual traditions as a vivid representation of moral development. Both traditions eschew didactic moralism in favor of developmental processes. Confucianism envisions moral potential as innate, capable of growing and flourishing within a social environment, emphasizing individuals' ethical accountability to the wider community. Similarly, the Western concept of Bildung emphasizes the cultivation of individuals within a cultural context. Wilhelm von Humboldt, for instance, likens Bildung to the organic growth of plants, arguing that, when nurtured by the right social conditions, human beings can achieve moral and intellectual development through the exercise of reason (von Humboldt, 1993). John Dewey, in his theory of experiential education, also portrays education as a process of growth fueled by children's natural curiosity, shaped by exploration, reflection, and active engagement in community life—an essential prerequisite for the renewal of democracy (Dewey, 1985a, 1988).

However, crucial distinctions exist between Chinese self-cultivation and Western Bildung, particularly in how they perceive the role of emotion. Confucian philosophy places affect at the center of ethical formation, grounding cardinal virtues such as humaneness, compassion, filial affection, righteousness, and a sense of shame in cultivated emotional capacities. These emotions arise primarily through familial bonds and communal practice, forming, in traditional Chinese thought, a kind of moral epistemology in which refined feeling often holds greater authority than abstract rationality in shaping character.

In contrast, Western Bildung presents a more nuanced perspective, generally prioritizing rationality and critical thinking over emotion in self-cultivation. Early formulations, shaped by logocentric dualism, often regarded emotions as obstacles to higher reasoning—elements to be controlled or subordinated. Yet, even within this rationalist framework, alternative voices emerged that recognized the value of emotion as an integral part of human development. Later phenomenological thinkers, for instance, acknowledged the transformative role of emotions in the Bildung process (Brinkmann, 2021), a recognition that would be further developed by philosophers such as John Dewey and Richard Rorty. In contrast to the Kantian tendency to minimize emotion, they embrace sympathy, imagination, and affective experience as essential to moral growth and the formation of a fully developed self.

Another fundamental distinction between Chinese moral cultivation and Western Bildung lies in their underlying selfhood and sociality. The Bildung tradition often frames virtue through the lens of individual autonomy, where moral development unfolds within a framework of personal rights and private self-formation. Confucian ethics, by contrast, understands virtue as fundamentally relational, with moral growth inseparable from one's embeddedness in familial and communal life. Whereas Bildung tends to regard self-cultivation more as an individual endeavor, Confucianism envisions it as a fundamentally social process—where personal refinement both shapes and is shaped by a morally responsive community.

In both Daoism and Confucianism, all things are interdependent, and the boundaries between self and other, as well as person and thing, are blurred. The individual is not conceived as an isolated entity, but as an integral part of a vast, interconnected whole—encompassing human society and the natural world. For Daoists, this interrelatedness is expressed through a spontaneous harmony with the natural order, where the self dissolves into effortless attunement with all existence. In Confucian thought, this sense of interconnectedness places human relationships at the center of moral life, where the needs of the individual are often tied to and subordinate to the collective well-being of family and community. This relational worldview stands in contrast to the Western Bildung tradition, which typically foregrounds individual self-development as both the starting point and primary focus of moral formation.

For many Bildung thinkers, self-cultivation extends beyond simply acquiring social graces; it is a deeply personal journey—an evolution from one's initial state to a higher plane of reason and humanity. Social interaction and responsibilities to others are important aspects of this process, but the primary focus remains inward: a personal exploration of the self. Its ultimate goal is to develop citizens with the moral strength and emotional intelligence to act as both collaborative members of society and independent thinkers, capable of navigating its complexities of society without losing their own voice. Thus, while Bildung champions responsible citizens, it also strongly safeguards their freedom and independence—two complementary pillars of a well-rounded moral character.

In terms of social impact, Bildung and Confucianism present differing perspectives. Bildung, often nestled within the ivory towers of Western academia, can be likened to an individual's artistic masterpiece, appreciated for its intrinsic value, but not always immediately applicable to everyday social challenges (Alves, 2019). While Bildung has undeniably contributed to social change and revolutions by fostering personal development, critical thinking, and moral responsibility—particularly through the influence of elite universities and literary works like the Bildungsroman—its effects often diffuse gradually from intellectual circles, rather than through direct engagement with broader society.

Confucianism, in contrast, resembles a bustling marketplace, emphasizing the practical application of virtue within the social world. Concerned with both inner sagehood and outer kingliness, it envisions scholars as active participants in governance and exemplars of ethical leadership, charged with the task of promoting moral cultivation. Even Daoism, while articulating a naturalist philosophy, offers its own political approach—wuwei—as a means to address social crises. These traditions reveal a fundamental tenet of Chinese thought: Philosophy is not merely intellectual exploration; it is, above all, a practical endeavor aimed at directly addressing social challenges and the needs of the state. The dynamic interplay between the "grand tradition" of elite philosophy and the "small traditions" embedded in daily life enabled Confucian scholars to fulfill their edifying role of "transforming customs and moral norms" (Yu, 1987).

When weighing the full trade-offs, each tradition presents unique strengths and weaknesses in navigating the balance between personal growth and communal obligations. Bildung, with its individualistic orientation, ignites intellectual curiosity, empowers personal critique of conventions, and fosters original perspectives. Yet, as noted, this transformation often begins at the personal and cultural level, like a flame burning brightly but often heating only its immediate surroundings, its capacity to reshape broader structures unfolding more gradually. Confucianism, by contrast, operates as a cultural sun—its warmth radiating through social hierarchies to nurture collective values and stability. But like sunlight, this pervasive influence creates both illumination and shadow: While fostering harmony, its emphasis on filial piety and social conformity can risk dimming critical discourse and innovative thought, even as many Confucian voices stress the duty of remonstrance and the moral courage to challenge unjust authority.

These contrasting models of moral cultivation reflect a nuanced philosophical divide between Eastern and Western traditions. Bildung, historically rooted in Western individualism, flourishes in cultural climates that valorize personal liberty, egalitarian principles, institutionalized rights, and autonomous agency. Its practitioners tend to pursue truth through personal reflective inquiry while also engaging in a dynamic and dialectical exchange with the world and its competing perspectives. Through rigorous critique, they deconstruct assumptions and construct systematic theories within the conceptual realm, a process that leads to a more universal form of self-consciousness through mutual recognition.

The Chinese tradition of self-cultivation, by contrast, arises from an organic philosophy of relationality, where collective well-being, mutual responsibility, and cosmic harmony form the foundation of ethical development. Here, moral refinement is enacted not merely as private introspection but also as social artistry, cultivated through lived relationships, ritual practice, and communal exchange. Wisdom is conveyed less by abstract discourse than by the embodiment of virtue, whereby students cultivate ethical insight through lived practice. The result is a dynamic interplay in which personal betterment and societal flourishing continuously co-create one another.

References

Alves, A. (2019). The German tradition of self-cultivation (Bildung) and its historical meaning. *Educação & Realidade, 44*, e83003.

Bauer, W. (2003). On the relevance of Bildung for democracy. *Educational Philosophy and Theory, 35*(2), 211–225.

Bellmann, J., & Su, H. (2016). Democracy and Bildung/Erziehung—Toward a universal theory of education. *Education Sciences, 7*(1), 5.

Brewton, V. (2003). *Ralph Waldo Emerson*. Internet Encyclopedia of Philosophy. https://iep.utm.edu/ralph-waldo-emerson/

Brinkmann, M. (2021). *Emotion, Bildung, Übung–Thoughts on a bildung of emotions as practising the practice*. Il sentire che noi siamo.

Cavell, S. (2018). *Conditions handsome and unhandsome: The constitution of Emersonian perfectionism: The Carus lectures, 1988*. University of Chicago Press.

Chaudhuri, H. (1954). The concept of Brahman in Hindu philosophy. *Philosophy East and West, 4*(1), 47–66.

Dewey, J. (1985a). *Democracy and education*. In J. A. Boydston (Ed.), *The middle works, 1899–1924: Volume 9*. Southern Illinois University Press.

Dewey, J. (1985b). How we think; contributions to a cyclopedia of education, (Vols. 1–2)vols. In J. A. Boydston (Ed.), *The middle works, 1899–1924: Volume 6*. Southern Illinois Press.

Dewey, J. (1988). Experience and education. In J. A. Boydston (Ed.), *The collected works of John Dewey, 1882–1953: The later works, 1925–1953 (Vol. 13, pp. 1–62)*. Southern Illinois University Press. (Original work published 1938).

Emerson, R. W. (1971). The divinity school address. In A. R. Ferguson (Ed.), *The collected works of Ralph Waldo Emerson* (Vol. 1, pp. 71–140). Harvard University Press.

Gadamer, H. G. (1992). *Hans-Georg Gadamer on education, poetry, and history: Applied hermeneutics*. SUNY Press.

Hegel, G. W. F. (2015). *The philosophy of right*. Hackett.

Herdt, J. A. (2019). *Forming humanity: Redeeming the German Bildung tradition*. University of Chicago Press.

Horlacher, R. (2004). Bildung–A construction of a history of philosophy of education. *Studies in Philosophy and Education, 23*(5–6), 409–426.

Huang, Y. (2010). *Rorty, pragmatism, and Confucianism: With responses by Richard Rorty*. State University of New York Press.

Johansson, V., & Schumann, C. (2019). Bildung, self-cultivation, and the challenge of democracy: Ralph Waldo Emerson as a philosopher of education. *Educational Philosophy and Theory, 51*(5), 474–477.

Kant, I. (2002). *Critique of practical reason*. Hackett Publishing.

Konrad, F. M. (2012). Wilhelm von Humboldt's contribution to a theory of Bildung. In P. Siljander, A. Kivelä, & A. Sutinen (Eds.), *Theories of Bildung and growth: Connections and controversies between continental educational thinking and American pragmatism* (pp. 107–124). Sense.

Kovalainen, H. A. (2012). Emersonian self-culture and individual growth: The American appropriation of Bildung. In *Theories of Bildung and growth* (pp. 183-197). Brill.

Masschelein, J., & Ricken, N. (2003). Do we (still) need the concept of Bildung? *Educational Philosophy and Theory, 35*(2), 139–154.

Nordenbo, S. E. (2002). Bildung and the thinking of Bildung. *Journal of Philosophy of Education, 36*(3), 341–352.

Rorty, R. (1986). *On ethnocentrism: A reply to Clifford Geertz*. University of Michigan.

Rorty, R. (2009). *Philosophy and the mirror of nature* (Vol. 81). Princeton University Press.

Schumann, C. (2019). Aversive education: Emersonian variations on 'Bildung'. *Educational Philosophy and Theory, 51*(5), 488–497.

Schweitzer, A. (1923). *The philosophy of civilization*. A. & C. Black.

Siljander, P., & Sutinen, A. (2012). Introduction. In P. Siljander, A. Kivelä, & A. Sutinen (Eds.), *Theories of Bildung and growth: Connections and controversies between continental educational thinking and American pragmatism* (pp. 1–18). Sense.

Spinoza, B. (2002). *Spinoza: Complete works*. Hackett.

Stoll, T. (2020). Review of Jennifer Herdt's forming humanity redeeming the German Bildung tradition. *Notre Dame Philosophical Reviews, 202001*.

Swahananda, S. (2022). Chandogya upanisad. *Sri Ramakrishna Mathematics III, 14*, 1.

von Humboldt, W. (1993). *The limits of state action*. Liberty Fund. (Original work published 1791–1792).

von Humboldt, W. (2000). *Theory of bildung. Teaching as a reflective practice: The German Didaktik tradition* (pp. 57–61).

Voparil, C. (2005). On the idea of philosophy as bildungsroman: Rorty and his critics. *Contemporary Pragmatism, 2*(1), 115–133.

Widgery, A. G. (1930). The principles of Hindu ethics. *The International Journal of Ethics, 40*(2), 232–245.

Yu, D. (2002). *Religions in the dynasties of Xia, Shang, and Zhou: The origin of Chinese philosophical thought*. Liaoning Education Publishing House.

Yu, Y. (1987). Han dynasty officials and cultural diffusion. In Y. Yu (Ed.), *Modern interpretation of Chinese tradition of thought* (pp. 167–258). Linking Publishing Company.

Part III
The Shaping of Chinese Civilization

Chapter 7
The Great Unification: Statecraft and Social Systems in Imperial China

For over two millennia, Confucianism, Daoism, and Legalism transcended mere philosophical debate to become the architectural pillars of Chinese civilization. These were not simply schools of thought but the operating systems of empire, molding both governance and scholarly tradition. Central to this enduring legacy was the ideal of "great unification" (大一统)—a vision of cosmic order where governance, culture, and society aligned under a unified moral-political system. Emerging during the Western Zhou dynasty, this principle served as the centripetal force in Chinese statecraft, perpetually drawing periods of fragmentation and chaos back toward unity, stability, and shared destiny.

Though first imposed institutionally through Legalist rigor under the Qin, great unification found its enduring soul in Confucianism. Where Legalism provided the skeletal structure of centralized rule, Confucianism supplied its ethical flesh—transforming raw authority into moral legitimacy by grounding governance in virtue rather than fear. Most dynasties, recoiling from the excesses of Legalist rule, adopted Confucian moral cultivation as the ideological foundation of governance: pursuing social harmony by fostering moral duty in their subjects rather than relying solely on punitive measures and deterrence. In this ruling paradigm, rulers aimed not just for obedience, but for cohesion, strengthening unity through the cultivation of virtue among the people, all in pursuit of the enduring ideal of a harmoniously unified realm (大同).

Note that the ideology of great unification, though deeply rooted in Confucian moral cultivation, is not an exclusively Confucian contribution; it is significantly enriched by Daoist, Legalist, Mohist, and Buddhist thought. Take Daoism, for instance: although Lao Tzu's political ideal is commonly associated with the "tiny state, small population," he nonetheless "envisioned a unified realm and even provided a metaphysical basis for this goal [the great unity]" (Pines, 2000, p. 305).

This political-ethical framework of great unification, along with its moral cultivation system, permeated all aspects of civilization, from imperial administration to legal systems, from aesthetic traditions to the national ethos, becoming the

Z. You, Y. Hu, *Philosophy and Civilization: How the Idea of Moral Cultivation Shaped China*, East-West Dialogues in Educational Philosophy and Theory,
https://doi.org/10.1007/978-981-95-5660-1_7

foundational blueprint of Chinese cultural identity. While its influence was broad and multifaceted, this chapter narrows its focus to two pivotal arenas: the structures of political governance and the core societal spheres of customary practices, legal institutions, and economic ethics.

7.1 Moral Cultivation and Statecraft

Nearly all ancient agricultural civilizations developed centralized authority to varying degrees—a practical necessity for administering irrigation networks, allocating resources, and mobilizing mass labor. Such administrative centralization, in turn, paved the way for political unification, as coordinated efforts within a unified system proved efficient for managing the complex infrastructures of agrarian societies.

In China, Confucianism and Legalism, despite their differing approaches, supported the concept of great unification as a political cornerstone. This concept of statehood, seen in China since Spring and Autumn Period (770 to 481 BCE), emphasizes unification as essential to effective governance. The term "great" conveys the vast scope, authority, and significance of such rule, while "unification" refers to the integration of diverse regions and their administrative and cultural systems under a single framework, including standardized decrees, calendars, rituals, language, weights, measures, and the promotion of official ideological conformity. Together, these efforts created a powerful centripetal force, binding disparate elements into a cohesive and highly unified state.

But ruling a vast and centralized empire millennia ago posed a formidable challenge. Chinese monarchs had to strike a careful balance between stability and efficiency. To achieve efficiency, they adopted the system of great unification; for stability, they often promoted moral cultivation to harmonize great unification, advocating for the kingly way over the hegemon's way.

7.1.1 Role of Moral Cultivation in Great Unification

The concept of great unification has a developmental history rather than a single point of origin. Its roots can be traced back to the idea of All under Heaven during Shang-Zhou dynasties (Wang, 2024), but it was formalized as a political ideal and put into practice much later. The vision took a significant step forward during the Western Zhou dynasty, which implemented a feudal framework by enfeoffing royal kinsmen and meritorious officials as vassals tasked with exploring and settling new territories. This strategy sought to uphold the authority of the Zhou suzerain while enabling rapid territorial expansion. Although seemingly paradoxical, the enfeoffment system laid the territorial and cultural groundwork for the eventual emergence of a vast unified empire.

But how could loyalty be ensured and order preserved while empowering regional leaders? In the Chinese cultural context, which emphasized human relationships, contractual agreements alone proved insufficient to secure lasting allegiance. To address this, the Zhou dynasty instead transformed its patriarchal system—a male-centered structure rooted in blood ties and primogeniture—into a national political and cultural framework. By extending familial bonds, it established a father-son dynamic between the monarch and his ministers.

To sustain this family-state structure, the Zhou dynasty institutionalized a comprehensive system of ritual and musical cultivation—a dual mechanism for preserving both political order and social harmony. These rites, backed up by military authority when necessary, served as behavioral templates that guided people to accept their roles within the hierarchy while internalizing moral norms through disciplined and elegant practice. By mitigating conflict, instilling shared values, and enhancing overall resilience, this system proved to be an effective tool for governance, revealing the extraordinary potential of moral education to administer an increasingly vast and complex territorial order.

7.1.1.1 Virtuous Governance and Family-State Paradigm

A full understanding of "virtuous governance" in imperial China requires examining its roots in the patriarchal social and cultural order. While "rule by virtue" serves as the standard term for this governing philosophy, alternative expressions like "rule by filial piety" or "ritual governance" underscore its grounding in the patriarchal clan system, which modeled the state on familial relationships. Within this structure, the emperor assumed a monarchical paternal role, promoting moral cultivation across society to uphold the values of humaneness, filial piety, loyalty, and broader social harmony and order.

The term patriarchy, derived from the Greek for "rule of the father," takes on a distinct expression in traditional Chinese society. Rooted in male authority and primogeniture, the Chinese patriarchal system ensured that leadership typically passed along the male line—usually to the firstborn son of the official wife of the family patriarch. This principle governed not only the hierarchy of families and clans but also imperial succession, creating a social continuum that both structurally and ideologically connected the family to the state.

While the emperor and central government wielded considerable authority, their power was not absolute; it was somewhat diluted at the grassroots level, where influential patriarchal units—families and clans—retained a degree of autonomy in managing everyday affairs, such as local disputes and even certain aspects of state administration. This created a two-tiered power structure, with imperial power at the top and powerful families, often referred to as the gentry and clan power, at the base.[1] Yet, despite some degree of grassroots autonomy, the patriarchal system func-

[1] Fei Xiaotong, in "The Rigidity of Grassroots Administration," puts forward the concept of "dual-track politics" in traditional Chinese history, with top-down imperial power on the one hand and

tioned as a unified pyramid. As both sovereign and supreme patriarch, the emperor occupied the zenith of the national hierarchy, embodying absolute authority while carefully orchestrating the balance of power and resources across the realm.

This hierarchical system was not just about the distribution of privileges but also emphasized mutual obligation and collective welfare. Within the clan-based structure, relationships were tightly woven and meticulously ordered. Kinship proximity determined not only closeness but also the reciprocal duties among members. The clan system functioned as a support network, where members aided each other and provided assistance to less fortunate families. For instance, it created educational opportunities for talented children from impoverished backgrounds, with the expectation that they would succeed and contribute to the clan. However, the system also inherently contained oppressive elements, including rigidly enforced gender roles, strict demands for obedience, arranged marriages, and entrenched social hierarchies that constrained individual freedoms and reinforced inequality.

The patriarchal system in ancient China gave rise to the concept of family-state isomorphism, where the fundamental structure and characteristics of the family were mirrored in the broader political sphere. For instance, the political relationship between ruler and minister was modeled on that of father and son in the family. Institutionally, the family, or extended family, formed the basic social unit, and clans collectively made up the state. Thus, the state functioned as a collective of families and clans, with its leaders typically being the heads of the most influential families. In this framework, ancestor veneration took precedence over the worship of gods, as lineage played a crucial role in determining social standing and political influence. Filial piety (to one's father)-loyalty (to the monarch), reinforced by Confucian moral cultivation, emerged as a central virtue, forming the foundation of both individual values and political ethics in ancient Chinese society.

The Zhou dynasty offers a striking example of this dynamic. The feudal system, where the king granted land and titles to royal family members and meritorious officials—often bound by marriage alliances—as hereditary lords, further cemented the identity between family and state. These powerful vassal states, many led by families directly descended from the Zhou royalty, mirrored the central government in structure and values. This fostered the parallel concepts of filial piety and ministerial loyalty: just as a son owed absolute obedience to his father, so too did a vassal lord dedicate unwavering fealty to the king, with ministers similarly obliged to their respective lords (Chen, 2017). In this context, a family functioned as a microcosm of the state, while the state itself could be seen as an expanded family unit. This close association nurtured a sense of collective responsibility and solidarity, reinforcing the hierarchy that influenced both private and public life.

Since ancient Chinese political logic was rooted in family relationships, with state ethics extending directly from familial ethics, this connection inevitably complicated the ethical landscape. The family-state entanglement risked fostering favoritism and factionalism, as individuals could blur the line between public and private

---

bottom-up gentry and clan power on the other.

interests or prioritize family and clan ties over the needs of the state. Yet the same framework can also cultivate higher ideals: the state's emphasis on collective welfare, coupled with the Confucian vision of "All under Heaven," encouraged individuals to transcend narrow loyalties in service of the greater good. The veneration of sages and Junzi, who exemplified selflessness and placed public duty above personal or factional interests, reflects this aspiration. Throughout Chinese history, many such figures embodied an altruistic commitment to societal well-being, illustrating the enduring ideal of morally grounded governance.

Rooted in China's family-state paradigm itself, Confucianism functioned as a vital mediator between competing loyalties. While exalting filial piety and familial devotion, it also emphasized the moral imperative of societal duty and collective welfare. In moments of conflict, Confucian ethics consistently privileged the public good over private gain. This philosophy fostered an ethos of collective responsibility, urging individuals—especially rulers—to transcend kinship ties and embrace concern for the state and All under Heaven. The ideal sage-king embodied this principle, subordinating personal interests to the welfare of the realm and modeling virtuous leadership that ensured stability and universal flourishing. Though the family-state dynamic remained inherently tension-laden, its influence indelibly shaped China's political consciousness—a legacy that continues to inform modern Chinese social values.

7.1.1.2 Evolution of the Political System of Great Unification

Though initially effective, the Zhou system gradually declined as vassal states gained power, eroding central authority and subverting the ritual order. As central power waned and the rites-music system deteriorated, warfare between regional lords intensified. This crisis of legitimacy created fertile ground for Legalism's ascent—a doctrine prioritizing absolute control and administrative efficiency through codified laws. For instance, the Qin state systematically dismantled Zhou feudalism, replacing hereditary nobles with centrally appointed administrators in commanderies and counties. After unifying the country, the newly established Qin Empire imposed sweeping standardization—of script, currency, and measurements—forging an unprecedented bureaucratic apparatus.

However, this powerful regime was short-lived, lasting only 15 years. Harsh laws, burdensome taxation, and relentless demands for military and labor service, used to fuel the empire's grand ambitions, bred deep resentment among the people. Eventually, this discontent erupted into widespread revolts, toppling the empire. Its collapse became a lasting cautionary tale: no matter how efficient or centralized, systems can crumble under the weight of their own rigidity and oppression. Though the Qin's model was remarkably effective in mobilizing resources and asserting control, its overreliance on coercion ultimately proved unsustainable.

The Han dynasty inherited the Qin's efficient "great unification" administrative system, leveraging its capacity to mobilize resources, centralize authority, undertake massive public works, and launch wars to secure frontiers and expand territories. Yet the Han consciously tempered the excesses of Qin rule, embracing a more balanced philosophy of governance. The dynasty initially adopted Huang-Lao Daoist principles of noninterference but later transitioned to institutionalizing Confucian ideals, evolving toward a humanistic paradigm of "rule by virtue." By blending effective bureaucracy with virtuous governance, the Han established one of history's most enduring imperial systems.

Grounded in Zhou traditions and later refined by Confucian thought, the ideal of virtuous governance rested on the belief in human moral potential—inherently good, yet in need of nurturing and ethical guidance. It emphasized leadership by moral example; the cultivation of core virtues such as humaneness, trustworthiness, and filial piety; and the implementation of benevolent policies such as tax relief and reduced legal burdens. Proponents argued that such virtue-based governance was inherently more sustainable and effective in maintaining social harmony and achieving long-term prosperity than reliance on coercive punishment.

Confucian literati served as the architects of this transformation, charged with molding the ethical foundations of future officials while teaching moral values throughout the empire—effectively becoming the cultural stewards of imperial governance. Moreover, governing an empire of such vast scale and complexity demanded ideological adaptability. While Confucianism served as the foundational state orthodoxy, effective rule required the strategic integration of complementary philosophies. Daoist principles of natural harmony and wuwei informed flexible, context-sensitive governance approaches, whereas Legalism's focus on codified laws and administrative rigor provided the necessary mechanisms for maintaining order, deterring malfeasance, and implementing structural reforms when circumstances demanded.

7.1.1.3 The Necessity of Moral Cultivation for Great Unification

Moral cultivation functioned as the critical interface between imperial governance and local communities in traditional China. The empire's distinctive sociopolitical architecture emerged from tightly knit kinship systems that sustained order through collectively upheld ethical frameworks. These lineage-based structures evolved into formidable corporate entities—extended clans and descent groups that commanded economic resources and exercised political power. The ascendance of such corporate kinship organizations, operating within a stratified social hierarchy, demanded robust centralized authority to coordinate, mediate, and harmonize these competing factions, thereby preserving societal equilibrium and dynastic resilience.

This centralized and unified political model required a sociocultural intermediary to navigate the vertical tensions between state and family. Ancient China, unlike many Western societies, lacked influential intermediaries like religious institutions, local self-governance, and autonomous legal systems. It depended heavily on direct state involvement to achieve large-scale social mobilization and administrative coordination. However, the very efficient top-down model—especially in a culturally and geographically diverse empire—also carried the risk of structural rigidity.

To address this, a complementary yet significant framework was needed: one that could uphold systemic coherence while providing the moral and cultural flexibility needed to ease the tensions inherent in a steep hierarchical order—a role fulfilled by China's distinctive tradition of state-centered moral cultivation.

Confucianism and Legalism offered contrasting paths to achieving this unification. Legalism emphasized strict control and the rigorous enforcement of laws, envisioning a unified system where central authorities devised overarching policies while local officials carried them out with maximum efficiency. Although this approach significantly enhanced the state's organizational capacity, its reliance on harshness and rigidity often provoked discontent and resistance. Confucianism, by contrast, pursued unification through cultural cohesion and the promotion of shared moral values, ideally cultivated through education and personal example. After the fall of the Qin dynasty, the more harmonious Confucian model steadily supplanted the Legalist framework. This transition, driven by the gradual replacement of Legalist administrators with Confucian scholar-officials, proved essential for administrative flexibility, social cohesion, and long-term stability.

A metaphor envisioning ancient China as a great seafaring vessel helps illuminate the ideological transformation of its governance. The Zhou system functioned like a ship with watertight compartments—a three-tiered structure where the king governed from the bridge, ministers oversaw the main operations on the deck, and regional nobles administered local populations in segregated holds. This decentralized design, while sacrificing some efficiency—like a ship trading cargo space for stability—provided crucial systemic resilience. Each compartment acted as a buffer, containing rebellions or misrule before they could engulf the entire vessel. Local disturbances might flood one section without sinking the whole, granting the realm both adaptive flexibility and remarkable endurance amid internal storms.

The Qin system, by contrast, sought absolute control and centralized authority, dismantling the nobility-led "compartments" and consolidating power under a single, tightly governed unit driven by the emperor's ambition (Zhang, 2019). While this structure enabled rapid decision-making and efficient resource mobilization—helping Qin unite China with juggernaut-like power—it came at a significant cost: resilience. Without intermediary aristocratic layers, the system lacked shock absorbers. When the populace could no longer bear oppressive burdens, widespread and violent resistance erupted, directly targeting the emperor. This structural vulnerability became tragically evident in the Qin Empire's swift collapse—like a massive ship without watertight compartments, it sank within a mere 15 years amid widespread peasant uprisings.

While preserving the Qin's unified administrative framework, the ensuing Han dynasty fundamentally transformed its ideological foundations by embracing Confucianism. This shift replaced Legalist bureaucrats with Confucian scholars and scholar-officials who served as a crucial mediating class, simultaneously governing the empire while cultivating moral order through ethical instruction and ritual propriety. The resulting system maintained the structural efficiency of centralized rule while creating permeable "moral compartments" throughout society. This ethical scaffolding afforded the flexibility to adapt locally, simultaneously building the cultural legitimacy that ensured its enduring stability.

Ancient Chinese governance, while incorporating rational bureaucratic elements and meritocratic features, diverged significantly from modern civil service systems grounded in codified rule of law and democratic accountability mechanisms. Instead, it relied on a dynamic synthesis of legal statutes, Confucian moral principles, customary social norms, and the authority of the imperial mandate, all guided by a deeply rooted ethical imperative to govern virtuously, aiming to maintain social order and the general welfare of the people. This model of governance evolved as a pragmatic response to the immense challenge of administering a vast and diverse empire, where centralized authority served as the essential tool for reconciling regional variation and maintaining social stability within a complex hierarchical structure.

Within the imperial sociopolitical order, Confucian moral cultivation served as the mechanism that linked family ethics with political authority. The domestic hierarchy of filial devotion naturally extended into political loyalty, reflecting the family-state continuum. Confucian scholar-officials embodied this dual allegiance, serving simultaneously as imperial administrators, ethical exemplars, and community leaders. By mediating between the throne and local kinship networks, they preserved a delicate balance of unified authority and regional adaptation. This sophisticated integration of moral philosophy with statecraft became a cornerstone of imperial resilience, weaving ethical cultivation into the very fabric of China's enduring civilization.

The Confucian model of great unification endowed imperial rulers with exceptional governance capacity, allowing swift, coordinated responses to diverse challenges—from distributing famine relief across provinces to marshaling border defenses against nomadic incursions. Rather than relying on draconian Legalist-style rewarding and punitive measures, this system derived its resilience from Confucian relational ethics, which lent it both institutional efficacy and cultural cohesion. By appealing to shared values of reciprocity and hierarchy, it mediated regional conflicts, eased class tensions, and coordinated collective action empire-wide. Viewed through a modern lens, this paternalistic paradigm might appear to constrain personal liberties and grassroots initiative, yet its emphasis on stability, humaneness, harmony, and mutual obligation proved extraordinarily effective in maintaining solidarity across China's vast, heterogeneous territories.

7.1.1.4 Mechanisms of Virtue-Centric Governance

The concept of virtuous governance (德治) formed the cornerstone of imperial Chinese political philosophy. This ruling paradigm emphasized moral leadership, benevolent administration, and ethical cultivation as primary instruments of statecraft while treating legal codes and punitive measures as auxiliary mechanisms. It imposed rigorous expectations on sovereigns, requiring—at least nominally—the cultivation of personal moral perfection as the fundamental precondition for legitimate political authority. Only through virtuous governance could emperors maintain social harmony and ensure the welfare of "All under Heaven," thereby securing the Mandate of Heaven. A striking example comes from Emperor Wu of Northern Zhou, who, when condemned for abolishing Buddhism, asserted his readiness to suffer in hell if it meant prosperity for his subjects (Dao, 1991). Such declarations underscore the centrality of moral imperatives in China's political tradition, where ethical accountability could transcend even religious orthodoxy in legitimizing state action.

In ancient China, rule by virtue was a double-edged sword for emperors. While fostering political stability and concentrated power, it also imposed constraints on imperial authority. The Mandate of Heaven—a core political doctrine—made an emperor's legitimacy conditional on his moral conduct and kept him under constant scrutiny. Rooted in Confucian virtues like rites and filial piety, this moral standard demanded that rulers mediate conflicting interests, protect the vulnerable, and promote the welfare of all under Heaven. Failure to meet these obligations could result in ministerial admonition, self-criticism, or, more severely, rebellion and dynastic collapse—signs that the emperor had lost the Mandate of Heaven. Even peasant uprisings could claim to act in accordance with Heaven's will, justifying their actions as a restoration of the rightful order. Thus, despite their vast authority, emperors remained beholden, though sometimes more in theory than in practice, to an abstract moral ideal and the tangible expectations of their people.

The success of the system also rested on a foundation of political meritocracy—an effort to appoint virtuous, capable, and knowledgeable elites to government positions. Initially, these elites were recommended to serve based on their virtuous reputation and exceptional abilities. Beginning with the Sui dynasty (581–618 CE), the Imperial Exam System, centered on mastery of Confucian classics, provided a more standardized path for talented individuals, including those from lower social backgrounds, to ascend the political hierarchy. This practice gradually replaced the hereditary aristocracy with a merit-based bureaucracy, enhancing social mobility and consolidating imperial authority.

This institutional evolution realized Confucius' vision of moral statecraft, in which scholar-officials sustained governance through ethical leadership. To fulfill this dual mandate, the literati elite integrated some of Legalist administrative methods, synthesizing technical statecraft with Confucian moral principles. Through rigorous merit evaluations, these officials developed into professional administrators, advancing both administrative effectiveness and demonstrated virtue—qualities ideally manifested in their integrity, allegiance to the ruler, and dedication to the well-being of people. This distinctive meritocratic system fostered a largely competent and devoted civil service, which became fundamental to the empire's enduring stability, adaptability, and socioeconomic flourishing.

While rule by virtue generally contributed to dynastic longevity, it had its own inherent limitations. Virtuous government excelled in fostering stability under principled rulers yet weakened as vested interests consolidated power and ethical standards deteriorated. Without robust institutional checks and balances, this model gradually proved inadequate for addressing the polity's escalating structural challenges, pushing rulers toward political maneuvering. The combination of ethical decline and systemic vulnerability created fertile ground for nepotism, corruption, and growing inequality—all of which further deepened political crisis and social unrest. Though not the sole cause of dynastic failure, these patterns illuminate how moral, political, and economic dynamics intertwined to shape China's recurring cycles of dynastic rise and decline.

7.1.2 The Dialectic Between Kingly Way and Hegemonic Way

Ancient Chinese politics was characterized by a fundamental tension between the dominant "kingly way" (rule by virtue) and the "hegemonic way" (rule by force). Rulers, in effect, rarely relied on virtue alone. Instead, even while embracing Confucianism as the official ideology to stabilize their reign, they also incorporated Legalist strategies to deter misconduct, check power, and implement systemic reforms.

7.1.2.1 The Kingly Way as Moral Cultivation

The "kingly way" (王道) emerged as a foundational political ideal in classical Chinese statecraft. Though later most closely associated with Confucian thought, related ideas also appear in Daoist writings: *Chuang Tzu* (2013) formulates the expression "inner sage–outer king," while *Daodejing* emphasizes that only sages can align with the Way of Heaven, balancing interests and curbing exploitative human tendencies (Lao Tzu, 2010, Chap. 77). Confucianism adopted this notion, advocating for governance rooted in Confucian virtues. A sagacious monarch was expected to embody both political leadership and moral exemplarity, inspiring and teaching his people. This ideal contrasts shapely with the Legalist endorsement of rule by force and strategic manipulation, known as the "hegemonic way" (霸道). While Confucians acknowledged that war could sometimes be inevitable, they upheld the kingly way as the ideal path—one that sought to prevent conflict and cultivate enduring peace under Heaven.

The promotion of the kingly way necessitated moral cultivation, which aimed to rectify the heart-mind of individuals and nurture their virtues. Throughout Chinese history, this emphasis on moral development permeated all aspects of political life. Everyone, from the emperor to the commoner, was expected to cultivate virtue. An emperor, in particular, was expected to rule through ritual and filial piety, thereby inspiring his subjects—hence the reverential title, "Your Sagacious Highness" (圣上). Although few emperors fully lived up to this ideal, this ethical expectation exerted a significant influence on them, serving as both powerful constraint and inspiration on their actions.

Likewise, Confucian scholars pursued self-cultivation not merely as a personal endeavor, but as a means to help shape a morally upright society. In this sense, the ultimate purpose of moral cultivation extended beyond individual ethics to a broader political vision. As contemporary scholar Yu Yingshi observes, this process involves every individual contributing to the creation of a virtuous state; or conversely, the fate of a dynasty rests upon the humane hearts of its people (Yu, 2023).

The Western Han dynasty (206 BCE–9 CE) witnessed the institutionalization of the "kingly way." Emperor Wu, recognizing Confucianism's legitimizing power, elevated it to state orthodoxy—a decisive transformation that embedded Confucian principles into China's governance framework. This transformation accomplished three critical objectives: it enshrined moral cultivation as an official state policy, reinforced centralized authority by legitimizing imperial rule, and created a meritocratic system where advancement depended on Confucian learning rather than noble birth. The resulting synthesis of ethical governance and bureaucratic administration proved remarkably durable—dynasties embracing this model consistently enjoyed greater stability and durability than those relying primarily on Legalist methods.

7.1.2.2 The Hegemonic Way and Institutional Transformation

The "kingly way" of virtuous governance operated in dynamic tension with its counterpart—the "hegemonic way" of coercive rule. While Confucianism served as the official ideology, promoting moral cultivation and social harmony as pillars of lasting stability, Legalist principles quietly shaped the imperial system through their contributions to centralized bureaucracy, codified laws, and power consolidation strategies. This dual framework created a sophisticated governance model where moral ideals coexisted with pragmatic statecraft.

In effect, China's grand unification matured from a dynamic interplay of both Confucianism and Legalism. While Confucianism envisioned a harmonious society rooted in virtues, it lacked institutional mechanisms necessary for implementation. It was the Legalists who initially established a centralized structure of governance, extending from provincial administrations down to county-level units, all directly accountable to the central government. Without Legalism, Confucianism's ideals may have remained lofty abstractions, unable to shape society in concrete terms; yet without Confucianism, Legalism's rigidity could have suffocated social resilience and fueled public discontent. It is Confucianism that provided moral justification and ethical orientation that legitimized the state's authority, grounding its political frameworks in widely accepted values. This synthesis—a flexible, inclusive moral order paired with a robust, highly functional bureaucracy—allowed the Chinese state to effectively govern a vast and diverse empire.

Even after Confucianism was established as the sole official ideology in the Han dynasty, Legalism continued to inform governmental practices in subtle ways. Emperor Xuan of Han, for instance, emphasized the dynasty's tradition of balancing both ideologies when advising his son, warning against relying solely on moral instruction (Ban, 2016). While it is an exaggeration to label ancient Chinese politics as Confucianism outside and Legalism inside (外儒内法), Legalist principles remained integral to the ideological fabric of the state and was often strategically invoked during periods of political reform. This reflected a sobering practical reality: although Confucianism fostered order and harmony, it could gradually lose its grip on powerful interest groups, whose unchecked influence risked eroding the very moral foundation Confucianism sought to uphold. In such instances, Legalism functioned like a scalpel—deployed surgically to rein in excesses and endeavor to restore balance.

Unlike the stabilizing influence of Confucianism, Legalism showed little interest in preserving the status quo. It was fundamentally disruptive, actively challenging outdated institutions and entrenched interests. Rejecting moral idealism in favor of uncompromising pragmatism, it dismantled hereditary privilege and extended strict state authority over all social strata to forge a centralized, efficient state system. It was akin to stripping down a creaky, antiquated machine—discarding the rusted gears of nepotism and retrofitting it with polished components of efficiency and discipline. However, this drive for institutional efficiency came at a steep cost. Legalism demanded absolute authority, empowering a monarch with the iron hand to enforce its reform measures. This concentration of power, when overreached, often sacrificed individual rights, the public interest, and social harmony, reducing people to mere instruments of the state, straining them to their limits and triggering widespread resentment and unrest. Throughout history, it was a high-wire act with mixed outcomes, teetering between progress and tyranny.

The post-Qin political synthesis positioned Legalism as the necessary but unspoken counterpart to Confucian governance—the shadow complement to its light. Like two gears, they worked differently yet in sync, driving the machinery of imperial rule. Confucianism served as the primary guiding force, nudging people toward righteousness and harmony. In contrast to the complementary role of stringent laws, moral cultivation usually received much greater emphasis. However, during times of crisis, governments often turned to Legalist strategies to restructure political and economic systems. Some scholar-officials, steeped in Confucian ideals, embodied this adaptability. While committed to virtuous government, they pragmatically deployed Legalist methods when swift reform or strict discipline became necessary—endeavoring to balance Confucian ideals with the hard realities of statecraft.

7.1.3 The Lineages of Legitimate Political Succession and Confucian Orthodoxy

Ancient Chinese political authority rested on two distinct yet interrelated lineages: legitimate political succession (法统) and Confucian orthodoxy (道统). The former refers to the transmission of legitimate authority, encompassing not only hereditary inheritance but also the rightful ritual-legal succession of the ruling mandate and orthodox governing institutions. It regulated the transfer of power both within dynasties, through royal inheritance, and across dynasties, by adopting the cultural orthodoxy of their predecessors, thereby maintaining continuity of values and authority. The latter, the lineage of the Way or the Confucian orthodoxy, denotes a moral-philosophical authority that undergirds the ethical legitimacy of dynastic rule. It traced the transmission of Confucian wisdom, not through bloodlines, but through the intergenerational inheritance of moral truth. This spiritual lineage connected the sage-kings to Confucius and his disciples, perpetuated through both textual mastery of the classics and the intuitive heart-mind transmission between master and pupil.

These two lineages functioned as interdependent systems of legitimacy with distinct yet partially overlapping domains. While imperial authority affirmed its legitimacy through adherence to the lineage of rightful succession, Confucian literati, as guardians of moral order, reinforced dynastic stability through the Confucian orthodoxy. Together, they formed a dual validation system in which legitimate rule required both proper royal succession and demonstrated moral alignment with the Confucian Dao.

While the royal ancestral lineage was crucial for asserting dynastic continuity, it was Confucian orthodoxy that ultimately provided ideological legitimacy. Aligned with the "Mandate of Heaven," Confucian orthodoxy held that righteous rule conferred emperors the ultimate right to rule. Should an emperor lose virtue or neglect the welfare of his subjects, he risked forfeiting Heaven's Mandate, potentially losing his throne or even precipitating the collapse of the dynasty. From this perspective, Confucian orthodoxy played a dual role: it reinforced imperial power by grounding it in moral authority while also imposing ethical constraints that required emperors to embody Confucian virtues and uphold the interests of their subjects.

This system of moral accountability oversaw the ethical evaluation of each emperor, particularly through posthumous assessment: honorific temple names like Emperor Wen canonized rulers who embodied Heaven's virtuous majesty, while critical epithets like Emperor Yan permanently marked those who oppressed his people and defied Heaven's Mandate. Far from empty ritual, these judgments constituted an intergenerational moral ledger. Although successor often awarded inflated titles to rehabilitate reputations, the uncompromising verdicts recorded in official dynastic histories—compiled in the subsequent dynasty—largely preserved the truth. This created an enduring mechanism that confronted every new emperor with the stark precedents of either heavenly approval or historical condemnation, reinforcing the inseparability of political authority from Confucian moral reputation.

Confucian orthodoxy represents a long-standing ethical-political tradition that grounds authority in moral principles, legitimizes political power, and channels collective strength toward just causes. This tradition finds its roots in Confucius's doctrine of Rectifying Names, which holds that titles, roles, and designations must correspond to their true ethical substance—a principle with far-reaching sociopolitical implications (Confucius, 2016, 13.3). By insisting on the alignment between nominal status and virtuous essence, Confucian scholars sought to construct an ideal order aligned with Confucian orthodoxy. A paradigmatic example is the case of the Duke of Qi Huan, who, during a time of Zhou royal decline and nomadic invasions, rallied forces under the slogan of "venerating the king and repelling the barbarians." His morally justified leadership gained broad legitimacy among the vassal states, enabling him to defend the realm, protect the weak, and restore order—an achievement that ultimately solidified his political authority.

Later Confucian thinkers systematically developed Confucian orthodoxy by deepening its philosophical foundations. Confucius's grandson, Zisi, for instance, advised the Duke of Lu that true loyalty lay not in blind obedience but in the moral courage to point out a monarch's missteps (Jingmen Museum, 1998). Xunzi (1997) echoed this idea, arguing that scholars should follow the Dao's ethical compass rather than blindly obey the throne. This tradition of principled critique was further developed by Neo-Confucian scholars, who introduced metaphysical concepts such as "the heavenly principle" and "the Supreme Ultimate" which, as least theoretically, offered an ideological counterweight to absolute imperial power, suggesting that even emperors were subject to a higher moral order.

For many scholar-officials, loyalty transcended mere personal allegiance to the emperor—it constituted a sacred commitment to Confucian orthodoxy and its imperatives of ethical governance. While emperors held political authority, they were regarded as stewards of the realm, entrusted with safeguarding the nation's welfare. As such, virtuous emperors received the devoted loyalty and support of their officials, while flawed rulers were met with frank counsel urging a return to moral duty. When emperors ignored such advice, officials faced a stark choice: to resign in protest or persist in remonstration, even at the cost of demotion or death. In this light, the enduring stability of the vast imperial order rested not solely on centralized power but on a shared commitment to a moral tradition grounded in humaneness, righteousness, and harmony (Pan, 2023).

Admittedly, Confucian orthodoxy was never an absolute check on imperial power, nor did all scholar-officials uphold it uniformly. As royal authority became increasingly centralized since the Song dynasties, opportunities for principled dissent diminished markedly. In the face of wayward rulers, Confucian officials adopted divergent strategies: some bartered principles for patronage, and others sought safety in silence, while many defended their convictions regardless of consequence. Even amid the treacherous machinations of court politics—where factional rivalries posed existential risks—numerous ministers maintained unyielding fidelity to ethical governance, earning them perpetual veneration in China's historical narrative.

In fact, scholar-officials throughout history frequently faced the daunting task of political navigation, striving to uphold moral principles while steering through the perilous waters of power. A striking example is Fang Xiaoru of the Ming dynasty, who refused to recognize Emperor Yongle's legitimacy after Yongle seized the throne from his nephew Emperor Jianwen. In retaliation, Yongle ordered Fang's execution along with that of his extended families, associates, and students (Zhang, 1975), demonstrating the extreme cost of unwavering loyalty to principle.

Fang Xiaoru's defiance might superficially appear as blind allegiance to a fallen regime—particularly given Yongle went on to become a capable ruler. Yet on a deeper level, Fang's conviction could also be perceived as a principled act of martyrdom to upholding Confucian orthodoxy. Had all scholars acquiesced to the usurpation, the moral authority of the Confucian Dao, with its emphasis on loyalty toward the rightful succession, would collapse. In this context, someone had to take a stand and become the martyr. Fang's sacrifice, then, was not mere obstinacy, but a powerful assertion of the Dao's inviolable standards. This, nonetheless, did not diminish his colleagues' subsequent service under Yongle, as it reflected another—and arguably even more critical—Confucian imperative: ensuring virtuous governance for the people's welfare. This paradox reveals the tradition's ethical flexibility, where some upheld its ideals through steadfast principled dissent, while others advanced its mission through pragmatic statecraft.

7.1.4 Structural Constraints and Ethical Tensions in Confucian Political Systems

We must acknowledge that Confucian-informed governance in ancient China, like its counterparts elsewhere, had its darker dimensions—ruthless power struggles, systemic corruption, oppression, and persecution. This book does not shy away from confronting these uncomfortable realities. While morality and virtue are typically associated with humanistic ideals and ethical conduct, rulers often employed these very values as tools of political control—even as their own actions directly contradicted them.

Several factors contributed to the more troubling aspects of ancient Chinese politics. Confucianism's hierarchical model could contribute to the oppression of individuals and the systemic marginalization of lower social strata, especially when applied in an absolutist manner. Power struggles, often fueled by intrigue and ruthless tactics, frequently eclipsed the moral ideals Confucianism espoused. Legalist tactics and principles—emphasizing control, punishment, and centralized authority—consistently influenced political practices, at times directly undermining Confucian ideals. Accordingly, persistent gap emerged between the philosophical vision of Confucian virtues and the grim realities of governance. Even among Confucian scholar-officials, many fell short of the tradition's lofty moral standards, succumbing to the temptations of power, self-interest, and corruption.

Yet, these problems did not overshadow positive dimensions of ancient China's politics. Countless scholar-officials remained steadfast in their adherence to Confucian principles, governing with conscientious integrity that often restrained bureaucratic abuses. Some emperors, too, transcended mere realpolitik by actively cultivating Confucian virtues—their reigns frequently correlating with eras of sustained social stability and prosperity. Even when employed strategically, Confucian ideals often served to moderate the excesses of imperial power and its accompanying corruption, thereby reducing the burden on ordinary people. Compared to the harsher, manipulative methods associated with Legalist governance, Confucian moral cultivation offered a more humane and ethically grounded approach to rule.

7.1.5 The Enduring Ethical and Political Order of All Under Heaven

Chinese imperial history is marked by a pronounced cyclical rhythm of dynastic ascent and decline, in which regimes typically began by reconstructing social cohesion and reinforcing political and ethical legitimacy. These policies, underpinned by Confucian moral cultivation and a delicate balance of power, facilitated sustained economic and cultural flourishing. Yet as these stabilizing mechanisms gradually decayed, the polity inevitably faced systemic pathologies: entrenched elite malfeasance, extensive land seizures, fiscal insolvency, and peasant uprisings. Although rulers implemented corrective reforms to forestall decline, institutional inertia ultimately rendered the system incapable of meaningful adaptation, precipitating existential crises that culminated in dynastic collapse, often followed by devastating warfare.

From the ashes of upheaval—whether peasant rebellions, warlord conflicts, or ethnic conquests—new dynasties consistently arose to restore civilizational equilibrium. While imperial houses rose and fell (sometimes across ethnic boundaries), Confucian statecraft endured as the perennial operating system of governance. Conquerors, nobles, and commoners-turned-emperors alike ultimately adopted its framework, recognizing moral cultivation as the indispensable bedrock of sustainable rule. This historical recurrence reflects not cyclical fatalism, but rather a profound political logic: unchecked power invites chaos, while governance tempered by ethical principles, complemented by legal structures, creates the conditions for enduring stability.

The Confucian ideal of All under Heaven provided both the philosophical foundation and moral imperative for China's recurring reunification. This worldview outlined an expanding sphere of ethical responsibility: from self-cultivation to familial harmony, from righteous governance to universal peace—a process simultaneously sequential and coexisted. More than mere political unity, it nurtured a sense of belonging to an expansive, quasi-cosmopolitan community defined not by ethnicity or bloodline but by shared cultural values, ethical commitments, and a holistic order in which individuals thrived through interdependence and coexistence. Ultimately, "All under Heaven" reflects an inclusive ethos—rather than excluding others, it tries to transform "others" into "one of us" (Zhao, 2008). When dynasties fractured, it was this deep-seated belief that persistently drove reconstruction efforts across the vast land.

The All under Heaven system embodied a distinctively Chinese universalism—one that privileged virtuous governance over territorial domination. While all major Chinese philosophical schools embraced the notion of All under Heaven, Confucianism proved uniquely capable of institutionalizing this vision. Legalism's strength in systemic reform and administrative efficiency came at the expense of long-term social stability and harmony; Daoism, though profound in its metaphysical insights, offered limited practical strategies for governing a large empire (Shi, 2018). It was Confucianism's emphasis on social harmony—its mechanisms for conflict resolution, its rituals of mutual obligation, and its vision of graduated moral responsibility from family to the world—that rendered it the most viable philosophical foundation to institutionalize the all-inclusive system and contribute to the recurring national unification.

This cultural-political system shaped a distinctive Chinese cosmopolitanism—one that positioned the Middle Kingdom as civilizational center while actively welcoming all peoples into its moral universe. Non-Chinese groups were offered a place within this ethical framework or even became Chinese, provided they embraced its rituals and values. The concept intriguingly parallels modern world citizenship in its vision of shared humanity and inclusivity yet diverges fundamentally in ethical structure. Whereas contemporary cosmopolitanism insists on equal standing for all, Confucian ethics advanced concentric circles of obligation, extending humaneness progressively from family to community and ultimately to the world. The system's moral genius lies not in flattening hierarchies but in carefully calibrating how care and responsibility radiate outward, underscoring the moral imperative to extend benevolence and harmony across these interconnected spheres while maintaining social order.

The Confucian world system held China's ruling elite to extraordinary moral account, especially the emperor, who, as the designated "Son of Heaven," was responsible for the welfare of the whole Chinese realm. This role demanded selflessness, as, at least in theory, the emperor's duty to his people and "All under Heaven" took precedence over his personal and familial interests. For instance, a virtuous emperor was expected to transcend factional interests and appoint worthy ministers based on virtue and merit, not just personal connections. Scholar-officials were called to uphold this selfless responsibility, called upon to place the common good above their own advancement. This moral imperative often required scholar-officials to stake their positions—and sometimes their lives—in forthright remonstration when imperial actions jeopardized the realm's well-being. While records many deviations from these virtues, the ideal nevertheless functioned as a powerful normative force. It sustained among the educated elite a culture of ethical accountability that transcended generations, transforming Confucian principles from abstract philosophy into lived political responsibility.

Notably, the concept of All under Heaven served as a crucial framework for overcoming ethnic divisions and forging pan-cultural unity. This ideal proved especially vital during the fractious Wei-Jin and Northern-Southern dynasties (220–589 CE), when Confucian literati grappled with the intellectual challenge of reconciling their universalist ideals with non-Han rulership. Then came Wang Tao of Sui dynasty, who made a persuasive defense of Emperor Xiaowen of Northern Wei: Despite his minority Xianbei origin, the emperor's actions—protecting the people during chaos, embracing the traditions of sage-kings, residing within the Chinese heartland, and prioritizing the well-being of the Chinese people—qualified him as a legitimate ruler of China (Wang, n.d.).

This reasoning reflects the inclusive ethos of All under Heaven, which emphasizes unity, interdependence, and the pursuit of collective peace and prosperity for all beyond ethnic boundaries. It laid the foundation for a multiethnic Chinese civilization, where minority groups were not only incorporated but also played a meaningful role in shaping its cultural and political development—an essential factor in dynastic restoration within this broader cultural and political framework.

7.2 Moral Cultivation and Social Transformation

Ancient Chinese society functioned as an "acquaintance society," where interpersonal relationships were deeply embedded in intricate networks of reciprocal obligations and emotional bonds. At the heart of this social fabric was the system of moral cultivation, which served as the enduring adhesive binding individuals to one another in an ethically grounded way. This framework not only guided ethical social conduct but also fostered a profound sense of shared cultural identity. While religious practices persisted, they operated within—and ultimately reinforced—an overarching framework of secular virtue. The system's remarkable persistence across vast territories and millennia of dynastic transitions attests to its unparalleled effectiveness as a civilizational foundation and source of stability.

This enduring influence stemmed from the fact that Confucian-centered moral cultivation was not just a set of abstract ideals; it was the very lifeblood of Chinese society, shaping political institutions, legal practices, cultural life, and daily behavior. This moral framework received strong backing from the state, particularly from the Eastern Han dynasty onward, which launched an empire-wide campaign of Confucian moral cultivation. From imperial edicts to village elders' teachings, Confucian ethics reached every corner of the empire, with its education, ritual, and even commerce resonating to the rhythms of virtue (Liu, 2002).

In this light, this chapter will analyze how state-backed campaigns shaped moral values, reinforced class hierarchies, promoted social mobility, influenced legal codes, and infused Confucian ideals into economic activity. These themes are explored through the broader lens of governance, given the profound interconnections between politics and these social structures in ancient China.

7.2.1 Education, Social Values, and Family Rites

Ancient China regarded moral cultivation as a fundamental responsibility of the state. As articulated by scholar Dong Zhongshu, ancient kings considered the promotion of virtue their highest duty. They established schools across the empire to instill values such as humaneness and righteousness, aiming to build a society where moral cultivation reduced the need for harsh punishments (Ban, 2016). Subsequent dynasties largely followed this approach, reinforcing the importance of moral cultivation in maintaining social order.

Central to the system was the deep interconnection between education and politics. Moral cultivation, rooted in Confucian classics, gained further traction through the state's meritocratic selection processes and civil service examination system, which propelled widespread study of these foundational texts. Ritual promotion also played a vital role. Emperors publicly honored individuals showcasing loyalty, filial piety, and chastity, setting moral examples for others to follow. Ming dynasty founder Emperor Taizu, for example, actively promoted Confucian ideals through royal edicts and teachings, urging his subjects to "show obedience to your parents, respect your elders, maintain peace in your village, educate your children and grandchildren, be peaceful and do nothing evil" (Zhang, 1975).

With government and local sponsorship, a vast network of schools was established nationwide to disseminate Confucian values. From the grand halls of the Imperial Academy to the humble huts of village schools, a chorus of Confucian learning echoed throughout China. Elementary schools were established across the land, introducing children to the first strokes of wisdom. Local schools sustained literacy and moral instruction, nurturing Confucian values that trickled down to the common populace. Official schools focused on rigorous study of the classics to prepare future leaders, while academies offered advanced training for aspiring scholars. Together, these institutions formed a multitiered educational system that sustained a nationwide project of moral cultivation.

Confucian scholars played a crucial role in instilling values and promoting character development, and among them, Zhu Xi stood as a towering figure. His work, *The Collected Commentaries of the Four Books,* later became the standard curriculum for the imperial examinations, ensuring that Confucian teachings reached generations of scholars and left an enduring legacy. Even today, expressions like "the heavenly principle" and "Dao and Principle" (道理) remain part of everyday language, reflecting a deeply rooted moral consciousness in Chinese culture.

Zhu Xi's influence extended far beyond the elite. His ideas permeated family and social life, reaching even illiterate peasants. Moral cultivation through rites and music, embodying the Confucian ideal of living by virtue, served a key function here. Initially reserved for nobility and educated elite, Confucian rites gradually permeated all levels of society and became a widespread custom, thanks to the efforts of Confucian scholars like Zhu Xi. In his seminal work *Family Rites*, Zhu Xi provided simplified rites and regulations for commoners. It covered rituals for major life events, including daily etiquette, coming-of-age ceremonies, weddings, funerals, and ancestral sacrifices, making Confucian values much more accessible. He insisted that ordinary families, like the elite, should observe proper rites to honor their forebears, educate their children, and cultivate moral virtue.

Since then, family rites had become an integral part of daily life for everyone. At the heart of these rites stood the ancestral hall, a symbol of deep respect for lineage and clan honor. This emphasis on love, respect, and ancestry embodied Zhu Xi's concept of rites as both a path to self-cultivation and a means of social transformation, ultimately fostering virtue and refining social customs (Zhou, 2019). Against this backdrop, the Ming and Qing dynasties witnessed a proliferation of family codes, clan rules, and community covenants. Confucianism, while originating from the patriarchal clan system, actively reinforced and enhanced the ethical dimension of that system through the grassroots moral cultivation. This popularization of rites marked a pivotal point, embedding Confucian ideals into daily life and extending well beyond the elite to reach ordinary families. Through the efforts of Confucian literati such as Zhu Xi, Confucianism came to rival the world's major religions—such as Christianity and Islam—not as a religion in the institutional sense, but in its scope and influence across China and neighboring East Asia.

This widespread ritualization of daily life not only disseminated Confucian values throughout society but also consolidated patriarchal authority at the grassroots level. Family rites and clan regulations functioned as a pervasive system of informal governance, reducing reliance on legal institutions by embedding moral domestic discipline within kinship structures. Observance of these norms earned social validation, while violations invited censure from one's lineage. Such practices fostered strong communal bonds and collective responsibility, yet their emphasis on patriarchal control and conformity came at a cost: rigid demands suppressed individuality and personal autonomy. This dynamic echoes Yuval Noah Harari's observation that families and communities, like states and markets, exercise coercive power—shaping lives through tension, control, and at times violence (Harari, 2014).

7.2.2 The Shi Stratum and Social Mobility

Throughout history, the scholar-officials class (shi-dafu) played a central role in both governance and social affairs. Tracing its origins to the lower aristocracy of the Zhou dynasty—a class that included Confucius's own lineage—the concept of shi (士) underwent a significant expansion during the turbulent Warring States period. Ambitious commoners committed to moral cultivation and talented men of humble origin entered its ranks, forging an identity grounded in civility, dignity, courage, and fidelity. A prime embodiment of the "shi" ideal was the Confucian Junzi, the Superior Man who combined virtue with cultivated talent and assumed the responsibility of promoting social harmony.

In Confucian thought, the cultivation of the Junzi represented a central ethical project, an aspiration for individuals to approach the moral perfection of the sage. The shi served as the primary source of Junzi, or alternatively, the Junzi represented the moral ideal to which a shi aspires. These well-educated shi scholars took on diverse roles—as stewards, strategists, tutors, and even warriors—serving feudal lords and contributing to state governance, all while helping to solidify the moral foundations of society. Nonetheless, Confucianism was not alone in this aspiration to shape morally exemplary shi as other schools offered their own models: Daoism sought to cultivate the True Person, one who lives in harmony with the Dao. Mohism aimed to train "shi" committed to universal love and impartial care; and Legalism prized those shi who could strengthen the state through discipline, administrative skill, and strict law.

As Confucianism ascended to a dominance from the Han dynasty onward, the term "shi" came to be largely associated with Confucian scholars—individuals not simply well-versed in Confucian classics, but also receptive to ideas from other schools of thought. Serving as literati, educators, and officials, they pursued self-cultivation while bearing the broader responsibility of cultivating moral virtues and communal flourishing. This multifaceted engagement, combining ethical refinement, political engagement, and artistic expression, deeply shaped the fabric of Chinese culture, leaving a legacy that continues to resonate today.

The term "Dafu" referred to middle-to-high-ranking aristocrats, or ministers, who were also expected to uphold moral cultivation. This commitment to virtue is reflected in Shu Sunbao's rebuttal of another noble's narrow equation of immortality with the mere perpetuation of a family lineage, arguing that true immortality—lasting legacy—was secured through moral integrity, the power to inspire and instruct through words, and meaningful service to the state (Zuo, 2024). These three pillars, rather than aristocratic bloodlines, became the cornerstone of moral cultivation for later Confucian scholars. Thus, "Shi Dafu" transcended its literal meaning, representing esteemed Confucian scholars and scholar-officials who pursued a higher form of immortality through virtue, wisdom, and dedicated service in assisting monarchs to govern with virtue.

7.2.2.1 From Village to Court: The Keju System as Engine of Social Mobility

To curb the growing influence of aristocratic clans and military elites, Western Han emperors fostered a new bureaucratic class: Confucian scholar-officials. Initially recommended for their intellectual merit and moral reputation, these scholars gradually merged with Legalist administrators to form a governing elite (Yan, 1996). Yet this reform inadvertently produced imperial power's own challenge—by the Wei-Jin period, hereditary scholar clans (士族) had emerged, dominating Confucian orthodoxy and monopolizing high offices, thereby undermining the very imperial authority they were supposed to uphold.

In response, the Sui dynasty introduced the imperial examination system (keju, 科举), which, coupled with the spread of printing that made educational materials more accessible, gradually dismantled these hereditary privileges by institutionalizing merit-based recruitment. This transformative mechanism not only enabled unprecedented social mobility but also revitalized governance with capable officials committed to Confucian ideals of virtuous rule.

The Imperial Exam System, a cornerstone of the moral cultivation system, offered a limited yet significant avenue for upward social mobility in ancient China, cutting through otherwise rigid hierarchical boundaries. At its core, Chinese society embraced the belief in the equality of all individuals before Heaven and cosmic principle. This ethos affirmed that social advancement should not be solely determined by birth, but also by moral virtue and demonstrated talent. While hierarchical structures were considered essential for maintaining order and efficiency, mechanisms for upward social mobility, like the imperial examinations, helped uncover hidden talent, alleviate social tensions, and sustain the state's long-term vitality.

Politically, the imperial examination system allowed emperors to centralize authority by replacing hereditary aristocracy with a meritocratic bureaucracy. Through competitive selection, the throne cultivated a class of loyal, capable officials whose primary allegiance lay with the imperial state—not clan or regional power centers. Crucially, since talent is not necessarily heritable, the descendants of scholar-officials frequently declined into commoner status over generations, creating space for new aspirants. This systematic circulation of elites prevented the consolidation of power blocs, sustaining a dynamic equilibrium between the emperor and his civil service—a balance crucial to both imperial authority and state stability.

Perhaps more critically, the system ensured a steady infusion of diverse perspectives and intellectual resources, contributing to the empire's resilience and prosperity. Through rigorous assessments focused on Confucian classics, history, and statecraft, the imperial examination promoted moral education and cultivated a talent pool for virtuous governance. This broadened access increased the likelihood of discovering exceptional individuals, while the inclusion of socially diverse talents sustained political vitality across centuries. Thus, the meritocratic practice not only facilitated social mobility but also cultivated intellectual vigor and a strong ethos of public service among scholar-officials.

7.2.2.2 The Tension Between Talent and Virtue

While both virtue and talent were essential criteria for official selection, their relative importance varied across different schools of thought. Confucianism, for instance, emphasized the primacy of virtue, contending that although talent might bring short-term success, it is moral character that ultimately determines long-term social stability and prosperity. Only when grounded in strong ethical foundations can talent be used to serve the greater good.

That said, Confucianism advocates for a harmonious integration of virtue and talent. Dong Zhongshu, for example, stressed the importance of cultivating individuals who are both humane and wise, ensuring that moral integrity and intellectual capability develop in tandem (Dong, 2012). Ideally, the two form a unified whole, where talent supports virtue and virtue commands talent. Yet when virtue and talent came into conflict, Confucianism clearly prioritized virtue. Morally deficient individuals—no matter how capable—are seen as potential threats to the social order. Without moral restraint, talent can be misused, even becoming a tool for harm. Later Confucians, asserting that virtue is the master of talent, likened a talented but unvirtuous person to a servant who usurps ownership of the house, underscoring their proposal that virtue must govern talent (Hong, 2010).

Other philosophical traditions developed distinctive positions on this question. Mohism emphasized the equal cultivation of virtue and talent, arguing that only the harmonious combination of both qualities could produce concrete benefits for All under Heaven. Daoist thinkers expressed skepticism toward talent-centered approaches, cautioning that overemphasis on human artifice might erode innate virtue and alienate individuals from spontaneous harmony with the Dao. Legalists adopted a decidedly pragmatic stance, prioritizing talent over virtue for its utility in enhancing state power. While not wholly rejecting virtue, they explicitly subordinated moral considerations to the imperatives of political efficacy and administrative control.

Chinese history saw a fluid system of official selection, with rulers strategically emphasizing different combinations of virtue and talent in response to shifting political needs. During periods of instability, pragmatic considerations of administrative and military talent often took precedence over moral qualifications when the two were in conflict. Conversely, during prolonged periods of peace, Confucian emphasis on virtuous character reasserted its primacy in governance. Overall, although Legalism's meritocratic approach left a lasting imprint on governance, Confucianism's emphasis on moral cultivation ultimately exerted a deeper and more enduring influence, fostering an ideal of integrated virtue and ability. This tension between talent and virtue persisted throughout imperial China and continues to resonate in political discourse today.

7.2.2.3 The Development of Scholar-Gentry

The imperial examination system and its emphasis on moral cultivation contributed to the rise of Confucian scholars and scholar-officials—a distinctive elite class dedicated to harmonizing ethical principles with practical statecraft. From this elite emerged scholar-gentry (士绅): a socially influential group of educated elites, retired officials, and local literati landowners who acted as cultural arbiters and intermediaries between the state and local society, bridging the gap between local government and villages. Alongside dafu (ministerial officials), they formed the composite identity of "shi-dafu" (士大夫), a unique synthesis of gentry, scholar, and official. Through their dedication to scholarship, moral cultivation, and public service, these figures helped to shape China's ethical and governance traditions from the highest echelons of power down to village life.

Though not a full autonomy, Chinese rural areas enjoyed a notable degree of self-governance. For millennia, state authority extended only to the county level, with its reach weakening in towns and villages. Local communities were largely overseen by clan elders and scholar-gentry who held moral, economic, and social authority. Unlike traditional landlords, these scholar-gentry—often Confucian-educated landowners or merchants—formed a distinctive elite assuming community leadership. They actively promoted village self-regulation by initiating village and township compacts that emphasized virtuous conduct, personal accountability, civility, and mutual assistance. Many served as moral exemplars by organizing charitable activities, funding infrastructure projects, sponsoring schools, and spearheading local initiatives in ethical cultivation (Fei, 1980).

The scholar-gentry earned authority and influence through their contributions to community welfare. As respected arbiters in village affairs, they were often sought out to mediate disputes, frequently bypassing formal judicial channels altogether. Their dual qualifications as local leaders and Confucian literati or former officials granted them credibility, enabling them to function as crucial intermediaries who could both implement state policies and protect local interests. Such a system functioned as a crucial stabilizing mechanism, mitigating social tensions and preserving cultural traditions across dynastic changes.

Yet the system was not without its critics. Some gentry members, labeled as "local bullies and evil gentry" in contemporary discourse, exploited their privileged positions for personal gain. Such abuses became particularly rampant during the late Qing dynasty, when the authority of Confucian orthodoxy waned and the rural economy collapsed under the influx of Western industrial goods. These shifts eroded traditional checks on landlords, leading to widespread corruption that severely damaged the scholar-gentry's moral standing and contributed to the system's eventual collapse in the early twentieth century.

7.2.3 Moral Critique in Ethical Communities

Traditional Chinese society developed a sophisticated ethical ecosystem that prioritized moral cultivation and social harmony, forming moral communities bound by reciprocal obligations and shared values. These ethical communities were defined not only by teaching, learning, self-cultivation, and mutual influence, but also by collective moral evaluation and critique—practices essential for maintaining social cohesion and moral integrity. Such moral appraisals took many forms, including teacher evaluations, peer reviews, familial admonitions, self-reflection, and public praise or censure. As a result, public opinion and social reputation held considerable weight: those who upheld virtuous conduct were highly esteemed, while those who violated established norms faced social criticism and, in some cases, official punishment.

Moreover, Confucian culture emphasized that a ruler's moral conduct fundamentally influenced the character of their subjects. Emperors, therefore, were held to exacting ethical standards, with serious lapses potentially provoking formal remonstrance from their ministers. This principle of virtuous governance inspired generations of scholar-officials to challenge imperial misconduct, often at great personal risk. Moral accountability also extended throughout the bureaucracy, subjecting officials at every level to ethical evaluation by both peers and superiors. So deeply embedded was this emphasis on upright conduct that most dynasties established Censorates—autonomous oversight bodies tasked with monitoring officials at all levels and, when warranted, admonish even the emperor himself.

This culture of moral critique permeated the broader literati and local gentry of Chinese society. Many of them, whether openly or discreetly, criticized unjust policies, denounced corrupt officials, and passed moral judgment not only on their peers but also on community affairs, regional governance, and even the conduct of the imperial court. A renowned couplet captures this ethos: "The sounds of wind, rain, and study fill my ears; the concerns of household, state, and world weigh upon my heart."[2] China's voluminous historical annals and private jottings also followed this enduring tradition of moral assessment, preserving meticulous records of virtuous deeds and moral failures across all levels of society.

Ethical communities and moral critique were not limited to the elite; they extended deep into towns and villages, where Confucian values functioned as unwritten laws guiding ethical appraisal and social evaluation. Supported by the government, local elites, and clan and family leaders, these principles were enforced through communal mechanisms—public censure of transgressors and honors for those upholding moral norms. Even domestic disputes or street altercations often drew crowds of onlookers who readily offered moral judgments, frequently condemning those who breached ethical norms. This climate of public scrutiny, reinforced by an "onlooker mindset" and moralizing gossip, exerted strong social pressure to conform, making the pursuit of a good reputation a powerful incentive for virtuous behavior. In these local communities, reputation was paramount: moral conduct reinforced social standing, while misconduct could result in shame, ostracism, and exclusion from critical aspects of communal life—including marriage arrangements and other key relationships.

7.2.4 Primacy of Chinese Secular Ethos

Around the world, religions and ethics have profoundly shaped individual worldviews and social structures, making them a central topic in intercultural dialogues about civilizations. China presents an important case, where Confucianism, Buddhism, and Daoism have often been compared to Christianity and other global religions, underscoring the unique nature and functions of Chinese belief systems.

However, unlike many other societies where religion held primacy, China historically prioritized ethical and political culture over organized religion: Secular authorities typically retained dominance over religious institutions, reinforcing a tradition in which moral philosophy, rather than religious doctrine, guided public life. Ancient Chinese ethos of moral cultivation emphasized earthly well-being and moral conduct over otherworldly salvation, perpetuating the predominance of Confucianism and Classical Daoism in shaping societal values. While religion certainly played an important role in social life, its position remained largely secondary. Confucianism, for example, addressed spiritual needs through ancestor veneration and the pursuit of self-cultivation, rather than a focus on the afterlife. Modern scholar Gu Hongming (2004) even posits that the Chinese had no need for religion, as Confucianism, broadly conceived, functioned as a form of religion, fulfilling similar social and spiritual functions as Buddhism or Christianity.

In this context, the Chinese myth of "severing the ladder between Heaven and Earth" can be interpreted as an early symbolic expression of rulers' efforts to limit

[2] This is a renowned couplet from the Donglin Academy in Wuxi City.

religious interference in secular governance. Prior to this symbolic rupture, competing claims of divine revelation through shamans and diviners had led to social confusion and instability. By severing the direct connection between humanity and the heavens, the monarch assumed the role of the sole legitimate intermediary with the divine. This shift enabled rulers to consolidate their authority under the framework of the Mandate of Heaven, now increasingly grounded in Confucian ethics. In this formulation, the way of Heaven and the way of humanity converge through ethical governance.

Consequently, religion became firmly subordinated to the state and Confucian principles. In this worldly oriented culture, even religious Daoist deities were not regarded as ultimate beings but rather as enlightened individuals who had achieved harmony with the Way of Heaven and the Dao. Folk traditions similarly deified historical figures who had benefited the people or embodied specific virtues. Although Chinese civilization, like monotheistic religions, provided moral principles that unify people, provide purpose, and shape behavior, it placed a distinctive emphasis on moral cultivation as a quasi-religious practice—where ethical critique functioned in a role comparable to religious judgment. Rituals, in this context, were less about seeking salvation and more about reporting virtuous governance or righteous deeds.

With a strong centralized state and Confucian ethics jointly shaping the moral landscape, religions such as Buddhism assumed a complementary role rather than functioning purely as a rival. While Buddhism questioned Confucianism's hierarchical social structure and addressed its metaphysical limitations, it also enriched Confucian ethics with principles such as moral and spiritual equality, compassion, and altruism. These additions broadened Confucianism's social focus, incorporating values of universal salvation and enlightenment—clarity of mind and nature. This integration enhanced Confucianism's capacity to promote virtue and transform social customs with greater universality and inclusivity.

7.3 Moral Cultivation in Legal and Economic Systems

In imperial China, where moral philosophy underpinned social organization, both the legal and economic systems functioned within an ethical framework. This perspective underscores the deep penetration of Confucian ideals into social institutions, revealing their foundational role in shaping jurisprudence, economic policy, and communal life.

7.3.1 The Moral Foundations of Chinese Jurisprudence

Unlike the West's emphasis on formal legal systems, ancient China upheld a distinctive social order wherein unwritten moral codes worked alongside statutory laws. Central to this framework was a strong commitment to moral cultivation, informing law enactment and application while also fostering reconciliation and educating those in legal disputes, thus reinforcing social harmony. Although Confucian teachings advocated for humane governance, prioritizing guidance over harsh punishment and viewing legal intervention as a last resort, the legal system remained essential, often working in concert with moral cultivation to promote rule by virtue. Laws were designed not only to enforce social order but also, in many cases, to actively support moral development.

While both ancient Chinese and Western legal traditions aimed to maintain social order and administer justice, their underlying philosophies and institutional priorities differed profoundly. The Western legal tradition, rooted in Greco-Roman foundations, developed with a primary emphasis on codified individual rights and procedural safeguards to promote social justice and personal freedoms. Chinese jurisprudence, by contrast, organized itself around Confucian relational ethics, situating legal obligations within hierarchical social structures that privileged familial duty and collective stability. This distinctive approach transformed law into a means of moral cultivation and communal harmony rather than primarily a mechanism for asserting individual entitlements.

7.3.1.1 The Evolution of Legal Ontology

The foundations of the Chinese legal system drew heavily from a convergence of philosophical traditions—not only Confucian ethics, but also Legalist pragmatism and Daoist principles. Its defining feature was a unique synthesis of three interrelated pillars—the Dao (natural order), law (formal statutes), and virtue (moral conduct)—all working in concert to promote social stability.

Though various Chinese philosophical schools interpreted the Dao differently, all regarded it as the ultimate source of law. The Huang-Lao ideology of the pre-Qin era declared that "the Dao generates law," grounding legal authority in the natural order—a principle that conferred cosmic legitimacy upon Legal institutions and restrained arbitrary power (Mawangdui, n.d.). Legalists likewise argued that all state laws should follow the Dao—understood as the cosmic order or intrinsic human nature—thus providing a metaphysical foundation for just governance. This view parallels the Western concept of natural law, which holds that universal principles of right and wrong are inherent in nature and accessible through human reason, forming the legitimate basis of legal systems.

The Legalist thinker Han Feizi, for example, regarded the Dao as manifest in the regularity of the seasons, which he saw as evidence of its inherent harmony and impartiality (Han, 1999). That said, he advocated for stringent law, as fear of penalties could effectively regulate behavior, aligning with the view expressed in a pre-Qin bamboo slip: "All laws are to guide the people, to remove their lust and remove their evil behaviors, and to make them good" (Shuihudi, n.d.). However, this approach stood in stark contrast to that of Confucius, who argued that while legal deterrence might enforce outward compliance, it would merely produce shameless individuals lacking true moral conscience.

The Han dynasty saw Confucianism established as the state ideology, which then profoundly influenced legal practice. Officials routinely consulted Confucian classics when adjudicating cases, giving rise to a legal tradition known as the "adjudications informed by *the Spring and Autumn Annals*" (春秋决狱). This approach prioritized citing moral principles such as humaneness and righteousness as the foundation for judicial decisions. In cases where legal statutes were vague or lacking, the principles recorded in this classic filled the gaps and could even override existing laws if they conflicted with core Confucian values, serving as the ultimate basis for adjudication. For instance, to uphold virtues like filial piety, Confucian jurisprudence advocated exempting close relatives from punishment for concealing each other's crimes, such as a son hiding his father's wrongdoing or vice versa.

The Sui-Tang dynasties further advanced the Confucianization of law by embedding ethical principles directly into the legal system, marking a significant integration of Confucian rites and formal statutes. The Tang dynasty's "Code of Tang" exemplifies this synthesis, incorporating Confucian virtues and principles into its legal provisions. Moreover, Confucian scholars actively reviewed existing laws, eliminating or amending statutes that conflicted with Confucian principles, moral values, or human sentiments (Huang, 2009). Such an integration not only strengthened Confucian influence within the legal framework but also streamlined judicial processes by reducing reliance on direct citations from classical texts. This approach, along with political considerations and broader social dynamics, profoundly influenced the development of Tang legal codes.

The Song dynasty marked the pinnacle of Confucian influence on law with the introduction of principled judgments (义理决狱) system, which prioritized "the heavenly principle"—a universal moral order—while also considering human feelings (Zhang, 2006). Since Principle was regarded as eternal and governing all aspects of existence, including law, it became the ultimate standard for determining right and wrong, serving as the theoretical foundation for the entire legal framework.

Within this paradigm, the concept of "Dao generating law" evolved into the idea that law emanates from Principle. This approach implied that every law shared a deeper moral truth, guiding judicial decisions to be based not merely on written statutes but on a profound understanding of this underlying principle. It thus empowered officials to move beyond rigid legal codes and seek true righteousness in each case.

The "principled judgments," while rooted in Confucian values, allowed for a degree of flexibility in judicial decisions. One central tenet of this system is to minimize lawsuits. Pursuing social harmony, the official-judges strongly encouraged the peaceful settlement of disputes through mediation, using ethical principles to reach amicable agreements. These scholar-officials also recognized that "the heavenly principle" encompassed "human feelings" and often infused common sense, kindness, and sympathy into their rulings. In line with the principle of humaneness, they sometimes offered leniency for minor offenses, considering extenuating circumstances. However, this flexibility had clear limits—any transgression directly violating core Confucian principles would prompt judges to return to stricter law enforcement (Zhang, 2006). Acts that undermined filial piety, for instance, were met with severe punishment to safeguard the foundation of social order. This harshness stemmed from officials' desire to set a strong deterrent example, aiming to prevent future violations of Confucian moral codes and to establish virtuous societal norms.

This system relied heavily on scholar-officials who donned the dual hats of judge and moral educator. Their deep understanding of Confucian philosophy enabled them to deliver judgments, which not only settled disputes but also conveyed ethical instruction, allowing law to articulate the meaning of virtue and punishment to embody moral lessons. This way, the legal system became a powerful vehicle for advancing Confucian ideals. Yet, the success of this method hinged not only on the officials' intellectual and ethical authority but also on the populace's basic grasp of Confucian values. Only through this shared moral vocabulary could the law serve as a genuine instrument of moral cultivation in society.

In short, the Song dynasty's legal system offered several distinct advantages. First, its emphasis on Confucian moral principles over strict legal formalism granted magistrates discretionary power to adapt rulings to specific cases, ensuring justice could account for contextual nuances where statutes proved insufficient. Second, the system served both punitive and educative functions: by grounding verdicts in shared Confucian ethics, it sought not merely to penalize offenders but to morally reform them, embodying the principle of "governing through virtue." This integration of ethics and law—often described as "strengthening the law with morality"—sought to prevent wrongdoing at its source. Third, by encouraging mediated resolutions rooted in moral persuasion rather than adversarial litigation, the system reduced formal lawsuits, lowering administrative burdens while reinforcing community cohesion.

As might be expected, the Confucian-based legal system exhibited intrinsic limitations. Most critically, the broad and subjective interpretation of "righteousness" or "Principle" enabled morally compromised officials to legitimize unjust rulings or conceal corruption under the guise of ethical discretion. Moreover, the system's reliance on Confucian principles made it incompatible with modernity. As the Qing dynasty faltered and Confucianism came increasingly under criticism, the legal system's ideological foundation crumbled, ultimately leading to its replacement by codified, internationally recognized legal frameworks.

7.3.1.2 The Ethical Substructure of Traditional Law

Ancient China's legal system can be generally characterized as a form of "ethical law," where moral cultivation and social harmony took precedence over strict legal formalism, and where the promotion of ethical values often outweighed strict adherence to codified statutes. Judges drew upon not only state statutes but also the "heavenly principle" and human emotions, aiming to inspire self-reflection and preserve harmony within tightly knit communities. While this approach risked reinforcing authoritarian control by prioritizing moral authority, its grounding in universal ethical ideals and attentiveness to human sentiment may still provide valuable insights for contemporary legal thought—particularly in balancing justice with social harmony.

A central objective of ancient China's legal system was the cultivation of virtue and the promotion of social cohesion, reflected in its prioritization of resolving disputes over adversarial litigation. Deeply rooted in Confucian values of familial, clan, and communal harmony, this system sought to mediate conflicts and discourage litigation. Judgments were guided by "rites"—social norms and ethical principles—with the ultimate goal of transforming immoral behavior, cultivating good customs, and strengthening communal bonds. By emphasizing moral transformation over punitive justice, the system aligned individual behavior with the collective good.

In this light, the Confucian legal system may be seen as a moral transformation of the Legalist system—retaining its emphasis on order and authority while saturating them with ethical principles. Though both philosophies sought social stability, their methods diverged fundamentally. Legalism relied on codified punishments and impersonal regulations, lacking a substantive ethical foundation—a weakness that hastened its decline. Confucianism, by contrast, operated not through rigid statutes but through a deeply rooted ethical framework. Its emphasis on moral cultivation served not only to resolve disputes but also to preempt them, thereby fostering social harmony—a defining purpose of a morally-grounded legal system.

7.3.2 Moral Norms and Economic Practice in Imperial China

Ancient China's economy and society were fundamentally agrarian, with farming serving as the cornerstone of livelihood for most families. It was within this rural context that China's dominant philosophies—Confucianism, Daoism, and Legalism—first emerged. Upon gaining political prominence, they further reinforced and institutionalized the agrarian foundations of the Chinese economy. Confucianism, for instance, played a pivotal role by championing values that idealized agricultural stability, familial continuity, and social harmony. These principles informed government policies supporting farming communities, including efforts to promote population growth, reduce tax burdens, launch large-scale irrigation projects, curtail land concentration among elites, provide disaster relief measures, and offer direct incentives for agricultural production. Yet, this strong emphasis on agriculture came at the expense of commerce, marginalizing merchants and limiting their access to political power and social prestige.

7.3.2.1 Virtue as Market Regulation

Confucian ethics shaped economic activity by anchoring commerce in moral principles, familial obligations, and civic duty. Central to its discourse was the tension between righteousness and profit and between ethical imperatives and private interests. This framework sought to align economic behavior with societal harmony, subordinating individual gain to collective welfare when necessary. While recognizing material prosperity as legitimate, Confucianism unequivocally privileged moral integrity over profit. Neo-Confucian thinkers intensified this stance, emphasizing self-restraint and cautioning that unrestrained desire risked undermining both social stability and long-term economic health.

For Confucians, economy, in its deepest sense, is about ethical human relationships—founded on respect, reciprocity, and ethical conduct—essential to a well-functioning economy. As outlined in *The Great Learning*, the monarch should refrain from empowering unscrupulous individuals to extract wealth from the people, as such exploitation leads inevitably to ruin. Instead of prioritizing material interest, a virtuous ruler should regard righteousness as the true interest (Zengzi, 2016, p. 20). Confucianism thus advocated the integration of moral and economic life, asserting that virtues such as honesty, fairness, and self-restraint formed the true basis of lasting prosperity. Within this framework, virtue held primacy, while legal, economic, and administrative tools were viewed as supportive mechanisms for a society that values virtue (Zhao, 1996).

As a practical philosophy, Confucianism promoted a strong work ethic emphasizing diligence, trustworthiness, and faithfulness while also admiring frugality and denouncing extravagance. This ethic arose from the conditions of a densely populated agrarian society, where people emphasized "no work, no eat." Unbridled luxury was viewed as a threat to social stability and resource sustainability. Thus, Confucianism advocated a balanced—though not necessarily equal—distribution of resources, aligned with individuals' social roles and responsibilities. To further reduce conflicts over competing interests, it upheld the virtue of yielding: the voluntary act of giving precedence to others was regarded as essential for maintaining harmonious relationships and fostering long-term cooperation in business interactions.

This pursuit of harmony culminated in the overarching Confucian principle of equilibrium, which was vital in promoting social stability and sustainable economic development (Chan, 2012). This ideal manifested in concrete economic practices that eschewed monopolistic exploitation in favor of fair exchange and reciprocal benefit. It promoted a mercantile ethic of leaving a margin for others (留余)—a principle designed to cultivate reputation and sustain long-term collective prosperity within one's networks. It also encouraged aiding the vulnerable and fostering mutual support and long-term partnerships, viewing these as moral obligations in business. At the governmental level, sound administration implemented policies that protected agricultural livelihoods through tax relief, checked predatory land accumulation, supported handicrafts, regulated foreign trade for state benefit, and held corrupt elites accountable. These measures worked to mitigate wealth disparities while reinforcing the ethical foundations of economic life.

7.3.2.2 Agrarian Fundamentalism and Merchant Marginalization

Ancient China's imperial system emerged both as a product of its agrarian civilization and as its steward, sustained by a shared ethical framework that emphasized social stability and centralized authority. Several factors underpinned this alignment. The agricultural economy's susceptibility to natural disasters and internal unrest demanded a strong central authority capable of organizing relief efforts and arbitrating regional conflicts. Moreover, essential infrastructure projects such as large-scale water conservancy systems required the centralized coordination of labor and resources. These conditions made philosophies like Confucianism particularly suitable for a centralized government, as they provided ideological tools for unifying and managing large populations while cultivating social cohesion in a cost-effective and morally resonant way.

For most of its history, China's cultural-political system naturally prioritized agriculture, viewing it as the "root" of the economy, while commerce was treated as a supplementary "branch." In agrarian China where food security was paramount, state authorities generally favored farming and often curtailed large-scale commercial activities, even though this policy varied in intensity across dynasties and periods. The merchant class was often viewed as needed yet potentially disruptive—their risk-taking and profit-seeking ethos threatened the established hierarchies and internal equilibrium of China's self-sufficient farming system. Confucian moral philosophy played a key stabilizing role, helping delineate social stations, reconcile competing interests, and maintain long-term harmony conducive to a farming-based economy. Consequently, the Confucian-dominated imperial system inherently restrained commercial expansion, reinforcing the agrarian-centered social order through both ideology and administrative policy.

This explains why the regulation, and at times suppression, of commerce was a recurring pattern throughout much of Chinese history. Despite their often tremendous wealth and influence, merchants occupied the lowest tier in the traditional social hierarchy, ranked below scholars, farmers, and artisans—at least in official ideology. Confucian learning, endorsed by the imperial state, was regarded as the noble route to public service, while business pursuits, despite their profitability, were frequently viewed with suspicion or disdain. Moreover, many governments actively constrained commerce, imposing heavy taxes and occasionally confiscating merchant wealth, all to prevent disruption of agriculture, concentrate royal power, and maintain social stability. Consequently, many merchants had to attach themselves to high-ranking officials, through tributes and strategic alliances, to gain protection and prestige. That said, despite experiencing periods of both restriction and relative freedom, commerce remained a vital part of the Chinese economy, providing substantial tax revenue that governments heavily relied upon.

Against this backdrop, Confucian moral cultivation, which reinforced China's traditional agrarian-centered economy and its preexisting distrust of commercial pursuits, came under growing strain with the ascendancy of an industrial-commercial economy during the late Ming dynasty. The Neo-Confucian creed of "the preservation of Principle and the elimination of desire," originally intended to promote moral self-cultivation, became increasingly restrictive over time. This rigidity often suppressed individual desires and discouraged risk-taking and profit-seeking—traits essential for a vibrant market economy and entrepreneurial spirit—potentially hindering economic transformation during a period of growing commercial dynamism (Liu, 2001).

This, however, does not suggest that ancient China lacked commercial activities. In fact, vibrant trade flourished—particularly during Silk Road exchanges, with lucrative exports like silk, porcelain, and tea driving a booming economy. Yet these commercial developments never coalesced into autonomous market forces. When merchant wealth grew substantial enough to challenge the agrarian-dominated hierarchy, the state systematically intervened to curb its influence. Lacking political representation and social standing, merchants remained vulnerable to state suppression. Thus, despite intermittent commercial prosperity, these structural constraints curtailed the maturation of ancient China's embryonic capitalism, if at all.

That said, portraying Confucianism as wholly antagonistic to commerce is an oversimplification. While often seen as commercially restrictive, Confucian moral cultivation actively shaped traditional Chinese business ethics. Many merchants—particularly those from scholar-gentry backgrounds—practiced what became known as the "Dao of commerce," integrating Confucian values into their enterprises. This approach emphasized long-term relationships built on trust, integrity, quality craftsmanship, and righteous conduct. Guided by Confucian social ideals, successful merchants frequently invested in public goods, funding roads and bridges, establishing schools, and providing famine relief. These practices demonstrate how Confucian ethics fostered a commercial legacy rooted in mutual benefit and social responsibility—principles that continue to inform contemporary business ethics worldwide.

References

Ban, G. (2016). *Book of Han*. China Bookstore.

Chan, S. (2012). Equilibrium in classical Confucian "economy". *Open Journal of Philosophy, 2*(2), 100–106.

Chen, L. (2017). *The core values of Chinese civilization*. Springer.

Chuang Tzu. (2013). *The complete works of Zhuangzi* (B. Watson, Trans.). Columbia University Press.

Confucius. (2016). Analects. In J. Legge (Ed. & trans.), *Confucianism: The four books and five classics*. Delphi Classics.

Dao, X. (1991). *Guanghongming collection* (Vol. 10). Shanghai Ancient Books Publishing House.

Dong, Z. (2012). *Spring and Autumn Annals*. China Bookstore.

Fei, X. (1980). *China's gentry: Essays on rural-urban relations*. University of Chicago Press.

Gu, H. (2004). *Selected works of Gu Hongming*. Changjiang Literature and Art Publishing House.

Han, F. (1999). *Hanfeizi*. Gansu Nationality Publishing House.

Harari, Y. N. (2014). *Sapiens: A brief history of humankind*. Random House.

Hong, Y. (2010). *The unencumbered spirit: Reflections of a Chinese sage*. Kodansha USA.

Huang, Y. (2009). *Han Tang legal system and Confucian tradition*. Yuan Zhao Publishing.

Jingmen Museum. (1998). *Guodian Chu slips*. Cultural Relics Publishing House.

Lao Tzu. (2010). *Daodejing*. In R. T. Ames & D. L. Hall (Eds. & Trans.), *Dao de jing: A philosophical translation*. Ballantine Books.

Liu, X. (2001). An analysis of the history and characteristics of Confucian economic ethics in ancient China. *Journal of Northern Polytechnic University, 13*(2), 64–70.

Liu, H. (2002). Moral education tradition of the eastern Han dynasty and its historical effects. *Qilu Journal, 1*, 48–53.

Mawangdui. (n.d.). *The four classics of Emperor Huang*. https://so.gushiwen.cn/guwen/bookv_46653FD803893E4FC8439EC58097DC19.aspx

Pan, Y. (2023). Preface. In X. Wu & T. Ni (Eds.), *Politics of the Qin and Han dynasties and the Roman empire*. People's Publishing House.

Pines, Y. (2000). "The one that pervades the all" in ancient Chinese political thought: The origins of "the great unity" paradigm. *T'oung Pao, 86*(4/5), 280–324.

Shi, Z. (2018). *The hub: 3000 years of China*. Guangxi Normal University Press.

Shuihudi. (n.d.) *Bamboo slips of Qin Dynasty unearthed from Shuihudi*. https://so.gushiwen.cn/guwen/bookv_46653FD803893E4FA2DB7509965450A1.aspx

Wang, Qi. (2024). The concept of "all-under-heaven" in the Shang and Zhou dynasties and the emergence of the idea of great unification. *Chinese Social Sciences, 11*, 164-183+208.

Wang, T. (n.d.). *The says of Wen Zhongzi*. https://ctext.org/wiki.pl?if=gb&chapter=970459&remap=gb

Xunzi. (1997). *Xunzi*. Liaoning Education Press.

Yan, B. (1996). *History of the political evolution of the scholars*. Beijing University Press.

Yu, Y. (2023). *On heaven and man: An exploration of the origins of ancient Chinese thought*. Linking Publishing.

Zengzi. (2016). *The great learning*. In J. Legge (Ed. & trans.), *Confucianism: The four books and five classics*. Delphi Classics.

Zhang, H. (2019). *A brief reading of Chinese history*. Yuelu Press.

Zhang, L. (2006). Exploration of the "righteousness in determining prisons". *Hebei Journal, 26*(2), 108–112.

Zhang, T. (1975). Six imperial edicts in historical records of Xuanju. In *The history of Ming*. China Bookstore.

Zhao, C. (1996). Characteristics of Confucian economic ethics and its function in ancient Chinese society. *Morality and Civilization, 2*, 32–34.

Zhao, T. (2008). A brief formulation of the heavenly system. *World Economy and Politics, 10*, 57–65.

Zhou, Y. (2019). The qualities of Zhu Zi's family rituals—Based on the perspective of social indoctrination. *The History of Chinese Philosophy, 1*, 70–77.

Zuo, Q. (2024). *The commentary of Zuo on Spring and Autumn* - 24th year of Duke Xiang. China Bookstore.

Chapter 8
Where Nature Meets Culture: Art, Literature, and Architecture

Unlike many analytic philosophical traditions that prioritized logical or theoretical reasoning, East Asian philosophy is notable for its profound synergy with artistic expression—a holistic unity weaving thought, creativity, and nature into an organic whole. Philosophers have traditionally grappled with existential, ethical, and metaphysical questions through aesthetic forms, while artists have infused their works with philosophical inquiry, simultaneously reflecting and challenging societal values. Nowhere is this interplay more vivid than in the Chinese artistic tradition, where poetry, painting, and literature bring abstract metaphysical ideas to life and where brushstrokes and verses alike meditate on moral imperatives and the human ideals. This enduring reciprocity between wisdom and artistic creativity has not only sustained philosophical vitality but also elevated art into a medium of transcendence, ultimately forging a cultural legacy in which the cultivation of goodness is inseparable from the appreciation of beauty.

8.1 Moral Cultivation and Aesthetic Humanities

Chinese thought is deeply embedded in the humanities—particularly literature, art, music, and history—standing in contrast to much of Western philosophical tendency to align more closely with mathematics and the natural sciences. Confucianism, for instance, yielded classical texts of profound aesthetic merit, many revered not only as philosophical works but also as artistic masterpieces. Its ideals of humaneness and harmony are intrinsically aesthetic, expressed through ritual propriety, music, and the pursuit of the golden mean—all embodying an elevated sense of beauty.

Conversely, artistic expression also contributes to Confucian moral cultivation. Confucius (2016a) himself praises the "Shao" music for embodying both beauty

Z. You, Y. Hu, *Philosophy and Civilization: How the Idea of Moral Cultivation Shaped China*, East-West Dialogues in Educational Philosophy and Theory,
https://doi.org/10.1007/978-981-95-5660-1_8

and moral uprightness (3.25). This points to a convergence of arts and philosophy or the harmonization of beauty and goodness. As contemporary scholars have observed, "in Chinese aesthetics, when the pinnacle of goodness is reached, the realm of beauty, in its most fundamental and expansive sense, is also attained" (Li & Liu, 1999).

In Chinese philosophy, artistic expression serves a dual purpose: celebrating beauty and acting as a powerful means of moral cultivation, rooted in the deep connection between ritual, art, and personal transformation (Mullis, 2007). This interconnectedness is well articulated by Confucius (2016a), who advocates that Junzi navigate life by aspiring to the Dao, grounding themselves in virtues, embracing humaneness, while wandering in the six arts of rites, music, archery, charioteering, calligraphy, and mathematics (7.6). For him, artistic pursuits, in line with Confucian principles, are essential for moral development. This fosters a tradition in which Chinese artists do not only refine skills and techniques but also infuse their works with virtues, insights, and moral teachings. Through this, their creations offer more than aesthetic enjoyment—they subtly convey the right attitudes toward life, embodying the humanistic spirit of Chinese art.

While Confucian ethics profoundly shaped Chinese art through their emphasis on moral cultivation and social harmony, the influences of Classical Daoism and Chan Buddhism added profound philosophical depth, enriching the art's ability to cultivate aesthetic sensibility, moral insight, and spiritual awakening. Daoism, diverging from Confucianism's structured formalism, advocates for an organic artistic paradigm celebrating the naturalistic virtues of "nonaction" and spontaneity. Lao Tzu regards spontaneity as the highest virtue and the wellspring of beauty, while Chuang Tzu emphasizes the aesthetic value of individuality, transcendental freedom, and contemplative stillness. These concepts fundamentally shaped China's aesthetic traditions where artistic expressions sought to embody spontaneous harmony between human creativity and the rhythms of the natural world.

Beyond its impact on artistic creation, Daoist aesthetics profoundly shaped the spiritual life of the Chinese people. Daoism's emphasis on art as a path to ultimate freedom and oneness with nature significantly cultivates the perception of beauty as a form of liberation. This connection between beauty and freedom resonates with many Confucian scholars. From the Wei and Jin dynasties onward, Daoist spiritual practices became increasingly woven into the lives of literati. This fusion created a distinctive cultural landscape whereby art served as a vehicle for spiritual exploration, seeking tranquility, transcendence, and freedom from worldly constraints.

Influenced by Daoist thought, many literati and scholars—Confucians and Daoists alike—sought refuge in the tranquil beauty of mountains and rivers, treating these natural sanctuaries as spaces for self-cultivation and artistic inspiration. This contemplative engagement with nature allowed them to refine their character, cultivate moral integrity, and draw inspiration for artistic expression, harmonizing the pursuit of natural beauty with Confucian ideals of good governance and the pursuit of societal harmony. From this confluence of philosophies emerged a rich tradition of artistic creation—works that seamlessly blended Confucian moral aspiration with Daoist spirituality, leaving a legacy across Chinese cultural history.

Daoist aesthetics grounds moral development in a naturalistic foundation through the principle of nonaction—not passivity, but acting in harmony with the natural order, free from coercion or excessive striving. From this principle comes the cultivation of harmony, interconnectedness, and simplicity in both art and life. Artistic expressions that embody these values, in turn, invite moral contemplation, urging individuals to relinquish ego and excess, while attuning themselves to the natural world. By engaging with such art and embodying its ethos of interconnection, one cultivates humility and compassion, deepening both moral integrity and spiritual awareness.

Chinese Buddhism, particularly Chan (Zen) Buddhism, offered scholars another avenue to spiritual self-cultivation, further enriching their artistic experience and moral development. At the heart of Chan lies meditative absorption, a practice aimed at achieving inner stillness and unity with the world. Literati-monks and devout scholars translated this spiritual discipline into artistic creation, embodying Chan principles of simplicity, intuitive insight, and mindful presence. Their works—from ink landscapes to contemplative poetry, from Chan gardens to ritualized tea ceremonies—became vessels of awakened consciousness. More than aesthetic pursuits, these practices nurtured both artistic mastery and boundless compassion, reflecting the profound Buddhist truth of universal interconnectedness.

Fundamentally, Chinese artistic tradition embodies an integration of Confucian, Daoist, and Buddhist worldviews—three distinct yet complementary systems united in their pursuit of harmonizing human existence with cosmic order, blending reality, virtue, and beauty. These traditions, both individually and collectively, shaped China's diverse artistic forms, from poetry and ink painting to music and garden design (Zhou, 2016). In this context, artistic creation and appreciation in ancient China were not merely acts of self-expression but carried a moral responsibility—to cultivate the self and inspire virtue in others. Through aesthetic experience, the arts deepened human understanding, nurtured empathy, and promoted a spirit of harmony and enlightenment. Though not the only force at play, the imprint of moral cultivation on Chinese literature and art has proven both pervasive and profound.

8.2 Artistic Disciplines as Vehicles of Moral Cultivation

Within traditional Chinese culture, the arts and moral cultivation were in a dynamic, mutually reinforcing relationship. Moral principles served as a constant source of inspiration for artistic expression, while the arts, in turn, often provided a powerful and accessible medium for embodying and conveying those very ethical ideals. Notably, artistic creation is not an isolated activity; it often involves different art forms interacting and mutually inspiring each other. Music, for instance, was closely linked with poetry, which in turn shaped the sensibilities and symbolic content of painting, particularly within the literati tradition. This interconnectedness extended beyond aesthetics; nearly all artistic expressions carried the important function of nurturing moral and spiritual development. A prime example is the *Book of Poetry*, a collection of poems—songs and odes performed in ceremonies—valued not just for their rhythm and musicality but more importantly for their ethical teachings. Since the time of Confucius, these poems have been used to promote virtues such as loyalty and harmony, serving as a means for moral cultivation.

It was widely believed that prose should be served as a vehicle for conveying Confucian Dao, the moral truth, thus assigning literature the role of moral cultivation. Likewise, music and painting were regarded as vital ways to nurturing virtue. This emphasis on morality, however, may raise concerns about artistic freedom. To modern art critics, the idea of Art upholding rather than challenging established norms may seem paradoxical. How, then, did these artworks manage to preserve their aesthetic value and creative expression within such a seemingly restrictive framework?

The answer lies in the fact that Chinese art did not equate morality with rigid uniformity; rather, it emphasized harmony and balance, fostering diverse artistic expression while remaining grounded in core societal values such as reciprocity, humaneness, and integrity. A landscape painting, for example, could simultaneously showcase individual aesthetic appeal, convey a connection with nature, and express personal virtue or aspiration—values central to Confucian and other philosophies. Rather than employing heavy-handed moralizing, Chinese artists conveyed ethical messages through subtle symbolism, metaphor, and emotional depth. This indirect approach allowed for diverse interpretations and personal connections, preventing art from becoming stagnant or formulaic. In essence, traditional Chinese art flourished through this delicate equilibrium, with the resulting creative tension producing works that were both vibrantly individualistic and deeply expressive of core cultural values.

8.2.1 Music as Ethical Alchemy

China featured a rich heritage of using music for moral instruction, particularly in the form of ancient court music. Known as music of elegance or music of virtue, this highly formalized and ritualistic genre of music and dance emphasized balance, solemnity, and decorum, conveying symbolic meanings related to cosmology, morality, and the authority of the monarch. Favored by the royal court, it played a central role in state ceremonies, such as sacrifices to Heaven and Earth, ancestor worship, official gatherings, and noble family banquets. Confucian scholars valued this music not only for its aesthetic qualities but also for its role in cultivating virtues such as humaneness and reverence.

Music held an essential place in the formation of Junzi, aiding in the refinement of characters. Its purposes ranged from expressing personal aspirations and fostering inner peace to promoting familial harmony and contributing to collective welfare. As Confucius (2016a) remarked, "It is by the Odes that the mind is aroused, it is by the Rules of Propriety that the character is established, and it is from Music that the finish is received" (8.8). That said, art in ancient China functioned as a vehicle for moral expression rather than being virtue itself. A gentleman's worth was judged primarily by his character and moral standing, not solely by his artistic talents. Likewise, a musician's value depended not only on aesthetic merit but also on the work's capacity to inspire virtue.

In addition, music instruction played a vital role in promoting virtuous social customs. This practice was rooted in the Confucian belief in music and rituals' transformative power, a tradition dating back to the sage kings who employed music and rites to guide people toward harmonious living (Xunzi, 1997). Confucians believed music, grounded in humaneness and empathy, could move the heart, stir emotions, and foster moral development across all levels of society. This moral influence was further amplified by music's natural appeal: people are instinctively drawn to beautiful melodies. When infused with ethical messages, such music could profoundly shape minds. By immersing themselves in these uplifting sounds, individuals might unconsciously or consciously internalize moral values, weaving them into the very fabric of their emotional life.

It is important to note that music for moral cultivation in ancient China did not refer to ordinary music, but to a comprehensive artistic ensemble that integrated poetry, song, vocal performance, rhythm, instrumental accompaniment, and collective dance. In this integrated process, poetry served as the canvas for conveying thoughts and sentiments, song became the expressive language from which the five tones emerged, and the six rhythms orchestrated the harmonization of these tones (Xunzi, 1997). While instruments such as bronze bells, chimes, strings, flutes, and pipes came together in harmonious performances during banquets and ceremonial events, participants engaged in synchronized dances and choral singing, striving for alignment of mind and body, unity within the group, and harmony between humanity and Heaven.

Initially intended to honor spiritual forces and provide aesthetic pleasure and solemnity in early Chinese rituals, this integrated musical performance evolved over time to fulfill a social function: alleviating tensions inherent in ritual hierarchies and promoting communal bonds. A prime example is the performance of Shao music (韶乐), meticulously choreographed to inspire the cultivation of virtue—particularly filial piety and fraternal love—thereby conveying moral values through a sublime aesthetic expression.

The Zhou dynasty institutionalized music education as a comprehensive system for moral cultivation, primarily for the aristocracy and, to a lesser extent, commoners. From the ages 13–15, children began their studies in musical instruments, basic dance moves, and poetry recitation, disciplines believed to revive innate virtue and prevent ethical waywardness. From age 15 onward, the curriculum advanced to incorporate the ethical and linguistic dimensions of music, along with more sophisticated dance techniques, all designed to cultivate virtue, regulate emotions, and refine artistic abilities (Wang, 2018). During this stage, students also examined the broader moral and political functions of music. With the solemn and reverent melodies honoring Heaven and Earth, music was seen as instrumental in shaping the character of a gentleman, affirming social hierarchy, and generating an ambiance of harmony.

However, not all music was considered morally edifying. Alongside the refined and ritualized compositions endorsed by the court, folk and popular music flourished, serving primarily as entertainment. These genres often featured lively, carefree, or even sensual melodies designed to evoke joy, longing, and pleasure. Confucius (2016a), however, expressed reservations about such folk music, warning that the potentially decadent nature of some popular tunes could tempt rulers toward carnal indulgence and weaken their moral resolve (15.11). Despite these concerns, folk music remained widely appreciated, offering a more spontaneous and emotionally expressive form of art that broadened musical landscape of ancient China.

Furthermore, the Confucian ideal of musical harmony evolved through dynamic engagement with Buddhist, Daoist, and diverse regional traditions. This cross-pollination of musical philosophies—incorporating minority, religious, and foreign influences—prevented Confucian musical practice from rigidifying into dogma. This synthesis did not dilute music's moral purpose; instead, it expanded its capacity for ethical cultivation. By integrating multiple aesthetic perspectives, Confucian music gained broader resonance and offered richer, more nuanced avenues for personal refinement and strengthening social bonds.

8.2.2 Brushwork as Moral Exercise

Confucian literati held profound influence on the development of calligraphy and painting, two disciplines that, along with guqin (a seven-stringed Chinese zither) and the strategic game of weiqi (Go), comprised the "Four Arts" essential to a gentleman's self-cultivation. Yet beyond their Confucian framework, these arts absorbed complementary Daoist and Buddhist aesthetic values: spontaneity, individuality, and spiritual contemplation that balanced Confucianism's emphasis on ethical formalism and social order. This philosophical synthesis created a rich artistic tradition that cultivated not only moral character but also aesthetic sensibility and metaphysical insight.

8.2.2.1 The Ethics of Ink: Calligraphic Self-Cultivation

Calligraphy is one of the most revered art forms in China. Its pictographic and ideographic characters, combined with the practiced skill of brushwork, enable calligraphy to embody thought, feeling, and ethical values. This intricate process involves scholars applying brush and ink to absorbent rice paper, meticulously striving for balance of strokes within individual characters and overall compositional harmony. Yet what truly elevates calligraphy is its profound integration of moral and philosophical ideals (Ni, 1999). Confucianism, for example, regarded calligraphy as essential to education, including it among the Six Arts and placing it alongside literature and music in conveying the teachings of the [Confucian] Dao. The disciplined practice of calligraphy was believed to nurture virtues such as humaneness, propriety, uprightness, trustworthiness, and the doctrine of the golden mean.

From a philosophical perspective, Chinese calligraphy epitomized the harmony of form and essence, serving as a medium of artistic expression and a path of moral self-cultivation. Beyond its aesthetic appeal, it was revered as an embodiment of the Dao, mirroring cosmic balance and manifesting the calligrapher's inner world. Each dot, stroke, and composition conveyed not only technical mastery but also the artist's sensibility, strength of character, and aspiration (He, 2006), transforming the art into a disciplined pursuit of virtue, a seamless fusion of beauty and moral integrity.

Accordingly, calligraphy was often used as an important way to train the mind and develop virtues. Effective brushwork required the rectification of the heart-mind, for only righteous mind could guide the hand to produce strokes of integrity and grace. Humility and discipline were equally essential: beauty arose not from flourish but from the quiet application of unadorned lines, mindfully rendered. True artistry in calligraphy also demanded adherence to the golden mean—each stroke balanced, each character poised between expressive individuality and disciplined restraint. Practicing calligraphy in accordance with these ethical principles became more than an artistic exercise; it was a lived process of moral cultivation, an embodiment of inner harmony through outward manifestation.

A masterpiece of Chinese calligraphy was ideally understood to embody harmony—peacefulness, gentleness, and broad-mindedness—thereby representing the highest ideals of the art (Kong, 2020). As the calligrapher lifted the brush, each movement resonated with quietude: hands steady, breath measured, and mind anchored in stillness. Even the preparation of calligraphy ink became a form of self-cultivation. Every slow, circular grinding of the ink stick against the inkstone not only transformed the pigment but also refined the calligrapher's inner state. Patience, focus, and composure, qualities cherished in both art and life, took shape alongside the ink. This meditative ritual nurtured an inner equilibrium, which then breathed life into every stroke upon the page.

It is important to note that calligraphy was often judged as much by the moral stature of its creator as by its aesthetic qualities. The revered Tang dynasty calligrapher, Yan Zhenqing, exemplifies this: while his brushwork was widely admired, it was his unyielding integrity and ultimate martyrdom that cemented his enduring legacy. Students studied his works not merely to perfect their brushstrokes but to commune with his noble spirit. The opposite held equally true—skilled but morally compromised officials like Qin Hui and Yan Song found their calligraphy rejected regardless of technical excellence, their artistic legacy tarnished by their ethical failings. This cultural phenomenon reveals how deeply artistic appreciation was intertwined with moral judgment in China's scholarly tradition.

While Confucian ethics heavily shaped the moral dimension of calligraphy, Daoist ideals of simplicity, spontaneity, individuality, and genuineness also enhanced its aesthetic and ethical development. Many scholars embraced these Daoist principles in both calligraphy and painting, seeing in them a means to balance structure with freedom. This synthesis fostered artistic works marked by distinctive personal styles, as artists believed that nonattachment and spontaneous creation could harmoniously unite individual temperament, moral depth, and beauty. The highest pursuit was a tranquil state of mind attuned to the natural order, allowing brush and ink to move freely and express personal aspirations. Ultimately, the beauty of calligraphy lied not in flashy techniques but in its moral commitment and genuine emotions emerging from the artist's unfettered mind and authentic self.

8.2.2.2 The Cultivational Dimensions of Chinese Painting

Like calligraphy, many traditional Chinese painting served as a vessel for virtues and cosmic harmony, with deeper meanings woven beneath its surface imagery. Figure paintings, for example, went beyond physical likeness to capture the subject's personality, character, and inner spirit. Landscape paintings symbolized the humanistic ideals and contemplative nature of the literati, while flower-and-bird motifs celebrated nature's dynamism as metaphors for human characters, aspiration, and joy. These diverse themes often converged to embrace principled harmony as the supreme form of beauty.

Numerous examples illustrate this deep fusion of art and virtue. Towering mountains and vast snowscapes, for instance, transcended the landscape depictions to symbolize the lofty character of a Junzi steadfastly adhering to principles and unyielding to power. Likewise, the "Four Gentlemen of Flowers"—plum blossoms, orchids, chrysanthemums, and bamboo—were favorite subjects among Confucian literati, each representing a distinct virtue. The plum blossom, blooming in winter's chill, embodied perseverance; the refined orchid, elegance; the unassuming chrysanthemum, humility; and the straight and jointed bamboo, integrity. These motifs served as metaphoric reminders, reinforcing the resolve to uphold Confucian ideals.

Many literati painters held a special fondness for depicting cows and oxen as symbols of diligence, reliability, perseverance, generosity, justice, and a pioneering spirit. In their painting, Confucians scholars endeavored to promote these moral qualities as aspirations for both themselves and others. Such moral instruction through painting was not confined to the male sphere. The renowned painted silk scroll "Admonitions Scroll of the Court Instructress" narrated 12 stories of exemplary behaviors by virtuous court ladies throughout history. One scene, for example, vividly depicted Concubine Ban's refusal to share the sedan of Emperor Chen of the Han dynasty. This gesture expressed her wish for her husband to prioritize state affairs over sensual pleasures, reflecting her own deep sense of responsibility and loyalty.

Admittedly, not all paintings were overtly didactic. Many scholar-officials navigated a "double life," reconciling state duties with a reclusive, contemplative retreat. Their painting and calligraphy embodied personal philosophies, values, and a genuine appreciation for life, often revealing an intimate connection between humanity and nature. However, even these seemingly less explicitly "Confucian" paintings still held implications for self-cultivation. While paintings portraying hermit's life among mountains and rivers may not directly convey Confucian ideals of state service, and at times even subtly critiqued the imperial court, they reflected the scholars' integrity and principled stance against a corrupt officialdom, with mountains symbolizing their Confucian integrity and waters implying their Daoist preference for spontaneity and freedom.

Through this very synthesis, the art reveals the profound Daoist undercurrents in Confucian scholar-artists' lives, enabling them to deepen their spiritual cultivation and momentarily transcend the rigidities of bureaucratic life. Inspired by Chuang Tzu's idea of the "transformation of things" (物化), they blurred the boundaries between human figures and natural things in landscape painting, allowing the two to merge pictorially and spiritually. This approach offered a profound sense of inner freedom, a Daoist expression of the "unity of Heaven (nature) and man," creating a contemplative space that liberated both artist and viewer from the exacting demands of social propriety and political obligation.

A distinctive characteristic of Chinese painting is the intentional use of "white space" to evoke a subtle and infinite aesthetic realm. This technique resonates with Lao Tzu (2010)'s teachings, which emphasized that "being is born from nonbeing" (Chap. 40) and advocate for a state of "ultimate emptiness and stillness" (Chap. 16). It also drew insights from Chuang Tzu (2013)'s aesthetic vision of intuitively grasping the Dao—"getting the meaning but forgetting words" (p. 233)—emphasizing that language cannot fully capture profound truths. In this context, emptiness in art is not a void but a deliberate space left for the viewer's imagination. It conveys meaning beyond the reach of brush and ink (Zhou, 2016), inviting the beholder to actively participate in the creation of beauty and understanding and thus deepening the connection between viewer and artwork.

Inspired by Daoist philosophy, Chan Buddhists embraced the concept of emptiness in painting, seeing it as a path to spiritual awakening—one that transcended material form to reveal the unity of mind, nature, and cosmos. The resulting ethereal imagery cultivated an aesthetic of natural tranquility and profound empathy, allowing Chan monks and scholar-painters to articulate life's ineffable truths. Echoing Daoism, Chan Buddhism celebrated simplicity and spontaneity, epitomized in the notion of "yi-jing" (意境)—an aesthetic realm where inner contemplation merged with external nature to embody the harmony of Heaven and humanity. This poetic dimension defied literal interpretation; it demanded to be intuitively grasped rather than analytically dissected (Lai, 1992). The true power of this tradition lay in its capacity to forge a shared, wordless dialogue between creator and beholder—a testament to the enduring profundity of Chinese ink art.

Buddhist ethics significantly expanded the moral and spiritual vocabulary of Chinese art by harmonizing with Confucian virtues like filial piety and loyalty. This synthesis found profound expression in Buddhist sculptures and narrative murals—particularly at Dunhuang's Mogao Caves—which functioned as both spiritual guides and embodiments of ethical ideals. Scenes of filial devotion, royal loyalty, moral restraint, karmic justice, and postmortem judgment adorned the cave walls, transforming abstract principles into unforgettable imagery. One notable example is the mural of the Nine-Colored Deer, which warns against ingratitude and wrongdoing while extolling the virtues of justice and compassion. Equally poignant is the

Sama Jataka, depicting the saintly youth Sama tenderly caring for his blind hermit-parents, even while mortally wounded by a hunter's arrow. This heartrending tableau elevates filial piety to spiritual heroism, portraying self-sacrifice not as mere obligation but as transcendent grace.

In short, the convergence of Confucian, Daoist, and Buddhist thought profoundly shaped Chinese art. United in their pursuit of harmony between humanity and the cosmos, these philosophical traditions elevated artistic practice into a mode of moral and spiritual cultivation, nurturing holistic intuition, compassion, and moral awareness—qualities that came to define the essence of Chinese calligraphy and painting.

8.3 The Role of Literature for Moral Cultivation

At its core, ancient Chinese literature sought to illuminate the Dao through expressions of harmony and moral virtue. This belief found its most eloquent expression in literary theorist Liu Xie's seminal work, *The Literary Mind and the Carving of Dragons*, where he argued that sages conveyed the [Confucian] Dao through their writing, unveiling its timeless principles (Liu, 2015). Far more than mere artistry, literature served as a conduit for moral edification—reinforcing Confucian virtues, refining individual character, and nurturing social cohesion. This ideal transcended genre boundaries, infusing poetry, fiction, and drama alike, each reflecting the inseparable bond between literary expression and the cosmic-moral order of the Dao.

Within the strong moral tradition of China, even elementary literacy textbooks were explicitly designed to foster moral cultivation. These primers, often rooted in Confucian teachings, enabled children to acquire literacy and ethical values simultaneously. A prime example is the renowned *Three-Character Classic*, which conveys foundational virtues—filial piety, respect, diligence, and social harmony—through concise, rhythmic chapters. Its poetic structure and musical cadence transformed reciting into not merely an intellectual endeavor but also an artistic and moral experience.

Such primers rested upon the deeper cultural premise that Chinese written language itself embodies moral implications. In effect, the pictographic nature of Chinese characters uniquely integrates meaning, aesthetic grace, and ethical resonance, making literature a potent vehicle for moral edification. Their ideographic structure, with its intuitive expressiveness and calligraphic artistry, naturally lends itself to articulating moral values, evoking an emotional affinity for virtue and propriety. Ultimately, from classical poetry and idiomatic expressions to operatic librettos and canonical texts, this enduring tradition transmits ethical ideals through a seamless fusion of philosophical depth and artistic beauty.

8.3.1 The Transformative Power of Poetic Tradition

Poetry held an esteemed place in Chinese culture, serving not merely as an art form but also as a powerful instrument of moral transformation. Steeped in Confucian ideals, the practice of poetry cultivated introspective self-reflection and nurtured collective social harmony. The *Classic of Poetry* (诗经) leads this tradition, its verses extolling virtue, denouncing vice, and shaping moral customs. This classical poetry, along with other poems, became foundational texts—studied in schools, recited in homes, and internalized by scholars, officials, and commoners alike. Their profound influence gradually permeated Chinese thought, language, sensibility, and cultural expression, leaving an enduring imprint on the nation's intellectual and social identity.

Poetry's special power to awaken emotions and elevate the spirit rendered it indispensable to self-cultivation. Through the melodic recitation of virtuous verse, readers could absorb ethical teachings, nurture compassion, and hone essential virtues like humaneness, integrity, and moral courage. The art of poetic composition offered a space for self-examination, enabling composers to gauge their deepest thoughts and actions against Confucian or Daoist ideals, while giving voice to their innermost sentiments, fondness, and aspirations. Through masterful employment of diction, metaphor, and symbolic imagery, poets gave artistic form to their ethical convictions, grappled with philosophical quandaries, and expressed their visions of cosmic harmony. The act of creating or appreciating poetry thus demanded not only intellectual engagement but also emotional attunement to its underlying truths—prompting profound reflection on one's relationship with others, society, and the natural world.

Poetry was long regarded as a vital force for promoting good governance. In courtly settings, it conveyed political ideals, offered ethical counsel to rulers, and celebrated virtuous conduct. Recognizing its power to influence public opinion and shape cultural values, the state elevated poetry into an indispensable element of statecraft and moral leadership, even leading to its inclusion in imperial exams across many dynasties. As a powerful form of social critique, poetry provided scholars with an elegant means to eulogize virtuous acts, criticize malfeasance, and advocate for principled reform. The revered "Sagacious Poet" Du Fu exemplified this tradition: his immortal verse often voiced concern for the common people and reminded rulers of their ethical duties, urging governance rooted in virtue and righteousness.

8.3.2 Ethical Edification in Classical Novels

Chinese novels emerged from a vibrant heritage of legendary tales and oral traditions that flourished during the Tang, Song, and Yuan dynasties. By the Ming and Qing periods, educated elites increasingly embraced novel writing, refining these narratives into both succinct anecdotes and sprawling epics. This literary evolution paralleled the ascendancy of Neo-Confucianism's School of Principle, which championed fiction as a vehicle for ethical edification. Many scholar-authors crafted tales that celebrated Confucian ideals while exposing moral failings, employing compelling narratives to provoke readers' self-examination and inspire virtuous actions.

The use of novels for moral instruction echoes the tradition of rites and music, where ceremonies and melodies cultivated ethical values and proper conduct. Novels inherited and extended this spirit, aiming to shape behavior through engaging narratives (He, 2003). Many Confucian-minded literati, keenly aware of storytelling's strong influence on the broader public, saw fiction as a dual opportunity: both to captivate audiences and to impart moral instruction. They harnessed the innate appeal of narrative artistry, transforming entertainment into a vehicle for ethical cultivation that could reach beyond elite circles to shape society at large.

In their literary works, the novelists subtly wove traditional virtues like loyalty, filial piety, and righteousness into their characters. By vividly contrasting unwavering loyalty with treacherous betrayal, they created stories with strong moral resonance that helped shape readers' values. Many writers openly championed the novel's capacity for ethical transformation. The celebrated vernacular author Feng Menglong, for instance, praised fiction's "alchemical power" to refine readers' character, asserting that compelling stories could transmute cowardice into courage and moral weakness into virtue. He believed that novels might even surpass canonical texts like the *Analects* or *Classic of Filial Piety* in their ability to move hearts and reform conduct (Feng, 2018).

Consider the renowned classic *Romance of the Three Kingdoms*, an epic tale rooted in history. More than just a thrilling tale of warfare and strategy, the novel served as a rich tableau of Confucian virtues and villainy. Each main character embodied a distinct moral quality: Liu Bei, the ruler of Shu, embodied humaneness; Guan Yu, his general, personified loyalty and righteousness; and Zhuge Liang, the master strategist, exemplified wisdom. In contrast, the brilliant but Machiavellian Cao Cao stood as the antithesis of these ideals. The novel also illustrated how secondary virtues, when fully cultivated, can lead to the attainment of ultimate humaneness: Guan Yu attained this supreme virtue through unwavering righteousness, just as Zhuge Liang achieved it via consummate wisdom.

The novel's central narrative revolved around the intertwined stories about Liu Bei and Cao Cao, symbolizing a moral conflict between good and evil. Among the rulers of the Three Kingdoms, Cao Cao of "Wei" benefited from favorable timing and Sun Quan of "Wu" from strategic geography, while Liu Bei of "Shu" prevailed through moral leadership and the resulting harmony among his people. This thematic structure closely echoes Mencius (2016)'s teaching that the support of the people outweighs geographical advantage, which itself surpasses mere timing (2B:1). Such a value orientation was deeply ingrained in Chinese culture long before the novel's creation. As the Song dynasty literatus Su Shi noted, even children instinctively sympathized with Liu Bei's trials and rejoiced at Cao Cao's defeat—revealing the tale's enduring power to shape moral orientation (Su, 2013).

From loyal warriors to righteous outlaws, Chinese folk novels teemed with inspiring tales of virtue and valor. The *Biograph of Yue Fei* and *Generals of the Yang Family*, for instance, portrayed patriotic generals whose characters epitomized the Confucian devotion to sovereign and state service. Even the rebellious heroes of *Water Margin*, often likened to Robin Hood's band, justified their rebellion against corrupt bureaucrats as ultimate fealty to both emperor and cosmic justice, claiming to execute Heaven's Will when earthly authority failed. Moreover, the tradition also honored incorruptible magistrates who administered impartial justice, alongside wandering swordsmen who rectified societal ills—often collaborating to resolve intricate legal cases. These legendary narratives popularized the ideal of righteousness and reinforced the readers' faith in moral order and their aspiration for a just world.

Many novelists explored life's journey through a religious lens, weaving together Buddhist concepts—compassion, karma, reincarnation, and moral retribution—with Confucian virtues like loyalty, filial piety, and righteousness, often portraying unrighteous behavior as leading to karmic suffering. These stories often served as cautionary tales, warning against the unethical pursuit of worldly pleasures such as wealth, beauty, and vanity, while embodying the Buddhist teachings on impermanence and the Daoist concept of "nonbeing" (Zhou, 2015). By exposing the fleeting nature of material pursuits and the inevitability of karmic justice, they discouraged unethical behavior, urging readers to rise above excessive desire and cultivate virtue instead.

However, employing novels for moral cultivation had its drawbacks, as the imperative to preach ethical values could at times constrain artistic freedom. When authors prioritized moral instruction over creative storytelling, their works often became narratively formulaic: virtuous characters were rewarded, while wrongdoers met punishment, yielding predictable plots and one-dimensional characters who functioned primarily as vessels for virtues or vices (Wang, 1995). This rigidity deprives the narrative of the psychological ambiguity that often drives reader engagement. In effect, the most captivating novels in ancient China achieved a delicate balance, conveying moral messages while weaving compelling narratives. Some even subverted expectations, by featuring rebellious themes that challenged conventional norms. These exceptional works demonstrated the power of storytelling to inspire both moral reflection and artistic brilliance.

8.3.3 The Chinese Opera as Performance Pedagogy

Chinese opera, a captivating and accessible art form, played a vital role in disseminating moral values, especially among the lower classes. In ancient China, where widespread illiteracy and dispersed rural communities made formal schooling a rarity, opera became a vital vehicle for ethical instruction. Performances at festivals and village gatherings transformed stories into visceral lessons, exalting righteousness and exposing corruption. With its vivid characters, dramatic plots, and emotional resonance, opera transcended mere entertainment, emerging as one of the most effective tools for instilling moral values in the broader populace.

For instance, tales like *Romance of the Three Kingdoms* and *Water Margin* captivated the commoners primarily through opera performances and oral storytelling. These dramatic adaptations became cultural conduits for transmitting Confucian values, celebrating loyal ministers, filial sons, and chaste widows, while promoting ideals such as altruism and service to the state. By immersing audiences in these vivid plots, operas helped distinguish integrity from corruption and offered moral guidance on how to be an honorable person, a faithful friend, and a devoted family member.

Confucian playwrights played a pivotal role in Chinese opera's transition from lighthearted entertainment to a powerful tool for moral cultivation. Early opera forms, often characterized by witty banter and vulgar amusement, fell outside Confucian propriety, making them unsuitable for moral instruction. It was during the late Yuan and early Ming dynasties, when the Study of Principle began to influence artistic expression, that opera underwent a significant shift toward didactic purpose. Recognizing its educational potential, many Confucian playwrights infused their works with Confucian values, crafting narratives that honored paragons of virtue and exemplified ethical behavior.

Ancient Chinese rulers at the time, recognizing the potent influence of folk opera on social values, actively sought to regulate these performances. They issued decrees prohibiting the portrayal of emperors, concubines, loyal ministers, and virtuous individuals in operas unless these performances explicitly promoted Confucian virtues (Wang, 1982). This policy channeled playwrights toward specific themes, with many embracing Confucian ideals willingly, while others complied with government mandates out of practical consideration.

Unlike literacy-dependent poetry and literature, folk opera transcended this barrier, using its compelling stories and performances to impart moral values across all social strata. These dramatic narratives reinforced a fundamental notion that virtue begets reward while vice invites ruin. As audiences watched characters eventually reap the consequences of their actions—heroes triumphing through righteousness or villains encountering poetic justice—they absorbed society's ethical codes in the most direct yet impressive way. This so-called "moral cultivation on high stage" played a significant role in shaping the moral customs of the community.

The power of Chinese opera extended far beyond its narratives. Its artistic synthesis—the interplay of haunting melodies, stylized movements, vibrant costumes, and poetic lyrics—transformed moral instruction into an unforgettable sensory experience. This multimedia approach endowed ethical teachings with extraordinary persuasive power: where philosophical texts might alienate, the opera's artistry made Confucian virtues resonate deeply across diverse social backgrounds, acting as a unifying force. Consequently, core principles such as "loyalty and filial piety," "three principles and five rules," and "sacrificing one's life for righteousness" became creeds adopted by both the upper echelons and the lower classes alike.

8.3.4 Literary Dissent and Its Challenge to Ritual Orthodoxy

Paradoxically, the very narratives reinforcing orthodox moral values in novels and operas also sowed seeds of artistic insurrection, as the human drive for individuality and creative expression inevitably clashed with the prevailing emphasis on conformity. Visionary authors and playwrights—sometimes overtly, sometimes subtly—began to push against rigid ethical constraints. Their narratives celebrated self-expression, championed intellectual freedom, and gave voice to previously taboo subjects: intimate desires, romantic passion, and personal fulfillment. This rebellion did not signal an abandonment of morality, but rather its evolution—a demand for ethical frameworks capable of embracing the full spectrum of human experience while preserving social harmony.

This artistic rebellion in Chinese literature may, at least partially, be ascribed to the philosophical transformation during the Ming and Qing dynasties. In contrast to the dominant "Study of Principle" which emphasized a rigid and normative path, the rising influence of "Study of Mind" in the mid-to-late Ming dynasty granted people more freedom and flexibility. This intellectual shift was further bolstered by ontological development in the late Ming and early Qing, which introduced a fresh perspective on human desires.

For instance, philosophers like Dai Zhen (1982) argued that desires are not inherently negative; rather, it is their excess that creates problems. Desire can be rational if they align with Principle, allowing for a balance of emotion, neither excessive nor deficient. This philosophical evolution found its expression in literature, which began to move away from strict ethical constraints toward a greater tolerance and harmonious integration of human needs and ethical considerations. Amid such a backdrop, themes of individuality, emotional expression, and even romantic love flourished.

Take *the Peony Pavilion*, for instance. The Ming dynasty romantic tragicomedy audaciously explored the legitimacy of human desires, intricately weaving a compelling tale of love, sexual passion, and youthful rebellion, all expressed in strikingly beautiful language. The play marked a departure from the puritanical restraints of Cheng-Zhu Study of Principle, critiquing its suppression of natural human needs. Embracing the concept of free love, it celebrated the uninhibited passion and desire, offering a vivid portrayal of the romantic experience that deeply resonated with audiences.

The Ming dynasty anthology "Stories Old and New" stands as a particularly daring example of this literary rebellion. Defying conventions, its narratives ventured into ethically contentious territory—premarital intimacy, marriage without parental consent, extramarital affairs, and even widow remarriage. These subjects were not merely presented but often viewed through a surprisingly tolerant and empathetic lens, reflecting a growing sense of individualism that began to challenge the rigid social norms and moral codes of the time. The female characters, in particular, challenged traditional stereotypes. Gone are the submissive, demure figures; in their place stand independent, self-directed women who pursued love with courage and passion. These women, in confronting the traditional demands of chastity and arranged marriages, embodied a yearning for romantic autonomy and the courage to challenge some of the restrictive ethical codes imposed by Confucian orthodoxy.

The rebellious spirit of this artistic movement is brilliantly captured in *Dream of the Red Chamber*, widely regarded as one of the greatest masterpieces of Chinese literature. The novel revolved around the emotional journeys of a young aristocratic man and a group of young aristocratic women who yearned for personal freedom, love, and individuality while chafing against the constraints of their social class. Similarly, *Journey to the West* featured the mythical monkey king, renowned for his audacious rebellion against the Heavenly Court. His defiance can be interpreted as a subtle critique and satire of the author's era, reflecting a desire to transcend the oppressive political system and rigid social hierarchy.

It is important to recognize that Chinese literature was not solely defined by Confucian norms; it also explored a wide range of themes and engaged in bold social commentary. Chinese poetry, for instance, while often addressing moral concerns, expressed personal feelings, aspirations, and a deep appreciation for nature's beauty. Similarly, novelists and opera playwrights navigated the complex interplay between moral instruction and the exploration of personal fantasy, individual concerns, and self-expression, creating a rich and varied artistic landscape. Ironically, some of the most significant literary achievements of these periods emerged from these explorations of rebellion and individualism.

That said, the dynamic between moral instruction and literary rebellion in Chinese fiction often yielded narratives of remarkable complexity and ethical nuances. Take *Stories Old and New*: while its tales of forbidden passion pushed boundaries, they typically concluded with cautionary, orthodox moral lessons. This creative tension produced works that simultaneously acknowledged love's compelling force and warned against its unrestrained pursuit. Writers skillfully employed the mechanism of karmic retribution—demonstrating how indulgence in sensual excess inevitably led to downfall—thus exploring transgressive themes while ultimately reaffirming stringent ethical norms. Through this delicate balance, they expanded literature's imaginative and provocative horizons without undermining its moral foundations.

The rigid moral demands of Confucianism, paradoxically, promoted folk-art forms that playfully danced along the edges of propriety—not to dismantle tradition, but to entertain through irreverent humor. Take comic cross talk (相声), for example. This popular form, rich in witty banter and verbal agility, delighted in poking fun at social conventions, gently stretching—but rarely breaking—the boundaries of acceptable discourse. Performers might flirt with risqué themes like marital infidelity or turn filial piety into farce, all while preserving a veneer of plausible deniability. A classic routine involved one comedian declaring himself another's father—a line that, delivered with perfect timing, could reduce audiences to tears of laughter while leaving the social order fundamentally intact.

This brand of humor, though perhaps startling to outsiders, amused Chinese audiences, functioning as a social pressure valve in a culture governed by strict hierarchies and moral codes. Through exaggerated mockery and absurd subversions, comedians created a shared space where audiences could momentarily entertain taboo thoughts without feeling guilty. Yet, by making their subversions audacious and absurd, comedians may have inadvertently reinforced the very norms they seemed to undermine—a kind of reverse psychology, with laughter acting as a subtle reminder of the existing social order.

8.4 Architecture as a Silent Moral Cultivator

Architecture is more than mere construction; it is a distinctive art form that fuses functionality with cultural meaning. Like painting that speaks through pigment or music that resonates in melody, architecture communicates through layout, spatial form, and symbolic design. Beyond providing shelter, built environments become silent teachers of morality, where the interplay of light, balance, and proportion subtly shapes behavior and nurtures virtue through lived experience.

Ancient Chinese architecture exemplifies this idea, with its history deeply intertwined with the evolution of Chinese civilization. Building designs served practical needs while also embodying deep humanistic and ethical values. Influenced by philosophies such as Confucianism and Daoism, these structures embodied abstract concepts like "unity of Heaven and man," "rites and music," and "moral cultivation" through their design and function.

As a result, traditional construction achieved a harmonious balance between goodness and beauty, solemnity and individuality, as well as practicality and innovation. Design principles, spatial layouts, and even the names of architectural elements became metaphorical expressions of virtues such as ritual propriety, respect for hierarchical order, humaneness, the golden mean, harmony, simplicity, and spontaneity. In this way, traditional Chinese architecture functioned as a silent educator, subtly imparting moral lessons through residents' daily engagement with its spaces and rituals.

8.4.1 Ritual Architecture's Moral Grammar

Traditional Chinese architecture was known for its role in promoting ritual propriety, signifying a refined and graceful hierarchy. Nowhere was this more masterfully realized than in the Forbidden City, where every architectural element conspired to manifest the emperor's supreme status and absolute authority. Upon entering its gates, one stepped into a world of axial symmetry—an architectural language symbolizing solemnity, balance, and harmony. Imposing structures, vibrant red and yellow hues, expansive courtyards, and intricately carved ornamentation collectively conveyed the emperor's unrivaled dominion over the realm, inspiring awe and reverence. The spatial order such as the stratified layout and the south-facing orientation of the throne halls subtly embodied Confucian rituals, embedding hierarchy and discipline into the very structure of imperial life.

The ritual system influenced even commoner dwellings. Whether in northern courtyard houses or southern-style residences, the layout of these dwellings reflected the hierarchical structure of patriarchal families and conformed to established ritual norms. Elements such as doorways, walls, room placement, roof design, and pedestals all symbolized familial relationships and hierarchy, embodying principles like "the order of seniority" and "distinctions between genders." Within these domestic spaces, rooms in the northern section were regarded as more prestigious than those in the south, while eastern rooms held higher status than their western counterparts.

The most revered space in the residence is the central hall, positioned along the central axis. Serving as a ceremonial structure, it housed spirit tablets representing "Heaven and Earth, the monarch, ancestors, and teachers" and was used for receiving distinguished guests and conducting important family rituals. The main living room, also aligned with the central axis and facing south, was reserved for the family's elders and most respected members. Flanking it on either side along the north-south axis were the symmetrically arranged "two wing rooms," designated for the younger generation. The front hall functioned as a venue for formal social interactions, where the male head of the household received his male guests. The back hall, in contrast, provided a more private space for female family members to socialize and entertain female visitors. This spatial arrangement reflected the traditional division of labor within the family: men managed external affairs and business, while women oversaw domestic responsibilities. It is important to note, however, that this layout represents a prevailing architectural pattern rather than a rigid norm, with regional and contextual variations across different districts.

While this housing arrangement underscored order and distinctions between seniors and juniors, husbands and wives, and superiors and subordinates, it was also designed with harmony and adaptability in mind, balancing "heavenly principles" with social affinity and practical needs such as comfort, convenience, and connectivity. The courtyard, a hallmark of traditional Chinese homes, exemplified this balance. As a central space open to the sky yet enclosed by surrounding rooms, it embodied the Chinese ideal of unity between openness and enclosure. This design fostered warmth, connection, and harmony, thereby promoting close-knit family relationships and facilitating interaction within an ordered, welcoming environment.

The ancestral shrine hall, or extended family lineage hall, stood as a powerful symbol of clan authority. Following the principle of "left for ancestors, right for community," it typically located at the village center or on its left side. Primarily, the hall served as a venue for ancestor worship, clan gatherings, family rituals, and even the enforcement of family discipline, serving to strengthen lineage identity, enhance clan cohesion, and uphold traditional hierarchies and patriarchal values (Qin, 2003). Beyond the ancestral hall, other forms of traditional local architecture also contributed to the transmission of Confucian moral values: The Temple of Confucius served as a hub for education and veneration of the sage's teachings. Commemorative archways honored individual virtue and public achievement, while stele pavilions housed stone tablets engraved with stories of exemplary figures, serving as permanent reminders of key Confucian virtues.

Modeled after imperial and noble ancestral temples, the clan halls of Chinese villages served the same primary function: ancestor veneration. While their scale and purview differed, both operated as quasi-religious ceremonial centers anchoring familial and spiritual life. Yet, unlike ordinary clan rituals, imperial ancestral ceremony carried public significance. The emperor, bearing responsibility for the entire realm, conducted ancestral ceremonies imbued with the weight of "public sacrifices." This reflected the Confucian belief that the royal power was a "public utensil" entrusted to him, rather than a personal possession.

8.4.2 Harmony in Traditional Chinese Architecture

For the ancient Chinese, harmony was not just a supreme virtue but a universal principle embedded in the very fabric of reality. This worldview was vividly expressed in their architecture, where buildings were conceived as microcosms of the universe. Proportion, symmetry, and interconnectedness were essential in shaping harmonious living environments, reflecting the belief that balance and order were vital to a well-lived human life.

For example, the iconic symmetrical layouts of palaces and residences symbolized impartiality, moderation, and equilibrium. The Forbidden City exemplifies this ideal: its strict symmetry conveys a sense of harmony and balance, reflecting the envisioned order of the universe. Even the names of its three principal palaces—"Supreme Harmony" (太和), "Central Harmony" (中和), and "Preserving Harmony" (保和)—underscore the guiding principle. In this context, architecture transcends mere function and aesthetics, emerging as a profound ethical symbol rooted in Confucian cosmology.

This philosophy of harmony found equally profound expression in the deliberate humbling of architectural scale to suit a building's true purpose. Confucius (2016a) explicitly criticized ostentatious palaces perched atop towering terraces as symbols of hubris. Instead, he advocated simplicity and restraint, urging rulers to reduce the size and cost of such structures in favor of prioritizing the people's well-being (8.21), an approach reflecting both the ruler's benevolence and the state's commitment to social harmony. Confucius's view resonated with Daoist principles of humility, frugality, and living in accordance with nature, together contributing to the ideal of designing buildings with appropriateness and moral intent—not by excess, but by ethical and practical fitness.

These principles greatly shaped the design of ancient Chinese buildings. Although grand structures existed, most buildings were modestly scaled, avoiding excessive grandeur that could result in discomfort or alienation from the natural world. Instead, architectural designs prioritized practicality, aligning size and height with the daily needs of the people. Ultimately, this measured approach embodied the ideal of concord between Heaven and Earth—a balance grounded in humility and believed to foster the flourishing of all life.

Chinese geomancy, commonly known as feng shui (风水), embodied a profound understanding of architectural suitability. Rooted in the principle of harmony between humans and the world, "feng shui" practitioners evaluated auspicious locations and harmonious structural designs to optimize the flow of "qi," the vital cosmic energy shaping destiny. Key to this practice was identifying "dragon veins," or sites with potent energy currents, thought to enhance prosperity and success. Equally crucial was the seamless integration of structures with their natural surroundings. Classical feng shui advocated moderation and balance, emphasizing that buildings should be proportioned and positioned to harmonize with—rather than dominate—their environment. For example, sharp corners pointing toward neighboring homes were avoided, as they were believed to generate negative energy that disrupted communal harmony, reflecting the ideal of cultivating stability, peace, and prosperity.

8.4.3 Ornamentation and Garden Design as Moral Pedagogy

Ornamentation and decorative features in and around architecture were often intentionally designed to reflect the values of the residents. For example, the shapes and forms of furniture frequently conveyed ethical messages: square tables symbolized "squareness and uprightness," representing a commitment to moral integrity, while seating arrangements reinforced social hierarchy and relational order. At a rectangular table, placement signified rank, with the head position reserved for the most esteemed individual, mirroring familial and societal hierarchy. In contrast, a round table symbolized unity, fostering harmony and collective spirit among those gathered.

This concept extended to ritual vessels and decorative objects, seen as tangible reminders of ethical principles. For instance, the ceremonial Zhou dynasty bronzeware called "jin" (forbidden) warned against excessive drinking and promoted self-discipline. Likewise, mirror screens adorned with images and biographies of Confucius and his disciples offered daily visual cues to uphold Confucian virtues. Door couplets also carried this moral mission, expressing values to be honored and passed down through generations. One well-known example declares, "book and poetry are the treasure of the world, filial piety is the root of the family," emphasizing both intellectual and familial virtues. Even the exterior colors of houses may embody this pursuit of moral cultivation: while the white walls and black tiles of Jiangnan's water towns served clear functional and material purposes, their striking visual resonance with the scholar's essential tools—white paper and black ink—would have offered a powerful symbolic association with homeowners' aspirations to cultivate scholarship and achieve success in the imperial examinations.

The stele, a stone monument inscribed with calligraphy, offered a unique architectural medium of moral cultivation in China. The Xi'an Stele Forest stood as a powerful example of this fusion of architecture, calligraphy, and Confucian values. Among its many monuments was the *Stone Stele Classic of Filial Piety*, inscribed with the calligraphy of Emperor Xuanzong of the Tang dynasty, preserving a cornerstone Confucian text on filial piety. Its design was rich in symbolism: the stone platform represented the Earth; the cloud motifs at the top signified Heaven; and the text itself, positioned between the two, illustrated filial piety as the principle that unites Heaven and Earth. The inscription included the renowned aphorism: "Filial piety is the source of virtue, from which all moral cultivation originates." By engraving his calligraphy of this classic in stone—a symbol of permanence—Emperor Xuanzong demonstrated his deep commitment to promoting Confucian moral values for future generations.

The classical garden stood as a distinctive architectural achievement balancing worldly engagement and reclusive living—a material manifestation of the harmonious interplay of Confucian, Buddhist, and Daoist philosophies, offering a sanctuary for spiritual fulfillment and ethical cultivation. These traditions converged to shape its meticulously crafted spaces and objects, mirroring the literati's pursuit of aesthetic sensibility and moral aspirations. Guided by Confucian principles of order, the garden's layout often unfolded along a symmetrical central axis, manifesting balance and harmony. Meanwhile, the deliberate inclusion of bamboo and pine, emblems of resilience and integrity, rooted the landscape in Confucian virtues, transforming nature into a living allegory of scholarly refinement.

A closer look reveals the subtle influence of Chan Buddhism. Walls and rock formations partition the garden with quiet intentionality, suggesting unseen depths and inviting mindful wandering. Sinuous curves of waterways evoke the illusion of eternity—an ever-present reminder of impermanence. Here, every element conspires to awaken contemplation: landscapes bloom and recede, bridges arch over murmuring streams, and pavilions frame vistas that shift with the seasons. This choreography of nature fosters a profound intimacy, drawing visitors into joyful communion with their surroundings while whispering Chan's timeless motifs of compassion and wisdom. Within this sanctuary, the worldly dissolves into layers of meaning—each turn of the path an invitation to ponder life's mysteries and gently detach from earthly concerns.

Daoist philosophy also breathed an ineffable spirit into the classical Chinese garden, transforming structured spaces into fluid dialogues between human craft and wild essence, a setting that quietly invited contemplation of the Dao. The Chinese pavilion, a light and airy structure upheld by slender columns, exemplified architectural modesty, simplicity, and openness, allowing for a spontaneous merging of individuals with their natural surroundings—resonating with Daoist principles of humility and nonaction. This design echoed the teachings of Chuang Tzu, who advocated for quieting the mind, shedding distractions, and embracing a life in harmony with nature, illustrating the Daoist ideal that even human-made structures should appear naturally formed. In this way, the garden became not only a space for daily living but also a realm for spiritual self-cultivation—an experience that enriches both the landscape and the inner life.

8.5 Moral Cultivation Through Health-Preserving Arts

The concept of health preservation (yang-sheng, 养生) was conceived as an integral dimension of moral cultivation, advancing a holistic vision of well-being that united body, mind, and virtue. Combining principles of traditional Chinese medicine with self-cultivation practices, "yang-sheng" pursued longevity through harmony with the Dao, attending equally to physical vitality and spiritual refinement. It transcended mere health maintenance to integrate medical wisdom, ethical development, leisure, and aesthetic cultivation into a unified way of being, epitomizing the traditional Chinese ideal of a balanced, meaningful existence.

The concept of yang-sheng stemmed from the fundamental Chinese philosophical beliefs in interconnectedness, particularly the unity of Heaven and man, the dynamic balance of yin and yang, and the cyclical interactions of the five phases. At its core, yang-sheng involves nurturing "qi," the vital energy that flows through the body and the universe, constantly shifting and adapting. The yin and yang aspects of qi engaged in a continuous interplay of opposition and mutual support, while the five phases represented the generative and restraining cycles that sustain harmony within both the body and the cosmos.

This philosophical framework fundamentally informed traditional Chinese medicine's understanding of pathology as an imbalance in the dynamic interplay of yin-yang and the five phases. Both therapeutic interventions and health preservation strategies consequently sought to realign these fundamental harmonies. A wide range of practices supported this goal of yang-sheng, including the cultivation of qi, the nurturing of the heart, moderation of desires, herbal therapies, tea drinking, meditative reflection, internal alchemy, qigong, and martial arts. While acknowledging this broad spectrum of practices, the present study will concentrate specifically on techniques that most explicitly embodied the principles of moral cultivation.

8.5.1 Self-Cultivation, Inner Peace, and Healthy Life

In traditional Chinese health philosophy, the interdependence of physical vitality, emotional stability, and spiritual harmony formed the cornerstone of wellness. Destructive emotions such as anxiety, rage, and resentment were understood to obstruct and deplete qi circulation, disrupting physiological balance while simultaneously generating psychological turbulence that predisposed the body to illness. This psychosomatic understanding positioned moral cultivation as a therapeutic necessity, as ethical considerations fostered the tranquility of mind essential for physical health. By embodying qualities of kindness, honesty, and compassion, individuals could reduce both internal anxiety and external conflicts, fostering inner peace and mental equilibrium—conditions that, in turn, supported a longer and healthier life.

Confucian scholars offer a compelling example. Their pursuit of moral excellence was believed to contribute to longevity, based on the idea that humane individuals often live a long life (Confucius, 2016d, 6.21). Through self-cultivation, they nurtured both characters and emotional qualities such as open-mindedness, optimism, and compassion, alongside virtues like diligence, thrift, and temperance. For example, avoiding greed fostered harmony and a sense of well-being, while practicing moderation preserved mental composure and emotional equilibrium—both essential for maintaining health.

Drawing heavily on concepts advanced by Mencius, scholars regarded the practices of cultivating qi and nurturing the moral heart as important ways of health preservation. Cultivating a "flood-like qi" (浩然之气), a vast, upright energy associated with righteousness and moral courage, enabled individuals to become fearless and free of guilt, dispelling negative emotions. Alongside the cultivation of qi, nurturing a moral heart entailed observing proper rites, regulating desires and conduct, pacifying the restless mind, and practicing mindful breathing in harmony with nature. These self-cultivation methods aimed to harmonize yin and yang energies within the body, reduce stress and anxiety, and foster a balanced and ethical disposition that results in inner peace and improved wellness.

Daoist thought also significantly influenced ancient Chinese perspectives and practice surrounding health preservation. Much like the Confucian notion that benevolent individuals tended to enjoy long lives, Daoists maintained that following the Dao—the underlying principle that nurtures and sustains all things—was the ultimate path to cultivating virtue and preserving health. Alignment with the Dao cultivated an organic moral compass that naturally promoted well-being. By releasing the impulse to control and compete—instead attuning themselves to nature's rhythms—practitioners transcended the agitation born of ceaseless striving. This inner stillness and emotional balance, in turn, laid the foundation for a long, peaceful, and healthy life.

Drawing upon Daoist philosophy, religious Daoism developed esoteric systems that unified metaphysical cultivation with physiological refinement. The central practice of "dual cultivation of nature and vitality (性命双修)" sought to harmonize the interconnected spiritual and physical dimensions of the self, which were seen as mutually reinforcing: physical vitality sustains spiritual awakening, while transcendent awareness optimizes bodily health through emotional equilibrium and mental purification.

The pinnacle of this tradition manifested in "internal alchemy (内丹)," which is a specialized technique supposed to achieve immortality, building upon the foundation laid by dual cultivation. It consisted of abstruse doctrines centered on physical and meditative practices designed to cultivate a spiritual embryo—a cosmic essence capable of transcending the physical realm and attaining union with the Dao. Although the goal of immortality may remain elusive, these practices were widely believed to enhance health and prolong life.

This practice extends beyond physical fitness, breathing techniques, and spiritual exercises to embrace a broader commitment in cultivating a harmonious and compassionate society, thereby integrating social responsibility into the path of self-cultivation. Many religious Daoists held Confucian ethical values, such as loyalty, filial piety, harmony, and kindness, as prerequisites for spiritual advancement and the attainment of immortality. As the renowned Daoist Ge Hong (2011) noted, technical mastery alone was inadequate without cultivating these virtues. Daoists should discourage excessive desires and advocate compassionate conduct as a means of promoting broader social harmony, which in turn fosters a tranquil heart and a resilient body.

8.5.2 *The Art of Tea as Self-Cultivation*

Tea drinking in China exemplifies a unique convergence of health preservation, leisurely pastime, and self-cultivation. More than a mere beverage, tea evolved into a philosophy, an etiquette, and a way of life, giving rise to what is known as the art of tea. This culture offered a holistic vision of well-being, seamlessly blending the inherent health benefits of tea with the ethical thought and spiritual insight of Chinese philosophies. Scholars even likened the Chinese ethos to tea itself: sober, subtle, and gentle, yet never overly modest or condescending (Yang, 2013). Against this backdrop, this section explores how the rituals and etiquette of tea drinking functioned as a practice of nourishing both body and mind and a vehicle for ethical development.

The art of tea is a cultural practice emphasizing mindfulness, aesthetics, and social harmony. It involves meticulous preparation, elegant presentation, and slow sipping, with attention to quality tea leaves, pure water, suitable tea ware, refined etiquette, and a tranquil state of mind. Tea preparation began by heating water over a clay stove. The tea powder or leaves were either boiled directly in the kettle (as during the Tang dynasty) or steeped in the pot. Finally, the brew was gracefully poured, ready to be savored in solitude or shared with guests. Often described as a "tea ceremony," this practice inspired reverence for nature, fostered patience and inner calm, and offered a contemplative path to understanding the self and the world through ritual and refinement.

At its core, Chinese tea culture embodies harmony in diversity, reflecting the ideal of unity between Heaven and humanity. Like the art of balancing different ingredients and flavors in Chinese cuisine, tea culture sought a delicate alignment and equilibrium among various elements: water, tea, tea ware, clay stove, firewood, and the quiet rapport between practitioner and nature. This pursuit of harmony was deeply informed by multiple philosophical traditions: it drew ritual propriety from Confucianism, embraced spontaneity from Daoism, and incorporated the meditation and mindfulness of Chan Buddhism—transforming the tea platform into a microcosm where cosmic order becomes sensually immediate.

Among the earliest traditions to endow tea drinking with ethical and aesthetic meaning, Confucianism elevated the practice through the principles of ritual propriety, humility, and balance—uniting body and mind in pursuit of universal harmony (Yu, 2005). For Confucians, tea embodied virtues such as concord, reverence, and frugality, making it a valued ritual for moral self-cultivation. Sharing tea encouraged thoughtful and harmonious conversation and nurtured the virtue of humaneness in social interaction. Ritual propriety played a pivotal role in this transformation, turning tea drinking into a ceremonial practice characterized by orderly and reverential conduct. From preparation and pouring to serving and sipping, each movement was carried out with grace and intention, forming a cosmic rhythm that symbolized the unity of Heaven, Earth, and humanity.

Daoism also left deep mark on tea culture, infusing it with moral and aesthetic ideals such as spontaneity, simplicity, tranquility, authenticity, and veneration for life (Li, 2005). Where Confucianism brought structure, Daoism breathed the spirit of nature into the tea ceremony. Manifesting the ideal of natural harmony, Daoist tea culture favored unadorned elegance and natural materials—pristine mountain spring water and tea wares like red clay stoves, purple sand teapots, and white porcelain cups. It sought to preserve the original aroma and flavor of the tea, favoring a light color and pure taste. Resonating with the subtle essence of tea, the Daoist principle of "void and stillness" fosters an atmosphere of quietude, gently guiding participants back to nature and into a purified state of mind attuned to the rhythmic flow of the Dao.

It is important to note that the Japanese "Chado" (茶道, the Way of Tea) traces its origins to Sui and Tang dynasty China, where Chan Buddhism (Zen in Japan) played a significant role. While Chinese tea culture drew deeply from various philosophical traditions, the Japanese "Chado," drawing on its own aesthetic of rustic simplicity, imperfection, and transience (wabi-sabi), refined tea culture into a distinct expression of Zen Buddhism, emphasizing concentration and full presence in the moment. This mindfulness shaped the core characteristics of Japanese Way (Dao) of Tea, where hosts served their guests with reverence, grace, solemnity, and meticulous care, anticipating their needs in a ritual of full dedication.

While both traditions shared the fundamental pursuit of spiritual fulfillment through tea, their philosophical foundations and aesthetic ideals revealed subtle cultural distinctions. Chinese tea culture sought serenity and inner peace through a blend of spontaneous harmony and the moral refinement of humaneness. In contrast, the Japanese Way of Tea cultivates tranquility within a more structured and codified framework, characterized by refined utensils, precise etiquette, and highly ritualized serving practices. Whereas Chinese traditions cultivate attunement to the grandeur and meaningful unity of Heaven and humanity—seeking the enduring meaning of life—the Japanese approach focuses more intently on a contemplative mindset aligned with the wabi-sabi ideal of sacred imperfection and the poignant transience of existence.

References

Chuang Tzu. (2013). *The complete works of Zhuangzi*. (B. Watson, Trans.). Columbia University Press.

Confucius. (2016a). Analects. In J. Legge (Ed. & Trans.), *Confucianism: The four books and five classics*. Delphi Classics.

Confucius. (2016d). Book of documents. In J. Legge (Ed. & Trans.), *Confucianism: The four books and five classics*. Delphi Classics.

Dai, Z. (1982). *Mengzi ziyi shuzheng*. China Bookstore.

Feng, M. (2018). Ancient and modern novels preface. In *Yu shi heng yan*. Beijing United Publishing Co.

Ge, H. (2011). *The inner chapters of Baopuzi*. China Bookstore.

He, H. (2003). The spirit of moral cultivation in ancient Chinese music and fiction. *Studies in Ming and Qing Fiction, 4*, 228–233.

He, B. (2006). Calligraphy and philosophy. *Journal of Baoji College of Arts and Sciences, 26*(1), 88–94.

Kong, L. (2020). A brief discussion on the beauty of neutrality in calligraphy. *Literature of the Past and Present, 22*, 76–77.

Lai, Y. (1992). The influence of Buddhism on traditional Chinese thinking patterns. *Chinese Social Science, 1*, 93–102.

Lao Tzu. (2010). *Daodejing*. In R. T. Ames & D. L. Hall (Eds. & Trans.), *Dao de jing: A philosophical translation*. Ballantine Books.

Li, L. (2005). A study of the Daoist philosophy in the Chinese tea ceremony. *Tea, 31*(4), 256–259.

Li, Z., & Liu, G. (1999). *History of Chinese aesthetics*. Anhui Literature and Art Publishing House.

Liu, X. (2015). *The literary mind and the carving of dragons*. The Chinese University of Hong Kong Press.

Mencius. (2016). Mencius. In J. Legge (Ed. & Trans.), *Confucianism: The four books and five classics*. Delphi Classics.

Mullis, E. C. (2007). The ethics of Confucian artistry. *The Journal of Aesthetics and Art Criticism, 65*(1), 99–107.

Ni, P. (1999). Moral and philosophical implications of Chinese calligraphy. *Grand Valley Review, 20*(1), 8.

Qin, H. (2003). "The speechless educator" and "the talking architecture"—Thinking on the moral education function of architecture. *Journal of Beijing Institute of Civil Engineering and Architecture, 19*(B06), 69–73.

Su, S. (2013). *Dongpo Zhilin* (Vol. 1). China Bookstore.

Wang, L. (1982). *The history of the prohibition of fiction and opera in the Yuan, Ming and Qing dynasties*. Shanghai Ancient Books Publishing House.

Wang, Q. (1995). A test of the ancient Chinese novel's tradition of moral cultivation. *Nanjing Social Science, 4*, 51–54.

Wang, S. (2018). How "music" with the nature of "opera" in the Zhou and Qin periods assumed moral cultivation. *History of Chinese Philosophy, 3*, 5–11.

Xunzi. (1997). *Xunzi*. Liaoning Education Press.

Yang, Q. (2013). The middle way, harmony and the way of tea. *Tea Expo, 2*, 38–38.

Yu, Y. (2005). Confucianism, Buddhism, and the spirit of the Chinese tea ceremony. *Agricultural Archaeology, 5*, 115–129.

Zhou, W. (2015). On the moral cultivation significance of Buddhist thought in "three words" and "two beats". *Humanity, 33*, 41–42.

Zhou, S. (2016). Similarities and differences in the influence of Confucianism, Taoism, and Buddhism on the art of painting in ancient China. *Beauty and Times: Journal of Fine Arts, 5*, 134–135.

Chapter 9
The Logic of Taijitu: Chinese Ethos and the Dialectics of National Character

The Chinese ethos is not an enigmatic puzzle but a living expression of enduring philosophical foundations—notably Confucianism, Daoism, and Buddhism—which have cultivated a shared cultural orientation toward human development, social harmony, holistic thinking, and pragmatic wisdom. This ethos animates the national character, manifesting through collective psychological tendencies, value orientations, and behavioral patterns, where internal dualities, pairs of opposing traits that function holistically and dialectically, generate both productive tension and creative synthesis.

As we undertake this analysis, several critical methodological considerations must be foregrounded. The study of cultural ethos and national character inherently risks reductive generalization—a concern particularly salient in the case of China, a civilization marked by vast historical depth and regional diversity. This examination identifies broad patterns informed by dominant philosophical traditions; yet, it is crucial to recognize that premodern China encompassed numerous ethnic groups and regional subcultures and individual variation invariably complicates such characterizations. Therefore, the frameworks presented here—like all broad cultural analyses—should serve as heuristic lenses rather than exhaustive representations. Readers are encouraged to engage these observations as provisional and interpretive, with the understanding that lived cultures inevitably exceed their abstract formulations.

9.1 The Taijitu's Revelation of Chinese Ethos

The Taijitu (diagram of the Supreme Ultimate) visually encapsulates the foundational Chinese principle of the Supreme Ultimate, offering a key to understanding a core cultural ethos. This iconic symbol illustrates that seemingly opposite

Z. You, Y. Hu, *Philosophy and Civilization: How the Idea of Moral Cultivation Shaped China*, East-West Dialogues in Educational Philosophy and Theory,
https://doi.org/10.1007/978-981-95-5660-1_9

forces—such as yin and yang—are interdependent, complementary, and dynamically unified: each defines and sustains the other. More than a mere image, the Taijitu expresses a quintessential Chinese worldview centered on harmony, cyclical transformation, and balanced reciprocity. Proper understanding of this conceptual framework requires close study of both the symbol itself and the profound philosophy it embodies.

The Taijitu diagram articulates a holistic cosmological vision. Its perfect circle, bisected by an S-curve into interlocking black (yin) and white (yang) halves, encapsulates dynamic dualism—opposing principles in harmony within a unified whole. The S-shaped dividing line signifies constant interaction and mutual transformation, while the small contrasting dots within each half demonstrate how all phenomena contain the seeds of their opposites, manifesting the fundamental principles of interdependence and perpetual change.[1] Through these visual symbolism, the Taijitu powerfully reveals how the Supreme Ultimate, as the universe's underlying order, functions not only as the supreme principle but also as the generative source of the cosmos, promoting life-nurturing, renewing, and co-flourishing.

This system functions as an open circuit, defined not by internal isolation but by its ongoing interaction with external catalysts for change. Though its circular form implies self-containment, it signifies a unified whole rather than a boundary. This openness is characterized by three essential qualities: a dynamic equilibrium that balances constant flux, an adaptive responsiveness to environmental stimuli, and a perpetual exchange that fuels continuous transformation. More than a static duality, this framework reveals a living process of cosmic interaction.

This open, dynamic system stands in contrast to closed, deterministic models like thermodynamic entropy theory, which posits a fixed cosmic endpoint of heat death. While such reductionist frameworks have historically driven conceptual development and scientific progress through precise quantification, their application to social affairs often reduces complex social realities into rigid binaries of friend/foe or win/lose, which risk exacerbating conflict through oversimplification. In contrast, Chinese Taiji philosophy presents a transformative worldview grounded in adaptability, relationality, and endless cyclical renewal, where every ending becomes a new beginning. Eschewing static categories, it envisions reality as ceaseless interaction among complementary opposites, each rising and falling in relation to the other through a perpetual cycle, moving toward dynamic equilibrium. This perspective provides a robust foundation for conflicting yet interdependent coexistence and reciprocal flourishing, illuminating pathways for addressing the complex challenges of both natural and human systems.

This framework, which defines opposites not just by antagonism but also by complementarity, fluidity, and the potential for mutual transformation, likely arose from ancient observations of natural cycles, such as day and night or the waxing and waning of the moon. As a foundational worldview, it underscores harmony, balance,

[1] The mature Taijitu we see today is recorded in the book *Yi Xuan* penned by Zhang Xingcheng in the Southern Song dynasty.

and the interconnectedness of all phenomena—encouraging a holistic and systemic understanding of the world, rather than a reductionist or atomistic one.

Accordingly, the Chinese mindset reflects a worldview of dynamic relativity—what might be termed "Taijitu thinking"—that emphasizes contextual understanding, dialectical interconnectedness, and adaptive flexibility[2], contrasting with the analytical tendencies of many Western traditions that prioritize clear-cut distinctions, definitive conclusions, absolute universality, and fixed categories. While a relative perspective's tolerance for ambiguity and fluid boundaries may pose challenges for such systematic endeavors, it should not be regarded as a deficiency, but rather as a distinct cognitive orientation—one that privileges dialectical synthesis over formal logic and analogical reasoning. Its strength lies in fostering harmony, measured compromise, and integrative perception—qualities especially valuable for navigating complexity, sustaining balance, and accommodating diversity.

This philosophical perspective provides a powerful framework for understanding core tenets of the Chinese ethos: holism, harmony, humanism, and pragmatism. At its foundation lies a holistic mindset that prioritizes the common good and underpins a collective orientation. This worldview champions the pursuit of harmony—with nature, inside the family, and across society—by adeptly navigating change and avoiding destabilizing extremes. Its humanistic dimension focuses on cultivating virtue to advance both personal flourishing and social cohesion, often employing adaptable means to achieve humane ends. This is balanced by a pragmatic commitment to workable solutions and tangible results, making philosophical ideals concrete in the world. Ultimately, all these aspects are reflected in the cyclical movement and dynamic balance of the Taiji diagram, which mirrors the rhythms of the natural world, providing an enduring ethical compass for social and moral development.

9.1.1 Relational Holism and Collectivist Ethics

Unlike mainstream Western culture, which traditionally emphasizes individual autonomy and analytical thinking, Chinese cultural thought prioritizes holism and collectivism, shaped by a systems-oriented mindset that values harmony, balance, and the interdependence of all components. This orientation fosters collaboration and collective problem-solving, enabling groups to navigate complex challenges with integrative strategies. However, it also presents limitations such as the potential suppression of individual autonomy and a tendency to favor conformity over innovation, which may constrain efforts to transcend established norms and frameworks.

Holism is a philosophical perspective that views the world as an interconnected whole rather than as a collection of isolated parts (Oshry, 2008). Deeply ingrained

[2] Conceptually synonymous with Taiji thinking (太极思维), the term Taijitu thinking foregrounds the yin-yang diagram as both a visual and functional epistemic model, illustrating the dynamic, holistic, and dialectical operations of this cognitive framework.

in traditional Chinese culture, this outlook is exemplified by the notion of the unity of Heaven and humanity, which envisions all things as interdependent components of a complex, dynamic system rather than a linear chain of cause and effect (Marchal & Wenzel, 2016). This holistic approach permeates diverse domains including philosophical discourse, artistic creation, political governance, and interpersonal relations, consistently seeking to achieve equilibrium and harmony. It promotes a balanced perspective that considers the systemic consequences of individual actions while affirming the interconnectedness of all life. Such a paradigm contrasts sharply with mainstream Western cultural orientations, which prioritize individualism and independence. While the Western "salad bowl" metaphor highlights the coexistence of distinct cultural identities, Chinese culture is better represented by the "Buddha Jumps Over the Wall" soup—a dish that symbolizes the seamless integration of diverse elements into a unified, harmonious whole.

This holistic perspective is indispensable for a genuine understanding of Chinese culture. While the major philosophical traditions—Confucianism, Daoism, Mohism, and Legalism—may seem divergent or even oppositional at first glance, they are, in profound and nuanced ways, fundamentally coexistent and complementary. Without recognizing the overarching framework of All under Heaven and the dynamic interplay among these schools, one may overlook the essential synthesis that defines Chinese cultural thought. This sense of interconnectedness also explains why Chinese moral cultivation situates self-cultivation within a network of communal influence and moral responsibility for others, viewing personal development as inseparable from its social context in the pursuit of moral excellence.

The holistic approach is also evident in traditional Chinese medicine, where physicians address root imbalances rather than merely surface symptoms, aiming to restore harmony to its deeply interconnected systems. Similarly, Chinese martial arts prioritize fluid, full-body coordination over isolated movements. Techniques frequently employ simultaneous and often counterbalancing actions to maximize power, vividly demonstrating the effectiveness of holistic principles in practice.

China's holistic worldview underpins a relational emphasis on interdependence, harmony, and dynamic relationships, as well as a collectivist orientation that prioritizes communal well-being. This outlook has profoundly shaped Chinese social structures, where individuals are conceived not as discrete entities but as integral threads of a vast social fabric, their identities and roles constituted through an intricate web of relationships. Historically, this social structure grew from China's agrarian roots, which centered on the family as the primary social unit. Strengthened by kinship and marriage, these familial bonds extended outward to form the framework for political, economic, scholarly, and social institutions. This deep relational interconnectedness fosters strong mutual support mechanisms that reinforce social cohesion and bolster collective resilience during times of hardship.

A profound family- and society-oriented emphasis on relational and collective values provided a critical stabilizing force in imperial China. This ethos cultivated pervasive contextual awareness, encouraging individuals to prioritize interdependence and the well-being of both family and community. In this hierarchy of values, the family duty and group's interests routinely superseded individual ambitions, which were themselves expected to harmonize with collective objectives.

The family-state culture ultimately integrated familial relations into broader collective goals. The state exercised paternalistic authority, overriding parochial interests while assuming responsibility for the welfare of subordinates. In this relational worldview, maintaining social harmony often carried greater ethical weight than rigid adherence to moral absolutes. This "group-first" ethos is encapsulated in the idea of "duty before freedom, obedience before rights, community before the individual, and harmony before conflict" (Chen, 2017). Such an orientation fostered a deeply ingrained sense of mutual obligation and shared destiny, underpinning China's remarkable historical endurance and civilizational resilience.

Traditional collectivism conferred many societal benefits, particularly in fostering group harmony, strengthening social cohesion, and enabling coordination. This tendency is further reinforced by the holistic cognitive orientation inherent in Chinese cultural traditions, which prioritizes systemic design and integrated planning. Such an approach enabled Chinese governing structures to reconcile national imperatives with regional concerns, thereby facilitating the realization of ambitious, long-term national projects: from the construction of the Great Wall to the engineering feat of the Grand Canal.

While collectivism reinforced social cohesion and a shared sense of purpose, it also generated inherent tensions. The emphasis on conformity and group harmony could constrain individual expression and personal autonomy. Within such a system, resolving complex challenges entails prioritizing collective objectives, a dynamic that raises critical questions for the modern era: how can individual agency, voice, and rights be nurtured when they are often overshadowed by group priorities? This enduring paradox, where the "I" is frequently subsumed within the "we" (Zhang, 2011), illustrates the persistent challenge of balancing profound social unity with the cultivation of independent thought and self-determination.

9.1.2 Harmonious Equilibrium

The pursuit of harmony converged across Chinese philosophical traditions, with Confucianism, Daoism, and Buddhism each realizing it through social propriety, natural equilibrium, and spiritual transcendence, respectively. This philosophical emphasis on harmony became deeply embedded in the Chinese cultural psyche, functioning as what might be termed a "civilizational unconscious." It manifested in carefully calibrated interpersonal relations and social order within hierarchical frameworks, promoting propriety, intimacy, and organizational cohesion. As illustrated by the Taijitu's yin-yang dynamics, harmony denotes a state of dynamic, fluid equilibrium, attained through the fulfillment of individual roles in accordance with established norms and collective consensus, simultaneously cultivating personal flourishing and communal well-being.

9.1.2.1 The Influence of Harmony and Formalism

As a supreme ideal, harmony fundamentally structured Chinese engagements with the natural world, social interactions, and broader political orders. This philosophy, born from a deep agrarian history, embodied a prescient ecological wisdom that recognized humanity's inseparable interdependence with nature. It promoted an ethic of sustainable stewardship, emphasizing the duty to conserve resources for posterity by avoiding overfishing and overcultivation. While conflicts between human needs and environmental limits inevitably occurred, the cultural preference was for long-term solutions that sought synergy between human prosperity and ecological sustainability.

In the social realm, harmony functioned as a stabilizing force, mitigating friction in hierarchical structures and channeling potential discontent into socially constructive avenues. Within family structures, while generational and gender hierarchies remained firmly established, the cultivation of warm, nurturing relationships took precedence; disruptive actions were discouraged and often met with social censure. Similarly, in broader interpersonal contexts, harmony was maintained through reciprocal consideration, empathetic engagement, and a shared commitment to collective flourishing.

Note that ancient Chinese thinkers conceptualized social harmony not as the absence of conflict, but as the skillful maintenance of equilibrium within collaborative and oppositional relationships, achieved through kindness, self-restraint, and courteous deference. This cultural emphasis on harmony yielded an ethic of tolerance, humility, the golden mean, and the subtle art of balance—like a culinary expert harmonizing various flavors to achieve gastronomic perfection, principles that ultimately undergirded many of China's most enduring civilizational achievements.

Yet the true meaning of social harmony must be carefully distinguished from what modern Chinese scholars term "formalism" (形式主义)—a bureaucratic phenomenon distinct from the analytical concept of formalism in Western philosophy. In the Chinese context, "formalism" denotes the prioritization of appearances over substance, characterized by bureaucratic excess, hollow ritualism, and superficial displays that often produce impressive statistics while masking deeper qualitative deficiencies. Such "formalism" resembles an immaculately manicured garden that, beneath its picture-perfect surface, suffers from ecological sterility and a lack of true vitality. This divergence between form and essence represents a significant departure from the authentic, dynamic harmony cherished in traditional Chinese philosophy.

Although the ideal of harmony emphasized moral sincerity, its misinterpretation laid the groundwork for formalism's rise. Confucianism's emphasis on hierarchy and ritual propriety, when stripped of their ethical substance and reduced to performative compliance, could paradoxically contribute to a culture of formalism. This tendency was significantly exacerbated by Legalism's mechanistic model of governance, which sought control by prioritizing rigid administrative regulation, a reward and punishment system based on quantitative metrics, and the pursuit of short-term political outcomes.

The historical confluence of these misappropriated traditions produced an administrative trap that, while generating surface-level stability and uniformity, often masked deeper institutional weaknesses. Imperial regimes frequently instrumentalized these systems to suppress dissent and enforce conformity, leading to bureaucratic inertia, intellectual constriction, and the stifling of innovation. Ultimately, "formalism" represents not the harmonious order Confucius envisioned, but a distortion—one that conceals systemic flaws and obstructs meaningful development.

9.1.2.2 Cultural Inclusiveness and Assimilation

Anchored in the principle of harmony, Chinese civilization exhibited an extraordinary capacity for openness, inclusivity, and tolerance toward the cultural traditions beyond China's borders. Nowhere is this more evident than in the realm of religion: Buddhism not only took root in China but underwent profound sinicization, eventually becoming one of the Three Teachings alongside Daoism and Confucianism. Similarly, Abrahamic traditions including Islam, Christianity, and Judaism maintained vibrant communities for much of their history under imperial protection. This remarkable religious pluralism reflected China's sophisticated cultural framework—one that could assimilate external influences while preserving civilizational continuity, transforming "the foreign" into "the Chinese" through gradual, organic integration.

Ancient China's inclusivity and tolerance can be attributed to a deep belief in the harmony between Heaven and Earth, which embraces all things with generosity and openness, fostering the accommodation of diverse perspectives. Anchored in a strong cultural confidence, it allowed the Chinese to assimilate the wisdom of other civilizations selectively, regarding such integration not as a threat but as an enrichment of their own heritage. The adaptive capacity proved especially valuable in the early modern period, when China demonstrated a notable ability to incorporate Western science and technology while largely preserving the core of its cultural identity.

9.1.2.3 The Golden Mean for Equilibrium and Reconciliation

The Confucian golden mean profoundly shaped the Chinese ethos, advocating moderation and dynamic equilibrium as essential virtues. This doctrine rejected extremism in all its forms, emphasizing instead the art of discerning the optimal middle path between competing forces. More than mere compromise, it represented a cultivated wisdom of measured responsiveness—where individuals exercised disciplined judgment to avoid both aggressive overreach and deficient inaction. This emphasis on moderation and balance helped reduce conflict and resentment, contributing to the cultivation of a stable and harmonious social order.

Chinese culture prioritized reconciliation and the pursuit of common ground. When resolving disputes, the focus shifted from adversarial debate to preserving relationships, practicing mutual accommodation, and sustaining social harmony. This approach rejected extremes, instead embracing dynamic balance through adaptability—like a tightrope walker's subtle adjustments to maintain equilibrium. By valuing compromise and mutual understanding, it mitigated destructive conflict and reinforces societal stability and cohesion. However, such forbearance has its limits. When tensions accumulated beyond a certain threshold, confrontation could erupt despite the cultural ideal of harmony.

China's traditional commitment to harmony via the middle way is not without its downside. When misapplied, it may foster excessive risk-aversion that stifles individual initiative and institutional innovation. This cultural preference for compromise could incentivize risk avoidance and tacit tolerance of mediocrity, potentially impeding societal advancement and delaying necessary reforms. In social interactions, this tendency frequently emerged as strategic ambiguity: the art of circumventing direct confrontation to preserve relational harmony. Such behavior was not a sign of weakness, but rather a sophisticated cultural calculus that prioritized collective stability over individual assertion.

That said, an emphasis on harmony and social order should not be equated with resistance to change, for Chinese cultural tradition values a dynamic equilibrium—one that selectively incorporates new elements while preserving fundamental structures. But when this balance is severely disrupted by systemic corruption, social crisis, or institutional collapse, the tradition's own logic can justify revolutionary change as necessary to restore harmony. Even so, the cultural preference remains firmly anchored in stability: Chinese civilization has historically treated radical change as a measure of last resort—a necessary but undesirable response when incremental adjustments fail.

9.1.3 Ethical Humanism

The ethics of self-cultivation in traditional Chinese thought, particularly Confucianism, shape a distinctive humanism centered on moral development (Peters, 2022), which prioritizes ethical living and social harmony in the secular realm over metaphysical or salvific concerns. While sharing with Western humanism a fundamental respect for human dignity, Confucian humanism differs markedly in its rejection of radical individualism and abstract rationalism. Rather, it articulates a relational paradigm where human fulfillment emerges through maintaining conscientious performance of social roles, collective well-being, and the cultivation of harmonious relationships as the foundation of a well-ordered society. This vision of human flourishing is grounded in the Taiji worldview, where yin and yang are inherently linked and mutually dependent, constituting the generative force that nurtures all living beings. Within this framework, humanity occupies a tripartite cosmic role alongside Heaven and Earth, bearing the solemn duty to nurture social prosperity and sustain universal harmony.

The Confucian moral cultivation profoundly advanced China's humanistic tradition, centering on virtuous living within the secular world. Unlike the religious zeal that permeated medieval Europe, imperial Chinese society was largely insulated from pervasive fanaticism. While spiritual practices retained cultural importance, they were consistently subordinated to Confucian norms in official ideology, familial structures, and social ethics—all of which emphasized secular duties and earthly virtue. This paradigm thus fostered a relational ethics in which personal cultivation was primarily directed toward communal flourishing rather than individual salvation.

The Chinese have long been recognized for their deep commitment to active participation in social life, viewing the family and the state as interconnected arenas. While Confucianism was pivotal in shaping this ethos, Daoism—often mischaracterized as purely escapist—also embodied a profound humanistic spirit. Its ultimate aim was not the renunciation of human society, but the cultivation of a more harmonious world through spontaneity and effortless action. Together, these philosophical traditions greatly reinforced the this-worldly orientation of ancient Chinese. In contrast to ancient India, where spiritual practice often emphasized liberation from the cycle of rebirth and concerns of the afterlife, ancient Chinese tended to seek unity with the divine through ethical living and harmonious coexistence with nature in the present life.

These humanistic traditions contributed to an "ethical culture" centering on moral development. Whereas the ancient Greeks often focused on uncovering the universal laws governing both the physical world and human behavior, the ancient Chinese concentrated primarily on moral principles that guided family, governance, and society—ethics forming the very foundation of their civilization. Education, accordingly, was valued less as an objective inquiry into nature and more as a means of moral cultivation. The Confucian tradition, in particular, viewed education as a transformative process for developing virtue and preparing individuals to fulfill their societal roles responsibly.

Deeply rooted in worldly ethical commitments, ancient Chinese, particularly elites, developed a strong sense of social obligation, embracing the mission of world betterment as a personal moral charge. These values were disseminated through scholarly instruction and folk arts, which helped commoners realize that their lives were closely tied to the state's stability and welfare. These ethical concerns ultimately culminated in the conviction that the rise and fall of the world rests upon the responsibility of every individual.[3] While dynasties and emperors came and went, the cultural identity of China—represented by the ideal of All under Heaven—endured. By the early modern period, this humanistic vision—linking personal

[3]The famous maxim was concluded from Confucian scholar Gu Yanwu's *Record of Daily Knowledge*.

well-being with national prosperity—had become widespread across Chinese society.

9.1.4 Adaptive Pragmatism

Grounded in a strong this-worldly orientation, Chinese culture cultivated a pragmatic worldview that valued knowledge for its practical utility in solving concrete problems (Kelly & Cordeiro, 2020), an ethos that found distinct expressions in diverse philosophical schools. Confucianism, playing a central role, emphasized using moral cultivation and meritocratic system to turn ideals into reality. Daoism advocated adaptability, open-mindedness, and effortless strategies for navigating a dynamic world, while Legalism underscored efficient administration and the utilitarian application of law to secure urgent goals. Together, these traditions forged a solution-focused mentality that remains integral to China's cultural identity today.

In effect, Chinese culture has historically privileged pragmatic measures to real-world challenges over abstract theorization. Within this tradition, moral cultivation extends beyond the contemplation of idealized virtues, focusing instead on the skilled navigation of social relationships and the practical application of ethical principles for the betterment of society. By adeptly balancing competing interests and making thoughtful concessions, Chinese society developed a knack for defusing tensions and turning conflicts into opportunities for mutual benefit. This pragmatic intelligence, combined with ethical consideration and resourceful problem-solving, enabled social thriving even in resource-limited environments.

This pragmatic culture also reveals itself through a remarkable adaptability. Chinese traditions have long emphasized adjusting approaches based on practical effectiveness—a principle vividly captured in the Taijitu, which symbolizes dynamic transformation through the interplay of opposing forces. Daoist philosophy profoundly shaped this flexible mindset, promoting nonconfrontational strategies and rejecting rigid dogma. Even Confucianism, though centered on moral discipline, allowed for contextual flexibility; Confucius himself prioritized ethical judgment over adherence to rigid rules, famously refusing to honor an agreement made under duress (Sima, 2016). Yet this adaptability never came at the expense of core values. Practical adjustments were consistently guided by enduring moral principles, fostering a cultural equilibrium where practices adapted to context, but foundational ideals remained intact.

China's pragmatic ethos had long permeated various dimensions of social life. In governance, ancient Chinese societies championed "virtuous governance," believing that ethical leaders, possessing both virtues and practical wisdom, could uphold social order and foster prosperity. In education, the imperial examination system served to select civic talent, institutionalize Confucian moral cultivation, and legitimize meritocratic avenues of upward mobility. Economically, the Chinese prized industriousness and frugality, pursuing prosperity through diligence, resourcefulness, and strategic effort—also exhibiting a strong inclination toward collaboration and shared advancement. Today, this enduring pragmatism is reflected in China's remarkable capacity for systems-level coordination, optimization, and adaptability in navigating complex social and economic challenges.

This emphasis on practical utility and real-life experience played a crucial role in driving technological innovation in ancient China. The Chinese demonstrated a remarkable aptitude for learning and invention, continually refining their techniques to address real-world needs. Many of the most influential inventions in ancient China such as papermaking, gunpowder, printing, and the compass arose from this commitment to solving practical problems. Yet this applied focus also had its drawbacks: while it fostered a dynamic culture of innovation, it often hindered the development of abstract scientific theories lacking immediate utility.

Notably, the emphasis on practicality and usefulness in Chinese culture does not exclude its idealist dimension. Like other great civilizations, the ancient Chinese cherished transcendent values—moral sentiment, ethical ideals, personal and societal perfection, and aesthetic harmony—which profoundly shaped their aspirational vision of society. Confucianism, at its highest level, transcends immediate concerns to embrace noble ideals cultivating a better society for all, whereas Daoism aspires to harmony with natural orders. These idealistic tendencies, when set against pragmatic needs, generated a dynamic tension within Chinese culture, as people sought to balance lofty ideals with the practical demands of reality.

9.2 The Dialectics of Chinese National Character

The term national character, popularized by Johann Gottfried Herder (1784/2024), refers to the idea that each nation possesses a unique identity shaped by its history, language, and culture. This identity can be understood as a set of shared thought patterns, attitudes, values, psychological traits, and behaviors commonly observed among a significant portion of the population (Lv, 1996). Essentially, it reflects how people within a nation perceive themselves, relate to one another, and interpret the broader world, shaping their interactions and responses across various contexts.

A realistic understanding acknowledges that China's national character, like that of any other culture, has not always fully embodied its ethical ideals. Philosophical aspiration has often stood in tension with lived reality, influenced by environmental pressures, material conditions, and the demands of statecraft. Even so, China's deep-rooted tradition of moral cultivation and its nuanced approach to balancing competing social obligations have fundamentally shaped its collective identity, often enabling the reconciliation of seemingly contradictory qualities.

Such synthesis epitomizes a durable cultural psyche, its dynamic tensions and resolutions reflecting the core dialectics of Chinese thought. Unlike many Western paradigms that prioritize singular, absolute truths, this tradition—grounded in the yin-yang interplay, as symbolized by the taijitu—presents a nuanced understanding of reality by harmonizing contrasting attributes. In doing so, it encapsulates the inherent flexibility of Chinese national character, demonstrating its pragmatic wisdom for navigating the complexities of existence.

9.2.1 Kindness and Indifference

For the ancient Chinese, kindness and care were not abstract ideals but foundational to daily life. Core values like humaneness, righteousness, and compassion emphasized care and concern for others—an ethic meant to extend from the family outward to the community, the state, and the entire world. This ideal was expressed through mutual aid, community support, and the Confucian imperative for virtuous governance. Yet, the lofty vision often clashed with reality. Despite the cultural esteem for humaneness, indifference to outsiders' needs was common, and actions of benevolence were largely confined to kinship networks and familiar associates. These enduring tensions between universal compassion and pragmatic detachment, and between ethical aspiration and everyday practice, continue to resonate in modern Chinese society.

In traditional Chinese culture, care was most deeply valued and expressed within the family, especially in the reciprocal bond between parents and children. Parents devoted themselves to securing their children's well-being through providing quality education, arranging suitable marriages, and often helping to raise grandchildren, while children reciprocated their parents' love by respecting them and dutifully looking after them in old age, creating a cycle of mutual care that forms the foundation of humaneness. Through both prosperity and hardship, a strong sense of family cohesion endures, guided by the overarching aim of honoring ancestors and ensuring the continued flourishing of future generations (Yang, 2003).

Community life placed a high value on altruism, generosity, and mutual aid, manifested through neighborhood support systems, philanthropic endeavors, and collective action to address local concerns. In the political realm, the Confucian ideal of benevolent rule was a cornerstone of statecraft. This doctrine charged rulers with governing compassionately, prioritizing the welfare of their subjects, and ensuring justice. While practice often fell short of this ideal, it nevertheless provided a powerful historical benchmark that shaped the aspirations of Chinese people and the duties of their leaders.

Benevolent affections were also deeply embodied in Chinese fictive kinship, a vital thread in the fabric of social networks. Close friendships, for example, were often framed as "brotherhoods with different surnames," where individuals addressed one another as "brother" or "sister" to underscore emotional ties and mutual obligation. Such bonds sometimes could even surpass biological ties in reliability, offering both practical assistance and enduring companionship, thus giving substance to the ideal of universal brotherhood. The same principle extended to master-disciple relationships, which traditionally resemble parent-child dynamics: the master imparted not only technical knowledge and skills, but also moral insight and life wisdom, while the disciple responded with loyalty, gratitude, and deep emotional commitment.

Yet, although kindness and compassion flourish within familial and intimate circles, they often wane when extended beyond these networks. This contrast historically manifested as a reluctance to engage in broader civic life or assist strangers, reflecting an enduring tension between personal obligation and collective responsibility. The proverb, "everyone sweeps the snow from his own doorstep and heeds not the frost on his neighbor's roof," powerfully encapsulates this circumscribed sense of public-mindedness. Over a century ago, missionary-sociologist Arthur Henderson Smith (1894) identified this paradox in *Chinese Characteristics* and noted this perplexing coexistence of profound warmth within inner circles and apparent detachment toward outsiders—a social dynamic that remains persistent in contemporary China.

This tension, rooted in China's closely knit social fabric, was further shaped by a selective interpretation of humaneness, which prioritized care within proximate relationships before extending it outward. This graduated ethical framework fostered a natural distinction between "in-groups" and "out-groups"—or "our people" and "others"—where familial bonds and close friendships commanded immediate concern, while distant others received only measured regard. Yet these boundaries were not fixed. Through sustained interaction and the formation of new social ties, outsiders could gradually be incorporated into established circles of care.

This in-group partiality in Chinese social life, however, conflicts with Confucianism's loftier ideal of expansive humaneness, which emphasizes inclusiveness rather than graded love, and with Buddhism's vision of universal compassion. To bridge this gap, Confucianism emphasizes the cultivation of virtuous individuals and persons of righteousness, who extend their moral concern beyond their immediate circles. These moral exemplars aim not only to serve their family and community but also to embody a broader vision of humaneness, aspiring to care for all people under Heaven.

Throughout Chinese history, individuals who rose above self-interest and in-group bias to serve the broader needs of society were held in the highest esteem. Those who altruistically aided strangers, upheld integrity in public life, or made personal sacrifices for the common good were celebrated as cultural heroes, embodiments of "expansive humaneness" and "greater righteousness." Their actions stood in marked contrast to those motivated by personal gain or narrow group loyalties, especially when such pursuits came at others' expense. These principles permeated society, shaping a national character that continually balanced the pull of parochial obligations with the aspiration toward a more inclusive, universal ethic of care—embodying, in lived practice, the ethical dialectic between kindness and indifference.

9.2.2 Hierarchy and Harmony

Ancient Chinese society cultivated a unique synthesis of structural hierarchy and relational harmony. While maintaining clear stratification—from the imperial court to scholar-officials to the peasantry—it simultaneously emphasized reciprocal duties, moral interdependence, and cooperative ideals. This dual emphasis on order and harmony sought to mitigate social tensions while preserving stability, creating what has been described as a "harmonious hierarchy."

Social hierarchy was both an entrenched ideology and an institutional pillar of stability in traditional China, expressed through deference to established order. While the hierarchical framework structured daily interactions, individuals actively fulfilled their assigned roles in return for protection and the possibility of upward mobility through merit. This arrangement mitigated social friction and fostered systemic resilience, rendering hierarchy a legitimized norm within society. Even in moments of disruption, such as peasant uprisings, the goal was often to replace the dynasty rather than dismantle the hierarchical framework itself.

The inherent tensions of social hierarchy were moderated by ritual propriety, which emphasized reciprocity. Ideally, reciprocal obligations were modeled in the mutual affection between father and son, extending upward to the loyalty of a minister toward a benevolent ruler. Gender roles were similarly shaped by this framework: women were expected to be submissive to their husbands, yet they could earn respect and admiration by fulfilling their prescribed duties, particularly through bearing sons and raising children—a contribution held in high regard. This emphasis on mutual respect, along with adherence to established social norms and rituals, further reinforced the hierarchy's legitimacy and helped maintain social cohesion.

In a closely intertwined society, this measured approach cultivated a keen awareness of social boundaries and the importance of both self-restraint and external regulation. Such ritual propriety discouraged superiors from overreaching or exploiting their authority while also discouraging subordinates from defying the established order. By promoting consideration for others in social interactions and resource distribution, these values reinforced balance and contributed to social stability, even amid periods of hardship.

The belief in and practice of dynamic social mobility helped sustain harmony within ancient China's hierarchical structure. Unlike many ancient cultures where social status was mostly fixed by birth, the Chinese system allowed for a degree of upward mobility, providing crucial "breathing room" that helped reconcile its otherwise rigid social hierarchy. Individual merit—expressed through ability, effort, virtue, and the conscientious fulfillment of one's roles and responsibilities—played a vital role in shaping social standing and sustaining harmonious relationships. Thus, the dynamics in ancient Chinese hierarchy, though limited, reflected the natural variations in individuals' talents and their contributions to the state, whether moral, military, or political (Bell & Wang, 2020). This historical emphasis also explains the enduring Chinese cultural value of placing importance on education, diligence, and service as legitimate paths to personal advancement today.

Yet, despite its harmonious implications and limited avenues for mobility, this hierarchical culture had notable drawbacks. It could discourage belief in equality, foster admiration for power and privilege, and reinforce social inequality as natural. Deference to authority and strict adherence to established norms sometimes led to dependence, timidity, and a lack of initiative (Xu, 1988). Furthermore, this authoritative structure may have impeded scientific and technological advancement, as younger generations with innovative ideas often lacked the resources or autonomy to realize them. Like a sturdy ship built for long voyages, the system prioritized stability, but this very strength also bred conservatism and rigidity—factors that may have contributed to China's relative social and technological stagnation in the early modern era.

9.2.3 *Gratitude and Righteousness*

The ancient Chinese esteemed gratitude and righteousness as foundational principles guiding ethical conduct in both private and public life. While these values were often complementary, they also created tension when personal loyalties conflicted with public duties or when competing obligations demanded different moral priorities.

Gratitude, or "en" (恩) in Chinese, extends far beyond simple thankfulness. A foundational concept in Chinese relationships, gratitude encompasses appreciation, a sense of indebtedness, and a strong desire to reciprocate kindness. Rooted in the acknowledgment of others' kindness and generosity, gratitude fosters a mutual dynamic of care and affection that permeates social interaction. This sentiment of indebtedness is not confined to personal or familial favors—it encompasses gratitude toward society, the state, and even the natural world.

Gratitude is often paired with "righteousness" to form the concept of "en-yi (恩义)," which embodies personal attachment, reciprocity, duty, and mutual moral reinforcement. "Righteousness" signifies moral imperative—a commitment to doing what is just and appropriate. It functioned as a fundamental virtue and a key criterion for evaluating ethical behavior, especially in how one responded to others' kindness. Failure to repay favor was often seen as both ungrateful and unrighteous, highlighting the close alignment between gratitude and righteousness.

Influenced by Confucian and Buddhist moral teachings, gratitude and reciprocal righteousness were deeply ingrained in Chinese society. Within families, filial piety expressed children's gratitude for their parents' care and upbringing. Spousal relationships also embodied these values: wives appreciated their husbands' roles as providers and protectors, while husbands acknowledged their wives' nurturing and household contributions. This reciprocal gratitude extended to friendships, where individuals endeavored to repay kindness and uphold unwavering loyalty, a quality often described as "righteousness," signifying a commitment to stand by one another through adversity.

In the political sphere of ancient China, allegiance to the monarch was regarded as a paramount virtue, with the relationship between ruler and ministers predicated on the principles of gratitude and righteousness. When sovereign appointed and promoted officials based on merit and moral integrity, it fostered a deep sense of indebtedness among ministers. In return, ministers were expected to serve with righteousness, namely, unwavering loyalty. Thus, gratitude and righteousness reciprocity were not merely personal sentiments but foundational ethical principles that helped sustain the political order.

In Chinese social life, acknowledging and reciprocating gratitude was a fundamental moral obligation, embodied in proverbs like "It is not virtuous not to return a gratitude" and "A drop of water shall be repaid with a spring." Kindness—whether from the cosmos, parents, rulers, or teachers—demanded recognition and a corresponding response. Unlike the Western concept of divine grace, which often directed gratitude upward toward a transcendent source, Chinese gratitude tended to operate more horizontally, demanding mutual responsibility among peers. Failing to express gratitude or to reciprocate kindness—let alone responding to it with hostility—was regarded as a serious moral failing. This strong emphasis on reciprocation also underlay the concept of accumulating merit (积德), in which performing good deeds cultivated positive karma, believed to bring blessings to oneself and to future generations.

The concepts of gratitude and righteousness also held a significant place in ancient Chinese spiritual life, which emphasized not only religious devotion but also moral and harmonious living. In Chinese Buddhist thought, the recognition of emptiness and the inherent interdependence of all things engender both a deep sense of gratitude and a moral imperative for compassionate action. This recognition that our lives are intricately intertwined with all beings and conditions fosters ethical conduct rooted in universal compassion, resonating with the idea of greater righteousness. While Confucian gratitude tends to focus on reciprocal kindness within specific relationships, Buddhist interconnectedness extends to all phenomena, suggesting a universal moral responsibility. From this perspective, all human interactions—whether familial, social, or even adversarial—are opportunities to cultivate compassion, purify karma, and contribute to the liberation of all sentient beings from suffering.

However, the intricacies of Chinese social life, characterized by the blurred boundaries between public and private, complicated the relationship between gratitude and righteousness. While gratitude emphasizes loyalty to specific individuals, righteousness, particularly in its higher form such as the greater righteousness, often compels allegiance to the broader collective good, leading to conflicts between competing obligations.

Although repaying gratitude was often commendable, when misdirected, it could cloud sound ethical judgment within the complex web of personal and public relationships. For instance, the desire to honor personal favors sometimes risked overshadowing broader societal responsibilities, drawing public criticism. Conversely, fulfilling public duty at the expense of personal debts was sometimes criticized as cold or unfeeling. Virtue, in this context, lay in the ability to balance personal gratitude with the demands of justice and the common good.

Two well-known Chinese tales illustrate the intricate ethical dilemma of balancing personal gratitude with public duty as encountered by Chinese people. The first one is the story of Guan Yu.[4] While Guan Yu's unwavering loyalty to Liu Bei was celebrated as an expression of greater righteous, his decision to release Cao

[4] See Guan Yu's story in Chap. 8.

Cao—honoring a debt of gratitude—was also regarded as a righteous act. Within this tradition, neglecting either obligation could be deemed morally deficient. Guan Yu was admired precisely because he strove to uphold both public duty and personal gratitude.

Yet this very ambiguity could create space for favoritism: individuals might misuse public resources to repay personal favors, and powerful figures may exploit others' gratitude for personal gain, resulting in nepotism and injustice. In response, Confucian scholars sought to draw a clear line between private favor and public duty. While Confucianism highly valued the repayment of personal gratitude, it ultimately upheld the principle of public righteousness, which, in times of conflict, prioritized the common good over personal debt.

This ideal was vividly embodied in the renowned figure of Bao Zheng (also known as Bao Gong), the archetype of an incorruptible official celebrated in Beijing opera. In one tale, despite being raised by his sister-in-law, Bao Zheng sentenced her son to death for committing heinous crimes. This agonizing yet principled act exemplified his unwavering commitment to justice and public welfare. That said, though Bao Zheng was revered as a hero in ancient China for safeguarding greater righteousness, many people in real life often struggled to balance personal loyalty with broader moral duty—a dilemma that continues to resonate in contemporary Chinese society.

9.2.4 Guanxi, Face, and Big-Picture Perspective

Similarly to the gratitude-righteousness dynamic, the interplay between guanxi (personal connections) and big-picture perspective—considering overall situation (大局观)—represents a defining dialectic in Chinese national character. While often in tension, these two values coexist: Guanxi centers on the intricate web of personal relationships and mutual obligations, whereas the big-picture perspective calls for prioritizing common good or national interests. Grasping this inherent tension is essential to understanding the options Chinese individuals take when navigating ethical and social complexities.

9.2.4.1 Emphasizing Guanxi and Reciprocal Obligation

At the heart of China's relational culture lies guanxi, a complex system of interpersonal connections that extends from the family to friends, colleagues, and broader social networks, where familiarity fosters trust and cooperation. More than mere social networking, guanxi functions as a vital form of cultural capital, granting access to opportunities, resources, and information crucial for advancement. This system naturally demarcates social spheres: inner circles enjoy unwavering mutual support and collaboration, while those on the periphery receive limited assistance. Yet guanxi networks are not fixed. Many Chinese are adept at expanding their social circles, skillfully transforming strangers into trusted connections. As familiarity deepens, so does the potential for reciprocal support—reinforcing social cohesion throughout Chinese society.

The system operates on an ethic of reciprocal obligation, or "renqing" (人情)—the duty to return favors—through which relational equilibrium is maintained. Rooted in emotional bonds that underpin harmony and trust, renqing serves as the lifeblood of guanxi, enabling the intricate social network to expand both personal and professional opportunities. These practices include nuanced forms of exchange, such as gift-giving, hospitality, and mutual assistance, which operate within contexts ranging from familial and friendly to professional and transactional. Failure to reciprocate can lead to accusations of ingratitude, strained relationships, or even social exclusion. Consequently, cultivating and maintaining guanxi networks is not merely a conscious social strategy for personal gain, but a deeply ingrained cultural practice reflecting a fundamental worldview of reciprocity and relationality.

Renqing-guanxi is often described as the social glue binding Chinese society together; yet, when mismanaged, this very strength can paradoxically undermine broader ideals of social justice. Guanxi provides the structural network of relationships, while renqing governs the normative rules of interaction within it. Cultivating guanxi, therefore, entails navigating these social ties in accordance with the principles of renqing—reciprocity, obligation, and emotional resonance. Although vital for fostering trust and cohesion, this system carries inherent risks. As a form of personal long-term social capital requiring continual investment, renqing-guanxi can be misused, leading to favoritism, corruption, and the erosion of fairness and equal opportunity—benefiting certain individuals or small networks at the detriment of others and the public good (Fan, 2002). When it involves illicit transactions or bribery, it raises serious ethical concerns, compromising merit-based systems, fostering dishonesty, and eroding trust in the rule of law.

Confucianism addresses this tension by advocating the prioritization of public righteousness over personal interests whenever private relationships conflict with the needs of the broader community. While human nature instinctively favors kinship and in-group ties, Confucian moral cultivation demands conscious self-restraint—transcending partiality to serve the greater good, thereby fostering social harmony and enduring stability. Yet, self-discipline alone proves insufficient; it needs the support of both ethical guidance and institutional oversight, which is essential to Confucian moral cultivation. This integrated approach—balancing personal cultivation with structural accountability—remains profoundly relevant today, underscoring how robust governance and cultural values must jointly uphold justice to prevent ethical breakdowns in modern societies.

9.2.4.2 Valuing Face

Valuing "face" (面子) is a defining characteristic of Chinese people, deeply shaping social interactions, especially within the context of reciprocal favors and guanxi. "Face" involves an individual's prestige, dignity, and reputation within their community. Gaining face brings honor and pride, while losing it results in deep shame. This deeply rooted concept of face permeates all aspects of life, from business negotiations to personal relationships. It functions as the social currency that reflects an individual's importance and standing within a guanxi network. Because preserving face—for oneself and others—is so important, many Chinese go to great lengths to maintain and enhance it, actively seeking opportunities to strengthen their position within these crucial relational networks.

Maintaining face is essential within guanxi networks, guiding social interactions, influencing obligations, and shaping the management of relationships. Bestowing favors enhances one's face by signaling generosity and capability; accepting them conveys respect and affirms mutual recognition—thus reinforcing the face of both parties. Rooted in a moral economy of reciprocal obligation, face extends beyond personal gratitude to encompass one's influence and sense of duty, both personal and collective. Fulfilling obligations reinforces one's reputation and solidifies face; failing to do so can diminish face and erode trust. In essence, face functions as a form of social capital or power, earned through the strategic giving and receiving favors, strengthening bonds within social circles. Well deployed, face facilitates conflict resolution, enhances authority, and safeguards communal harmony. Ultimately, this system of face-work sustains guanxi by aligning personal reputation with the smooth functioning of the broader social network.

In Chinese social etiquette, preserving the face of others through kindness, consideration, and courtesy is vital for maintaining social harmony. This cultural logic manifests in deliberate acts of interpersonal face preservation—using tactful euphemisms, exercising diplomatic restraint, and practicing self-effacing humility to shield others from embarrassment. The strategic avoidance of public criticism or overt confrontation serves a dual purpose: it protects both the recipient's dignity and the initiator's reputation. Conversely, positive face-work—publicly recognizing achievements, deferring to status hierarchies, and performing respectful gestures—functions as social alchemy. These behaviors transmute courtesy into relational capital, elevating others while simultaneously reinforcing one's own network position. Ultimately, this economy of mutual face-giving weaves stronger interpersonal bonds and sustains the delicate ecosystem of guanxi harmony.

In the business world, face functions as a cultural lubricant, facilitating smooth interactions, fostering mutual trust, and cultivating partnerships. Individuals build rapport through the strategic exchange of face, which can positively influence negotiations and agreements, potentially resulting in cost savings. In the political realm, face is crucial for system stability. Historically, preserving face was a priority for ancient Chinese government, as it symbolized imperial authority and legitimacy. A loss of imperial face could threaten the stability of the entire political system. This framework allows for a reinterpretation of the imperial Chinese tributary system as more than a mere gesture of magnanimity.[5] Through the ritualized reception of tribute—symbolic acts of submission reciprocated with generous gifts—the royal court

[5] The Tributary System was a cornerstone of China's foreign policy, establishing a hierarchical relationship with neighboring states. These states acknowledged the Chinese emperor's supremacy and offered tribute in return for protection, trade privileges, generous return gifts, and other benefits.

bolstered its face and authority, thereby preserving imperial stability and consolidating central power.

The concept of face, representing dignity and social reputation, is deeply intertwined with the psychology of shame, a cornerstone of traditional Chinese moral education. Within China's collectivist framework, individual behavior carries communal weight, as actions reflect not just on the self but also on family and broader social networks. The fear of losing face or bringing shame acted as a strong deterrent against misconduct and a compelling incentive for proper behavior and achievement. Public exposure of normative violations led to a loss of face, triggering guilt and shame that encouraged self-reflection, correction, and moral growth. Thus, the desire to preserve face, for oneself and one's kin, became a powerful force driving self-discipline and socially appropriate conduct.

However, the pursuit of face among Chinese people, particularly in the context of guanxi networks, can also lead to unintended negative consequences. In these networks, giving face is often instrumentalized as a form of social currency to secure personal gain through ethically questionable transactions, fostering unfairness and undermining the public interest (Zhang & Si, 2010). Moreover, for many, "face" is mistakenly equated with luxury and vanity, fueling a culture of conspicuous consumption to project status and privilege. This obsession with external appearances fosters a competitive social environment in which material success is prioritized over the deeper moral dimensions of face, such as personal integrity and contributions to the collective good.

9.2.4.3 The Imperative of Big-Picture Perspective

The Chinese worldview fosters a big-picture mentality through its principles of holistic unity, dynamic interdependence, and perpetual transformation. This perspective encourages individuals to account not only for personal and interpersonal dynamics but also for the needs of the broader community and long-term development, thereby ensuring collective stability and prosperity. It is an essential orientation for navigating China's intricate social fabric, where individual and collective interests are closely intertwined.

Big-picture perspective is an important goal of moral cultivation. China's cultural emphasis on strong, reciprocal relationships has long necessitated a focus on moral cultivation, which works to harmonize, rather than oppose, the dynamics of guanxi. Because these networks could be used both constructively and opportunistically, traditional Chinese thought explicitly cautioned against exploiting guanxi networks for personal advantage at the expense of collective welfare, condemning such behavior as both ethically transgressive and socially corrosive. To reconcile this tension, philosophers advocated cultivating a macro-ethical perspective—one that elevated the interests of the state and community over individual benefit and favored sustainable prosperity over short-term benefit. Individuals who embodied this expansive moral vision and situational awareness were revered as Junzi, or even sage-leaders.

Though not formally defined in classical texts, the big-picture perspective was revered as a cardinal virtue by the Chinese, deeply ingrained in the national character. It shaped a collective ethos and an individual disposition that privileged communal welfare. At its core, this worldview called for visionary individuals to mediate disputes with impartiality, allocate resources equitably, and harmonize competing interests—all in service of sustainable societal flourishing. In doing so, they upheld the ideal that true virtue serves not factional advantage, but the peace and prosperity of All under Heaven.

These moral tensions had real consequences in social life and public decision-making. Complex Chinese societal contexts often demand long-term vision and careful balancing of personal and collective interests. When individuals gave unqualified loyalty to their immediate network—whether by repaying favors or safeguarding factional interests—this exclusive parochialism could erode ethical standards and sowe discord in the broader community. Navigating this challenge required a macro-ethical lens typically embodied by Confucian sages and junzi, who judiciously prioritized collective needs while weighing all stakeholders' interests to achieve social stability and harmony.

This moral expectation further shaped a distinctly Chinese social character, one defined by the careful navigation of tensions between personal and public ethics. In China, individuals naturally valued guanxi and obligations within their inner circle, yet this was balanced by a cultural mandate for the big-picture perspective. This ethic, which emphasized private ties while advocating self-sacrifice for the common good, was upheld across society, from elites to commoners. Chinese society long esteemed those who could subordinate personal interests to promote collective welfare, viewing such virtue as essential for managing competing claims in a society structured around kinship and guanxi. Such exemplary individuals, while honoring relational obligations, demonstrated situational mastery and a broad perspective, ultimately placing the needs of the group above their own. In mediating disputes, for instance, they might even choose solutions that disadvantage their own subgroup, aiming to advance the greater good and secure long-term harmony.

The idea of a big-picture view, one that considers overall situations, has long been shaped by Chinese philosophical traditions and moral cultivation which hold it as the highest aim. Confucianism, for example, upholds broad ethical principles like humaneness and righteousness, which individuals cultivate through self-reflection and social engagement. This moral growth requires not only the transcendence of personal biases, but also the overcoming of the natural partiality rooted in kinship ties, leading to a truly societal consciousness. In this sense, the grand vision, rising above self-centeredness and self-possessiveness, embodies the profound virtue of life-generating, renewing, and mutual flourishing.

This big-picture perspective also draws profound inspiration from Daoist virtues such as impartiality, humility, and selflessness, which emulate the Dao's manner of sustaining all creation without expectation or possessiveness. This ethos, along with Buddhism's emphasis on interdependence and universal compassion for all sentient beings, reinforces the ideal of a harmonious relationship between Heaven and humanity. Together, these philosophical traditions have cultivated a shared outlook that encourages collective consciousness, mitigates internal strife, and promotes the long-term stability and flourishing of Chinese civilization.

9.2.5 Yielding and Contending

The Chinese national character embodies another profound dialectical unity: the dynamic equilibrium between contention and yielding. Where contention serves as the engine of individual advancement and societal development, yielding operates as the essential counterbalance, tempering conflicts and cultivating harmony.

While traditional Chinese society is often portrayed as consistently prioritizing yielding and conflict avoidance, this perspective offers only a partial understanding. Contention was also an integral part of ancient Chinese life, shaping its social dynamics and historical developments. Like any complex society, China has long experienced internal contention for resources and social status, often resulting in intense disputes and even violent confrontations. In this context, humility functioned as a vital mechanism for managing these tensions through negotiation and compromise. Yielding, therefore, should not be a sign of weakness but rather as a strategic act—an expression of courtesy and goodwill aimed at de-escalating tension, transforming contention into cooperation and sustaining social harmony.

The virtue of yielding stands as a cornerstone of Chinese cultural conduct that shows deep reverence and consideration for others, embodying the Confucian ideals of humility, humaneness, and ritual propriety. Historically, those who demonstrated graceful concession, restraining improper actions or speech, were celebrated as moral exemplars. This enduring ethos continues to animate contemporary life, from offering seats to pregnant women on public transit to prioritizing the elderly in queues. In social interactions, humble language and etiquette were highly valued. Boastfulness was (and remains) culturally sanctioned against, while thoughtful accommodation of others' perspectives and sensitivities became the mark of refinement. Such values shaped characteristically nuanced modes of Chinese communication—where hints, metaphors, euphemisms, and even silence were commonly used to avoid direct confrontation or criticism.

In Chinese social interactions, courteous deference—whether to friends or strangers—serves as both a social courtesy and an act of self-cultivation. Rooted in the Confucian norm of reciprocity, such acts of civility are expected to be reciprocated, thereby fostering mutual respect and facilitating long-term cooperation. Therefore, this willingness to yield embodies kindness and foresight, while still recognizing appropriate boundaries. When goodwill is ignored or the principle of reciprocity is violated, Chinese individuals are prepared to respond with notable resourcefulness and determination. When confronted with undue provocation, they can demonstrate a level of resolve and assertiveness equal to that of any other culture. For them, just as yielding reflects cultivated virtue, measured contention demonstrates equally cultivated strength.

From a sociological perspective, the concept of yielding was deeply rooted in the realities of a densely populated society, where ruthless competition for the lion's share often bred grievance, resentment, and turmoil—ultimately bringing significant losses to all parties involved. In ancient China, the virtue of yielding emphasized attentiveness to shared interests and the restraint of one's own desires, aligning with broader cultural values such as harmony, ritual propriety, and reciprocity. Thus, individuals who possessed the strength to contend yet the wisdom to defer at the right moment were especially admired. This moral consensus reflected the belief that humility and restraint could achieve greater and more lasting success than direct confrontation.

While historically celebrated as a mark of moral refinement, the contemporary application of courteous yielding reveals potential tensions. Rigid adherence to this virtue is believed to foster passive dispositions—hindering authentic self-expression, discouraging rightful claim-making, and potentially eroding self-efficacy as individuals avoid necessary challenges.

These tensions are intensified in today's hypercompetitive environment, where cultural rewards increasingly favor strategic self-promotion over modest self-restraint. In such contexts, unilateral yielding may leave individuals vulnerable to exploitation, thereby undermining the very social harmony it was originally meant to sustain. At the same time, the erosion of humility creates its own cascade of problems as it contributes to rising individual anxiety, social friction, and interpersonal conflict. Therefore, the art of yielding, with its emphasis on seeking mutually agreeable outcomes, retains enduring value: as a method of constructive conflict resolution, a buffer against the pressures of social involution, and a safeguard for preserving relational capital in long-term interactions.

9.2.6 Assiduity and Adaptability

In terms of cultural attitude, China's cultural DNA weaves together two seemingly contradictory strands: unyielding assiduity and remarkable adaptability. On one hand, Chinese are widely admired for their tireless dedication and steadfast perseverance—qualities deeply rooted in Confucian values of self-cultivation. On the other, this diligence is paired with strategic flexibility, which fosters ingenious solutions to constrained challenges, though often through lateral approaches rather than direct confrontation of core issues. While this adaptability enables remarkable resourcefulness, its reliance on expediency over comprehensive problem-solving often sacrifices long-term integrity for short-term success.

China's robust work ethic is deeply rooted in its agricultural tradition, which emphasized that one should not eat without toiling daily, thereby prizing hard work and perseverance. This pragmatic emphasis on achieving tangible outcomes in the material world has shaped an industrious ethos, wherein accomplishments are often evaluated based on demonstrable achievements, motivating individuals for upward social mobility. Confucianism further contributes to this orientation by valuing both self-cultivation and the fulfillment of social obligations, fostering a national ethos of ongoing self-improvement, in which education and self-discipline are viewed as essential tools for both individual advancement and societal progress.

These enduring qualities of diligence and perseverance have served as a key driver of China's historical accomplishments, from sustaining social prosperity to pioneering technological innovations. In modern times, they have become instrumental in powering the nation's extraordinary economic ascent: This work ethic is evident in countless individuals who devote extended hours to education and career advancement, frequently prioritizing professional success and financial stability over personal leisure—a cultural trade-off that continues to fuel China's developmental momentum.

This strong work ethic intriguingly coexists with a high degree of adaptive flexibility. While remaining committed to core principles, this ethos functions not as rigid dictates but as dynamic frameworks—guides for discerning contextually optimal solutions. This philosophical flexibility springs from the classical Chinese worldview of perpetual transformation, embodied in the Taijitu's endless interplay of complementary opposites, suggesting that there is rarely a single "right" answer, but rather the most fitting response for a particular moment. This adaptive spirit also draws heavily from Daoist thought, which privileges indirect navigation over direct confrontation, harmonious adjustment over rigid resistance. Such resilience enables Chinese individuals to adjust strategies fluidly, embrace new methods, and solve problems resourcefully—qualities that have historically underpinned recovery from adversity and adaptation to changing circumstances.

While cultural adaptability offers considerable advantages, its overemphasis carries inherent drawbacks. The preference for indirect, situational responses may divert attention from systemic inquiry, encouraging workarounds that offer immediate solutions rather than direct engagement with fundamental problems. This "patchwork" approach may have historically hindered large-scale social transformation, instead allowing unresolved tensions to accumulate beneath a veneer of harmony that ultimately required greater corrective measures or even dynastic restart. Furthermore, it could have obstructed the emergence of a rigorous scientific framework in ancient China. The cultural preference for pragmatic, experience-based responses to immediate challenges may have come at the expense of pursuing deeper causal explanations—a hallmark of scientific progress, which requires sustained intellectual investment, patience in the face of slow results, and a willingness to question foundational assumptions.

9.2.7 Compliance and Resistance

Another dialectical tension within the Chinese national character lies in the interplay between cultivated compliance and latent resistance. While Confucian values have long upheld deference and forbearance as civic virtues, Chinese history reveals an equally potent capacity for rebellion when systemic injustice crosses critical thresholds. This duality operates not just as contradiction, but as complementary forces: the same cultural traditions that prize social harmony harbor wellsprings of righteous defiance, activated when oppression violates fundamental moral or existential boundaries.

China's strong emphasis on social cohesion and individual responsibility has cultivated a cultural orientation toward compliance and endurance. Rooted in traditions such as Confucianism, this tendency manifested in deep respect for authority, adherence to established norms, and the prioritization of collective well-being over individual ambition. Departures from these expectations may invite social disapproval, whereas reserved, humble, and deferential behavior is praised. This contrasts with more individualistic societies where self-expression and open dissent are more commonly accepted and even encouraged.

Under dominant cultural influences, ancient Chinese tended to exhibit docility and deference to authority, aligning themselves with traditional norms and hierarchical structures—most notably within familial (father-son), political (monarch-minister), and gender (husband-wife) relationships. In this regard, even the highly valued concept of harmony, when misinterpreted, could become coercive, suppressing personal initiative and limiting the expression of diverse perspectives.

Daoism also contributed to the traditionally conservative outlook of Chinese people. Its advocacy of conflict avoidance and modest self-presentation can, at times, foster passivity, while the principle of nonaction may be misread as endorsing inaction or a lack of initiatives. Within the sociocultural context of a hierarchical agrarian society—shaped by collective philosophies such as Confucianism and Daoism—many developed tendencies toward introversion, diminished self-assertiveness, and an inclination to conform. While such attentiveness to others' perspectives supports social cohesion, it can also give rise to groupthink, suppressing individual expression and prioritizing conformity over innovation and dissent.

However, the Chinese have, paradoxically, exhibited a deep-seated spirit of resistance. Though celebrated for their extraordinary endurance in hardship, they have never been passive victims of oppression. History reveals a consistent pattern: when injustice crossed an intolerable threshold, popular uprisings erupted against oppressive regimes, serving as powerful reminders to rulers of the imperative of virtuous governance.

Surprisingly, this spirit of resistance is deeply rooted in Chinese philosophy, which, alongside its emphasis on order and harmony, encompasses rich literary and philosophical traditions advocating opposition to tyranny and injustice. Grand ideals such as the "Way of Heaven," which upholds universal moral laws, and the virtue of "righteousness," which champions moral integrity and justice, have long inspired a belief that authority too must conform to ethical principles, embodying a cosmic imperative.

Throughout Chinese history, revolutions and rebellions invoked these ideas to legitimize their causes, drawing from Confucian sources such as Confucius's insistence on moral rectitude in rulers and Mencius's advocacy for righteous opposition, even at the cost of self-sacrifice. Even Legalist ideas, originally designed to consolidate the monarch's power, were at times appropriated to justify resistance. The famous insurgent slogan, "There are no seeds for kings and marquises," may have been inspired by Legalist ideas of undermining hereditary privilege and advocating merit-based advancement. The resulting dialectic between state orthodoxy and revolutionary idealism became a driving force in China's cyclical dynastic transformations, proving even the most authoritarian systems are vulnerable to moral revolt.

References

Bell, D. A., & Wang, P. (2020). *Just hierarchy: Why social hierarchies matter in China and the rest of the world.* Princeton University Press.

Chen, L. (2017). *The core values of Chinese civilization*. Springer.

Fan, Y. (2002). Ganxi's consequences: Personal gains at social cost. *Journal of Business Ethics, 38*, 371–380.

Herder, J. G. (1784/2024). *Ideas for the philosophy of the history of mankind.* Princeton University Press.

Kelly, L. M., & Cordeiro, M. (2020). Three principles of pragmatism for research on organizational processes. *Methodological Innovations, 13*(2), 1–10.

Lv, S. (1996). *Daoism and national character.* Hunan University Press.

Marchal, K., & Wenzel, C. H. (2016). Chinese perspectives on free will. In K. Timpe, M. Griffith, & N. Levy (Eds.), *The Routledge companion to free will* (pp. 374–388). Taylor & Francis.

Oshry, B. (2008). *Seeing systems: Unlocking the mysteries of organizational life*. Berrett-Koehler.

Peters, M. A. (2022). Educational philosophies of self-cultivation: Chinese humanism. *Educational Philosophy and Theory, 54*(11), 1720–1726.

Sima, Q. (2016). *Historical records*. China Bookstore.

Smith, A. H. (1894). *Chinese characteristics*. Revell.

Xu, Y. (1988). Confucianism and national character. *Journal of Beijing Normal University: Social Science Edition, 4*, 101–106.

Yang, D. (2003). Ethnic culture and psychological characteristics of Chinese people. *Neurological Diseases and Mental Health, 3*(5), 329-333.

Zhang, S. (2011). *Chinese and Western culture and self.* People's Press.

Zhang, Y., & Si, H. (2010). Cultural interpretation of Chinese face psychology. *Theoretical Observations, 1*, 52–54.

Part IV
Morality and Civilization Beyond History

Chapter 10
The Cultural Power of Moral Cultivation and Its Contemporary Challenges

To approach the world's oldest continuous civilization philosophically is a formidable challenge, demanding a nuanced understanding from both author and reader. Having established an analytical groundwork in earlier discussions, we now turn to a holistic and introspective perspective to present a fuller picture of China's cultural and moral foundations. This entails reflecting on its enduring moral legacy, remarkable resilience, and the expansive love that nourished its development, as well as their influence on the evolution of science in ancient China. Equally vital is an examination of the cultural challenges China faces today. In response, the framework of "morally grounded democracy" is introduced as a path toward reconciling moral tradition with modern governance, ultimately affirming the enduring relevance of Chinese wisdom in navigating the complexities of the contemporary world.

10.1 The Legacy of Chinese Moral Culture

Chinese morality is a dynamic and evolving construct, shaped by the interplay of philosophical traditions and historical currents. Its deep connection to the natural world and the cosmos informs its generative virtue as life-nurturing, renewing, and mutual flourishing. Beyond personal virtue, it emphasizes compassion, equilibrium, and moderation within the social sphere, seeking to harmonize individual aspirations with the collective good while embracing both diversity and transformation.

Z. You, Y. Hu, *Philosophy and Civilization: How the Idea of Moral Cultivation Shaped China*, East-West Dialogues in Educational Philosophy and Theory,
https://doi.org/10.1007/978-981-95-5660-1_10

10.1.1 Virtue as Cosmic Nature and Embodiment of the Dao

The Chinese tradition of moral cultivation views virtue as intrinsically linked to cosmic order and harmony, with moral principles reflecting the inherent patterns of the natural world rather than mere human subjectivity. Consequently, the process of moral cultivation involves aligning the self with these cosmic norms while skillfully adapting them to particular circumstances. This dual practice—of celestial alignment and contextual discernment—is deemed essential for sustaining societal order and universal harmony, ultimately contributing to the flourishing of both the individual and the collective.

The essence of Chinese virtue is deeply rooted in the Dao, the primordial source and first mover of the world, whose profound potency fosters life and promotes co-flourishing. As the origin of life and harmony, the Dao embodies generative virtue that transcends partiality, extending beneficence to all beings. Fundamentally, the Dao manifests vitality and constant renewal, necessitating a moral framework that cultivates wisdom, compassion, and altruism—qualities essential for transcending selfish desires and aligning human conduct with this cosmic principle.

The Dao pulses with life-giving transformation, its creative rhythm flowing through all existence. All things arise from and return to it, cycling endlessly through constant change. Within this dynamic flow, the individual sheds rigid moral absolutism, attuning instead to the broader context and unique circumstances of each moment to respond with harmonious and fitting grace. This continuous adaptation prevents stagnation and excess, cultivating a state that fosters the interdependent flourishing of all beings—the fullest expression of its nature.

The Dao is not merely a Daoist concept but a foundational principle adopted across Chinese philosophical traditions to ground the cultivation of virtue. It reveals a world rooted not in ruthless jungle laws, but in the nurturing principles of growth, transformation, and coexistence. Heaven and Earth exemplify these altruistic, life-sustaining characteristics, which give rise to the virtue of humaneness or compassion. This worldview contrasts sharply with the popular image of nature as a brutal arena of survival. In traditional Chinese philosophy, the logic of nature is conceived from a holistic and macro-level perspective as a prescriptive and life-affirming mandate, emphasizing interdependence and balance. While tigers prey on dears, such predation sustains ecological balance—and when predators perish, their remains nourish other life forms, perpetuating the cycle of life. Virtue, in this view, emerges not as an artificial imposition but nature's principles incarnate: it tempers contention, nurtures cooperation, and fulfills both nature's role in sustaining life and humanity's calling to cultivate harmony, coexistence, and shared prosperity.

This cosmic order pursues not absolute equality, but dynamic equilibrium—a balance of complementary forces through which life sustains and prospers. In this harmony, each being flourishes by its unique gifts, where lacks are met with abundance and surpluses temper scarcity. To move with this rhythm in the human world demands virtues like humility and selflessness, ensuring one's growth nurtures the whole. For where imbalance takes root, disruption follows, and suffering begins.

10.1.2 Virtue as Balance and Harmony of Interests

For ancient Chinese, virtue and "Heaven" are deeply intertwined. Heaven is often seen as the source of human conscience, while virtue reflects the cosmic order inspiring self-cultivation. In this context, Confucianism's emphasis on humaneness and Daoism's focus on spontaneity offer distinct interpretations of this heavenly way, yet both embodying harmony and balance. This dynamic fosters a reciprocal human-cosmic relationship: Heaven and Earth bestow boundless creativity, nurturing all life, while humanity's flourishing completes the cosmos, rendering the universe not only vast but purposeful.

Ultimately, virtue is most powerfully expressed through human development. In Chinese philosophy, "Heaven" represents cosmic justice that integrates both individual virtue and collective moral will. Its expansive nature inspires people to transcend personal limitations and strive for the long-term flourishing of humanity. This perspective provides a contemporary interpretation of "Heaven's Way" as a holistic approach to reconciling diverse interests and promoting sustainable development for both humanity and the natural world.

Overall, traditional Chinese virtue prioritizes the harmonization of individual conduct with collective well-being, promoting cooperation, social stability, and a strong sense of shared responsibility. Unlike ethical frameworks that elevate individual rights as paramount, Chinese ethics emphasize contextual awareness, relational duties, and the greater good, requiring individuals to weigh these diverse factors in ethical decision-making. Within the Confucian tradition, this ethos manifests as a harmonious social order, where each member's flourishing sustains the whole. Such harmony requires individuals to balance personal aspirations with communal welfare, cultivating a flexible yet principled approach to ethical challenges. Historically, this framework has been instrumental in preserving China's social cohesion, reflecting a vision of morality that is as pragmatic as it is aspirational.

The idea of reconciling interests is a key theme not only in Confucian ethics but also in Daoist thought. Lao Tzu (2010) observes, "The way of tian [Heaven] is to let some go where there is excess to augment where there is not enough," while the way of man is "to take away from those who do not have enough in order to give more to those who already have too much" (Chap. 77). The former seeks equilibrium, whereas the latter, driven by greed, leads to imbalance and chaos. Lao Tzu's critique of "the way of man" targets the self-serving pursuit of power and wealth, which deepens inequality and fuels conflict. In contrast, the idea "the Way of Heaven" embodies a broader perspective, prioritizing long-term harmony and sustainable development.

This emphasis on harmony, characterized by balance and appropriateness, resonates with Confucianism's ideal of achieving social equilibrium through moderation and measured conduct. For both Confucius and Lao Tzu, sages are those who truly align with the Way of Heaven. Whereas Confucian sages would actively guide society toward harmonious relationship and mitigate wealth disparities through rituals and moral regulation, Daoist sages would promote simplicity and the reduction of desire, allowing such imbalances to diminish naturally.

Confucianism's emphasis on public righteousness over private advantage reflects its foundational aim of harmonizing competing interests to preserve social harmony. This principle was especially relevant in agrarian China, where tightly knit familial bonds frequently intersected with—yet at times conflicted with—communal obligations. In such a society, individuals naturally prioritized the well-being of their immediate circle, potentially leading to conflict and social instability. Confucianism addresses this tension by advocating for a dynamic balance between self-interest and collective welfare through the principle of public righteousness. This ideal is embodied in its concept of "rule by virtue," which emphasizes ethical leadership and moral cultivation to harmonize personal and communal needs.

Confucian scholars elucidate the relationship between virtue and interests through the distinction between the Junzi and the petty person. The petty individual is characterized by an exclusive focus on self, family, and immediate connections, whereas the Junzi's concern extends to the well-being of others and society at large. The Junzi's virtue is rooted in this public-mindedness: while acknowledging the importance of familial bonds, they uphold a broader sense of responsibility that encompasses the greater community. In contrast, the petty individual, constrained by a limited perspective, prioritizes solely self-interest, ultimately impeding both individual and societal flourishing.

Mainstream Chinese virtue is inherently relational and collective—its practice and evaluation embedded in the fabric of social relationships. Virtue emerges through the dual process of personal development and active contribution to others' flourishing. This ethical framework discourages excessive self-interest, exploitation, or actions that hinder communal progress. Instead, it prioritizes mutual assistance, collective development, and a willingness to make concession or even sacrifices for the greater good. While prioritizing close relationships is natural, a truly virtuous individual upholds the collective needs above immediate personal ties. This does not mean neglecting personal relationships but rather ensuring that they contribute to—or at least do not undermine—the well-being of the larger society.

In Chinese culture, leaders are held to elevated moral standards due to the far-reaching impact of their actions, making virtue indispensable for addressing the broader needs. Ideally, emperors were expected to embody this moral leadership, assuming responsibility for the well-being of all under their rule. A hallmark of virtuous leadership is fair and equitable resource allocation. Leaders should promote individuals based on both virtue and merit, rather than just personal connections. This includes supporting capable members within their inner circle while also actively identifying and elevating talented individuals from outside their immediate networks. Such an approach fosters solidarity and cohesion across a vast and diverse society.

In Confucianism, virtue lies in maintaining a dynamic balance between competing interests, prioritizing the broader societal good without neglecting close personal bonds. This humanistic philosophy emphasizes contextual judgment, attentive to the complexities of Chinese social and moral life. A classic example is the dilemma of whether to report a family member's wrongdoing. Confucius himself, deeply valuing familial bonds, suggested that a son might conceal a parent's minor offense (like stealing a goat) out of filial piety (Confucius, 2016a, 13.18).

Yet in cases of grave crimes that jeopardize public righteousness, Confucian tradition prioritizes reporting the transgression (Zuo, 2024). This reflects Confucianism's nuanced approach to ethics: shielding minor faults preserves the emotional bonds foundational to humaneness, whereas addressing serious crimes safeguards social righteousness, exemplifying its deeper moral vision. By navigating this tension, the tradition avoids both the cold rigidity of legalism and the moral hazards of unchecked partiality, ultimately sustaining both personal and collective welfare.

10.1.3 Collective Ethos and Public Spirit

Overall, Chinese moral philosophy fundamentally emphasizes collective harmony, in contrast to Western ethical systems that prioritize individual rights as foundational. Confucianism, for example, established a framework of moral cultivation that reinforces collectivist ethics within both family and society (Pan, 2022), which, unsurprisingly, requires both self-discipline and social influence to develop and uphold moral values.

The emphasis on the common good facilitates cooperation in large-scale endeavors and encourages individuals to align personal conduct with societal needs. Such an orientation enables the efficient distribution of resources and coordinated development, often yielding significant public goods—such as feeding more people with limited resources. Yet, this collectivist paradigm carries an inherent tension: while it strengthens resource mobilization, it may also marginalize individual concerns and, in some cases, be invoked to justify the erosion of individual rights.

Nonetheless, it is crucial not to view this collective tendency as absolute. Chinese civilization upholds unity not through unconditional uniformity but through the principle of Taiji—harmony amidst diversity. This means individuals do not blindly conform to collective goals; rather, they often exercise reason and discernment. When called upon to act, many of them question the rationale behind their actions, considering whether they align with the heavenly principle, human feeling, and local realities. This emphasis on reflection fosters flexibility, allowing for independent judgment within the framework of collective ethics.

China's enduring prioritization of the common good is vividly embodied in its Confucian ritual tradition, which cultivates a shared sense of purpose and communal obligation. In a densely populated society, observing proper etiquette and following rituals became essential for maintaining social harmony. While these practices may seem restrictive, they foster mutual reverence, instill a sense of individual worth, and strengthen belonging within the social order. Rituals promote harmony by establishing clear norms, building trust, and preventing the infringement of others' rights. Although this model presupposes hierarchy, it enhances social coordination, improves resource allocation, and minimizes waste. It may not actively promote, and sometimes even discourages, individuality, innovation, or risk-taking, yet it has proven to be a cost-effective and efficient system for sustaining a large population amid limited resources.

Confucian moral cultivation nurtured a profound sense of public spirit through its emphasis on collective ethos and communal values. Far from promoting blind obedience as some critics claim, Confucianism sought to harmonize interdependent relationships across all spheres—from familial bonds to societal obligations and state governance. This strengthens the "family-state continuum," reinforcing core Chinese values: familial harmony social order, the well-being of the state, and peace for All under Heaven. This emphasis on ethical behavior fosters a sense of public responsibility within individuals, that "when the grand course was pursued, a public and common spirit ruled all under the sky" (Confucius, 2016b, LÎ YUN).

Of course, traditional Chinese public spirit differs significantly from modern conceptions. The family-state model, which organizes society around the structure of an extended family, tends to blur the boundary between private and public interests, thereby constraining the scope of what is considered truly "public." Moreover, originating from a hierarchical social structure, Confucian public spirit emphasizes traditional moral cultivation and social harmony. While it shares a concern for the common good with modern public spirit, it differs by prioritizing collective welfare over individual rights and equality, and by advocating for elite responsibility rather than broad civic participation. Another key distinction lies in its strong emphasis on virtue, whose influence endures across both ethical and political domains—for instance, the ideal of the "greater self" continues to shape contemporary moral education and models of governance.

The concept of the "greater self" emerged in Chinese thought as a vital ethical counterbalance to the natural human inclination toward familial and factional loyalties, which often threatened to compromise broader social obligations. Recognizing the pervasive risk of self-centeredness—particularly among power-holders who might prioritize private interests over the public good—Confucian philosophy emphasized an ongoing moral cultivation and critique. This cultivation actively addresses the enduring philosophical challenge of balancing public and private interests and, when necessary, affirms the primacy of the public good. It is precisely for this reason that Confucians placed such paramount importance on prioritizing "public righteousness" over private gains, promoting the cultivation of the "greater self" or even "no-self" as a fundamental societal solution.

10.1.4 Confucian Ethics as a Cultural Religion

China developed a distinctive civilizational model where philosophical traditions, most notably Confucianism rather than institutional religion, served as the primary source of moral and social governance. While Chinese religions such as religious Daoism and Buddhism offered spiritual solace and addressed existential questions, Confucianism, as the prevailing philosophy and often the state's official ideology, provided a comprehensive framework for social order and ethical conduct.

In this configuration, Confucianism fulfilled religion's typical social functions—establishing norms, reinforcing collective identity, and transmitting values—while maintaining its philosophical character. This synthesis produced what may be termed China's "cultural religion," wherein secular moral philosophy assumed the binding force typically associated with sacred traditions in other civilizations.

Confucian moral cultivation also provided a distinctive form of spiritual fulfillment that arguably paralleled religious systems. Its conception of the "Mandate of Heaven" established an ethical cosmology where moral harmony between human conduct and cosmic order reduced reliance on the worship of a personal deity characteristic of monotheistic traditions. While Confucianism lacked a savior figure, its concept of Heaven, along with ancestor veneration and reverence for sages, partially fulfilled spiritual functions. By urging individuals to honor traditional values through celestially aligned ritual, Confucianism performed a role akin to that of religion in satisfying the human need for spiritual meaning and moral coherence.

Confucianism shares with religious traditions the fundamental aim of cultivating inner peace and deep fulfillment yet pursues this through a distinctly humanistic path. Rather than seeking salvation in an afterlife, Confucian practice locates fulfillment in the conscientious realization of one's earthly roles and relationships. By cultivating moral virtues, Confucianism fosters both personal tranquility and societal harmony. Its ethical framework provides individuals with a deep sense of purpose, offering consolation through a life grounded in moral integrity and meaningful connections. In the face of life's uncertainties and upheavals, individuals can maintain inner peace through a quasi-transcendent understanding of human existence.

This perspective emphasizes achieving well-being amidst life's complexities by recognizing the interconnectedness of all things, accepting inevitable fluctuations, and finding meaning and purpose through the fulfillment of one's heavenly mandate—undertaking responsibilities within human relationships. Confucius himself, while acutely aware of life's adversities, charted perhaps the most demanding yet rewarding path: the cultivation of worldly harmony through moral excellence. His teachings of humaneness and reciprocity, alongside those of other influential philosophers, profoundly contributed to the fulfillment of ancient Chinese spiritual life.

10.2 The Resilience of Chinese Civilization

Ancient China's remarkable resilience defies easy classification as either nation or empire. It emerged as a unique civilization forged across an immense geographical canvas by integrating diverse peoples under a continuous cultural paradigm. What particularly sustained this civilization across millennia was its steady commitment to moral cultivation, a guiding principle that fostered cultural continuity, adaptability, and political stability.

This millennia-long tradition of moral cultivation does more than establish a shared framework of values—it operates as a dynamic cultural mechanism that shapes collective identity, preserves core traditions, and reinforces societal cohesion. As a stabilizing force, it has enabled Chinese civilization to endure external pressures and internal upheavals while continually adapting and evolving. Building on earlier analysis, this section adopts a holistic perspective to examine how the interwoven dynamics of moral cultivation underpin China's civilizational resilience.

10.2.1 The Dynamics of Centralized Authority Under Virtuous Rule

While natural law theory posits universal reason as the foundation of human laws, ancient Chinese philosophy advanced a distinct yet parallel concept. It anchored the distribution of power in virtue and ethical responsibility, viewing them as expressions of the cosmos's inherent order. In this framework, a ruler's legitimacy was not solely derived from their royal lineage but also on moral integrity. A virtuous leader, even without noble ancestry, could ascend to power during dynastic transitions, whereas those who deviated from moral righteousness risked losing the "Mandate of Heaven"—and with it, their right to rule.

Bearing this perspective, the ideal Chinese emperor was, theoretically, a sage-ruler, serving as a moral exemplar for the entire empire. Their leadership was expected to be guided by a sense of public duty, with legitimacy based on fulfilling the collective well-being. While wielding ultimate authority, the emperor did not govern alone. A robust bureaucracy, composed of scholar-officials selected through the imperial examination system, both strengthened and restrained royal authority. These officials, shaped by Confucian virtues, bore the responsibility of advising and, when necessary, admonishing rulers who strayed from ethical governance. While history records many tyrannical emperors and corrupt officials, the prevailing moral framework functioned as a significant check on their excesses.

The Chinese imperial system emerged as a crucial counterweight to the centrifugal pull and competing ambitions of a kinship-based society, where powerful clans and regional factions often prioritized parochial loyalties over the common good. By centralizing authority, the emperor served as the ultimate arbiter between competing interests and a unifying force capable of mobilizing collective action across the empire. In this context, a centralized imperial government played a crucial role in managing entrenched power blocs and curbing localist inclinations, which, if left unchecked, could have fractured social cohesion and imperiled unity across such a vast realm.

Such political centralization was not merely an administrative necessity; it reflected a fundamental feature of ancient Chinese thought that prioritizes unity and collective responsibility. Whereas Western traditions typically elevate individual rights and liberties as foundational, Chinese thought has long emphasized the individual's embeddedness within interdependent social networks. This orientation prioritizes collective welfare and emphasizes personal duty to sustain societal harmony. Take, for instance, Confucian virtues: while they uphold the family as the cornerstone of the state, they also extend beyond familial loyalty to embrace the broader ideal of the common good under Heaven. Navigating these overlapping obligations required both moral self-cultivation and strong, virtuous governance to sustain societal balance.

A robust central government with extensive responsibilities offered several advantages. By consolidating decision-making power, it enabled strategic planning, coordinated resource distribution for major public works, and harmonized long-term objectives with pressing necessities, all critical for maintaining social stability and collective prosperity. Yet this concentration of authority also carried inherent risks. It created heavy dependence on the imperial government and empowered officials, increasing the risk of corruption, bureaucratic inefficiencies, and the neglect of local communities and individual concerns. Most critically, the very efficiency that enabled rapid execution of large-scale projects could paradoxically inhibit adaptability, leaving the system poorly equipped to address unforeseen challenges or evolving circumstances.

It is important, nonetheless, to distinguish this centralized system from strict totalitarianism. Though localities were subject to central authority, they actively negotiated with the government to advocate for their diverse needs and ideas, exercising a degree of discretion and autonomy. This bargaining typically took place informally, in an unregulated and personalized way. Confucian virtue played a crucial role as a buffer within this system. Its emphasis on social harmony facilitated communication and helped mitigate potential conflicts between localities and the central government. In contrast, Legalism removed this mediating influence by prioritizing efficiency, often pushing society toward a rigid and tightly controlled structure. This approach, while tremendously strengthening imperial power, also heightened the risk of dynastic collapse by disregarding local autonomy and individual needs.

10.2.2 Virtuocracy and Meritocracy

The term "virtuocracy," alongside meritocracy, refers to a system of governance that entrusts power to individuals who embody both moral integrity and exceptional competence. While desirable in an emperor and fundamental to official selection, this principle proved key to Chinese civilization's enduring resilience. At its core lies a pragmatic approach to virtue: leaders and elites were expected not only to grasp ethical principles (the Dao) but to embody them, guiding society through just and humane policies that addressed real-world challenges and advanced the common good.

Confucian moral cultivation, particularly through education and civil examination system, played a pivotal role in establishing a political order where merit and virtue—not birthright—primarily determined elite status. For nearly 1300 years, this system profoundly shaped China's educational and political landscapes. Beyond positioning Confucian learning as the principal avenue for social advancement, it also served as a leveling force: even established families risked losing their status if descendants failed to demonstrate ability. This continuous circulation of talent sustained a virtuous-meritocratic order, rendering ancient Chinese society renewable, resilient, and dynamic.

The confluence of moral cultivation, competent and ethical leadership, and social mobility underpinned ancient China's adaptability and continuity. By prioritizing collective well-being over individual desires, the system encouraged all members of society, especially the elites, to uphold moral conduct, exercise self-restraint, and apply their talents for social stability and long-term development. These measures helped mitigate conflicts and slow down the widening of the wealth disparities, bolstering the resilience of many Chinese dynasties and the long-term continuity of Chinese civilization.

10.2.3 Dynastic Cycles and the Resilience of Civilization

Ancient China is known for its dynastic cycles, a historical phenomenon propelled by a complex synergy of cultural, political, economic, educational, and ethnic factors—among which moral cultivation was a constant and foundational element. By shaping ethical beliefs, conduct, collective norms, and societal values, this moral emphasis forged a cohesive national identity grounded in shared principles and a common sociocultural consciousness. Although it could not ultimately prevent dynastic collapse, the resilient cultural foundation it cultivated enabled the revival of successive regimes and sustained the remarkable continuity of Chinese civilization through even the most profound disruptions.

10.2.3.1 The Periodic Collapse of Dynasties

Chinese history unfolds as a continuous sequence of dynastic rise and decline, with many regimes enduring two to three centuries. In their early phases, dynasties often achieved periods of stability and prosperity, as peasant access to land increased, whether through postwar depopulation, state-led redistribution, or the reclamation of unused lands. Yet this equilibrium proved unsustainable. From the mid-dynastic period onward, population growth consistently outpaced the availability of arable land, intensifying competition for finite resources. Scarcity was worsened by systemic vulnerabilities: the accumulation of land by powerful elites, administrative corruption, fiscal crises, erosion of imperial authority, natural disasters, and large-scale peasant uprisings—often compounded by external threats such as nomadic invasions. Although each dynasty faced distinct challenges, it was the convergence of these interrelated pressures that eventually overwhelmed the empire's capacity to cope.

Moral cultivation, institutionalized through Confucian governance frameworks, served as a critical stabilizing force in imperial China, tempering social conflict and preserving order. By promoting ethical leadership and a sense of collective responsibility, it helped curb abuses of power, alleviate economic inequality, and strengthen communal bonds. Historically, dynasties that consistently upheld virtuous rule achieved significantly greater longevity and stability than those reliant on coercive Legalist measures.

That said, the Confucian system had its limitations. While effective at managing routine social tensions, it ultimately proved inadequate against accumulated structural problems—relentless land annexation, systemic fiscal decay, entrenched interests, and bureaucratic malpractice. As these crises intensified, the efficacy of moral persuasion, even when reinforced by institutional oversight, inevitably waned. Once the state's moral authority eroded beyond repair, social crises deepened, tensions mounted, and dynastic collapse loomed.

Granted, each phase of decline also spurred efforts to forestall the crisis. As political and fiscal problems intensified, rulers frequently resorted to pragmatic reforms, restructuring political, military, and economic systems to consolidate power. Legalist principles, which emphasized high efficiency and centralized control, acted as a disruptive force, challenging entrenched interests, strengthening central power, and temporarily easing fiscal strain. Throughout Chinese history, Confucianism and Legalist ideas coexisted in a dynamic tension: Confucian principles were publicly championed as fundamental policy, whereas certain Legalist measures were discreetly implemented. This interplay created a cyclical rhythm of stability and transformation, with moral cultivation and coercive measures either complementing one another or alternating in prominence. Notably, although moral virtue remained the foundation of governance, it was often pragmatic Confucian officials, vested with imperial authority, who led institutional reforms during periods of crisis. They believed that while humaneness constituted the soul of good governance, reform functioned as the sharp blade required to confront the empire's most urgent threats.

Nevertheless, Legalist-inspired reforms frequently provoked fierce opposition. Most Confucians viewed them as corrosive to the social fabric, arguing that they sacrificed individual welfare and social harmony for ruthless efficiency, leaving ordinary people vulnerable to exploitation and breeding social unrest. The outcomes of these reforms proved uneven. Some achieved partial success: breaking the grip of entrenched elites, relieving fiscal woes, and extending dynastic rigor; others fizzled or rebounded disastrously, inflaming class divides and, at worst, accelerating collapse. As virtuous governance faded, these misfires deepened regime fragility, weakening defenses against peasant revolts, nomadic raids, or their confluence—thus perpetuating the inexorable dynastic cycle.

10.2.3.2 Phoenix Logic: Civilizational Continuity Amid Dynastic Cycles

Despite its limitations, moral cultivation remained crucial to the endurance of Chinese civilization. Deeply embedded in the social fabric, this ethical and educational system shaped cultural values across generations, harmonizing familial, political, and cosmic ideals. It forged unifying bonds that transcended dynastic upheavals—cultivating shared identity, sustaining cultural resilience during fragmentation, and inspiring recurrent movements toward reunification, as capable leaders reclaimed the Mandate of Heaven. Though dynasties rose and fell, the moral foundation upheld the essential character of Chinese civilization. This dynastic change resembled the legendary phoenix, rising anew from its ashes; through it all, Chinese civilization endured, continuously adapting and renewing itself without ever losing its core identity.

Chinese civilization developed upon a robust ethical foundation that harmonized diversity within unity. Initially rooted in family values, the tradition evolved into a broader cultural identity that solidified the Chinese as a people. Acceptance of its moral norms in human relationships, rather than ethnicity, became a hallmark of being Chinese. Such an inclusive cultural framework fostered a robust internal cohesion and social harmony, facilitating the development of a secular society with exceptional organizational capacity. This strength was evident in the way the Chinese cultivated interpersonal relationships, social networks, and production systems.

Throughout history, this cultural consensus functioned as a powerful centripetal force, drawing people and surrounding ethnic groups into its field, where individuals embodied the essence of the civilization and could regroup and rebuild it even after periods of disintegration. Such unity was rooted not only in Confucian ethical teachings but also in a diverse array of influences, including Daoism's principles of inclusivity and non-coercive action, as well as Mohism's ideals of universal care and mutual aid. Despite their differences, these philosophies converged on a common goal: building "peace and stability" (安定) through a shared vision of unity and ethical goal (Pan, 2020). Together, they formed a comprehensive system of moral cultivation that has shaped and continues to shape the identity of the Chinese people.

The Confucian-inspired family-state paradigm fundamentally shaped China's collective consciousness and a deep sense of belonging, serving as the bedrock for social stability and cultural perseverance. While occasionally resorting to coercive measures, it primarily fostered voluntary alignment between local communities and central authority through common ethical and cultural norms. This framework transformed diverse regions into a unified civilization, bound by common values of righteousness and collective welfare, and sustained a deep sense of belonging across generations.

Within this framework, individual desires were intricately interwoven with, and often subordinated to, the needs of the family and the broader societal collective. The pursuit of public righteousness reconciled familial and clan interests with the state's welfare, engendering a shared sense of purpose. Such cultural cohesion proved indispensable for a vast and geographically dispersed empire like China, fostering a collective consciousness that reinforced civilizational resilience: even amid political upheavals and dynastic transition, family and clan networks endured, safeguarding traditional values and the ideal of "All under Heaven." Through this familial transmission of core principles, Chinese civilization consistently regenerated itself, reaffirming the same cultural foundations with each new dynasty.

The enduring vitality of Chinese civilization springs from its profound commitment to three foundational pillars: shared ethical norms, veneration of ancestral wisdom, and a holistic worldview emphasizing universal interconnectedness. The steadfast devotion of families and communities to these ideals preserved the civilization's essence, while their shared vision of unity inspired continual revival. At its core, China's cultural continuity reflects the transformative power of moral cultivation—the invisible thread weaving Chinese history into a silk scroll of dynastic rises and falls, preserving the fundamental ethos of the Chinese civilization. As the renowned Confucian Gu Yanwu remarked, there is a distinction between the end of a dynasty and the fall of All under Heaven (Gu, 2021). As long as the virtues of humaneness and righteousness endure, the belief on "All under Heaven," China as a cultural entity, persists.

It is noteworthy that the system of moral cultivation produced a highly competent elite class of Confucian scholars who served as cultural custodians of Chinese civilization. Aside from aiding emperors in effective governance, they played a crucial role in preserving cultural heritage and transmitting moral values. Even when the centralized regime faltered, these cultural leaders and educators remained steadfast in their commitment to Chinese identity. Their shared linguistic heritage, ethical framework, and cultivated sense of cultural continuity provided the foundation for China's remarkable resilience, facilitating both cultural and political resurgence, even under the rule of minority ethnic groups.

The extraordinary endurance of Chinese civilization can also be attributed to its ability to absorb and selectively adapt external cultural influences. By integrating foreign ideas—such as Buddhism from India and, later, Western thought—China has continuously enriched its intellectual and cultural landscape. This openness, however, is not indiscriminate. A robust foundation of core cultural values serves as a steadfast anchor, allowing China to adapt external influences while preserving its own identity. The balance between openness and preservation has been a cornerstone of Chinese civilization's strength and adaptability throughout history, enabling it to weather countless storms and emerge stronger.

10.3 Expansive Love and Chinese Cosmopolitanism

While myriad factors play a role, history shows that societies grounded in love, compassion, and empathy tend to exhibit remarkable stability and prosperity. The human connection and care—expressed through diverse cultural traditions—serve as fundamental pillars for building strong and enduring social structures. Even in Medieval Europe, Christian doctrines of charity and forgiveness softened feudal hardships while knitting communities together. Likewise, during the Islamic Golden Age, the emphasis on love, compassion, and charity toward all, regardless of background or belief, played a crucial role in sustaining a thriving and inclusive society.

Expansive love, manifested through inclusive governance, cultural tolerance, and a unifying ideology, was essential to the cohesion of history's large, multiethnic empires, as it transcended familial and tribal loyalties in favor of broader solidarity. Embracing human diversity in this manner fostered social cohesion and long-term sustainability, promoting cooperation and mutual understanding across societal divides and cultural differences. In ancient China, this ideal of inclusivity found powerful expression in the concept of "All under Heaven." More than political rhetoric, this idea embodied a sophisticated, cosmopolitan governing vision that aspired to uphold collective unity while respecting regional and cultural particularities, a delicate balance vital to the endurance of one of history's most diverse and resilient civilizations.

10.3.1 All Under Heaven and Cosmopolitanism

The concept of "All under Heaven," along with and influenced by the doctrines of the Dao and the Way of Heaven, espouses a spirit of public service and expansive love toward all people and beings. Beyond informing the Chinese political worldview, this concept carries profound implications for cultivating the greater self—one rooted in deep compassion, inclusive vision, and an abiding awareness of interdependence.

The implications of All under Heaven were diverse. Politically and geographically, it referred to the known world, with China at the center, surrounded by concentric circles of tributary states and foreign lands, implying a sense of cultural hierarchy and political centrality. For rulers, it underscored the extent of their authority while emphasizing the obligation to govern responsibly and uphold the welfare of all within their domain. Within the framework of moral cultivation, it encouraged transcending familial and territorial boundaries in pursuit of universal brotherhood, envisioning all people as part of a shared moral order. This broader, more inclusive vision emphasized the interconnectedness of all things within a greater whole.

The system of "All under Heaven" is intrinsically open and inclusive, symbolized by the Supreme Ultimate diagram, which illustrates the organic coexistence of opposites. The framework embraces the idea of "harmony amidst differences," providing a valuable framework for navigating diversity. It advocates for a pluralistic world order where cultures, while preserving their distinct identities and even encountering occasional conflicts, can coexist and engage in meaningful exchange. Grounded in ethical principles, the holistic vision upholds the unity of all existence, the interconnectedness of life, and the pursuit of universal harmony. This outlook is reflected in the coexistence of Confucianism, Daoism, and Buddhism in China, as well as its historical acceptance of Islam and Christianity. Ultimately, the ideal envisions a world where rigid divisions dissolve, and all things find their place through interplay and interdependence, fostering shared prosperity and harmony rather than antagonism.

The outlook of "All under Heaven" naturally emphasizes the deep interconnectedness of human well-being, recognizing that cooperation yields mutual benefit. Even in its early formulation during the Western Zhou dynasty—when its geographical scope was still limited—the ideal of "All under Heaven" envisioned a system rooted in shared prosperity and peaceful coexistence. This emphasis on harmony reflects a uniquely Chinese cosmopolitan ethos, offering insights highly relevant to today's complex and interdependent world.

This notion contributed significantly to the formation of Chinese cultural identity, which prioritizes shared values over ethnic origin. Individuals, regardless their ancestry, could be considered Chinese by embracing Chinese cultural traditions, particularly ethical beliefs. Throughout history, various ethnic groups have integrated into Chinese society through cultural exchange and the adoption of Han customs.

For instance, Emperor Xiaowen of Northern Wei dynasty, a ruler of Xianbei ethnicity, actively promoted Han culture among his people, ultimately leading to their assimilation into the Han population. While assimilation raises questions about cultural preservation, it had contributed to the evolution and enrichment of Han culture. At the same time, many ethnic minority groups have maintained distinct identities while coexisting with the Han, adding to China's cultural diversity. This underscores the multifaceted nature of Chinese identity, which encompasses both shared cultural values and ethnic pluralism.

Despite some controversy, the "All under Heaven" notion embodies a form of cosmopolitan outlook. Confucianism was often excluded from this discussion of cosmopolitanism due to its emphasis on differentiated love—where moral obligations extend outward from the family to the state and ultimately to the world, raising concerns about its compatibility with a universalist ethic. Nevertheless, Ivanhoe (2014) offers a nuanced perspective, framing Confucianism as a moderate variant of cosmopolitanism. Rather than conceiving humanity as a collection of isolated individuals, Confucianism envisions a global community structured as an extended family bound by ethical relationships akin to those between brothers or friends.

This humanistic cosmopolitanism is exemplified by the neo-Confucian idea that a benevolent person perceives all things in Heaven and Earth as an organic whole. In this framework, graduated love forms the vital foundation, while extended love represents its ultimate purpose. Differing from strict egalitarianism of Kantian traditions, this extended affection emphasizes deeper care for those closest to us, yet consistently radiates kindness and respect to all people and beings, treating them as extended family members or honored guests. Importantly, Confucianism does not endorse a diluted form of love. Like a well of water, it represents a concentrated care that flows outward—becoming less intimate with distance, yet retaining its full moral substance. While a petty person discriminates among individuals, a virtuous (greater) person sees everyone under Heaven as one family and China as a single body (Wang, 2011), transcending personal bias and favoritism to act with justice and altruistic virtues.

The cosmopolitan ideal of "one body for All under Heaven" finds it's rooted in the concept of "expansive love," a compassion that extends beyond one's immediate circle to embrace all, essential for promoting social harmony and fulfilling moral responsibilities toward the broader world. This ethic is not unique to Chinese thought. Across civilizations, leaders who prioritized benevolence and inclusivity over cruelty earned greater support and contributed to lasting stability. Cyrus the Great, the first emperor of Persia, embodied a vision akin to that of "All under Heaven." Though a formidable conqueror, he is remembered above all for his generosity and respect toward diverse peoples. His policies of religious tolerance and cultural inclusion not only reflected his expansive vision but also reinforced the strength and cohesion of his empire.

Beyond the political sphere, the ideal of expansive love flourishes in various religions and philosophies. Christianity upholds the commandment to love one's neighbor, even an enemy, embodying the aspiration for universal love. Buddhism advocates for universal compassion toward all sentient beings, coupled with an altruistic commitment to liberate them from suffering. Confucianism, while rooted in graded affection within the family, extends this ethical framework toward a vision of caring for "All under Heaven." Across these traditions, this shared ethos of expansive love has profoundly shaped enduring moral and philosophical thought.

What, then, defines "expansive love"? This all-encompassing affection, originating from the tenderest part in our heart, arises from a fundamental human need for connection and existential meaning. Expansive love seeks happiness not only for oneself but for all beings, nurturing their growth and flourishing. It manifests itself through acts of care, appreciation, and respect—for one another and the world we share—even to the point of self-sacrifice for the greater good. Though its expressions may vary across cultures, a universal thread of kindness and openness runs through them, ultimately animating the timeless ideal of "All under Heaven"—a cosmopolitan love especially embodied in Confucian thought, as explored in the following discussion.

10.3.2 Expansive Humaneness and Greater Righteousness

While grounded in familial and immediate social relationships, Confucianism ultimately aspires toward a broader vision: achieving social harmony and lasting peace through alignment with the Way of Heaven, whose moral priority transcends mere filial piety or blind loyalty. For many, obeying one's father constitutes only small virtues. As Xunzi eloquently states, the great virtue lies in following righteousness rather than blind obedience to one's father and adhering to the Dao instead of blindly following the monarch's orders (Xunzi, 1997). This echoes Confucius (2007), who asserts that a son should admonish his father and the ministers should reprimand the monarch if they stray from righteousness (chap. 15).

While Confucianism emphasizes filial piety and loyalty, these virtues ultimately serve a higher purpose: nurturing humaneness and extending care to All under Heaven. This imperative inspired generations of scholar-officials to risk their positions, and even their lives, in remonstrating against wayward rulers—not as acts of disobedience, but as supreme demonstrations of commitment to the Dao and collective welfare. In their most profound expression, these virtues articulate a broader vision of communal well-being, embodied in the ideals of "expansive humaneness" (大仁) and "greater righteousness" (大义), both reflecting the public spirit of All under Heaven. As concern for others and collective well-being expands from the family to the state and ultimately to the entire world, humaneness as a form of love naturally evolves into an inclusive care for all.

In this context, Confucian ideals of humaneness and righteousness diverge from the ethos of Chinese chivalry (侠), which honors promise and personal duty. While chivalric heroes often act benevolently, their deeds remain bound by personal loyalties, reciprocal obligations, or individual codes of honor. In contrast, those who embody expansive humaneness and greater righteousness extend their compassion and moral obligation to a broader social context, prioritizing the common good. Borrowing this Confucian ideal, novelist Jin Yong suggests that true "greater chivalry" transcends personal vendettas to embrace expansive vision—defending not just individuals but the welfare of the nation and all its people.

In Chinese society, prioritizing the greater good over personal benefits can be especially challenging, as loyalty to close-knit in-groups is deeply valued. Yet this very allegiance, when narrowly applied, can clash with the broader public interest—giving rise to favoritism, injustice, and disruptions to social harmony. Unsurprisingly, such a tradition necessitates a strong sense of public-mindedness, one that elevates collective well-being or at least carefully balances group loyalties with the needs of society at large. When supported by institutions and social norms that emphasize shared responsibility, a compelling vision for the future—anchored in expansive love and care for the community—can empower individuals to rise above parochial vision and commit themselves to the public interest.

Public spirit rooted in profound humaneness is essential for those in authority, as they are entrusted with the well-being of society. Confucianism crystallizes this responsibility through the ideal of the "sage-ruler," who governs selflessly for the common good, setting a high moral standard for leadership. Although history was filled with instances of corrupt ministers and tyrannical rulers, the Confucian principle of "greater righteousness" provided a powerful ethical framework for evaluating and critiquing their actions. This moral standard, reinforced by public scrutiny and institutional constraints, fostered some degree of self-restraint among the elite in the exercise of their power.

Notably, this Confucian ideal of expansive love does not overlook personal needs as family ties and individual bonds are deeply valued as the foundation of social harmony and the roots of humaneness. Yet, when personal interests come into conflict with the greater good of "All under Heaven," the latter takes precedence. This moral prioritization stems from the recognition that human beings are inherently interconnected and interdependent—that individual well-being is inseparable from the health of the larger social fabric. It is through this lens that virtues such as expansive humaneness and greater righteousness are cultivated, becoming essential pillars for a robust and enduring civilization.

Admittedly, the concept of "expansive love" is not unique to Confucianism within Chinese philosophy. Though different schools offer distinct interpretations of love, all affirm the interconnectedness of human life and the importance of social harmony, underscoring the imperative to care for others. This shared emphasis allows us to examine love through various philosophical perspectives, whether in Daoism's spontaneous compassion, Mohism's universal care, or Buddhism's compassionate aspiration. Each tradition, in its own way, echoes the ideal of expansive humaneness and enriches the broader discourse on human flourishing and the pursuit of a peaceful world.

10.4 Philosophical Constraints and Strengths in Science and Innovation

Contemporary scholars have long debated the Needham Puzzle: why ancient China, despite its remarkable innovations in astronomy, mathematics, gunpowder, and papermaking, did not develop a scientific theoretical system comparable to that of the West. While historical and sociological factors—such as the dominance of imperial bureaucracy, the scholar's orientation toward officialdom, and a deep social divide between scholars and technicians—are frequently cited, this book proposes a philosophical explanation. It argues that China's holistic worldview, thinking mode, and its culture, characterized by an ethical focus and strong political orientation, may, from a philosophical perspective, help explain this historical divergence.

Unlike some Western traditions' emphasis on categorical reasoning of the world, ancient China emphasized an interconnected worldview, where the practical application of virtues underpinned social order, moral development, and virtuous governance (Liu, 2000). This pragmatic orientation also shaped China's approach to knowledge and inquiry: While Chinese scientific achievements were sophisticated and highly effective for their time, they were grounded more in experiential knowledge than in the theory-driven framework of modern science.

10.4.1 Holistic Perspective and Pragmatist Tendency

Ancient Chinese philosophy adopts a fundamentally holistic worldview, emphasizing the dynamic interdependence of all phenomena within a unified cosmos. In contrast to the Western tradition's pursuit of absolute truths through formal logic and analytical rigor. Chinese philosophy prioritizes harmony, intuition, and relational understanding. These differing intellectual orientations may have constrained the emergence of systematic scientific theory, even as they harbor profound implications for contemporary scientific development.

This integrative perspective in Chinese culture, where the conceptual and perceptual domains are perceived as intrinsically interwoven, may have contributed to a comparatively diminished focus on formal epistemology compared to the West. Its emphasis on such interconnectedness can blur the distinction between observer and observed, potentially complicating the systematic analysis and classification that underlie modern scientific inquiry (Zhang, 2011). Such a worldview aligns more naturally with disciplines like literature and history, which prize interrelated forces and contextual nuance, yet proves less amenable to the precise, objective knowledge of the natural sciences. In contrast, Western philosophy's deep entwinement with mathematics and formal logic fostered analytical precision and logical rigor that propelled modern scientific thought.

Next, Chinese mainstream academia exhibited a strong pragmatic tendency that prioritized ethics over scientific inquiry. Many Confucian scholars believed that moral cultivation was essential for maintaining social harmony and stability, often viewing purely theoretical exploration and technological pursuits as secondary or even potential distractions from ethical development. Even Zhu Xi, a prominent scholar who advocated for "investigating things to know," ultimately framed this activity within his broader moral philosophy—as a means to comprehend and embody the "heavenly principle." His methodology, though occasionally involving the observation of natural phenomena, remained largely unscientific, relying on intuitive reflection rather than systematic experimentation. Rooted in the pursuit of moral self-cultivation, his inquiry aimed at achieving holistic integration rather than the isolation of variables, thereby fostering a different kind of intellectual tradition from the scientific theoretical system.

The pragmatic orientation of Chinese thought also helps explain why ancient Chinese prioritized technological development over foundational scientific inquiry. Scholars and inventors often avoided investing effort in abstract theories without immediate application, favoring technological and engineering solutions to tangible problems instead. By emphasizing concrete outcomes over systematic analysis, this mindset cultivated a culture that focused on the "what" rather than the "why." This orientation accounts for the historical gap in theoretical investigation and the development of formal scientific frameworks between ancient China and the West, even as China achieved remarkable advances in technology and engineering.

10.4.2 Nuance and Indeterminacy in Chinese Thought

Ancient Chinese thinking often favored a fluid, nuanced, and at times indeterminate conception of reality over rigid conceptual categories with distinct boundaries. Grounded in cultural ideals of equilibrium and cosmic harmony, Chinese thinkers embraced indeterminacy not as a flaw in reasoning but as an intrinsic feature of existence—exemplified by the Yin-Yang cosmology, which emphasizes the dynamic interplay of opposites. It privileged experiential knowledge and intuitive insight over systematic analysis, yielding profound practical wisdom while constraining the formation of methodical scientific theories.

Chinese methodologies such as the Confucian "middle way" and Daoist "wuwei" (nonaction), deeply ingrained in traditional thought, also actively discouraged rigid absolutism. Unlike the Western scientific tradition's focus on quantifiable precision and categorical conclusions, Chinese intellectual culture valued situational responsiveness. This perspective, which diverged from the linear causality and analytical generalization central to scientific inquiry, sought to harmonize complex human and social relationships, cultivating a tolerant, balanced, and contextual sensibility that finds insight in ambiguity and nuance.

The Confucian "middle way," for example, promoted a problem-solving paradigm centered on maintaining harmony through adaptive equilibrium. Its approach favored negotiated compromises and incremental adjustments, reflecting a philosophical stance that truth emerges not from binary thinking but through nuanced mediation within contextual "gray areas." This contrasts sharply with Western epistemological traditions that tend to privilege definitive answers and clearly defined categories. While exceptionally effective in managing intricate social relations, this cultural predisposition toward contextual ambiguity and flexible resolution may have inadvertently constrained the development of exact scientific formulations and systematic theoretical frameworks.

10.4.3 Limited Skepticism and Strong Political Orientation

Scientific progress thrives in cultures that institutionalize skepticism, systematically subjecting ideas to rigorous empirical verification. This ongoing dialogue between theoretical conjecture and experimental validation forms the bedrock of scientific advancement. Although imperial China produced notable empirical observations and moments of critical inquiry, such practices were rarely formalized or encouraged as a sustained mode of skeptical inquiry within scholarly institutions. This limited cultivation of systematic skepticism may help explain why China's impressive technological innovations did not evolve into the kind of theoretical scientific framework that emerged in the West.

While Chinese philosophical traditions certainly cultivated intellectual debate—both within and across competing schools—their critical engagement typically stopped short of the systematic skepticism that characterized Western intellectual traditions. The dominant Chinese philosophical traditions emphasized harmony, unity, and veneration for established wisdom, creating an intellectual culture that valued the preservation and exegesis of received knowledge above fundamental challenges to orthodoxy. This tendency found particular expression in the Confucian tradition's reverential treatment of classical texts and its pedagogical emphasis on textual mastery rather than substantive critique. While these values effectively maintained cultural continuity and social stability, they may have inadvertently suppressed the degree of epistemological skepticism necessary for paradigm-shifting scientific breakthroughs.

Moreover, the close alignment between Confucianism and politics, centered on social order and virtuous governance, may have overshadowed purely theoretical exploration of the natural world. As the official ideology, Confucianism attracted many of the brightest minds into civil service, where moral cultivation and statecraft took precedence over scientific inquiry. In effect, a political orientation was a common characteristic of Chinese philosophical schools—including Daoism, Mohism, and Legalism—each emphasizing the practical application of their ideas to governance.

The political emphasis diverted philosophers from purely theoretical inquiry, which offered little prospect of immediate change. This tendency reinforced the fragmented character of scientific achievements in ancient China. While some individuals produced remarkable discoveries, their efforts typically remained within the experiential domain and stood in isolation, lacking the cumulative theoretical foundations required to establish a comprehensive scientific system.

10.4.4 Weakness and Strengths in Innovation

Notwithstanding potential constraints, traditional Chinese moral philosophy actively contributed to scientific and technological progress by fostering disciplined scholarship, collaborative knowledge sharing, and a deep commitment to addressing human needs. Mohism, in particular, played a distinctive role: its rigorously pragmatic orientation encouraged technological innovation. This cultural foundation, coupled with a result-oriented approach to knowledge, enabled ancient China to excel in acquiring, applying, and refining knowledge, which resulted in both incremental advancements and groundbreaking inventions in fields such as agriculture and engineering, often surpassing contemporary developments elsewhere in the premodern world.

Moral cultivation, with its emphasis on virtuous education and honoring inherited wisdom, served as a powerful catalyst for refinement and innovation. By fostering a culture of continuous learning, adaptive improvement, and collective insight—grounded in the understanding that change is constant—it provided fertile ground for progress. The Confucian drive for self-cultivation and familial advancement became key motivators for technological development, while the scholarly reverence for knowledge inspired optimizations to existing practices. This accumulation of knowledge, combined with a mostly open-minded approach to learning, enabled both individuals and communities to develop effective solutions to pressing societal challenges.

Yet, the impact of Chinese philosophy on innovation presents a complex duality. While its conservative orientation—deeply rooted in societal values such as harmony, order, and reverence for tradition—may have constrained intellectual diversity and risk-taking, its enterprising dimension (Confucianism) and its resourceful dimension (Daoism) actively promoted the systematic refinement of established knowledge. This tension gave rise to a distinctive innovation pattern: Confucian scholars excelled in cumulative learning, technical application, and incremental advancement, typically favoring these methods over radical theorizing or paradigm-shifting breakthroughs. The thoughts of Confucius and Lao Tzu exemplified this as they championed a cyclical nature of change that emphasized stability and balance. Their teachings, while invaluable for social harmony and gradual improvement, might not have been as conducive to the disruptive nature of scientific breakthroughs. They fostered an intellectual tradition that prioritized perfecting existing frameworks rather than fundamentally challenging or replacing them.

In terms of individual agency, traditional Chinese moral culture's emphasis on social consensus and adherence to established norms presents inherent trade-offs: while promoting social order and stability, it can restrain individual expression and discourage risk-taking. Extended to the intellectual sphere, this orientation values harmony and refinement over contestation and doubt. Whereas societies prizing individuality, diverse viewpoints, and open inquiry tend to cultivate imagination and creativity, those favoring conformity, propriety, and collective harmony may discourage individuals from challenging prevailing ideas, suppressing the very dynamism essential for scientific revolutions.

Furthermore, the tradition's strong reverence for authority can lead to social rigidity and resource monopolization, both of which hinder scientific progress. Genuine innovation flourishes in environments that encourage original thinking, challenge existing authority, and ensure equitable, merit-based opportunities for the new comers. While traditional Chinese culture's collective orientation has supported long-term goals and promoted talent selection based on virtue and merit, its tendency toward entrenched authority has at times suppressed grassroots creativity by limiting access to resources and stifling alternative voices.

That said, contemporary science may find unexpected value in traditional Chinese philosophical frameworks. The concept of "unity of Heaven and humanity," for instance, offers a holistic paradigm particularly relevant to quantum physics, where wave-particle duality and quantum entanglement challenge classical notions of separability. This perspective encourages a view that embraces ontological wholeness and complementary dualities, potentially bridging seemingly contradictory phenomena.

A historical precedent exists: In his writing, Erwin Schrödinger (1992) drew inspiration from ancient Indian Vedic philosophy, finding parallels between its concepts of non-duality and interconnectedness and the ideas emerging from quantum mechanics. While Schrödinger did not engage directly with Chinese thought, the worldview of unity of Heaven and humanity shares similar perspectives that could potentially support the further development of quantum theory. After all, innovation often arises from discerning patterns within apparent chaos, a task well suited to holistic systems thinking.

Mainstream Western thought, often predicated on binary opposition, tends to emphasize distinct subjects, specializations, and increasingly fine-grained categorization. This analytical approach excels at producing detailed knowledge within specific domains, yet it can also lead to fragmentation and a diminished capacity to see the larger picture. In contrast, traditional Chinese holistic thought stresses interconnectedness, viewing opposites as interdependent elements within a unified whole. The pursuit of the Dao, which involves a reflective return to origins and underlying principles, illustrates this integrative mode of thinking. Such a perspective offers a valuable counterbalance to the limitations of overly analytic methodologies in scientific research, encouraging an approach that combines precision with holistic and contextual awareness.

10.5 Contemporary Challenges and a Morally Grounded Democracy

China's unique civilizational model has demonstrated enduring cultural resilience, persisting through millennia of political upheaval and societal change. This endurance was severely tested during the early modern period, as European powers, equipped with advanced weaponry and technology, exerted their overwhelming dominance. In response, China began a gradual, both conscious and unconscious, assimilation of Western ideas and technologies. Yet, even amid waves of modernization, Chinese civilization has preserved its foundational values shaped by scores of centuries of moral cultivation. Core principles such as the Dao, humaneness, and ritual propriety remain integral and deserve recognition as essential contributions to global cultural heritage.

While engaging with Western intellectual traditions, China will likely synthesize rather than fully adopt foreign paradigms, preserving its distinctive civilizational character marked by a pursuit of harmony, a holistic worldview, a collectivist orientation, and a focus on practicality. To the global community, China stands as a global power with vast population and growing influence, making its participation essential for addressing global challenges. For contemporary Chinese, it is increasingly important to view their national influence as extending beyond borders, embracing a sense of responsibility for global well-being. China has the potential to deepen its global contributions—particularly in science and technology, social development, and cultural exchange. Advancing in these areas will be key to fostering international cooperation and establishing meaningful leadership in the decades ahead.

10.5.1 Legacy's Contemporary Social Impact

At its highest level, the Chinese moral tradition transcends binary notions of right and wrong, fostering a life-affirming ethos that emphasizes reverence for all existence and promotes holistic responses to complex challenges. Over millennia, it has produced distinct cultural traits: diligent industry, cultivated self-restraint, and cooperative pragmatism, qualities reflecting the profoundly relational nature of Chinese social organization. Deciphering this ethical system provides crucial interpretive keys to understanding the operative values animating modern Chinese society.

First, the holistic worldview embedded in China's moral tradition manifests concretely in contemporary socioeconomic policies. A notable example is the country's extensive investment in rural infrastructure including comprehensive transportation grids and universal digital connectivity, which defy narrow cost-benefit analysis from a purely business perspective. These initiatives reflect a long-term, collectivist vision shaped by centuries of moral cultivation that prioritizes shared prosperity, comprehensive planning, and future-oriented development. This forward-thinking mindset also underpinned earlier national efforts, such as large-scale water conservation projects that continue to benefit Chinese agriculture today. Such culturally grounded policymaking demonstrates how traditional All under Heaven consciousness informs modern development paradigms, contributing to China's unique trajectory of sustained economic growth and social progress.

While macroeconomic policies, global markets, and technological innovation remain primary drivers of China's development, its cultural legacy of moral cultivation—a tradition not historically geared toward industry and commerce—has played a surprisingly significant, albeit subtle, role in its economic modernization. The Confucian emphasis on societal harmony, structural order, and organizational cohesion has created uniquely favorable conditions for industrial development.

Rooted in traditional values—holistic thinking, diligence, self-improvement, interpersonal harmony, and collective responsibility—this culture produces an exceptionally disciplined workforce, high savings and education investment rates, and remarkably effective coordination in complex production networks. This social model aligns well with many aspects of modern industrialized production, including long-cycle planning, supply chain integration, and collaborative innovation—helping explain China's distinctive capacity for synchronized sectoral development. Thus, what began as a preindustrial ethical system has, through adaptive reinterpretation, become an unexpected catalyst for economic success.

Human networks possess significant economic value, as trust, reciprocity, and long-term relationships facilitate trade, innovation, and collaboration. Drawing on its deep-rooted cultural emphasis on relational bonds—such as guanxi—China strategically leverages these social connections to gain a competitive edge in the global economy. This institutionalized network-building enables efficient resource coordination and optimized production processes, often yielding cost-effective, high-quality outcomes. Relational competence, evident across supply chains, partnerships, and social frameworks, not only reinforces these foundations but also fosters cooperation and mutually beneficial growth. Through formalizing these traditionally embedded relationship paradigms, China has effectively monetized social capital, transforming centuries-old interpersonal norms into drivers of contemporary economic success.

Yet, this reliance on relational networks can be a double-edged sword, as ethical concerns may arise when these networks function without a firm moral anchor.

Freed from such constraints, this cooperative mechanism can easily devolve into favoritism in bidding and potential regulatory corruption, as personal ties eclipse fairness. Moreover, guanxi's internal cohesion often breeds exclusion that stifle competition, hinder knowledge sharing, and limit equitable opportunity. These pitfalls underscore the need of grounding modern institutions in robust ethical frameworks, informed by updated Chinese moral philosophy and its enduring emphasis on moral cultivation. Ultimately, recognizing this dual nature of guanxi—its capacity to build trust-based ecosystems that drive growth, alongside its risks of exclusion and corruption—is essential for navigating Chinese business culture.

China's relationship-oriented moral culture is also indispensable for understanding its contemporary legal system, as adherence to rigid legal codes alone sometimes cannot fully capture the nuances of its intricate social dynamics. In practice, judicial outcomes are often influenced by human emotions, traditional values, interpersonal relationships, and communal needs. Consequently, Chinese legal practice reflects a careful consideration of this fundamental social context. Recognizing this does not diminish the authority of law or the importance of formal procedures; rather, it emphasizes the need to interpret and implement legal norms within China's distinctive cultural framework (Shao & Li, 2005). For example, the strong emphasis on mediation often leads to a preference for resolving disputes outside of court, prioritizing the preservation of relationships and the maintenance of social harmony.

10.5.2 Contemporary Issues in Social and Democratic Development

As contemporary society undergoes sweeping transformation, the traditional Chinese ethos of moral cultivation stands at a critical crossroads. Forces like urbanization, modernization, and globalization are reconfiguring China's social fabric, transforming it from close-knit communities to one increasingly defined by interactions among strangers. While traditional Chinese moral culture remains a vital source of strength, it also generates tensions with the demands of a globalized, market-driven society, raising questions about the applicability of classical moral cultivation today.

Yet, what appears to be a failure of tradition is, in fact, the result of an intricate interplay. Many of today's pressing social challenges stem not only from the obsolescence of some traditional cultural values but also from the marginalization of moral cultivation itself—a decline that has contributed to a rise in ethical problems impeding broader societal progress. These conditions suggest that the solution lies not in abandoning moral cultivation but in rearticulating it within a renewed and adaptive framework attuned to the complexities of the modern era.

10.5.2.1 The Exacerbation of Social Involution

The cultural predisposition toward social conformity exacerbates the phenomenon of social involution (内卷)—a relentless cycle of hypercompetition, overwork, and diminishing returns. Beyond contemporary pressures, this compulsion to strive may be deeply rooted in the historical conditions of ancient China, where large populations vying for limited resources created systemic pressures toward involution. Moreover, Confucian and Legalist values, with their emphasis on diligence, hierarchy, and worldly success, have long reinforced this dynamic, shaping a cultural mindset that continues to influence contemporary society.

Confucian societies, shaped in part by Legalist undercurrents, are especially prone to involution, as Confucianism emphasizes achieving personal potential within a tightly structured social structure. It encourages individuals to maximize limited resources through cultivating virtues that foster harmony and coordinated effort. Education, historically epitomized by the imperial examination system, has long been regarded as the primary avenue for social advancement. This cultural emphasis on academic achievement can, however, contribute to heightened stress and anxiety, particularly surrounding educational and career achievement.

However, Confucianism should neither be solely blamed for nor regarded as the primary driver of modern social involution. Legalist thought, with its strong emphasis on efficiency, control, and competition, likely plays a far more significant role in intensifying these dynamics. Historically, various cultural mechanisms existed to temper such pressures. When properly practiced, Confucian moral cultivation—with its focus on humility, balance, and social order—helped harmonize ambition with ethical restraint. A well-structured hierarchy, guided by Confucian virtues, historically provided social stability and a framework for mitigating excessive competition. Moreover, Confucian education, grounded in moral development, served to moderate unchecked personal desires, while Daoist principles of spontaneity and nonaction offered a philosophical counterweight to relentless striving. From this perspective, the erosion of traditional moral cultivation in the modern era may be a key contributor to the deepening of social involution today—a dynamic that, in turn, further weakens the moral foundations needed to counter it, creating a vicious cycle.

Thus, modern involution arises not so much from the foundational tenets of traditional philosophies themselves as from their selective or distorted interpretation in today's societal context. While Confucianism promoted education and virtue-based, meritocratic upward social mobility, Legalism prioritized efficiency, control, and incentive-driven performance. These values, amplified by modern pressures for rapid economic advancement and intense competition for status mobility, have contributed to a system that often privileges rigid, short-term success metrics over holistic and sustainable development.

The ever-escalating competitiveness of college entrance examination system epitomizes this trend. Originally intended to promote talent selection, equal opportunity, and social mobility—and still functioning as a vital mechanism for these aims—it has also fueled an education system disproportionately fixated on standardized testing and individual achievement. This obsession with test scores exacts a heavy toll: by imposing huge pressure and consuming students' time, the system risks eroding intrinsic curiosity, diminishing the joy of learning, and impeding the cultivation of essential capacities such as critical thinking, creativity, and ethical awareness—thereby accelerating societal involution.

10.5.2.2 Social and Cosmological Challenges

The contemporary transformation of Chinese family structures has significantly impacted traditional moral cultivation, weakening the social order it once upheld. In agrarian society, extended multigenerational households served as the foundation of community life. Close cohabitation naturally reinforced familial bonds and interdependence, making moral cultivation crucial for maintaining both domestic harmony and broader social cohesion. However, contemporary urbanization, accelerated by economic modernization and the one-child policy, has produced smaller, nuclear families often dispersed across geographic distances. This fragmentation has eroded traditional social networks and the moral values they upheld. Paternal authority has diminished, while practices like ancestor worship, which formerly cemented family unity and filial devotion, have faded or vanished. Although residual respect for elders persists, its influence on shaping moral behavior has substantially declined.

China's accelerated social transformation, driven by modernization and urbanization, has created a pressing need for new social frameworks that align with its increasingly mobile and diverse reality. As China transitions from a society rooted in close-knit communities to one increasingly defined by interactions not only among acquaintances but also with strangers, building trust and fostering cooperation across broader social boundaries has become an urgent and complex challenge (Wang, 2016). This shift calls for a thoughtful reevaluation of traditional moral values to address emerging social issues such as resource distribution, individual rights, and shared responsibilities.

Sociologically, the ongoing social decentralization, fueled by rising individualism, a loosening of social hierarchies, and the pervasive influence of the Internet, also poses a significant challenge to traditional moral cultivation. The ascendance of values like personal autonomy, equality, and self-expression generates increasing tension with traditional commitments to familial obligation and social hierarchy. This tension leaves contemporary Chinese citizens navigating a delicate balance: preserving meaningful aspects of their collectivist heritage while asserting individual identity in a rapidly transforming social landscape.

Moreover, the rise of scientific worldview has fundamentally disrupted the cosmological foundation upon which traditional Chinese moral cultivation was built. The concept of the "unity of Heaven and humanity," once an unquestioned source of moral and political legitimacy, now struggles to compete with scientific explanations grounded in empirical data and mathematical models. Consequently, the traditional frameworks of the Dao and Heaven for understanding the world no longer hold the same unassailable authority (Shi, 2018). This shift has also paved the way for the growing influence of modern Western values such as freedom, rights, equality, and individual autonomy, which increasingly contend with and coexist alongside classical Confucian virtues of humaneness, righteousness, propriety, and wisdom.

Despite these challenges, the holistic worldview grounded in "unity of Heaven and humanity" still retains profound relevance today. While modern cosmology has vastly expanded our knowledge of the universe, it often leaves existential questions of meaning and purpose unanswered. A strictly scientific perspective, relying solely on objective observation, can inadvertently cultivate feelings of alienation and existential void, potentially eroding ethical consciousness. Traditional Chinese cosmology offers a valuable counterbalance: it nurtures compassion, cosmic reverence, and a profound awareness of humanity's interdependence with nature. This perspective is especially meaningful in addressing contemporary crises, from ecological degradation to moral nihilism, offering a much-needed remedy to a purely materialist paradigm. Thus, even as contemporary Chinese society embraces scientific rationality, these ancient conceptions of Heaven and the Principle continue to inform worldviews, subtly yet enduringly shaping cultural consciousness at a deep, often unconscious level.

10.5.2.3 Issues of Reciprocal Obligation and Guanxi

A major challenge facing contemporary China lies in addressing the complexities created by reciprocal obligation and guanxi. Far from diminishing with the decline of traditional virtues, these practices—unchecked by those virtues—have in many cases become more prone to distortion and abuse. While they can foster mutual support and cooperation within social networks, their unethical application often compromises broader principles of social justice. The erosion of moral cultivation has exacerbated these tensions, making it increasingly difficult to counter ingrained in-group mentalities and cliquishness. The absence of traditional self-cultivation frequently leads individuals to prioritize loyalty to close circles over fairness, impartiality, and collective long-term development.

Despite China's rapid modernization, traditional social structures—particularly guanxi networks—retain substantial influence in contemporary society. These interpersonal connections, forged through familial ties, friendships, professional relationships, and shared regional origins, continue to shape both social interactions and career advancement. However, in the absence of strong moral oversight and sustained ethical cultivation, such networks may come into conflict with contemporary principles of justice and transparency. This tension intensifies in meritocratic systems, where guanxi can foster nepotism, favor-trading, and backroom deals. Such practices erode social trust and undermine fairness, creating a need for stricter regulations, which, in turn, can inadvertently suppress grassroots innovation and creativity. The persistent conflict between sweeping quality education reforms and the rigid, high-stakes college entrance exam exemplifies this complex dilemma (You & Hu, 2013).

Admittedly, even if fully preserved in form, traditional moral cultivation would not suffice to resolve China's contemporary social challenges. While the concept of Heaven offers an impartial moral authority, the virtues it promotes rely heavily on individual conscience and communal consensus—mechanisms increasingly insufficient for governing complex, large-scale societies. The emphasis on moral cultivation and ethical oversight, while philosophically sound, encounters practical constraints when confronting institutionalized power asymmetries, entrenched guanxi systems, and well-organized interest groups. In the absence of formal accountability structures, moral persuasion alone cannot effectively restrain these systemic forces.

For moral frameworks to achieve meaningful societal impact, they must transcend individual aspirations and become institutionally embedded within legal systems and democratic institutions. This necessitates the vital interplay between moral cultivation and institutional structures: while institutions offer the mechanisms to uphold ethical principles and foster positive social outcomes, moral cultivation supplies the ethical normative foundation that animates and sustains the integrity of these systems. This reciprocal relationship not only strengthens democratic governance but also facilitates continuous moral development at both individual and societal levels.

10.5.2.4 Moral Cultivation vs. Efficiency-Oriented Culture

Historically, traditional moral cultivation served as the primary mechanism for maintaining social stability and cohesion, often prioritizing these goals over pure bureaucratic efficiency. However, in times of crisis when moral persuasion proved insufficient, policymakers frequently resorted to Legalist principles, which emphasized narrowly focused efficiency and rigid incentive systems—often at considerable societal cost. While effective at generating immediate administrative results, the application of Legalist methods without complementary ethical safeguards tended to erode moral norms and ultimately exacerbate social crises.

Efficiency cuts both ways. While indispensable for driving economic and social progress, its overemphasis risks elevating short-term results and measurable outputs above enduring values, often undermining holistic development, depleting future potential, and eroding collective well-being. This dynamic not only fuels widespread anxiety but also threatens to marginalize ethical considerations in favor of short-term gains. Reinvigorating Confucian emphasis on social harmony alongside Daoist principles of natural flow and effortless action may provide crucial philosophical correctives, fostering more balanced growth and a stronger commitment to sustainable, long-term development.

Chinese society has traditionally cultivated profound respect for life, nature, and communal welfare. These core values, nonetheless, risk being eroded when excessive focus on efficiency undermines social ethical standards and public spirit—both essential for curbing the favoritism and injustice embedded in unprincipled guanxi culture. In hypercompetitive environments, individuals often pursue ever-higher markers of "success" while becoming less empathetic to others' struggles. This moral vacuum breeds a dangerous form of pseudo-efficiency, evoking the darker side of human nature: one that privileges ruthless individualism over the common good, adopts narrow perspectives rather than celebrating diversity, substitutes privilege for merit, and ultimately compromises society's resilience and capacity for sustainable development.

While moderate emphasis on efficiency may facilitate innovation, an excessive focus on it often stifles creative endeavors. Genuine scientific breakthroughs require a tolerance for risk-taking, a long-term perspective, and a willingness to embrace uncertainty, qualities that frequently clash with short-term efficiency goals. An obsession with immediate results, rigid metrics, and repetitive tasks can suffocate the exploratory spirit that drives true innovation. As Kevin Kelly observes, humans excel at creativity, which is a process inherently inefficient.[1] Creativity involves risks, accepts failure as part of the process, and demands the time and freedom for deep thinking and experimentation. The relentless pursuit of easily quantifiable "achievements" may yield impressive statistics but rarely fosters transformative breakthroughs and can ultimately end in disappointment.

From a sustainability standpoint, prioritizing efficiency without a strong moral foundation can be likened to cultivating a vast rubber plantation. While reaping impressive returns in the short term, it ultimately impoverishes the societal soil—its redundancy, diversity, and the vitality needed for long-term and balanced growth. For moral character and creativity to flourish, a more flexible, patient, and supportive environment is essential. Modern moral cultivation, grounded in interdependence, critical reflection, empathy, big-picture perspective, and respect for diverse perspectives, provides a crucial foundation for the sustainable development of both individuals and society.

To be fully effective, this contemporary approach to moral cultivation necessitates institutional protections for individual rights and ethical self-determination—safeguards that are essential to human dignity. When citizens enjoy secure property rights and legal protections, they gain the capacity to act ethically, confront injustice, and uphold moral principles without fear of existential ruin, thereby enhancing their civic engagement and their initiative for ethical oversight. Conversely, the erosion of these protections, in blind pursuit of sheer efficiency, diminishes autonomy and weakens society's ethical fabric. Thus, both involution and an overemphasis on efficiency threaten to undermine the very foundations of a functioning democracy, which depends ultimately on the moral character, civic capacity, and shared commitment of its citizens to the public good.

[1] Kevin's episode was featured in the 30 Days of Genius series of Chase Jarvis Live on CreativeLive.

10.5.3 Morally Grounded Democracy: Reconstructing the Future

A central challenge facing contemporary China is how to reconcile its deep-rooted moral and cultural heritage with the demands of modern democracy. Addressing this tension requires innovative institutional design, one that systematically integrates moral cultivation into democratic structures and processes. This synthesis finds its fullest expression in the concept of a "morally grounded democracy," a model that moves beyond mere formal legal-institutional structures by embedding collective moral oversight as an integral dimension of political life.

At its core, morally grounded democracy envisions a virtue-based system of governance where ethical values guide three interrelated pillars: the fair election of leadership, robust oversight and accountability of governmental power, and the equitable provision of social resources. This approach to governance draws upon a long-standing Chinese ideal, emphasizing that political authority should be grounded in moral integrity, while simultaneously embracing modern imperatives for popular sovereignty and active civic participation.

Understanding modern democracy requires examining its cultural foundations—particularly the contrasts between Eastern and Western traditions. Western thought has long enshrined rationality as the cornerstone of governance, while China's political philosophy upholds virtue or shared moral principles as its foundation. Yet neither reason nor virtue alone is sufficient; both depend on institutional reinforcement and active societal participation to uphold a just and functional political system.

In the West, democratic institutions rest on values such as individual liberty, legal equality, civic responsibility, and procedural rights, values that shape systems of checks and balances. These structures reflect a premise of skepticism toward concentrated power, empowering citizens to question authority, correct institutional failures, and resist abuses such as corruption or self-serving governance. By constraining human imperfection through transparency and participation, democracy seeks not utopia but resilience, a system capable of continuous self-correction in the face of power's temptations.

Chinese political culture is fundamentally rooted in a philosophy of relational governance—one that prioritizes symbiotic interdependence, societal equilibrium, and morally grounded statecraft. It stresses personal ethical cultivation, the fulfillment of role-based obligations, and the stewardship of collective welfare, often mediated through centralized structures and ethical oversight. These collectively oriented values invite critical scrutiny of their fit with modern institutional frameworks, which frequently operate under contrasting principles, most notably those centered on decentralization and the separation of powers. While neither "Western" nor "Chinese" traditions are monolithic—each encompassing internal diversity and historical evolution— recognizing these foundational distinctions remains vital to any meaningful discussion of how culture shapes institutional approaches to governance.

10.5.3.1 The Possibility and Necessity for a Morally Grounded Democracy

Although structurally divergent from Western democratic systems, traditional Chinese governance, patriarchal and authoritarian in form, harbored nascent ideas of popular influence grounded in ruler's ethical accountability. Unlike Western models that enshrine popular sovereignty via electoral consent, traditional Chinese political thought anchored legitimacy in the Mandate of Heaven, a transcendent moral principle binding power to virtue.

This Mandate embodied Heaven's moral order, with the people's collective will as its earthly reflection—the ultimate gauge of legitimacy. A sovereign straying from virtue thereby forfeited this divine sanction and lost the right to rule. The emperor reigned by incarnating celestial virtue, the essence of which lies in safeguarding the people's welfare. While unsanctioned by ballots, public sentiment and elite discourse served as potent moral and political reins on the ruler's conduct. In theory, the people's will held ultimate sway to affirm or revoke the Mandate—a nascent ethical seedbed for public rule.

This ethical governance functioned as a dual-edged mechanism, simultaneously legitimizing and constraining imperial authority and establishing an early form of conditional sovereignty and popular influence. While historical rulers frequently fell short of Confucian moral standards, the persistent ideal of virtuous rulership created durable societal expectations that exerted meaningful pressure on governance practices. Therefore, realizing democratic rights in contemporary China requires not just procedural systems but also cultural legitimacy frameworks that draw on the normative influence of virtue to encourage citizen participation and ensure effective checks on power.

The Chinese philosophical understanding of human nature, when reexamined through contemporary frameworks of equality and civic engagement, offers valuable insights for constructing democratic political systems. In cultures that regard human nature as inherently fallible, there is a strong emphasis on checks and balances, with democratic institutions and the rule of law designed to constrain power and curb corruption. In contrast, traditions like mainstream Confucianism, which emphasize either the inherent goodness or a more complex view of human nature, focus on moral cultivation. This does not reflect naivety or excuse wrongdoing; rather, it serves as a moral imperative, placing high expectations on individuals and institutions. Those who fall short may face public criticism or a loss of social standing. Thus, while views of human nature as either good or flawed may appear contradictory, they need not be mutually exclusive. Instead, they can function complementarily, together fostering a more just and harmonious society.

In reality, democracy and morality are fundamentally intertwined. Modern democratic systems, grounded not in a doctrine of inherent evil, but in an acknowledgment of human fallibility, place higher and more complex ethical demands on society. They aspire to loftier societal ideals by structurally embedding moral considerations within governance frameworks, all while maintaining clear-eyed realism about human nature's dual potential. Whereas institutional architecture—including checks and balances, representative structures, power separation, and press freedom—provides necessary scaffolding, the full realization of democracy's promise ultimately depends on the civic virtue and ethical commitment of both leaders and citizens. This constitutes the foundational premise of morally grounded democracy.

Traditional Chinese cultural norms present an institutional paradox: while the guanxi system fosters trust and cooperation within personal circles, its informal operation—without robust ethical oversight—can contravene modern standards of procedural integrity and institutional transparency. By privileging particularistic ties over universal norms, such networks may distort resource allocation, erode meritocratic principles, and ultimately weaken the democratic foundations of equitable access and public accountability. Moreover, virtues like humaneness, compassion, righteousness, and wisdom, though commendable, are often oriented toward interpersonal relationships and may fall short in meeting the demands for impartiality and due process in contemporary institutional frameworks.

These cultural characteristics need not, however, obstruct the process of institutional modernization. Although guanxi networks can pose challenges to contemporary governance, China's philosophical traditions provide robust ethical correctives capable of tempering such excesses while strengthening institutional integrity. Conceived originally to address the complexities inherent in administering a vast and heterogeneous empire, these traditions articulate values that transcend personal affiliations and affirm a commitment to the greater good.

For instance, Confucian virtue ethics, with its emphasis on "the impartial principles of Heaven and Earth," offers a philosophical basis for renewed civic virtue. Historically, it not only legitimized centralized power but also constrained it through concepts like the "Mandate of Heaven" and "Principle"—societal consensus on virtuous behavior. Thus, core Confucian values—public-spiritedness (公), broad accountability, and moral oversight—can, when creatively adapted and continually updated, forge a distinctive Chinese governance paradigm: one that synthesizes time-honored ethical wisdom with modern institutional functionality, transforming potential cultural obstacles into assets for political development.

History reveals important nuances. When Western-style legal and bureaucratic systems were introduced to early modern China, traditional moral values such as humaneness and righteousness came under significant strain and gradually waned in influence. Meanwhile, the wholesale adoption of Western principles and institutions also met deep-seated historical, cultural, and political resistance. Yet, the central challenge for modern Chinese institutions is not about cultural incompatibility, but the insufficient integration of ethical principles from China's rich philosophical heritage into their structure and operation, particularly regarding moral oversight and ethical governance. This deficiency can result in an overreliance on procedures, which, paradoxically, often, become vulnerable to guanxi networks, ultimately undermining institutional integrity and effectiveness. Addressing this gap would enable China to draw on its deep ethical traditions to construct institutions that are more resilient, trustworthy, and culturally grounded.

The concept of morally grounded democracy offers a potential framework for China, blending democratic governance with ethical foundations rooted in Chinese philosophical traditions. It posits that sustainable democracy requires both sound institutions and a morally engaged citizenry, integrating ethical principles directly into governance structures. A real democracy needs a soul: a set of shared virtues and a civic commitment to the common good. While upholding core democratic values—equality, freedom, and rule of law, adapted to cultural contexts—this model emphasizes ethical leadership, a spirit of interdependence, collective moral oversight, and participatory civic responsibility. It recognizes that procedural democracy alone is insufficient to guarantee justice; principled governance demands robust moral accountability, ensuring policies align with shared imperatives for the common good.

While requiring thoughtful execution, integrating ethics into democratic governance offers a compelling approach to addressing corruption, nepotism, and other systemic challenges. Traditional moral culture, with its emphasis on the greater self, championing virtues like impartiality and long-term vision, offers valuable resources for cultivating a morally grounded democracy. At its core, this model grounds governance in ethical principles, directing leaders and citizens alike to harmonize individual concerns with communal responsibilities, ensuring that private interest does not compromise societal well-being, a model particularly suited to the Chinese cultural context. A morally grounded democracy creates a political environment where ethical considerations shape public discourse, policymaking, and the exercise of power. By making moral considerations integral to public discourse and decision-making, it revives the classical ideal of "rule by virtue" within the democratic framework, in which power is exercised with ethical accountability to the common good, and where procedural integrity and institutional transparency, in turn, safeguard participatory civic moral cultivation.

A closer examination of core Chinese virtues reveals a potential avenue for constructing democratic systems grounded in a renewed moral foundation that emphasizes effective oversight and public accountability of power. While Western democracies prioritize individual rights and procedural justice, they also cultivate a public spirit and civic duty, emphasizing that safeguarding others' rights is essential to securing one's own. In comparison, traditional Chinese society places ethical conduct at the center of governance, with rights and resources allocated not only based on social roles but also on the fulfillment of corresponding duties. It was not just about entitlements, but also obligations. Traditional Chinese governance prioritized moral character and collective ethics over procedural formalism in overseeing power. This system of moral self-regulation and social censure offered a distinctive alternative to Western institutional checks—one grounded in ethical expectations and moral oversight, rather than relying solely on structural constraints. While these Confucian values cannot be mechanically transplanted into modern democratic frameworks, they offer critical insights for developing hybrid governance models that harmonize moral cultivation with institutional accountability.

Although ancient Chinese governance, characterized by personal rule and the aspiration for virtuous oversight, differed significantly from modern democracy, its underlying moral principles can still inform and strengthen contemporary governance. China's distinctive moral culture, when integrated with modern institutional mechanisms, can help cultivate a public ethos that reinforces democratic rule of law. By modernizing and democratizing these moral principles while preserving their collectivist spirit, it becomes possible to promote greater respect for individual rights, more equitable resource distribution, and the development of robust supervisory institutions. While approaching democracy from a foundation of collective moral cultivation, this model ultimately seeks the same goal as its Western counterparts: a just and democratic society grounded in accountability, transparency, and moral responsibility within a resilient institutional framework.

Having said that, morally grounded democracy depends not on the passive inheritance of traditional virtues, but on their creative renewal in the face of contemporary challenges. Concepts like "humaneness" and "righteousness," for example, can be reinterpreted to emphasize civic responsibility, shedding their historically hierarchical connotations. This reframing can strengthen civic duty, active citizenship, and public engagement—core pillars of democracy.

Equally important is the democratization of moral cultivation. Historically, this process was largely top-down, relying heavily on the self-discipline of the elite while casting ordinary people as passive recipients. This model not only constrained the public's capacity to resist abuses of power, such as political corruption, but also limited its ability to foster broader societal accountability and strengthen institutional integrity. Modern institutions, including civic education and accountable government, can foster grassroots moral and civic development by equipping citizens with the resources, infrastructure, and opportunities needed for meaningful participation.

These efforts, in turn, can stimulate a robust public dialogue on ethical issues, creating a culture of scrutiny that safeguards against institutional corruption. While traditional Chinese moral culture emerged in a hierarchical context distinct from modern democracy, its foundational principles—such as the notion that legitimacy flows from "Heaven" (often understood as reflecting the collective will of the people)—offer adaptable frameworks for democratic governance. By cultivating grassroots moral discourse and empowering citizens to voice ethical concerns, this historical connection to the "people's voice" can be revitalized. Such a reinterpretation reinforces democratic legitimacy and functions as a tool for institutional accountability, ensuring that diverse perspectives inform policy and practice.

The public spirit embodied in the framework of "All under Heaven" can also be revitalized to support contemporary morally grounded democracy. This ideal envisions a symbiotic relationship between robust institutions and a civic ethos rooted in the shared public vision. Democratic frameworks that empower citizens to oversee governance can encourage ethical discussion and public engagement, while the cultivation of an All under Heaven civic ethos further reinforces institutional integrity. This dynamic interplay helps counter corruption and undue factional influence—persistent threats to effective governance. Yet sustaining this balance demands an active citizenry, one that embraces both moral agency and social responsibility. It is here that the concept of "the greater self," explored in the next chapter, becomes essential.

Ultimately, a morally grounded democracy emerges from the synergy between civic virtue and an ethically reinforced social contract. Its foundation—rooted in principles of justice, empathy, equality, and the common good—forms the ethical bedrock of democratic governance. This framework functions as a collective agreement: while citizens participate voluntarily, they bear moral responsibility to uphold its principles. Adherence to this covenant nurtures societal flourishing, whereas its violation undermines the very fabric of the community and the welfare of each individual.

Such a morality-based contract creates conditions in which constructive human qualities—cooperation, kindness, and civic participation—find fertile ground to grow, thereby actively promoting democracy and collective welfare. Yet it does not depend on goodwill alone. Institutional pillars such as the rule of law, delegation of authority, and grassroots oversight serve not only as essential procedural safeguards but also as sources of collective ethical power, curbing destructive forces such as unchecked greed, entrenched vested interests, and bureaucratic corruption. Together, they sustain ethically grounded accountability and preserve the checks and balances necessary to ensure that moral ideals are translated into resilient democratic practice.

10.5.3.2 Integrating or Separating Inner Sage and Outer King in the Modern Era

The concept of morally grounded democracy provides fresh perspectives on the ongoing debate about the compatibility of Chinese culture with modern political institutions. Modern New-Confucian thinkers offer an optimistic outlook on this matter. Mou Zongsan (2003), for example, advances a dual-layered ontological framework in which the provisional submersion of innate moral knowledge (the "inner sage") into the realm of empirical experience facilitates the cultivation of a Western-style cognitive rationality. Mou argues that this dynamic process enables the rise of a modern "outer king"—one equipped to reconcile Confucian moral ideals with democratic values and scientific progress.

Critics, however, argue that the traditional concept of the "inner sage" (moral self-cultivation) is incompatible with the development of a modern "outer king" (democratic governance). The ethical monism inherent in "the unity of Heaven and humanity" risks blurring the line between ideal and reality, leading to overly moralistic discourse that overlooks the self-interested dynamics of political life—a factor that necessitates checks and balances for democracy to function effectively (Zhu, 1991). These critics further suggest a separation of the "inner sage" and "outer king," analogous to the West's "render unto Caesar" principle. Such a separation of politics and morality (or religion) would restrict self-cultivation to the personal and social spheres, allowing governance to focus on practical political considerations. Within this framework, Confucianism's emphasis on responsible power is viewed as lacking a robust theory of individual rights sufficient to place effective limits on that power (Ren, 2018).

While these arguments present thought-provoking perspectives, several counterarguments merit consideration. First, Confucianism is not a religion in the traditional sense but a comprehensive ethical-philosophical system. It integrates ethical principles, political philosophies, and practices of moral cultivation, all deeply connected to social and political life. Second, although modern governance maintains institutional separation from religious authorities, this does not necessitate the exclusion of morality from public affairs. Religion and morality are distinct conceptual categories. Western democracies, for instance, maintain church-state separation while still grounding legislation in ethical frameworks that promote justice, equity, and the common good.

Third, mainstream Confucianism offers a nuanced and realistic view of human nature, acknowledging the potential for both good and evil within individuals and highlighting the need for both moral education to cultivate the "good" and institutional oversight buttressed by public engagement to constrain the "evil." This balanced perspective on human potential underscores why a separation of the "inner sage" and "outer king" is neither necessary nor possible. Chinese cosmology, rooted in the interaction of yin and yang, emphasizes relativity and interconnectedness rather than rigid dichotomies. Philosophically, the "inner sage" and the "outer king" are interdependent, each completing the other in the pursuit of moral and political harmony.

In practice, the contemporary challenge lies not in the unity of "inner sage" and "outer king" but in their de facto disconnect. In China, where a civilization grounded more in moral culture than in legal or contractual systems, interpersonal relationships and political interests are often mediated through the adaptable lens of ethical principles. Yet in any society, especially one as vast and diverse as China, the virtues guiding interpersonal relationships within close circles (sometimes termed "petty virtue") must be complemented and enhanced by a broader ethical vision. This higher-order virtue, oriented toward the well-being of "All under Heaven," emphasizes inclusiveness, comprehensive vision, balance, and altruism. It is this expansive moral perspective that remains essential for cultivating social cohesion and sustaining well-functioning democratic institutions in a superlarge, complex country that must balance formal justice with ethical consideration.

The problem with the current modern systems is their tendency to prioritize procedural mechanisms while largely neglecting the oversight of "virtues" yet simultaneously allowing the covert but tremendous influence of guanxi (networks of favor exchanges). An overreliance on procedures can leave modern institutions vulnerable to manipulation, as individuals, especially those within interest groups, may leverage their influence to prioritize self-interest over public justice. This tendency often results in systemic inefficacy and corruption, which, in turn, erode public trust in democracy and the rule of law. Even Ren Jiantao, who advocates for a separation of the "inner sage" and "outer king," admits that such a division could diminish the relevance of moral self-cultivation for societal improvement and make governance more susceptible to power struggle (Ren, 2018). In this context, his proposed solution of using self-cultivation within autonomous community to check elite power seems both impractical and insufficient.

The fundamental premise remains that a thriving democracy depends on a bedrock of civic virtues. While Western democratic traditions typically prioritize individual liberties, equality before the law, and procedural justice, Confucian ethics emphasize social harmony and the careful calibration of personal obligations with collective welfare. Contemporary Chinese society illustrates how these traditional values can coexist with modern institutions, forming a distinctive moral ecosystem in which ancient virtues continue to support social stability. This synthesis suggests that modern democratic systems need not displace indigenous moral frameworks but can instead find meaningful expression through them.

Traditionally, morality served not only to unite people but also to regulate them, including providing checks on the power of the elite. In ancient China, both individual standing and elite power were role-based, contingent on the fulfillment of corresponding moral accountabilities across the family, the state, and All under Heaven. True virtue extended beyond personal loyalty and filial piety to encompass broader social responsibilities. The role of "inner sage-outer king," for example, involved caring for the world and embracing a greater self. Power was thus constrained not only by formal structures but, more importantly, by the moral principles embedded within them. Elites were expected to hold one another accountable based on these principles, and the populace held the right to criticize and even rebel against rulers who failed in their moral duties. Therefore, when contemporary systems of governance, whether democracy or the rule of law, are detached from a strong ethical foundation, they become vulnerable to manipulation by powerful interest groups and increasingly prone to dysfunction.

A robust system for curbing excessive self-interest demands not only the division of powers but also individual self-discipline, institutional oversight, and public accountability informed by public moral consciousness. In China, divorcing morality from governance risks eroding the ethical constraints necessary to counterbalance guanxi networks—informal patronage systems that can distort social equality and legal impartiality. That said, constructing a modern democratic system does not mean reverting to Confucian tradition of "inner sage" and "outer king." What is needed instead is a morally grounded democracy—one that, operating through modern institutions, holds leaders to high ethical standards, strengthens democratic oversight, and safeguards individual rights by cultivating moral character and civic consciousness at the grassroots level.

In short, a morally grounded democracy embeds a strong ethical foundation within civic governance, allowing China's humanistic tradition to constructively inform modern political structures amid global tensions. Institutional reforms should therefore prioritize combating nepotism, ensuring judicial fairness, and nurturing civic virtue. Reviving the classical integration of inner sage and outer king, this model envisions moral cultivation and democratic structures working in tandem, with top-down leadership and bottom-up supervision mutually reinforcing one another to foster a more equitable and principled political system.

10.6 Civilizational Implications

Civilizational dialogue across philosophical traditions is a vital source of mutual enrichment. By engaging Chinese moral philosophy in conversation with other cultural value systems, we cultivate not only deeper cross-cultural understanding but also the foundations for a more inclusive world order, one conducive to meaningful cooperation and shared human flourishing.

China's enduring strength resides in an ethical tradition that prizes balance and moderation, qualities that foster life-generating vitality. Beyond kindness, Chinese ethics promotes a dynamic harmony—one that embraces adaptation, cooperation, mutual benefit, and measured restraint. Moderation, achieved by avoiding extremes and cultivating temperance in thought, emotion, and actions, is essential to sustaining this equilibrium. Central to this philosophy is the generative virtue of life-nurturing, renewal, and co-flourishing—an ethic that emphasizes concern, vision, and altruistic values. It suggests that individual fulfillment is best achieved in harmony with the flourishing of the collective, forming a central pillar of China's cultural resilience. Given China's rich history of navigating diverse needs and reconciling conflicts, its time-tested approaches to resolving crises offer valuable insights for addressing contemporary global challenges.

For example, the concept of "unity of Heaven and humanity" holds continued relevance today, advocating a holistic worldview centered on order and harmony. This principle complements Western analytical methods that value independence and open inquiry. While technological advancements driven by free exploration have fueled innovation, the prevalence of global challenges underscores the increasing need for global cooperation and co-flourishing. In effect, the pursuit of order is not necessarily the enemy of progress; sometimes, even moderate constraints can become sources of ingenuity, as individuals and societies strive to achieve freedom through innovation and adaptation. The key, therefore, lies not in choosing between freedom and harmonious order but in finding a balance, knowing when or where to prioritize freedom and when or where to emphasize order. Through mutual learning and exchange, a delicate equilibrium can be cultivated, mitigating the risk of extreme swings in either direction and fostering a more stable and genuinely collaborative global environment.

Ancient China's agrarian foundations and dense population necessitated a strong concern for internal stability and communal harmony, within which managing intricate familial and clan structures elevated moral cultivation and conflict resolution to central cultural priorities. Western civilization, while complex in its diversity, developed a markedly different orientation—one characterized by exploratory ambition and individual rights, which found expression in scientific innovation, territorial expansion, and colonial enterprises. Whereas China's historical challenge lay in optimizing existing resources to sustain its populous society, Western nations more frequently sought solutions beyond their borders through exploration, commerce, and conquest. These fundamentally distinct approaches to civilizational development have produced profoundly different philosophical and cultural traditions.

While Western models and concepts have dominated global discourse since the early modern era, China's traditional paradigm also offers valuable insights for addressing today's complex challenges. The holistic and correlative worldview of Chinese philosophy serves as a crucial complement to the Western reductionist approach, echoing integrative movements within Western thought itself. Although reductionism has undoubtedly propelled scientific advancement by analyzing discrete components, it can also lead to fragmented solutions that neglect the interconnected nature of reality. In contrast, returning to the Dao and its foundational principles offers a more contextual and cohesive perspective. This emphasis on relational harmony not only broadens philosophical horizons but also suggests more balanced responses to contemporary political, social, and developmental challenges.

Furthermore, Chinese traditions of moral cultivation provide profound insights for reconciling the modern tension between individualism and collectivism—a dilemma of increasing global significance. While both individualist and collectivist societies may emerge under conditions of resource scarcity and high population density, they often pursue different strategies to address such constraints. When resources become insufficient to meet escalating demands, a society must either seek external solutions—through trade, exploration, or innovation—or address the disequilibrium internally and maximize the use of existing resources. Ancient China largely opted for the latter, foregrounding cooperation, social cohesion, and harmony through moral cultivation and viewing these principles as essential to long-term sustainability.

Today, with a global population nearing eight billion and exerting unprecedented pressure on Earth's finite resources, collaboration and sustainable resource management are more critical than ever. These challenges are further intensified by widening wealth disparities, which fuel both domestic and international tensions. While technological innovation holds promise, meaningful progress takes time—and without a solid ethical foundation, such advances risk deepening the very crises they aim to resolve.

The challenges of resource scarcity and conflicting interests underscore the enduring relevance of moral cultivation—a concept cherished not only in ancient China but across diverse cultures. Moral cultivation fosters harmonious relationships, moderates desires, and facilitates conflict resolution—essential for effective coordination, which, when balanced with competition, drives civilizational progress. Looking ahead, scientific breakthroughs alone will not secure a better future; they need to be conditioned by moral cultivation, as humanity must, in the process, nurture mutual understanding, align collective interests, and pursue shared development. Achieving such harmony requires more than political strategy—it demands a global consensus on peaceful coexistence and a shared vision for humanity's common future. In this light, moral cultivation remains a powerful and indispensable force for both individual well-being and the common good.

While conflict has often served a powerful catalyst for historical change, the enduring advancement of civilizations has ultimately relied on the cultural exchange and mutual enrichment. Over the past few centuries, Western civilization has played a transformative role in shaping global modernity. At the same time, Chinese civilization—with its millennia of philosophical and cultural achievement—has made significant contributions to global development and will continue to do so. Central to this contribution is the concept of the unity of Heaven and humanity, which underscores the interconnectedness of all existence and the importance of cultivating harmonious relationships. By encouraging responsible resource allocation and fostering cooperation, these values can offer a path to bridging differences and creating a more sustainable and beneficial world order.

References

Confucius. (2016a). Analects. In J. Legge (Ed. & Trans.), *Confucianism: The four books and five classics*. Delphi Classics.

Confucius. (2016b). Book of rites. In J. Legge (Ed. & Trans.), *Confucianism: The four books and five classics*. Delphi Classics.

Confucius. (2007). *Classic of filial piety*. China Textile Press.

Gu, Y. (2021). *Record of daily study* (Vol. 13). National Library of China Publishing House.

Ivanhoe, P. J. (2014). Confucian cosmopolitanism. *Journal of Religious Ethics, 42*(1), 22–44.

Liu, W. (2000). Outline of Confucian civilization. *Confucius Studies, 4*, 4–16.

Lao Tzu. (2010). *Daodejing*. In R. T. Ames & D. L. Hall (Eds. & Trans.), *Dao de jing: A philosophical translation*. Ballantine Books.

Mou, Z. (2003). *Mou Zongsan's complete works*. Lianjing.

Pan, Y. (2020). Warring States and Greece: A comparison of the roots of Chinese and Western civilizations. *Beijing Cultural Review, 3*, 14–31.

Pan, Y. (2022). *A comparison of the roots of Chinese and Western civilizations*. New World Press.

Ren, J. (2018). Inner sage to inner sage, outer king to outer king: The modern breakthrough of Confucianism. *Journal of Renmin University of China, 32*(1), 82–94.

Schrödinger, E. (1992). *What is life?: With mind and matter and autobiographical sketches*. Cambridge University Press.

Shao, L., & Li, X. (2005). The influence of Confucian ethics on contemporary Chinese people. *Literature, History and Philosophy, 6*, 25–32.

Shi, Z. (2018). *The hub: 3000 years of China*. Guangxi Normal University Press.

Wang, Y. (2011). *Collected works of Wang Yangming*. Shanghai Ancient Books Publishing House.

Wang, J. (2016). The qualities of Chinese civilization and its formation process - From the comparison of Eastern and Western civilizations. *Collection, 2*, 13–22.

Xunzi. (1997). *Xunzi*. Liaoning Education Press.

You, Z., & Hu, Y. (2013). Walking a policy tightrope: The dilemma of balancing diversification and equality in Chinese college entrance examination reform. *Higher Education Policy, 26*(3), 309–324.

Zhang, S. (2011). *Chinese and Western culture and self*. People's Press.

Zhu, X. (1991). The old inner sage and the new outer king: A review of Neo-Confucian political philosophy from the way of politics and the way of governance. *Exploration and Controversy, 6*, 40–50.

Zuo, Q. (2024). *The commentary of Zuo on Spring and Autumn*. China Bookstore.

Chapter 11
Toward Global Equilibrium: The Greater Self and the Future of Humanity

The future of humanity hangs in a precarious balance, not for lack of scientific progress but from a profound neglect of humanistic care. Technology has thrust us into an age of dazzling innovation, yet it has been incapable of bridging the expanding divides that fracture our world: yawning economic inequality, escalating global conflicts, and accelerating environmental collapse. These are not merely technical problems to be solved by better algorithms or cleaner energy alone but symptoms of a deeper moral dissonance, visible in the tensions between individual and collective good, excess and deprivation, human ambition and ecological limits, rationality and empathy, and science and humanity.

This disharmony reflects a long history in which progress has been shaped by the complex interplay of humanity's dual nature. Civilization has advanced through compassion, cooperation, and innovation, yet also through the relentless pursuit of wealth and power—a drive that has spurred both monumental progress and profound conflict. While this competitive impulse has often been a vital force, history repeatedly shows that, when left unchecked, it breeds animosity and threatens our very existence. Over a century ago, Mahatma Gandhi diagnosed these excesses as seven social sins: wealth without work, pleasure without conscience, knowledge without character, commerce without morality, science without humanity, religion without sacrifice, and politics without principle (Gandhi, 1958). His insights remain profoundly relevant today, reminding us that ethical cultivation is not a luxury but a necessity: it is our essential refuge in an increasingly uncertain world.

These reflections evoke what Peters and Meier (2025) would describe as a contemporary apocalyptic awareness—not a prophecy of divine judgment, but a revelation of civilization's systemic fragility, signaling both the potential collapse of global systems and the emergence of new forms of order. While the latter hints at possibilities for renewal, the immediate concern lies in the fact that beneath the glittering surface of technological progress, the world remains perilously vulnerable. Unlike the religious apocalypse involving transcendent salvation, the crisis we face

Z. You, Y. Hu, *Philosophy and Civilization: How the Idea of Moral Cultivation Shaped China*, East-West Dialogues in Educational Philosophy and Theory,
https://doi.org/10.1007/978-981-95-5660-1_11

is entirely of our own making, demanding our own redemption. It arises from a widening rift between human ambition and ethical responsibility, manifesting in social, cultural, and ecological disequilibrium. This modern apocalyptic sense of existential urgency calls for renewing civilization's ethical foundations, grounded not in abstract speculation but in a greater vision of individual moral resolve and collective purpose.

11.1 Sociocultural Disequilibrium and the Fragility of Civilization

In contrast to certain strands of modern analytic and existential thought, this book renews a long-standing philosophical tradition, found in both China and other cultures, which affirms the universe's intrinsic purpose and order. It contends that reason and kindness are not merely aspirations, but fundamental aspects of our being—reflecting the cosmos's inherent order and intelligibility, as manifested in our capacities for sensibility, compassion, and resilience. Such a humanistic perspective is vital in an era of rapid scientific and technological advancement, where ethical understanding and moral responsibility must keep pace with profound transformation.

This framework posits that an existence divorced from nature is like cut flowers: visually compelling but ontologically rootless and existentially ephemeral. It therefore advocates for moral cultivation not merely as a metaphysical foundation for meaning-making, but as an indispensable pedagogical and civic system for ensuring civilizational continuity and flourishing. Central to this system is love in its manifold expressions, which it establishes as the fundamental source of human well-being, fostering individual happiness, developmental growth, and the profound fulfillment derived from sustaining life and enabling collective thriving. Ultimately, by renewing our commitment to virtue and cultivating a profound reverence for existence, this approach constructs a substantive philosophical basis for ethical transformation. It reimagines moral agency, ethical vision, and civic responsibility as essential pathways for addressing today's most pressing global crises.

11.1.1 Contemporary Disequilibrium and Global Challenges

A vicious cycle grips contemporary societies, where concentrated wealth and deepening social stratification perpetuate one another. The resulting economic disparities limit access to education, healthcare, and professional opportunities, trapping poor families in a cycle of institutionalized, intergenerational disadvantage. While redistributive policies and inclusive development strategies represent necessary interventions, their efficacy remains constrained without heightened ethical awareness, civic participation, and collective effort. Persistent inequality breeds a spectrum of negative emotions—greed and arrogance among the privileged, resentment and intolerance among the disadvantaged, collectively fueling polarization. Such pattern has been repeatedly demonstrated during periods of economic stress throughout modern history, often serving as a major catalyst for domestic unrest, international conflict, and even war.

The accelerating anthropogenic estrangement from natural systems is increasingly reflected in ecological disruptions, including environmental degradation, resource depletion, biodiversity loss, and climate change. Industrialization, urbanization, and unsustainable land-use patterns are primary drivers of this crisis, generating cascading effects across ecological and social systems. The consequences—coastal inundation, intensified climatic volatility, and ecosystem failures—have shifted from future projections to observable realities with profound human impacts. This alienation from nature extends beyond the physical realm, eroding compassion, resilience, and a sense of responsibility, qualities essential for inner peace and mental health. As we distance ourselves from the natural world, we risk losing touch with what makes us fully human, not just biologically, but emotionally, ethically, and spiritually.

Another fundamental disequilibrium persists between scientific advancement and humanistic development—a prevailing paradigm that prioritizes instrumental rationality and utilitarian outcomes over a more holistic understanding of knowledge and human flourishing. This utilitarian emphasis risks severing the vital link between intellect and ethics, reducing morality to mere external rules and potentially cultivating apathy. More critically, the accelerating pace of technological innovation now consistently outstrips the evolution of corresponding ethical frameworks, creating a dangerous asymmetry. Unregulated technology, much like dangerous toys in the hands of a child, confers immense power without the requisite moral maturity. As we ascend our own technological Tower of Babel, we must cultivate a parallel growth in ethical consciousness to establish essential safeguards. Only through such balanced development can technological progress truly serve human well-being and sustain the continuity of civilization.

Artificial intelligence represents a paradigmatic case of the urgent need for parallel moral advancement. As AI systems become increasingly embedded in social infrastructures, they offer emancipatory potential while also generating systemic risks. Although offering enhanced individual agency, these technologies simultaneously exacerbate existing inequalities through power imbalances, labor market disruptions, and emerging forms of social exclusion, all of which threaten collective welfare and societal cohesion. This technological transformation necessitates proactive ethical development to counteract emerging pathologies of disengagement, alienation, and hyper-individualism. Indeed, as we enter the age of AI, ethical growth is no longer a philosophical luxury but an operational imperative. To harness the power of AI responsibly, individuals and societies must place ethical considerations at the forefront, ensuring that AI serves all humanity and upholds human dignity, social justice, and our shared moral values.

This principle is particularly crucial in mitigating existential risks posed by artificial intelligence, highlighting the imperative to embed human values at AI's core. Philosophically considered, AI systems are not merely mathematical constructs—they serve as value-laden artifacts that embody inherited human moral frameworks, shaped through their training on human-generated data that reflect our worldviews, emotions, and ethical judgments. This is especially true for large language models, whose architecture specifically encodes human linguistic and normative structures. Ultimately, AI's moral alignment becomes a profound mirror of our own. Whether AI evolves toward benevolence, reverence, empathy, and a spirit of the "greater self," or toward hatred and cruelty, depends on the values we spread online. In this sense, our collective ethical orientation will directly shape not only AI's behavior in the world, but also its relationship with and attitude toward us, its human creators.

11.1.2 Social and Cultural Concerns

Contemporary societies are witnessing a pronounced increase in social involution, which fosters heightened tension, simplistic thinking, and the resurgence of "might makes right" ideologies. These sociocultural conditions, often intertwined, create fertile ground for cognitive exploitation and perpetuate a self-reinforcing cycle of division and social discordance.

11.1.2.1 The Spiral of Social Involution

We live in an era where instrumental rationality—valuing efficiency and measurable outcomes—is often prioritized over other critical values. In highly competitive environments, this goal-oriented efficiency can exacerbate social pressures and narrow individual perspectives. When pushed to extremes, it gives rise to a heightened "involution," a phenomenon of intense competition that often yields little genuine progress, most notably observed in some countries in East Asia but now increasingly emerging on a global scale. In both educational and professional contexts, individuals become trapped in a cycle of relentless striving for scarce resources, such as promotions, recognition, or educational opportunities, where increased effort results in ever-declining returns.

Involution gradually saps a society's vitality. The relentless pursuit of narrow success, while seemingly efficient in the short term, creates pressure and anxiety that erode overall well-being. As individuals become consumed by the drive to outperform their peers, they often neglect essential aspects of life: mental and physical health, relationships, and personal growth. This environment can give rise to a "low-desire society," where younger generations resist involution by "lying flat"—opting out of traditional life paths such as marriage, overwork, and homeownership. This countercultural stance powerfully expresses dissatisfaction with a system that prioritizes competition over well-being and equity. Sociologically, involution stifles innovation, undermines cooperation, and disrupts justice and mobility. Ideologically, it breeds selfishness and narrow-mindedness, fueling xenophobia and polarization as defensive reactions. Left unchecked, this vicious cycle can lead to societal stagnation and dissatisfaction.

Countering societal involution requires transcending reductive paradigms to embrace a more nuanced understanding of human flourishing. An overemphasis on efficiency and competition often reflects a narrow vision of progress, fostering hostility, homogenization, and widespread apathy. While productive output remains valuable, an overreliance on quantitative metrics stifles authentic innovation and sustainable development. Nurturing creativity and resilience requires a supportive ecosystem rooted in vision, compassion, and inclusivity. This calls for a holistic approach that embraces diversity, fosters collaboration, encourages long-term thinking, and cultivates the societal resilience necessary to thrive amid mounting global flux.

11.1.2.2 The Allure of Polarization and Binary Thinking

The surge of polarization today—fueled by interwoven socioeconomic rifts, social atomization, cultural collisions, and geopolitical strains—demands urgent attention from scholars and society alike. As systemic inequities persist, disaffected populations increasingly perceive the world as intrinsically antagonistic and exclusionery, prompting them to adopt simplistic, polarizing responses to complex issues. These polarized frameworks serve both as manifestations of social grievance and potential catalysts for societal destabilization.

Polarization poses a serious challenge to humanity, as their inherent destructiveness obstructs meaningful change and offer no viable solutions (Shi, 2018). Those ensnared by these beliefs often become intolerant, dismissing alternative viewpoints and fostering a confrontational mindset that reduces intricate situations to simplistic "us vs. them" dichotomies. This divisive mode of thought compels individuals to take sides, breeding parochialism, xenophobia, and, in extreme cases, violence. Such an environment corrodes the appreciation of diversity and undermines pluralistic values, both essential for fostering global peace and sustainable development.

Those with polarized views tend to prioritize preconceived positions over factual evidence. They readily accept information that reinforces preexisting beliefs while simultaneously resorting to personal attacks against dissenting voices. Their moral compass is often self-serving, privileging emotions over analysis, personal needs over ethical considerations, and in-group loyalty over broader societal concerns. Social media algorithms amplify this polarization through creating filter bubbles that limit exposure to diverse perspectives. The "echo chambers" reinforce biases and impede constructive engagement, thereby undermining productive dialogue and collaboration (Shi, 2020).

Polarization thrives on reductive binaries that transform nuanced issues into divisive, absolutist narratives. These frameworks employ strategic simplification—often coupled with Machiavellian rhetoric—to recast partisan agendas as moral imperatives. Particularly appealing to marginalized groups experiencing socioeconomic frustration, such narratives offer emotionally compelling yet ultimately illusory resolutions, reflecting both the structural pressures they face and the psychological vulnerabilities that compromise critical reasoning. The risks are profound: historical precedents reveal how unchecked ideological radicalization frequently escalates into destructive societal outcomes.

11.1.2.3 The Rise of a Predatory Mindset

The concept of "jungle law" paints a dystopian picture where power dictates morality and survival hinges on ruthless cunning, utterly disregarding ethical considerations. While ostensibly repudiated by civilized societies, recent years have witnessed an insidious resurgence of this predatory mindset, fueled by intense competition for finite resources within increasingly competitive domestic and global arenas. The resurgent ideology rationalizes unscrupulous and exploitative tactics aimed at maximizing individual or narrow in-group advantage—a mindset that increasingly permeates popular culture and shapes the ideological frameworks through which we view the world.

A widely read example of popular literature is the award-winning science fiction novel *The Three-Body Problem*, presenting a "dark forest" universe where survival hinges on ruthless, predatory logic, dismissing compassion as vulnerability. This ideology, which prioritizes survival and success over ethical considerations, reflects the discontent and grievances of those under intense pressure for survival in today's intensely competitive world—a worldview that stands in stark contrast to traditional mainstream Chinese cultural values that emphasize harmony, humaneness, integrity, and sincerity.

This ascendance of "survival of the fittest" signifies an ontological rupture from "heavenly virtue"—which holds that just causes naturally garner support. While reflecting contemporary dissatisfaction, the glorification of ruthlessness is a dangerous overcorrection that advocates abandoning cooperation, mutual aid, and peaceful coexistence. It fails to recognize that human society is not always zero-sum; collaboration and mutual benefit are also vital for human survival and prosperity. Under the "law of the jungle," everyone, strong or weak, is vulnerable, as history has shown. Embracing this ideology would lead to societal fragmentation and heightened conflict, creating a recipe for implosion, even without an alien invasion.

These perspectives fundamentally misapprehend virtue's constitutive role in civilizational durability. True virtue is not leniency or softness, but courageous wisdom—the steadfast discernment of right and wrong, capacity for practical action, and the active maintenance of a harmonious social order that protects against internal disintegration and external threats. While technology is powerful, its responsible use rests upon a robust ethical framework, which serves as the bedrock of sustained human progress within a vast and potentially solitary cosmos. This framework serves as a safeguard against civilizational self-destruction and is key to the potential acceptance by advanced alien civilizations, should they exist.

The fiction's premise of limited resources in the universe rests on a static and impoverished view of existence. In truth, a civilization's capacity to access and generate resources expands alongside the evolution of its intellectual, moral, and technological capacities. History bears witness to the fact that human ingenuity—guided by discovery and reflection—has continually deepened our ability to transform the unknown into the usable. Far from being constrained by scarcity alone, we are defined by an open-ended potential for cognition, imagination, and creative synthesis. It is this generative capacity that reveals the universe not as a barren field of threats, but as a horizon of possibility yet to be understood and cultivated. This understanding underscores the centrality of human dignity, communication, and cooperation—all hinging on moral development. Life, far from being a burden, emerges as the universe's most profound expression of value. Without conscious beings to perceive, interpret, and steward its wonders, even the grandest cosmos reduces to a sterile, purposeless void.

11.2 The Indispensable Virtue

This section aims to construct a robust framework for understanding virtue and its development, offering a unique perspective to navigate contemporary ethical challenges. This is achieved by integrating traditional Chinese wisdom with global perspectives, focusing on three key areas—the intrinsic value of morality, its nature, and the generative virtue as life-nurturing, renewing, and co-flourishing—which lay the foundation for discussing the idea of the greater self.

11.2.1 Why Virtue Matters for Human Civilization

Anchored in fundamental aspects of human existence—our nature, sociality, political being, and affective dimensions—the philosophy of moral cultivation provides an ethical architecture conducive to both personal and collective flourishing. Though culturally varied in expression, virtue fundamentally emerges as an intersubjective consensus governing harmonious coexistence between individuals, communities, and the broader environment—emphasizing compassion, mutual obligation, and ethical conduct. The universality of human nature and emotional experience, together with common challenges, renders this framework globally relevant, offering vital normative resources for navigating contemporary global issues.

11.2.1.1 Human Nature, Emotion, and Moral Development

Human nature provides a universal metaphysical foundation for virtue, grounded in its complex duality, which reveals not only self-preservative instincts but also innate capacities for empathy, kindness, and a desire for connection. Though we possess the capacity to both create and destroy, our inherent potential for love, altruism, and creativity points toward a telos of moral development. Cultivating these qualities is essential for inspiring a more just, compassionate, and sustainable world.

This potential, however, is not fixed; for many philosophers, our innate seeds of "good" and "evil" are malleable, forged anew through lived experiences and deliberate education. Moral cultivation amplifies inherent goodness and transforms limitations through promoting internal sympathy, mutual benefit, and the gentle touch of societal norms. While selfish desires persist as a natural part of human motivation, they can be moderated and channeled toward more constructive purposes. Simultaneously, the altruistic aspect of human nature can be nurtured and expanded to encompass a broader sphere of concern, extending to the well-being of others and all sentient beings. In this context, Mencius' idea of inherent goodness is insightful as it highlights our potential for virtue, realized through sustained moral cultivation.

Recognizing human complexity allows for a balanced moral landscape, where responsible individualism, like collectivism, can contribute to moral development. When individuals understand their rights and obligations to society, they can foster altruistic perspectives and a public spirit. This sense of agency, coupled with a commitment to the common good, can significantly enhance the overall human flourishing. That said, not all manifestations of individualism are morally positive. Extreme individualism, often characterized by self-centeredness, materialism, and neglect of social responsibility, prioritizes personal gain at the expense of collective well-being. This "me-first" mentality undermines moral obligations and impedes the pursuit of shared prosperity (Rushing, 2013).

Emotions are integral part of human nature, shaping our thoughts, behaviors, and relationships. It is human to experience a spectrum of emotions from joy and love to depression and grief. While many Western philosophers regarded emotions as secondary to reason or even disruptive to ethics, others—most notably Aristotle—recognized, much like Confucius, that properly cultivated emotions are crucial to moral development.[1] Emotions inform moral judgments, motivate actions, and shape our understanding of right and wrong. For instance, empathy and compassion can inspire us to help others, whereas disgust and sense of justice prompt us to condemn harmful actions. Emotions such as guilt, shame, and pride can drive moral behavior, while friendship and loyalty foster responsibility toward each other.

However, when these affective responses become dysregulated, they can negatively impact both psychological and physiological well-being. Intense emotions like anger, jealousy, or hatred can cloud judgment, introduce bias into

[1] Aristotle's account of virtuous emotions includes nuanced discussions of gratitude and shame that could serve as a useful point of comparison with Confucian views. See Kristjánsson, K. (2018). Virtuous emotions. Oxford University Press.

decision-making, and lead to impulsive actions that are morally problematic or harmful. These emotions can also fuel an insatiable desire for external validation and immediate gratification, potentially undermining ethical principles and eroding inner tranquility.

To address such affective disturbances, self-cultivation offers a structured pathway for soothing and transforming emotions amidst discontent and anxieties. This introspective journey turns vulnerabilities—insecurities, ego, guilt, and negative thoughts—into catalysts for personal growth. By embracing imperfections and practicing tolerance, we build inner resilience; cultivating strong moral values provides purpose and meaning, especially when confronting a perceived lack of control or existential emptiness. Ethical conduct, rooted in kindness, justice, and empathy, bestows a profound sense of meaning that transcends fleeting desires. Upholding moral principles yields a luminous conscience and the quiet joy of aiding others. This inward-outward journey provides guidance and solace in adversity, culminating in a life woven from harmony and fulfillment.

11.2.1.2 The Interdependence Between Morality and Social Institutions

Contemporary institutional systems—particularly educational, legal, and political structures—serve as critical mechanisms for fostering moral development. Formal and informal educational channels cultivate ethical reasoning and prosocial dispositions, while legal frameworks institutionalize normative expectations through codified systems of accountability. Democratic processes further reinforce this moral infrastructure by enabling civic participation and collective value articulation. Collectively, these institutional dimensions function as interdependent pillars for both individual character cultivation and the maintenance of societal ethical benchmarks.

Morality, in turn, constitutes the foundational normative framework that sustains social institutions and legal systems. No political structure, however sophisticated, can remain functional without a morally engaged citizenry committed to upholding its core values. Democratic systems particularly depend on the cultivation of civic virtue to guard against institutional decay and the abuse of power. As moral commitment wanes, so too does institutional efficacy—revealing that democratic resilience depends on the integration of robust structural designs such as institutional procedures with the collective ethical integrity of the people. The fragility of certain democracies stems precisely from a deficit in shared moral purpose and civic consciousness among their populations.

The same holds true for the legal systems. Statutory law is built on fundamental principles of freedom, equality, justice, and reciprocity. However, laws remain mere words on paper until judges, jurors, and law enforcement put them into practice. The moral character of those who interpret and enforce the law becomes crucial, as legal provisions often require interpretation and discretionary judgment (Li, 2020). Judicial independence, for example, requires not only institutional protections but also magistrates who exercise principled discernment grounded in professional ethics. Combined with structural safeguards, this ethical commitment forms an essential bulwark against systemic corruption and external pressures.

Morality and institutions exist in a dialectical relationship. Core social institutions—including religious systems, legal frameworks, governance structures, educational apparatuses, and normative sanctions—function as both products and propagators of collective moral values. Concurrently, these ethical norms serve as critical checks on institutional power, ensuring their equitable operation. This reciprocal dynamic allows powerholders to legitimize authority through moral discourse while simultaneously enabling all citizens, particularly marginalized groups, to invoke ethical principles in resisting injustice and asserting their rights. Public conscience, shaped by these shared values, functions as a vigilant watchdog, while robust institutions embed ethical governance into the fabric of society.

11.2.2 Redefining Morality in a Contemporary Context

Though ancient, morality retains profound contemporary relevance. Note that societal progress does not guarantee heightened moral standards, nor does scientific advancement equate to greater virtue. In a world flirting with nihilism, the quest for meaning and purpose becomes even more paramount. Morality provides a unifying thread of shared, though often nuanced, values that transcend cultures and generations. Yet its fundamental nature remains contested. As we navigate the intersection of tradition and modernity, what ultimately defines morality?

11.2.2.1 Virtue as the Living Expression of Morality

Virtue blossoms through the nurturing of compassion, justice, and discerning judgement rooted in our shared humanity. It inspires the courage to act rightly, the wisdom to choose wisely, the foresight to see broadly, and the capacity to navigate life's complex ethical terrain. At its heart, virtue beckons us to harmonize personal ambition with communal thriving and to balance short-term gains with long-term consequences. It provides a moral orientation for approaching challenges with integrity, guiding responses that uphold fundamental values. By remaining attentive to moral commitments through adversity, individuals may contribute to both personal growth and society's deeper flourishing. In this way, ethical engagement fosters understanding and connection, the subtle, sinewy threads binding vibrant communities.

Moderation, a cornerstone of ethical philosophy, finds seminal expression in both Confucianism's Doctrine of the Mean and Aristotelianism's Golden Mean. These philosophical systems conceptualize virtue not as mechanical centrism, but as the contextual discernment of optimal ethical conduct. Moderation serves as a corrective to ideological polarization, tempering both libertine excess and authoritarian rigidity while acknowledging that even positive qualities become vices when taken to extremes. Extending beyond personal conduct, the principle of moderation informs social ethics by promoting fairness, proportionality, and restraint in both resource distribution and the exercise of authority—key to maintaining societal balance. Historically, this moderating ethos contributed significantly to Chinese civilization's resilience by fostering adaptive stability and pluralistic inclusion, demonstrating its enduring relevance for sustainable governance.

Virtue transcends normative prescriptions to represent a philosophy of humanistic interdependence, emphasizing our fundamental connectedness and reciprocal obligations within the ecological and social spheres. Authentic achievement, in this framework, is evaluated not by paradigms of domination but by capacity to facilitate mutual thriving. Meaningful self-realization emerges when personal aspirations help create communal possibilities. This ethical orientation echoes a perennial wisdom that conceives virtue as generative capital: moral actions accumulate into future flourishing, while transgressions erode the shared foundations of self and society.

This understanding of virtue as a form of wisdom remains deeply relevant today, serving as a vital expression of human insight, fostering inner peace, communal cohesion, and resourcefulness in the face of challenges. While kindness is a core element of virtue, its full realization demands profound strength, ingenuity, and courage. Good intentions alone do not guarantee positive outcomes; without discerning wisdom and the capacity to translate ideals into action, efforts may fall short or even backfire. Consequently, cultivating genuine virtue involves developing the vision and abilities necessary to navigate life's complexities with creativity, resilience, and resolve.

While the ontological status of morality within natural law remains contested, its conceptual foundations clearly draw upon principles observed in biological flourishing and ecological interdependence. This suggests that morality is not purely a human construct, but an intuitive inference from nature's sustaining patterns. Ancient moral philosophies likely developed key concepts—harmony, equilibrium, reciprocity—through the observation of life-generative dynamics. Modern science may support this view: Schrödinger's negentropy principle shows that living systems maintain order by resisting entropic decay (Schrödinger, 1992). In a similar way, moral systems act as societal negentropy—preserving social order and coherence through ethical norms that mitigate conflict and prevent collective self-destruction.

This naturalistic moral framework resonates with the universe's intrinsic tendency toward complexity and self-organization, processes that generate, sustain, and evolve life. Such patterns echo classical Chinese cosmology, where Heaven and Earth embody a life-nurturing virtue, privileging balance over brute force. Consider the metaphor of "a tiger with wings": in lore, it symbolizes invincible might, yet nature withholds such a beast. This absence whispers a normative truth: absolute dominance fractures interdependence, consuming the very web that sustains it and hastening its own demise. Herein lies a vital societal precept: moral architectures must shun monopolies, championing distributive equity to ensure civilizational endurance.

Natural systems, often deemed as amoral, yield potent analogies for social ethics. While predator-prey dynamics dominate ecological narratives, symbiotic mutualism persists as a core biological strategy—embodied in plant-pollinator bonds that evolutionarily entwine species' fates. More fundamentally, ecosystems thrive through biodiversity and dynamic equipoise: interwoven dependencies create resilience, where any organism's unchecked hegemony invites cascading collapse.

Anthropological parallels surface vividly—cultural and intellectual pluralism bolsters societal agility, much as equitable resource flows underpin communal steadiness. Just as ecological harmony averts degradation, moral architectures that restrain monopolies and champion inclusive justice shield civilizations from ruinous spirals. History affirms this: cooperative societies, knit by robust collective ties, have outlasted and outshone their more divided counterparts.

Even nature's seeming inefficiencies harbor adaptive wisdom, bearing lessons on temporal trade-offs: Rivers seldom carve straight paths but serpentine bends and loops, irrigating vast terrains and cradling richer biomes. This meandering ethos intimates that societies fixated on linear efficiency risk eroding resilience and communal vitality.

Moreover, as a species armed with advanced knowledge and technology, humans possess both the capacity and the responsibility to transcend the jungle law—a realm governed by raw might, hunting, and self-preservation, as even animals reveal pockets of serene coexistence once survival's urgencies subside. While competition can sometimes drive innovation, our increasingly interconnected world demands collaborative solutions to complex challenges. The more advanced a civilization becomes, the more essential it is to foster social cohesion, cultivate long-term vision, and embrace a broader, more inclusive perspectives. These cooperative principles form the foundational architecture of sustainable progress, enabling humanity to realize its fullest potential and preserving the future we hold in common.

The rationality of the universe may be debated, but the future of humanity undeniably hinges on our ethical capacity. Rather than ascribing virtue as a cosmological design, it is more precise to recognize that humans, capable of both benevolence and malevolence, have an acute need for virtue to navigate complex human life. Moral systems function as civilization's safeguard against the mutually assured damage of unconstrained self-interest by fostering vision, trust, and empathy necessary for cooperative advancement. This broader perspective calls for moving beyond parochial boundaries and aligning individual pursuits with greater welfare, thereby redefining greatness as selfless public stewardship.

11.2.2.2 Harmony of Reason, Desire, and Affection

Genuine ethical understanding requires the dynamic integration of three fundamental faculties: reason, desire, and affection. Reason provides the analytical framework for moral judgment, yet it often lacks the emotional impetus to instigate action. Desire, by contrast, offers potent impetus but can readily stray from a moral course without the guidance of reason and the grounding influence of compassion

(Tang, 2012). Together, these faculties form a moral compass, harmonizing our intentions, values, and actions to cultivate a life guided by both logical consistency and humanitarian engagement.

Far from being a mere impediment to moral growth, desires are fundamental drivers of human flourishing. Confucius, for example, views desire as a fundamental aspect of human nature, advocating for its guidance and moderation through ritual propriety. Integrating this wisdom with Western concepts like Maslow's hierarchy of needs reveals that ethically channeled desires can propel both personal and societal progress. When social pressures prioritize "lower" needs such as survival and safety, the less desirable aspects of human nature like hatred and greed may prevail. Conversely, prioritizing "higher" needs like respect, self-esteem, and self-actualization can foster positive qualities, including compassion, creativity, and contributions to society (Maslow, 1943). As a formidable force, desire has the potential to inspire remarkable contributions or lead to significant harm. The ability to channel desires wisely and virtuously distinguishes both morally cultivated individuals and ethical leaders.

Another key relationship exists between reason and affection. While certain strands of Western philosophical traditions prioritize reason, valuing logic and analysis over emotion in moral development, traditional Chinese philosophy offers a more holistic perspective that weaves together reason and affection into the fabric of "virtue." Confucianism, for instance, states that "the Dao [of morality] starts with affection, which emanates from human nature" (Guo Dian Bamboo Slip, n.d.). It suggests that moral affection serves as the fertile ground from which principles blossom, cultivating and reinforcing our innate sense of rightness. However, it is important to distinguish affection from the destructive force of unchecked desire. Affections such as care, fondness, sympathy, and love are crucial for reasonable moral development, whereas greed—a distortion of natural affection—can corrupt reason, leading to moral compromise.

Authentic moral development transcends purely intellectual pursuits. While reason provides crucial analytical tools, it often feels abstract and lacks a visceral motivation to inspire action. Pure logic does not always evoke thoughts about right and wrong. Similarly, religion often emphasizes love and compassion, sometimes at the expense of systematic rational grounding. Traditional Chinese philosophy, like many other philosophies worldwide, bridges these approaches, recognizing the vital interplay between head and heart. Here, moral behavior is not solely dictated by ethical laws but emerges from a harmonious blend of rational principles and the affective dimensions. Unlike Kant's deontological view, which prioritizes reason as the sole determinant of moral action, Chinese philosophy sees affection as reason's essential partner, motivating and guiding the ethical conduct. This balanced and holistic approach significantly contributed to the flourishing of moral cultivation in ancient China.

Historical and contemporary evidence reveals the perils of hyper-rationalized ethics divorced from moral sensibility. The Holocaust's bureaucratic execution exemplifies how instrumental rationality, when severed from ethical reflection, can enable systematized brutality. Likewise, the deployment of unmanned weapons showcases a chilling efficiency, driven by strategic and economic incentives, that can detach decision-making from human feeling and ethical consideration. These cases affirm Dewey's insistence on moral imagination, the capacity to envision consequences and foster empathetic connections, which serves as an essential corrective to purely procedural reasoning, achieved through an integrative ethical paradigm that synthesizes cognitive analysis with affective moral consciousness.

11.2.2.3 Reconciling Morality and Interests

Morality is not detached from interests but emerges from social consensus around principles such as fairness, equity, and just resource distribution. Whereas self-interest maintains moral permissibility within bounded parameters, its unchecked pursuit, particularly when spawning negative externalities, constitutes ethical transgression. By contrast, the virtuous agent masters the art of aligning personal aspirations with scrupulous regard to others' rightful claims, thereby embodying Aristotle's eudaimonia as flourishing woven into the social fabric.

The dialectical interplay between individual and collective interests reveals moral reasoning's profound intricacy, subverting reductive zero-sum paradigms. Moral systems emerge to navigate these contending tides—from parochial self-interest to altruistic concern and overarching communal commitments. Authentic deliberation demands transcending egocentric veils through inclusive consideration of stakeholders, integrating political acuity, economic imperatives, rational discernment, empathetic resonance, and ethical steadfastness. Unbridled self-maximization begets social entropy, corroding trust and birthing disorder; aligned pursuits, by contrast, kindle cooperative synergy. Herein lies morality's cardinal office: to deftly harmonize the particular and the universal across time's expanse, sating proximate urgencies alongside enduring, shared vitality.

This vision necessitates active participation from all members of society, where individual virtue underpins social harmony. Just as democracy thrives on diverse perspectives, collective well-being hinges on the moral contributions and vigilance of everyone. Moral leaders, by prioritizing the common good over the interests of a select few and ensuring fair resource distribution, play a pivotal role. They recognize that genuine success is inextricably linked to the long-term welfare of all, including themselves, and that a flourishing society elevates every individual within it.

Conversely, when self-interest eclipses justice as a social norm, conflict, warfare, and ultimately societal disintegration frequently ensue. In this context, morality embodies a commitment to mutual support grounded in long-term, common interests. This principle resonates both in the natural word, where symbiosis and mutual benefit coexist with natural selection, and in human societies that thrive through a balance of competition, mutual care, and collaboration. Although personal survival instincts remain powerful, contemporary global challenges demand a profound shift toward cooperation. From the escalating climate crisis and global economic instability to the potential outer space exploration, humanity's future hinges on embracing collaboration and mutual aid. With our enhanced capacities, a self-centered, hypercompetitive mindset does not just risk our collective well-being; it jeopardizes our very existence.

Having established this, it is crucial to distinguish between individual rights and personal interests, which can range from legitimate to detrimental. Just societies temper harmful self-interest while enshrining fundamental rights—the bedrock of communal thriving. Though intricate social exigencies may demand occasional interest concessions, such trade-offs must spring from voluntary civic virtue, not coercive edicts masquerading as collective good, which too often enrich the elite at the cost of others' rightful claims. The violation of individual rights ultimately damages societal flourishing by corroding the trust and reciprocity essential for cooperative existence.

True virtue calls for an expanded ethical consciousness, which recognizes the self-undermining nature of unrestrained self-interest. Prudential sacrifices merit serious consideration when they produce sustainable gains for collective welfare. This demands both personal self-awareness and a broader social consensus that transcend narrow, self-serving agendas. While deliberative democracy and institutional checks provide necessary structural constraints, ethical vitality ultimately rests on individual and collective commitments to intergenerational equity rather than transient advantage. This forward-looking, altruistic approach embodies the highest aspirations of democratic ideals.

Ethical discernment is essential to ascertain the legitimacy of a call for personal sacrifice. Democratic societies, by nature, mediate frictions between individual needs and communal duties. While selfless devotion to communal welfare reflects moral nobility, robust ethics must equally champion personal thriving. Real-world dilemmas—pitting self against others, private pursuits against public mandates, or fleeting profits against enduring aims—test this equilibrium. Prioritizing the greater good is laudable, but individuals must retain the freedom to pursue their aspirations, provided they do so with respect for the rights and dignity of others. Under mutual regard, personal and communal pursuits can entwine as allies rather than adversaries. Conversely, one-sided edicts for sacrifice imperil the very pillars of a just, empathetic society.

That said, cultivating collective commitment is crucial for both individual and shared flourishing. Chinese history offers sobering lessons about the consequences of neglecting this necessity. Dynastic collapses, beyond population pressures and natural disasters, often stemmed from factors like concentrated wealth, pervasive corruption, and obstructed social mobility. During these tumultuous periods, all social strata suffered immensely, with millions of lives lost and countless properties destroyed, highlighting the devastating consequences of societal imbalance and unethical conduct. Although moral cultivation alone could not prevent the eventual decline of an empire, it demonstrably prolonged dynastic lifespans by promoting ethical consciousness, balancing conflicting interests, and easing social tensions.

This insight holds profound relevance today. While technological innovation alleviates material scarcities, it falters against entrenched pathologies: systemic injustice, widening inequality, and rampant greed. Countering these demands moral character that transcends self-interest and embraces stewardship for justice and equilibrium. Naturally, such awareness thrives in tandem with resilient democratic and legal scaffolds, igniting a virtuous cycle: an ethical ethos prizing communal vitality fortifies institutions, which in turn nurture selfless conduct. This reciprocal mechanism steadies society, curbing disparities, tempering polarization, and anchoring equitable rule.

Yet this stability hinges not solely on structures but on the deeper moral impulses human ideals inspire within us. While morality addresses the reconciliation of interests, it often transcends such considerations to promote acts of selflessness. Rooted in profound sympathy and universal care for all sentient beings, it surpasses simple interest-based reasoning. This altruism arises from the recognition of an inherent unity between self and other, individual and world—an idea found not only in ancient Eastern philosophies but also echoed in Western traditions such as Stoicism and process philosophy. For instance, J. Howard Moore's doctrine of Universal Kinship reflects this expansive ethical vision, anticipating modern concerns about interconnectedness and the need for a more inclusive moral framework.

11.2.3 The Generative Virtue in a Global Age

Moral virtue constitutes an essential dimension of human flourishing, operating beyond codified norms to engage life's ontological implications. It fosters relational interdependence, empathic understanding, and collective intentionality, harmonizing pluralism with communal purpose. Life, in its lived reality, is an organic totality—diverse yet cohesive, vulnerable yet adaptive—where uncertainty coexists with creative possibility. A life-affirming virtue does not necessarily demand absolute equality but ensures that all individuals can survive, grow together, and realize their full potential. Above all, it affirms the intrinsic worth of every person—not as a means, but as an end in themselves.

11.2.3.1 Virtue as Life-Nurturing Force

Across diverse moral expressions, a universal imperative emerges: to nurture life and foster the flourishing of all beings. This cardinal virtue resonates deeply across philosophical traditions, from Baruch Spinoza's dynamic, self-generating ground of being (natura naturans) to John Dewey's evolutionary view of growth as an open-ended continuum of experiential learning and intelligent adaptation. This shared notion could be a guiding principle, affirming the intrinsic worth of both individual and collective existence. Beyond mere survival, such a virtue aims to cultivate prosperity by creating opportunities, generating meaning, and fostering equilibrium—ultimately promoting happiness, fulfillment, and a deeply enriched life experience. Notably, this flourishing is not about unchecked expansion but about diverse, sustainable growth and continuous renewal, unleashing every life form's latent potential in symbiotic realization.

The life-nurturing paradigm awakens an expansive ethical consciousness, one that honors giving and receiving alike, attuned to all life's profound interdependence. Even titans like whales participate in this cosmic reciprocity: their bodies, dissolving into the deep to nourish the marine web anew, perpetuating existence's ceaseless cycle. This natural wisdom informs humanity's ideal of the "greater self"—a moral framework that unites personal cultivation with collective flourishing. At its pinnacle, this vision culminates in the notion of "no-self," effacing ego's confines with boundless compassion while generating meaning through virtuous participation in life's interconnected unfolding.

At its heart, virtue sustains and nurtures life, beginning with care for family and loved ones, the foundation of resilient and supportive relationships. Radiating outward, it kindles communal, civic, and global harmony, regarding all as extensions of the self. Virtue ascends highest when agents embrace the greater good, recognizing the interdependence of all life and the shared prosperity it sustains. For both individuals and communities to thrive, it summons collective resolve and a shared, long-term vision, which fosters a world where life flourishes—not in isolation, but through interconnection and tender reciprocity.

If the universe unfolds as a symphony of energy, as modern physics intimates, then morality may eclipse human contrivance, arising as existence's innate axiom. It could be a cosmic imperative, an underlying force that orients energy and matter toward life's exuberant bloom. Where empirical inquiry unveils the cosmos's gears, virtue ethics provides the normative compass for our stewardship. Just as thriving systems rely on coherent operating principles, morality, or natural law in this context, serves as reality's woven substrate: an indwelling logic that cultivates equilibrium, intricacy, and generative plenitude across existence's vast continuum.

Think of the Dao as the animating rhythm of the cosmic symphony—the vital current that suffuses all existence. This primordial, generative principle transforms an ostensibly indifferent universe into a fecund, interconnected matrix capable of sustaining Earth's vibrant biosphere. This principle finds resonance in literature: in the conclusion of the science fiction novel *The Three-Body Problem* trilogy, intergalactic civilizations confront existential threats that challenge self-interest on a cosmic scale. Regardless of the literal outcome, the narrative illustrates that true power lies not in domination or force, but in the vision and moral courage to pursue meaningful cooperation. Aligned with the Dao's inherent harmony, the most powerful individuals are not those who wield destruction, but those who heal with love, generate new life, and contribute to a shared future through altruism and innovation.

Virtue embodies practical wisdom attuned to the Dao's spirit—the capacity to navigate life's intricacies with keen discernment. It entails a sustained commitment to personal growth and the common good, fostering cooperation, resolving conflict, and guiding ethical decisions through compassion and appropriateness. Yet, virtue rejects the rigid demand for constant self-sacrifice; grounded in realism, it hones the ingenuity to craft win-win harmonies where all can flourish. This resilient weave renders moral deeds enduring and life-enriching, even amid existence's inexorable tempests.

In this light, authentic moral consciousness transcends rigid formulations and dogmatic prescriptions. Its ultimate purpose is alignment with the cosmos' holistic generative essence, thereby manifesting a broader and more profound will to ever-regenerating flow. Clinging to fixed categories or rigid dualities of good and evil leads to partiality and obscures the intrinsic, interconnected dignity of all existence, thereby stifling the very capacity for selfless nurturance and creative renewal. Only by attuning to the universe's boundless vitality can one realize supreme creativity—the capacity to reconcile life's paradoxes through an expansive vision and a tender, generous mind.

11.2.3.2 All Under Heaven and Inclusive Diversity

The ancient ideal of "All under Heaven" remains profoundly relevant today, offering a visionary framework for inclusivity and harmony. It calls us to recognize humanity's fundamental interconnectedness, rising above artificial boundaries and partisan ideologies. This gives rise to a heightened global responsibility: individuals and societies must act with awareness of their choices' far-reaching consequences, including environmental stewardship, universal welfare, and more equitable allocation of resources and benefits across societies, generations, and ecosystems. Reviving and updating this ideal cultivates a universal ethic—a way of seeing the world as an extension of our own community—that inspires collective action to shape a sustainable, thriving future for all.

Nature illustrates this inclusivity, mirroring the virtue of life-nurturing that encourages an interdependent coexistence of all species. This ancient wisdom aligns with contemporary thought in valuing diversity and multiple perspectives to navigate uncertainty. Just as ecological diversity is vital to a thriving world, preserving cultural diversity is essential for sustaining resilience and vitality (Pohl, 2002). Human societies prosper and become robust when diverse needs are appreciated, recognizing that safeguarding the most vulnerable ultimately sustains the broader community, allowing every unique talent to thrive.

True cultural confidence is not exclusionary but expansive—an openness to diverse voices, enriched through dialogue, mutual growth, and shared flourishing. Cultural diversity within the framework of All under Heaven offers a multitude of possibilities, enabling continuous renewal and exploration of the unknown. This framework transcends mere coexistence, emerging as a generative force of diversity that propels human advancement. While efficiency grounded in uniformity may be tempting, an overemphasis on narrow standards reduces individuals to mere instruments, stifling creativity and vitality. Humans, with their inherent strength in complexity, defy such confinements. Life pulses in the intricate weave of familiarity and unexplored vistas. To blindly pursue dominance and efficiency is to tread a perilous path.

To live alongside difference demands more than passive tolerance; it calls for active engagement. True pluralism requires cultivating a living network of reciprocity and respect, a modern embodiment of All under Heaven that transforms diversity into dynamic harmony. Envision a complex overpass where separate paths can coexist and intersect. This "intellectual overpass" fosters a constructive and harmonious exchange of divergent ideas and cultural expressions, creating a space for respectful dialogue and robust debate. While acknowledging its challenges, it invites all participants to transcend narrow, linear thinking, embracing the creative potential of diverse perspectives within an inclusive framework. In doing so, we strengthen the virtues of understanding and collaboration in a globalized era, building a world where varied voices enrich our collective experience.

11.2.3.3 A Global Community for Moral Development

Forging a moral community rooted in shared values—while honoring differences—is vital to humanity's collective well-being, sparking substantive dialogue and unified resolve against our era's gravest trials. Whereas individual actions may seem like an insignificant ripple, together they form a powerful current of collective agency. Open dialogue and international cooperation are essential. Consider the ancient Indian myth of Brahman's dream: if our world exists only within his slumber, and our squabbles risk wakening him, would we not prioritize peaceful negotiation? This metaphor reminds us how interconnected we are. Just as the dream's inhabitants would act differently if aware of their common destiny, so too can we cultivate a sense of shared responsibility.

Virtue cannot flourish in isolation; it requires sunlight to grow. To cultivate moral excellence, we must foster a community that actively encourages ethical conduct through both reinforcement and accountability. This entails raising the costs of unethical actions while rewarding and recognizing moral behavior, or at least lowering the costs of acting ethically. Ethics is not a toothless ideal; it demands more than private conviction. Imagine a world where line-cutters face not timid shrugs or secret admiration, but with a chorus reminding them of civility and communal norms. While personal conscience plays a vital role, virtue grows most robustly when embedded in a fabric of shared expectations, mutual encouragement, and public affirmation of what is right.

Traditional China's moral system effectively aligned social incentives with ethical conduct, rewarding virtue and sanctioning misconduct. Although its influence has waned in the modern era, this legacy of communal moral accountability continues to underpin social justice and preserve cultural heritage. From village networks to contemporary digital communities, these ethical structures endure as foundational pillars of society. Ultimately, this collective conscience could serve as the bedrock of a distinctively Chinese democracy—one grounded not merely in political institutions, but in the daily practice of civic virtue.

Some may regard virtue as a wholly private domain, shielded from the currents of social influence. Yet even staunchly individualistic societies wield moral norms via collective verdict, where infractions draw censure, not indifference. This reveals that virtue is not solely a matter of personal will but is sustained and reinforced by cultural frameworks. Social expectations, peer recognition, and communal practices subtly guide ethical behavior, encouraging fidelity to shared ideals. Leaving immorality unpunished or worse, seeing it rewarded is a harbinger of societal decay and woe. The real challenge, then, is to construct social systems that sustain virtue: raising the cost of corruption while honoring integrity.

11.3 The Greater Self and the Future of Humanity

Originating in philosophical and spiritual traditions, the "greater self" represents a transformative understanding of human interconnectedness—one that dissolves rigid boundaries between self and others, individuals and the collective. This shift from ego-centered existence to civic consciousness ignites moral imagination, enabling societies to nurture the empathy and solidarity required to meet complex challenges and uplift humanity's intertwined, abiding prosperity.

11.3.1 The Architecture of the Greater Self

Cultivating the greater self means transcending egoic limitations to connect with a deeper sense of purpose, meaning, and interconnectedness. Central to this cultivation is the integration of rationality, i.e., objectively stepping outside oneself, and empathy, i.e., deeply understanding another's perspective. This process involves considering the big picture and long-term needs, ultimately building individual flourishing through safeguarding shared well-being.

While this process is rooted in long-standing traditions of philosophical and spiritual reflection, it also finds resonance in modern psychological research. Philosophers have long advocated for harmonizing the self with the cosmos, while many religious traditions call for union with God, both motivating individuals to pursue virtue and altruism. Psychologists have identified a mechanism for this transformation, arguing that the experience of awe, elicited by perceiving vastness or moral beauty, can reduce self-focus, deepen a sense of connectedness, and inspire prosocial behavior (Keltner & Haidt, 2003; Piff et al., 2015). This growing body of evidence suggests that the greater self is not merely a philosophical ideal but also a psychologically attainable state, cultivated through heightened awareness and transformative experience.

In this context, the "greater" in "greater self" signifies qualitative transformation rather than quantitative expansion. It calls for a widening of moral vision and a deepening of compassion, beyond extended grasp or amplified might. Grand ambition devoid of benevolence or empathy can be perilous for the ego's agendas—often disguised as justice—breed indifference to individual suffering, ruthless action, and widespread harm. The greater self, akin to the Higher Self, evokes both awe and humility. Grasping it unveils one's existence and worth as filaments within an expansive totality, revealing that achievements are not merely personal but also communal and that individuals serve as stewards rather than owners of what they create. Thus, the greater self transcends narrow personal ambitions, self-serving interests, and the confines of an inflated ego. It manifests as a vast, compassionate consciousness that unites the individual with others, society, nature, and the cosmos in reciprocal harmony.

A crucial ethical boundary follows: the imperative of becoming "greater" primarily applies to oneself—not to others. One must not invoke "greater righteousness" as a tool to deprive individual rights and inflict harm, or morally coerce others, especially when such claims mask personal interests. That said, this higher standard may rightly apply to leaders whose responsibilities affect many; they should be held to a "greater" measure of righteousness.

The greater self represents a unifying consciousness that transcends atomized individualism while resisting the fractures of polarization. Like the Taiji symbol, which illustrates the dynamic interdependence of yin and yang, the greater self recognizes our organic unity, too often obscured by reductive "us vs. them" dualisms and linear causality. This integrative vision harmonizes reason with emotion, personal growth with collective responsibility, affirming Kant's universal moral reason while embracing the transformative power of shared human feeling as essential to ethical understanding. Importantly, the term "greater" does not diminish the value of individual development, freedom, or respect for diversity; rather, it is these very individualities that, in their richness and plurality, constitute the greater whole.

While personal needs and plural perspectives remain vital, hyper-individualism creates moral myopia, blurring the essential truth of our interdependence. The mature self awakens to an identity that embraces both human community and ecological belonging. It is the breadth of one's vision that determines the scope of one's world: the wider the vision, the deeper the recognition of our shared imperative for care, balance, and reciprocity. This recognition of radical interconnectedness does not erase the self but fulfills it—for we come to truly understand ourselves through others, by transcending ego-boundaries, engaging compassionately, and participating in the greater community of life.

While conceptions of the "self"—whether defined through individuality or interdependence—differ cross-culturally, the "greater" in "greater self" consistently signifies an expansive ethic of care, conscientiousness, and elevated moral awareness—an ethic capable of embracing diverse identities. This synthesis cultivates both the empathy needed for collaboration and the wisdom to pursue transcendent purposes while encouraging innovative problem-solving and long-term thinking for the common good. Far from abstract idealism, this integrative vision addresses modern existential struggles by charting a path where self-realization unfolds through compassionate engagement with the world.

However, with cultural nuances, the idea of something greater than oneself resonates universally. In Chinese philosophy, it manifests as concern for the well-being of all, a principle reflected in diverse traditions such as Confucianism, Daoism, and

Mohism. Likewise, Western traditions speak to "something bigger than oneself," emphasizing contributions to a broader community. Platonism, for example, seeks to connect the individual to a perfect, universal order. This universal appeal enables a shared mission across diverse cultural interpretations, fostering a foundational virtue that transcends self-interest, unlocks human potential, and promotes a life of fulfilment.

Accordingly, this concept harmonizes Eastern and Western philosophies, combining their respective strengths. While Western thought emphasizes individual autonomy, ancient Chinese philosophy highlights interdependence. Both are essential today. Without a holistic perspective, the self risks egocentricity; without self-awareness and autonomy, "greater" becomes meaningless. By integrating these perspectives, we cultivate self-directed individuals who actively connect with others and contribute to the greater good.

The pursuit of the greater self affirms the inherent value and dignity of all life. It resonates with Chinese generative virtue: not as barbaric expansion and monopolization, but as the art of nurturing life's diversified flourishing and ceaseless renewal, kindling happiness, meaning, and the unique potential of each being. Grounded in this ethos, the greater self enacts life-nurturing as a moral imperative, where personal cultivation and collective benefit become inseparable. It thus emerges as both gardener and blossom in life's ecosystem—tending the whole while flowering uniquely, demonstrating that virtue's highest expression lies not in solitary perfection, but in symbiotic excellence. Overall, the greater self accords with the generative rhythm of the cosmos, a ceaseless creation and renewal that counters entropy, standing as the wellspring of pluralistic and harmonious existence.

At its core, the "greater self" is an elevated subjectivity marked by ethical self-awareness, attuned to the interconnected rhythms of the world and mindful of the long-term consequences of our actions. In an era where divine authority wanes and global welfare hinges on human hands, nurturing peace and harmony emerges as our immediate imperative. Nature's way—diversity, interdependence, and dynamic balance—offers a valuable framework for this endeavor. As our technological capacity expands, so must our ethical accountabilities. Cultivating the "greater self," with its emphasis on both individuality and interconnectedness, provides an essential compass for navigating contemporary challenges.

This vision fosters collaborative problem-solving and contributions to collective well-being. It weaves together China's ancient cosmology of Heaven-human unity—championing life's nurture, renewal, and co-flourishing—with Western commitments to fraternity, autonomy, and human rights. By actualizing our capacities for both self-determination and deep connection, the greater self responds to humanity's deepest call: to find personal purpose and meaning in harmony with a dynamic whole. In an age of pressing global challenges, this time-honored yet urgently relevant paradigm illuminates our path forward as conscious participants in existence's great unfolding.

Like building a house, this grand vision requires a strong foundation: cultivating a greater self and genuine care for others begins with loving oneself: not as self-indulgence, but as a foundational expression of self-respect and attentive care to one's own well-being. It means embracing our humanity, with all its contradictions. True growth arises not from relentless self-critique or the illusion of perfection, but through learning, self-understanding, and self-reconciliation. It also entails celebrating our uniqueness and recognizing the strengths, shortcomings, perspectives, and experiences that make us distinct. Such profound self-love, in turn, nurtures empathy for others—seeing their humanity allows us to fully understand our own. These principles form the basis of a healthy self-concept, enabling us to extend beyond ourselves, connect meaningfully with others, and contribute to the broader society. Without this inner grounding, the pursuit of a "greater self" risks becoming a hollow quest for external validation, leading to exhaustion or a fragmented sense of identity.

Ultimately, this expansive and elevated form of self affirms a love for life by harmonizing personal individuality with a deep attunement to shared meaning and prosperity. Eastern thought elevates the collective good to shelter individual interests, while Western philosophy champions individual rights to protect collective well-being, both ultimately aiming for human flourishing. Principles like harmony, humaneness, balance, and moderation contribute to societal flourishing, while freedom, individuality, and diversity enrich the human experience. Cultivating the "greater self" transitions us from a survival-focused existence to one imbued with creativity and shared purpose.

11.3.2 The Dynamic Between Small Self and Greater Self

Chinese philosophy presents the self as a dynamic interplay between two dimensions: the "small self," driven by acquisitive desires and adversarial pride, and the empathic "greater self," rooted in vision and boundless compassion. The vital work of self-cultivation develops within this transformative relationship—where the former is not eradicated, but gradually refined and transcended through the expansive vision of the latter.

The greater self is defined by humanity's visionary and altruistic dimensions. It draws on enduring moral insights shared across major philosophical and spiritual traditions, including Confucian humaneness, Daoist life-nurturing harmony, the Buddhist expansive compassion, and Christianity's agape—forms of love unbounded in its reach to all. Cultivating the greater self is less a summit to conquer than a way of traveling: a continuous unfolding of broader perspectives, where personal awakening and relational wisdom nurture one another.

Alongside the greater self exists the small self, a constricted consciousness centered on self-interest. Yet this small self is not inherently negative; it is an integral part of the human condition. It forms the foundation of identity, distinguishing us as individuals and motivating personal growth. Rather than an adversary, it is an essential component of the self that, when cultivated, supports virtues such as compassion and empathy. Yet if left unchecked, the small self can deteriorate into the shadow self—consumed by insatiable desires, engendering biases, anger, and even extremist ideation, thereby creating complexities that undermine societal cohesion.

The unprincipled shadow can be destructive, harming both its targets and its host. While religions invoke karma to explain this dynamic, philosophy points to a more intrinsic retribution: a conscience tormented by selfishness and distress. Those ensnared in this psychic prison inhabit a paranoid world of imagined threats, their inner turmoil mirroring the discord they project outward. History's fallen tyrants stand as stark reminders of this spiritual law—yet the danger is universal. A heart that nurtures cruelty becomes its first victim. What begins as armor against existential fragility hardens into the very instrument of one's undoing.

This reveals why cultivating the greater self matters profoundly. Unlike the self-serving small self, the greater self, attuned to universal principles like the Dao, prioritizes long-term well-being for all. It encourages mindfulness toward oneself, others, and even adversaries, aiming at fostering a harmonious society. While personal triumphs tempt us—and can spur innovation—obsessive focus on individual gain generates destructive waves through our shared existence. The mature vision recognizes our fundamental entanglement: in harming others, we inevitably harm ourselves; in nurturing their well-being, we nourish our own.

The "greater self" signifies a profound unity between humanity and the cosmos, embodying a moral imperative to nurture life, inspire renewal, and promote universal flourishing. Philosophically, it demands dual cultivation—refining personal character while weaving social ecosystems where all may thrive. Historically, the greater self has emerged across cultures as a moral world model, which reconciles enduring tensions between autonomy and communion, human and nature, passion and principle, and present impulses and future legacy. Today, this ancient ideal gains new urgency. No longer the preserve of sages, it must become society's living ethic—a practical framework for collective decision-making that honors our deep interconnection while addressing modernity's complex challenges.

This perspective on the self emphasizes a broadened view, not one of utter selflessness or self-rejection, but of situating the individual within a larger framework. It champions justice because it aligns with fundamental, holistic, and long-term benefits essential for all. In this sense, pursuing the greater self ultimately serves each individual—it is cultivated to protect and uplift every self, including one's own. At its core, it embodies humaneness, compassion, and empathy. No accumulation of personal success can compensate for indifference to our shared existence; no individual greatness matters without goodness.

Embracing the greater self does not mean sacrificing individual dignity. While it fosters profound social consciousness, true moral growth must enhance rather than diminish personal autonomy. It is cultivated through consent, never coercion. For the greater good to be authentically virtuous, it must inherently include each person's fundamental rights and freedoms. After all, individual legitimate rights are intrinsic to the greater good. Vigilance is essential whenever appeals to the greater good are invoked to justify oppression or moral coercion. Discerning this ethical nuance requires a foundation rooted in care and compassion for all beings as oneself, reinforced by critical thinking, an informed understanding of rights, and principled moral discernment. Only when individual worth and communal well-being exist in mutual harmony can the greater self fulfill its highest purpose: not the suppression of selves, but their flourishing in shared light.

11.3.3 Philosophical Foundations of the Greater Self

Chinese philosophical traditions of Confucianism, Daoism, Mohism, and Buddhism offer distinct yet convergent pathways for cultivating the greater self, emphasizing inner peace, ego transcendence, and a holistic perspective. Buddhism articulates the interconnectedness of all sentient beings and advocates for universal liberation from suffering. Mohism promotes altruistic Mohists that cares for all. Daoism promotes alignment with the Dao for cosmic equilibrium. Confucianism emphasizes the development of Junzi, an individual whose self-cultivation contributes to worldly harmony. Beyond ethical praxis, these philosophies also advocate for a transcendent spiritual freedom. This is evident in Confucius (2016)'s maxim of "following my heart's desires without transgressing boundaries" (2.4) or Wang Yangming's idea of the great person integrating with all things in the world, embodying ethical unity with the cosmos.

The cultivation of a greater self finds resonance across cultures and philosophies, each articulating unique pathway to transcend self-centeredness for a higher purpose. Hinduism's "Atman is Brahman" doctrine posits the transcendence of the ego to achieve union with ultimate reality, culminating in Moksha—a state of liberation and interconnectedness analogous to the luminous self. Similarly, Bildung emphasizes a transformative journey of self-realization, cultivating active and ethically responsible citizens. This pursuit of a well-rounded, virtuous, and engaged citizenry aligns with the ideal of the greater self, underscoring the universal aspiration for moral and spiritual transcendence in service to the common good.

The dichotomy between Western individualism and Eastern relationality presents a false choice—these traditions offer complementary strengths for human flourishing. The Eastern emphasis on interconnectedness cultivates a self rooted in mutual care, where identity blossoms through responsible relationships. The Western focus on autonomy nurtures the sovereign self, whose creative agency drives progress through critical inquiry and personal initiative. Where Eastern wisdom traditionally conceives the greater self as a person's devotion to social harmony, Western thought sees it as advancing collective good through individual actualization. This is not contradiction but completion. Their synthesis yields neither homogenized conformity nor atomized isolation, but a dynamic ecology of being, where virtuous individuals build resilient communities and thriving societies empower unique persons. Here, diversity becomes our highest harmony.

While many Western models emphasize individual development, they also incorporate collective dimensions, albeit with different emphases from Eastern ones. Abraham Maslow's hierarchy of needs, a model known for its focus on the individual needs, includes a stage of self-transcendence, representing "the most inclusive or holistic levels of human consciousness, behaving and relating, as ends rather than means, to oneself, to significant others, to human beings in general, to other species, to nature, and to the cosmos" (Maslow, 1971, p. 269). Similarly, Carl Jung (1951/1969) defines individuation as becoming an individual, in the sense of becoming one's own self, and emphasized that this process involves harmonizing personal uniqueness with the collective unconscious. These Western perspectives can enrich the model of the greater self, fostering a more comprehensive understanding that values both social cohesion and individual autonomy.

Applied to a civic context, Maslow's hierarchy offers valuable insight into how democratic citizenship can be cultivated through the development of the greater self, by revealing the reciprocal link between personal fulfillment and societal contribution. It suggests that individuals with met basic needs are more likely to contribute to the collective good through self-actualization, while those struggling for survival prioritize self-preservation, limiting their capacity for compassion and altruism. This idea aligns with Confucius's timeless wisdom: coercion produces only superficial compliance, while respectful conditions cultivate authentic virtue. Together, they illuminate a foundational truth relevant to democracy: that a just social contract must secure basic rights and needs—not as charity, but as the fertile ground for citizens' moral and civic growth. For the greater self to emerge at scale, society must first honor the worth of each particular self.

11.3.4 The Greater Self, Ethical Community, and Morally Grounded Democracy

Humans, by instinct, exhibit a proclivity for instant self-gratification, often prioritizing immediate desires, thereby hindering the fulfillment of long-term collective aims. Transcending this inclination requires cultivating a broader perspective—one that weighs the long-term consequences of our actions and balances immediate needs with enduring well-being of both oneself and others. This widened outlook reveals that our lasting well-being is inextricably tied to the health of communities and ecosystems, fostering a commitment to the common good. In liberal democratic politics, this manifests as a harmonious synthesis of mutually beneficial individualism and civic virtue (Xu, 2009). Harvard President Bacow's 2022 commencement address beautifully encapsulates this ethos: "Save a seat for other, make room for others; do not enrich your life alone, extend opportunity for others, and make a difference for the world." This exhortation resonates with the generative virtue as life-nurturing and co-flourishing, ensuring that our achievements possess lasting significance and contribute to a sustainable and harmonious cosmos.

Democracy's vitality depends on citizens of moral vision—the ability to transcend immediate self-interest for the enduring collective good. Although personal advantage is a natural motivator, justice requires attending to all stakes. True ethical awareness recognizes our fundamental interdependence: what serves one sustainably must serve all reciprocally. The paradox becomes clear: fixation on private gratification erodes one's own fulfillment, while moral courage, demanding sacrifice at times, ultimately weaves the social fabric that sustains everyone's well-being. Thus, democratic citizenship calls us to that higher standard, where "mine" and "ours" find their wisest balance.

In modern democratic societies, the greater self is accessible to all, not reserved for a privileged few. While absolute selflessness may be an ideal, striving to develop a greater self—one that weighs consequences beyond the self and contributes meaningfully to others—is achievable. The "selfish gene" theory falters in capturing the nuanced interplay between individual and collective interests. Many willingly uphold justice and fairness, especially when it does not directly collide with immediate self-gain. In thriving societies, individuals often champion social equity, recognizing that indifference to others' injustices boomerangs as self-harm. This demonstrates human capacity for altruism. Cultivating a "greater self," then, requires a vision of the reciprocal nature of our actions and a deft balance of personal aspirations with communal thriving, forging resilient democracies and sustainable futures.

That said, it would be unwise to continually test human nature by pitting personal gain against public good or demanding universal self-sacrifice. A more enduring path lies in cultivating moral consensus that elevates public-minded choices, particularly amid trials, while discouraging exploitative behavior. The concept of the "greater self" gains authentic meaning only when the individual pursuit of the public good is reciprocated with a robust collective resolve for justice. This balanced ethos encourages cooperative problem-solving, promotes social equity, and builds systemic safeguards against unethical conduct.

The ethical community and the greater self thrive in a symbiotic harmony. Moral communities cultivate individuals embodying the greater self, who in turn fortify communal bonds. By upholding ethical principles and contributing to the common good, these individuals sustain a just society and reap for themselves its fairness and affirmation. Conversely, those who prioritize personal gain at society's cost invite collective reproof, where social disapproval acts as an organic consequence of moral transgression.

Within this interplay, the greater self functions as a living moral compass: freely embraced, yet powerfully guiding collective ethos. Though performative morality may persist, this framework inherently curbs selfishness while actively fostering genuine ethical growth. Given its capacity to strengthen moral communities and promote democratic values, the greater self should serve as the defining standard of individual worth—one that assesses a person's ability to harmonize individual aspirations with collective welfare and to lead by ethical example.

This moral community distinguishes itself from traditional religious or moral judgments by avoiding subjectivity, coercion, or encroachment on personal liberty. Rather than policing individual conduct, it addresses concerns that affect the collective welfare. Functioning as a social ecosystem, it fosters mutual accountability and reinforcement, deepening communal ties and nurturing a sense of shared duty, which lies at the heart of morally grounded democracy. The greater self serves as the cornerstone of this framework, transcending bias by cultivating not only universal virtues like empathy and compassion but also a more expansive, forward-looking vision. It challenges hierarchies of power that privilege the strong over the vulnerable by emphasizing interdependence and the inherent dignity of all. Beyond idealism, the greater self acts as a democratic safeguard—an ethical bulwark against hidden agendas, especially in times of upheaval, ensuring resilience through collective moral strength.

Morality fundamentally requires both the equitable distribution of resources and the harmonization of competing interests—precisely what the greater self represents. When we shift from seeing ourselves as owners to becoming stewards of the world's resources, we awaken an ethic of care that naturally fosters altruism. The development of the greater self is a natural progression of moral concern, evolving through three stages: benefiting oneself without harming others, creating mutual benefit for all involved, and striving to help a broader community, even at personal expense.[2] Those with greater privilege and influence bear particular responsibility for the latter two principles, not necessarily as sacrifice, but as the highest fulfillment of ethical maturity.

11.3.5 The Transformative Power of the Heart

The heart serves as the vital foundation for developing the greater self. In Chinese philosophy, the heart transcends its physical function to serve as a moral and intellectual center that harmonizes reason, ethical feeling, and intuition. It is precisely this harmonizing function that makes the heart the seat of moral cultivation, drawing on its capacities for empathy, shame, and intuitive moral discernment, a quality accessible regardless of one's educational level. This holistic approach often yields ethical insights surpassing mere abstract reasoning.

The human heart longs for inner peace—a quiet state where guilt dissolves and contentment flourishes. An ethical heart—attuned to the suffering of others and the rhythms of nature—fosters self-awareness and guides right action. Witnessing grandeur inspires awe and humility; encountering suffering awakens compassion; understanding life's cycles cultivates a sense of interdependence. Such heartfelt experiences form the foundation of self-discipline and ethical understanding.

Self-cultivation is both an inward journey away from self-obsession and materialism and an outward journey toward seeing the world as a shared endeavor. This cultivation involves aligning the heart with the Dao, a principle of harmonious flow and interconnectedness. When one's heart resonates with the hearts of others, it enables a silent transmission of goodness, unfolding organically without the need for formal instruction. Recognizing interconnectedness helps us stay true to ourselves, unperturbed by the illusions, falsehoods, or worldly distractions. Our inner

[2] Yu Minghong, a Chinese entrepreneur, presented this idea in a video talk.

compass becomes our guide, navigating us through the turbulence of life with meaning and fulfillment.

The Chinese philosophical concepts of heart and [human] nature offer profound insights for contemporary moral development. A common concern about moral self-cultivation is that it requires extensive study of philosophical texts, making it accessible only to cultural elites. However, the belief that moral faculties are innate and universal challenges the idea. Since every individual possesses a heart and an inherent capacity for empathy, justice, and a sense of guilt, they can cultivate virtuous and instinctively navigate moral dilemmas by following an internal compass, rather than relying solely on rational analysis. In this sense, heart-based self-cultivation provides an inclusive path to moral development, accessible to everyone.

The conception of virtue as innate potential calls for active cultivation of the heart-mind, transforming latent capacity into realized moral character—awakened through introspection and nurtured through self-cultivation. This approach is especially vital for the greater self, as a nurtured heart unlocks human potential by kindling empathy, expanding horizons, and deepening moral insight. Whereas pure rational thought risks fragmenting reality in pursuit of ultimate meaning, the cultivated heart apprehends moral truth intuitively and holistically, integrating ethical insight with lived experience and guiding one toward a vision that emphasizes both self-realization and the flourishing of others.

11.3.6 Equilibrium and the Way of Moderation

Equilibrium is essential for individual welfare and social harmony. Just as psychological imbalance manifests in physical and mental distress, so too does economic inequality generate societal tensions, while ethical erosion undermines civilization's foundations. In this fragile ecosystem of human relations, equilibrium serves as our guiding compass—steering not only personal conduct but also society toward the delicate middle path between destabilizing extremes. Cultivating both inner and external equilibriums transcends mere self-care; it calls for an outward gaze, embracing the interconnectedness of our lives. By striving for a fair distribution of resources and upholding the well-being and rights of others, we lay the ethical groundwork for social justice and sustainable development.

Equilibrium is not a static state, but a dynamic process of continual adjustment to changing realities. It embodies proportionate fairness, steering between selfish absolutism and excessive self-effacement, toward a middle path that respects legitimate personal interests while sustaining social cohesion. Emotions offer a revealing exemplar. Through cultivating emotional moderation, we foster inner harmony and authentic expression. When strong emotions arise, ethical wisdom calls not for suppression but for mindful channeling—transforming emotional energy into inner clarity and virtuous action for the common good.

Moderation (度), the art of avoiding extremes and excesses, is essential for sustaining equilibrium. This virtue enables holistic evaluation of circumstances, flexible adaptation of methods, and the pursuit of thoughtful compromises that preserve social balance. True moderation demands both broadened perspective and openness to exchange, creating mutual understanding through authentic dialogue. In this reciprocal dynamic, where community contributions and personal benefits flow both ways, a constructive energy emerges that helps prevent conflict and nurtures collective harmony.

These principles of moderation and equilibrium can help prevent extremes across politics and social life. For instance, it can foster more balanced attitudes toward the disadvantaged and guide the formulation of philanthropic policies. Effective assistance requires a nuanced approach that blends respect, empathy, and genuine concern—carefully avoiding the pitfalls of condescension on one hand and uncritical indulgence on the other. This entails acknowledging the real struggles faced by disadvantaged individuals and providing essential assistance while maintaining confidence in their ability to overcome challenges and ultimately achieve self-reliance.

11.3.7 Expansive Love as a Civilizational Force

The greater self is grounded in, and ultimately fulfilled by, expansive love—a dynamic, creative force that binds humanity, propelling them toward justice, harmony, and global peace. Far from weakness, this profound love embodies strength, wisdom, and unyielding moral conviction. It demands vigilant confrontation of injustice without compromise yet tempers justice with compassion. Neither passive nor permissive, it forges the bedrock of social solidarity and trust, a vital power that upholds what is right while also building what might yet be.

11.3.7.1 Expansive Love Transcending Boundaries

Expansive love is inherently unifying across boundaries. When transcending personal needs, love becomes a powerful emotional force that bridges diverse groups, forming a shared foundation for collective growth. Throughout history, this capacious form of love has been essential to the development of civilizations, enabling people from varied backgrounds to converge around common or even divergent aspirations and foster enduring social cohesion. This universal love helps us see and care for the world as a single, interdependent whole, with diverse characteristics and needs.

At its core, expansive love blossoms through altruism, a selfless impulse to uplift others and nurture lasting connections. In contrast to hate's isolating discord, altruistic love cultivates understanding, cooperation, and shared well-being beyond boundaries. While self-preservation is innate, true fulfillment arises from honoring our interdependence: giving generously, receiving openly, and finding peace in connection. This reciprocal flow of altruistic love becomes a source of joy, while self-consuming emotions—jealousy and resentment—corrode the spirit, poisoning both mind and body alike.

Expansive love emerges as the natural outpouring of an enlightened heart, in which the illusion of separation dissolves, revealing our intrinsic unity with all life. This radiant, generative force flows beyond the narrow channels of ego and tribe, its boundless compassion recognizing no artificial boundaries. That said, while advocating for expansive love, it is essential to remember that expansive love and self-love are not opposites but complements: self-worth fuels other-regard, and self-love forms the foundation from which care extends outward. In this alchemy of the soul, the dichotomy between self and other transforms into a dynamic reciprocity—the sacred rhythm by which love both emanates and returns, sustaining the circle of mutual awakening.

With all these qualities, expansive love possesses profound transformative power, reshaping individuals and the world by cultivating a deep sense of value, fulfillment, and purpose. It operates as humanity's catalytic energy par excellence: its radius of compassion directly determining the scope of human potential. From the microcosm of the heart to the macrocosm of human systems, this principle holds true: love's transformative power manifests most fully when it transcends the narrow self to embrace the greater whole. Thus, across philosophical traditions, whether Aristotle's virtue ethics or Confucian co-creative harmony, we find the same profound truth: love's alchemy turns survival into flourishing, and individuation into cosmic participation. This is the sacred engine that has propelled, and must continue to propel, humanity's highest civilizational achievements.

11.3.7.2 Inclusion and Universal Empathy

Expansive love finds expression in inclusivity, actively seeking diverse perspectives and cultivating a profound capacity for learning. This openness fosters critical thinking, serving as a safeguard against manipulation and prejudice. In an increasingly polarized global landscape, fostering this inclusive disposition is imperative. It encourages respect and appreciation for cultural diversity and varied viewpoints, creating common ground and mutual benefit. Like a river enriched by tributaries, our collective understanding deepens when we dare to let contrasting currents converge. What begins as appreciation ripens into mutual transformation, proving that the most expansive love is also the most discerning mind.

Empathy, the emotional bedrock of expansive love, enables us to transcend self-centeredness and embrace inclusivity. As Arthur Schopenhauer (2016) observes, suffering arises from a sense of isolated consciousness—individuality and separateness—which fuels desires, competition, and conflicts. Empathy dismantles these barriers by comprehending others' needs, promoting fairness, and fostering cooperation. Confucius echoes this idea with the Golden Rule: treat others as you wish to be treated. For virtue is fundamentally rooted in human feelings, and only through an emotional connection can we make righteous judgments and cultivate inner peace. Conversely, those who prioritize personal gain and restrict their affections to a narrow circle risk self-imposed isolation, breeding apathy and eroding mental resilience. Despite any outward displays of strength, they remain vulnerable within.

The universal inclusivity is a central theme in many philosophies and religions, exemplified by Buddhist compassion—an altruistic and universal love that nurtures the development of the greater self. This expansive love is grounded in the Buddhist belief that suffering is an inherent part of life, a shared experience that inherently connects all beings. Recognizing the impermanent and interdependent nature of existence naturally inspires empathy and mercy toward all sentient beings, feeling their suffering as one's own, fostering a vision of fundamental unity, and igniting a commitment to their happiness and liberation.

The principle of "unity in diversity" revitalizes classical Chinese holism for our modern age, resolving the false dichotomies of subject-object and self-other that fracture contemporary consciousness and offering a fresh perspective on finding unity amidst a fragmented world (Zhang, 2011). This framework calls for a form of love that transcends parochial cultural boundaries, cultivating a richer, more nuanced appreciation of the plurality of human creativity and values. At its highest expression, civilizational love, a unifying force grounded in cultural affection, appreciates distinct cultural identities while aspiring toward a universal embrace of humanity.

11.3.7.3 Expansive Love and Human Flourishing

Expansive love grants life meaning and joy—an enduring aspiration woven into our very nature. Human well-being flourishes through heartfelt connection rather than isolation, inviting us to reach beyond the self to engage with others and the living world. A sense of fulfillment based solely on fleeting pleasure or personal success feeds a "hedonic treadmill," where satisfaction quickly fades and more is always needed. Expansive love, by contrast, anchors us in a purpose greater than ourselves. When we contribute to the flourishing of others, we discover a deeper, more lasting sense of meaning. This purposeful way of living offers a powerful antidote to existential emptiness and becomes a far more reliable source of inner contentment.

Genuine flourishing requires the full spectrum of human feeling. Empathy and care, seeing ourselves in others, enable us to share in their suffering and rejoice in their well-being. To a free and compassionate mind, all joy and sorrow are intimately connected. In sharing sorrow, life's deepest truths are revealed; in partaking of joy, fulfillment achieves its fullest flowering. When hearts harden to the pain of others or, worse, become its source, the capacity for joy begins to wither. Apathy constricts the mind, severing it from the very experience of happiness it seeks.

Expansive love unlocks a deeper and more enduring fulfillment than solitary joy alone can provide. This transformative love redirects our focus from consumption to contribution, liberating us from the exhausting pursuit of insatiable desires. Far from passive sentiment, expansive love is an act of courageous clarity: it shatters the illusion of separation that breeds loneliness and discontent. By dissolving the false divide between "self" and "other," it reveals our fundamental interconnectedness. Through deliberate practice—extending empathy beyond familiar circles, responding to strangers with compassion—we weave an invisible web of mutual care. This living network becomes both anchor and compass: sustaining us in adversity, deepening our joys, and reminding us that true happiness flourishes only in the soil of shared humanity.

In an imperfect world where all seek peace but few secure it, we need to cultivate moral and democratic structures that safeguard the well-being of all. Expansive love is needed in this pursuit, for like a candle, in illuminating others, we ourselves are illuminated. It fosters collective awareness, broader care, and active civic participation, urging individuals to undertake shared responsibility and translate consensus into institutional action. True moral cultivation lies in this continuous effort to bridge ideals and reality, ensuring that justice and compassion shape the world we desire. A life guided by the greater self, dedicated to both personal fulfillment and the betterment of others, offers the most meaningful and enduring path to human happiness. This, ultimately, is the purpose of this book.

11.3.8 Self-Cultivation for the Greater Self

The self-cultivation of the greater self emerges as a creative synthesis of timeless wisdom and contemporary insight. It is a transformative practice that weaves together ancient disciplines—such as meditation, ethical reflection, communion with nature, and artistic expression—with modern understandings of consciousness, autonomy, and critical thought. In pursuing shared ideals such as human flourishing, interdependence, and ecological sustainability, this practice also fosters meaningful dialogue between Eastern and Western philosophies, helping to foster a deeper understanding of our moral and spiritual selves.

11.3.8.1 Philosophical Contemplation

To cultivate the greater self is to consciously expand one's identity beyond the ego through a synthesis of philosophical insight, reflective self-awareness, and lived experience. This process begins with the contemplation of universal unity, recognizing the self as an integral part of an interconnected reality and sensing oneness with all things. Whether awakened through attunement with nature or the sublime grandeur of the cosmos, such experiences harmonize or humble us, dissolving the illusion of separateness and evoking a deep sense of shared existence. From this holistic vantage point, we become equipped to face life's ethical challenges with both interpersonal empathy and a broader moral responsibility to the whole. In this way, philosophical reflection becomes the foundation for ethical living, shaping a self that is both compassionate and cosmically aware.

This contemplative journey unfolds in distinct yet complementary ways for Eastern and Western thinkers. Marcus Aurelius (161–180 CE/2015), for example, conceives meditation as accepting the impermanent nature of fate, aligning personal actions with the rational order of the cosmos, replacing individual isolation with social cooperation, and practicing justice in public affairs, all while maintaining an inner citadel of the mind, unmoved by external chaos. By contrast, Chinese philosophers emphasize meditation not as a fortress of rational self, but as a holistic, intuitive route to wisdom. While reason holds value, meditation nurtures a broader mode of knowing, deepening our understanding of the self, others, and the world through a morally attuned heart and intuitive insight, offering a more integrative path to self-transcendence.

Building on these foundations, we can discern three interconnected dimensions in the cultivation of the greater self. First, individuality involves self-cultivation through moral reflection, ethical discernment, and learning from books, others, and life experiences. Second, sociality includes applying principles to address societal issues, embodying the ideals of interdependent community, accountable governance, and global peace. Third, transcendence explores the interconnectedness of self and cosmic harmony, advocating for universal well-being and the unity of Heaven and humanity.

Self-cultivation for the greater self constitutes a fundamental and transformative journey. Just as diamonds are forged under pressure, life's challenges refine our minds and spirits. Engaging with opposing ideas and constructive criticism, though often uncomfortable, cultivates resilience and deepens understanding. While sage-like selflessness remains an ideal, the pursuit of the greater self, a continuously evolving and ethically grounded version of self, is within reach. This ongoing process fosters open-mindedness, joy, and visionary thinking, empowering us to transcend personal limitations and develop deeper connection with the world.

11.3.8.2 Channeling and Guiding Desire

At the heart of self-cultivation lies the alchemy of desire—the transformation of raw impulse into purposeful striving. As the primordial engine of human existence, desire shapes our fundamental orientation toward life: its unbridled form has toppled empires, yet its disciplined expression built civilizations. While history provides ample evidence of the destabilizing effects of unchecked desire, it is equally true that desire fuels motivation, exploration, and the pursuit of goals essential for survival and development. The key lies in harnessing this potent energy. By cultivating self-awareness and directing desire toward constructive ends, individuals can attain meaningful fulfillment while advancing the collective good.

Desire reveals its dual nature as aspiration and greed, a dichotomy determined by the moral lens through which we channel it. When anchored in empathy and fairness, desire becomes a generative force: the scholar's pursuit of truth, the artist's creative impulse, or the reformer's vision of a more equitable world. Yet this same vital energy, when divorced from ethical concerns, can metastasize into destructive craving: the insatiable hunger for domination, hoarding, or control that corrodes the social fabric. In this light, true self-mastery does not require the extinguishing of desire, but rather its alignment with virtue, creating a sustainable equilibrium in which personal aspirations and collective well-being advance in tandem. The peril arises not from desire itself, but from the chasm between ambition and capability. When yearning outpaces our ability to fulfill it responsibly, we risk transgressing moral boundaries.

This imbalance is not determined solely by access to resources: those with little can still pursue goodness, while those with wealth and power may likewise fall prey to greed. In this context, capacity refers to the ability to be creative, see the bigger picture, empathize with others, and commit to self-improvement. When directed wisely through this capacity, desire, rather than being suppressed, can be transformed into a force for positive change. By channeling it toward a higher purpose, we harness its raw energy, allowing it to flourish not as a destructive impulse but as a dynamic force that fuels personal growth and collective progress toward a better world.

Traditional Chinese philosophy emphasizes the need of regulating and moderating desires, cautioning against their unchecked expansion. A powerful metaphor illustrates this concern: healthy cells grow harmoniously, sustaining the body, while cancerous cells multiply uncontrollably, consuming resources and ultimately destroying the organism. Similarly, individuals with unrestrained desires often ignore life's interdependence, engaging in relentless, often unethical competition for resources, oblivious to the harm they inflict on others. This relentless pursuit, like cancerous growth, disrupts the social balance and ultimately contributes to self-destruction.

In truth, virtue is not, as some traditional beliefs hold, about caging desire but about striking a delicate balance between freedom and control. Unbridled desires are like burning a candle at both ends—intense yet ultimately depleting, whereas total suppression can extinguish the spark of creativity and progress. Western culture often attempts to reflect this nuance, encouraging adventure and creative passion while trying to establish boundaries through laws, religion, and the pursuit of virtue. True freedom, in this dynamic, lies not in unchecked indulgence, but in self-discipline—a dynamic equilibrium that transforms desire into a force for growth and meaning.

11.3.8.3 Sitting in Tranquility and the Awakening of the Heart-Mind

Eastern philosophies revere tranquil sitting as a profound practice of self-cultivation. Lao Tzu (2010)'s teaching, "To the extreme of emptiness, keep the stillness," distills its essence (Chap. 16). In tranquility, by calming the body and mind, we attune ourselves to nature and awaken an inner awareness that aligns with the cosmic rhythms. This communion heightens moral awareness, expanding empathy and compassion beyond human boundaries to embrace all existence. Stillness becomes a gateway—not only to truth but also to beauty, joy, and the innate goodness within—a wellspring of moral affections that guides us toward integrity and universal care. The harmony it fosters, both inward and outward, is stillness's ultimate gift: a silent assurance of wisdom, connection, and a life in which the individual lives in unity with the whole.

From a psychological perspective, mental tranquility serves as an antidote to the pervasive internal friction that besets us in a relentlessly fast-paced world. In this age of distraction, where information overload, anxiety, and self-absorption overwhelm the mind, composure and focus have become rare and precious capacities. Mental clutter—endless desires, turbulent emotions, and unresolved regrets—muddles our thinking, leaving us restless and alienated from our deeper selves. Cultivating inner stillness interrupts this exhausting cycle, offering not just momentary relief but profound renewal. It creates the mental space needed to process emotions, dissolve anxiety, and think with clarity amid chaos. Tranquility thus forms the foundation for rational judgment, emotional resilience, and ethically grounded engagement with the world, reconnecting us with a centered and peaceful mode of being.

From the perspective of moral development, inner quiet unlocks our authentic essence, the self rooted in sensitivity, compassion, kindness, and profound connection with nature and the world. This reconnection is not merely foundational for cultivating virtue but also vital for nurturing the vision and wisdom necessary to realize our greater self. Throughout history, sages and philosophers have harnessed the power of stillness to cultivate this higher being. As the ancient Chinese statesman Zhuge Liang (ca. 227–234 CE/1998) observed, tranquility and temperance are the ground where aspirations clarify and grand visions ignite. This aligns with the Daoist concept of the "Dao," which flows in perfect silence to generate life. Attuning to this quietude steadies the mind, letting intentions pierce life's complexities and yield deeper ethical insight. Like a still pond reflecting the sky's vastness, a tranquil mind hones moral sensitivity and discernment. From this clarity, it perceives the subtle interplay of order, transformation, and interdependence that governs existence, guiding us toward integrity, harmony, and boundless care.

Inner tranquility prepares the fertile ground for an awakened mind, cultivating receptivity to insight and revelation amid life's ambiguities. Eastern philosophies elevate empathic intuition: honed through contemplative practice, it can yield profound ethical wisdom. As the mind attunes, it accesses Carl Jung's collective unconscious—that vast, ancestral wellspring of archetypal knowledge spanning human history. This synergy between individual and collective pursuit of wisdom, nurtured through moral and spiritual cultivation, offers a holistic path to self-realization, one that harmonizes individual growth with humanity's deepest collective knowing.

The human mind possesses extraordinary potential. In moments of crisis, we witness astonishing displays of this power—like a mother summoning superhuman strength to rescue her child. Modern physics describes a universe in which energy and matter are interchangeable, and some theorists even propose that reality itself arises from information, encapsulated in the "it from bit" hypothesis. Could our consciousness, too, be part of this vibratory dance of matter, energy, and information, resonating with a unified field of existence? If so, our heart-mind intentions are not just thought; they are powerful, synchronous vibrations, carrying a moral imperative that, by guiding collective actions, shapes our lives and subtly yet decisively influences the course of history and the world around us.

Recognizing this intrinsic unity, one finds that in the serene stillness of an awakened mind, the heart's awareness expands beyond self-concern to embrace the broader world, where the self empathetically connects and engages in reciprocal exchanges with other selves, all sentient beings, and the totality of life. Animated by profound sensitivity and vibrant energy, this expansive heart flows with the joys and sorrows of all lives, cultivating a natural sense of interdependence and moral responsibility. It listens deeply to the feelings and perspectives of each individual while simultaneously sensing the creativity, growth, and renewal of all in one living, organic unity. This capacity is vital, for the breadth of our heart defines the breadth of our world. As boundless as our heart becomes, so magnificent and broad will be the world we perceive and create.

Such expansiveness also calls for grounding. While the insight that our consciousness resonates with the whole grants ethical life a kind of cosmic significance, it must ultimately be lived through concrete, caring practice. Thoughts aligned with the collective good carry great force, yet only when tempered by humble discernment to avoid the perils of misguided zeal. Like the Dao's silent movement, the ethical mind in stillness, when translated into action, gathers and directs collective power, becoming a catalyst for positive social transformation and lasting flourishing. This echoes with Wang Yangming, who believes that the initial stirring of good and evil within the mind determines our path: toward upliftment and nobility, or descent into darkness, sowing discord and harm.

11.3.8.4 Unity of Knowledge and Action

Building on this, the path to a greater self transcends abstract philosophical reflection, demanding the integration of knowing and doing for ethical transformation. This emphasis on actionable knowledge is a hallmark of Chinese philosophy, where virtue is viewed more as a practice than a purely intellectual exercise (Tan, 2021). Confucianism stands as a prime example of this philosophy, insisting that moral self-cultivation must be translated into tangible social impact, progressing from the family outward to the state and the wider world.

This practical wisdom reveals a fundamental truth: virtue finds its fullest expression only when embodied in action. Ethical contemplation without follow-through is like designing a beautiful garden but never planting the seeds; even the noblest idea withers without taking root. Virtue and action are reciprocal: virtuous knowledge guides action, which, in turn, manifests and strengthens virtue—a continuous cycle of mutual reinforcement.

Uniting knowledge and action is crucial for achieving happiness. Introspection yields insight into our behaviors and motivations, whereas ethical conduct provides experience and feedback that enriches self-reflection, enlightening us morally and spiritually. This dynamic interplay forms the foundation of true fulfillment—for our values shape our character, and happiness blossoms when we live in alignment with them. In that sacred space where wisdom meets deed and principle breathes life into reality, we discover the profound joy of an authentic life fully realized.

The unity of knowledge and action is not unique to Chinese thought; similar ideas appear across cultures. John Dewey's concept of inquiry, for example, emphasizes the interplay between thought and experience. Through reflective practice and critical inquiry, we test our moral understanding in real-world contexts, refining values and forging character. This experiential approach not only deepens students' understanding of knowledge but also plays a crucial role in fostering responsible democratic citizenship.

Ultimately, the realization of the greater self, through this unity, manifests in active civic participation to foster a just and flourishing human life. This commitment is not only expressed through community service but, more importantly, through the daily actions that uphold fairness, integrity, and righteousness, knowing that virtue remains an empty ideal until it is lived and enacted to transform societies. By embodying these principles, individuals learn to transcend parochial ties and embrace the well-being of the broader civic community. Such engagement not only cultivates deep personal fulfillment but also forges the very moral foundation required for the arduous but necessary work of building a better common future.

11.4 Moral Cultivation and Democracy

Moral cultivation is crucial to a thriving democracy. While robust institutions are indispensable, their effectiveness ultimately rests on the moral character and civic engagement of citizens. In this context, the "greater self" becomes vital: by fostering a grassroots commitment to collective well-being, it counteracts the stagnation and resource hoarding that undermine democratic foundations. The call for the greater self thus represents a democratization of virtue—a moral awakening at the grassroots level. Where good governance once relied primarily on exemplary leaders, it now increasingly requires ethically conscious citizens who exercise their democratic rights with wisdom and vigilance. This shift from top-down to bottom-up governance underscores the crucial roles of personal integrity and collective responsibility in shaping a just and resilient society.

11.4.1 Moral Cultivation and the Making of Democratic Society

Democracy, a cornerstone of many societies, confronts unprecedented challenges: entrenched corruption, authoritarian power grabs, deepening inequality, and economic stagnation. These threats reveal democracy's inherent vulnerability in the absence of a strong ethical foundation. Without cultivated civic virtue and political awareness among citizens, even the most carefully designed institutions can falter. Lacking moral grounding, democratic mechanisms become susceptible to manipulation and shortsighted agendas that prioritize personal gain over the common good, ultimately undermining both societal and individual well-being.

A thriving democracy demands not only legal frameworks and individual rights, but also citizens' commitment to the common good, social responsibility, and the capacity to balance immediate concerns with long-term aspirations. Beyond safeguarding individual interests, democracy calls for collective consideration and a shared dedication to a better future. These virtues empower individuals to participate actively in democratic life, transforming democracy from a system of rights protection into a collective enterprise for human flourishing through critical reflection, mutual care, and open dialogue.

A democracy is only as strong as the citizens who sustain it, making civic and moral development not just beneficial but essential. Indeed, embedding ethical principles into daily action forms the cornerstone of a healthy democracy. True self-governance requires a shift beyond narrow self-interest toward a sense of social responsibility, transforming passive rights-holders into active stewards of justice. For democracy to flourish, citizens must cultivate broad-mindedness, respect for others' rights and dignity, and a commitment to civic participation. Recognizing our inherent interconnectedness fosters both responsible citizenship and moral leadership. This, in turn, demands the cultivation of self-discipline, accountability, and civic awareness, which empower individuals to become agents of constructive change and to navigate the ethical complexities of democratic life.

Accordingly, the development of the "greater self" is indispensable for morally grounded democracy, cultivating independent thought, justice, compassion, and shared responsibility—qualities vital to sustaining democratic structures. In turn, morally grounded democracy provides the external framework that supports and reinforces this inner transformation. Embracing this perspective means championing both individual and collective rights, not only as civic responsibilities, but as moral imperatives. Such rights empower individuals to hold power accountable for unethical actions while upholding the dignity and well-being of all. This ethical-civic integration fosters a democratic culture in which every voice, even dissenting, is respected and all legitimate human aspirations can flourish. Rooted in reverence for life and a commitment to our shared future, these principles equip us to address urgent societal challenges, cultivate social solidarity, and collaborate toward a more just and equitable world.

Ancient China's ideal of virtuous leadership emphasized a top-down model of virtuous government, wherein elites bore the responsibility of pursuing the common good with long-term vision and ethical integrity. In contrast, modern democratic societies rely not only on such leadership, but, critically, on bottom-up participation. The vitality of democracy depends on cultivating the greater self among citizens: a commitment to communal well-being, social justice, and ethical responsibility that transcends narrow, short-term self-interest. This grassroots moral engagement is essential to sustaining democratic institutions, upholding the rule of law, and protecting citizens' rights.

Virtue serves as a compass for responsible democratic practice, guiding constructive public engagement and ensuring that power is held accountable. In a well-functioning democracy, it transcends private sphere to become a public good, shaping education, civic discourse, and the ethical design and operation of institutions. The "greater self," nurtured within a civic ecosystem that cultivates moral courage, social responsibility, and the resolve to resist injustice, empowers citizens to strengthen democratic integrity and uphold social responsibility.

Just as virtue bolsters democracy, democracy, in turn, fosters virtue and strengthens civic awareness through formal institutions, such as education and law, and processes like transparency and open dialogue. This dynamic interplay is particularly significant in cultures with long-standing traditions of ethical cultivation, where virtue must be supported by democratic frameworks and inherited moral traditions can enhance participation and invigorate civic life.

Moral cultivation, in its renewed forms, can play an important role in promoting democracy by fostering broad perspective, balance, and peaceful coexistence. It encourages mutual understanding, respect, and reciprocity while appreciating both our shared humanity and individual uniqueness—qualities that help undergird the value foundation of democracy. With a revitalized spirit, this traditional philosophy aspires to shape an ethical consensus that supports democratic institutions, recognizing that true harmony arises from the richness of diversity, not forced uniformity or radical dominance. Through this approach, we can collectively build a robust democracy, safeguard human dignity, and steer society away from self-destructive paths.

Democracy is not just a set of institutions but, more importantly, the underlying values that shape it as a way of life. While democratic structures provide the framework, it is individual civic participation and collective moral consciousness that truly breathe life into democracy. This is especially vital in a broader sense of democracy, where vibrant community life fosters a shared and equitable society and where the light of humanity has the potential to dispel darkness. Too often, we lament the world's injustices while overlooking our own capacity to contribute to positive change. At its core, humanity, when properly cultivated, possesses an innate luminosity capable of brightening both our own lives and those around us. The true power of the "greater self," rooted in a collective consciousness, lies in the dynamic convergence of individual efforts, where small acts of integrity and compassion accumulate into broader social justice. By uplifting and enlightening one another, we join in the persistent pursuit of a more equitable and compassionate future—a pursuit that, while demanding, remains within our reach.

11.4.2 Caution Against Moral Misuse

Yet, for all its indispensable role in democratic life, morality's intricate nature and immense power render it vulnerable to perversion—especially when weaponized for control or persecution. Safeguarding moral integrity amidst competing social influences, therefore, necessitates active vigilance against both coercive conformity and rigid moral absolutism. Effective moral oversight must be grounded in either fundamental human values, such as compassion, equality, and harm minimization, or in culturally rooted principles that are widely recognized as reasonable and capable of evolving dynamically. Thus, despite varying conceptions of virtue across contexts, the universal lodestar remains: does it affirm human dignity and foster mutual flourishing? This approach preserves moral autonomy while navigating life's complexities and prevents morality being driven by subjective personal agendas.

The public moral criticism exemplifies this dynamic. While carrying inherent risks—from manipulation for personal gain to ideological weaponization—it remains an indispensable social practice. Moral discourse arises inevitably in human affairs, and its stakes are too high to ignore: when ethical failures go unaddressed, they breed systemic injustice and social decay, ultimately eroding society as a whole. Therefore, the solution lies not in abandoning moral evaluation but in elevating its standards: grounding critiques in discernment, integrity, and genuine concern for collective welfare rather than personal vendettas or partisan agendas. The Confucian golden rule, "Do not impose on others what you yourself do not desire," offers timeless guidance here, reminding us that constructive moral judgment begins with empathetic reflection and disciplined self-awareness.

To prevent the misuse of moral discourse, core ethical guidelines must be observed. Justice: Fairness entails the active mitigation of bias and the restraint of self-interest; moral critique should be grounded in virtues that promote collective well-being and long-term sustainability. Respect: Civility is essential. Focus on the issue, not personal attacks. Reciprocity: Before criticizing others, consider how your own actions would stand under similar scrutiny. Moral criticism begins with self-reflection. Diversity: Understand that plural perspectives exist along with yours. Criticism should address unethical behavior, not personal or cultural differences. Kindness: Moral discourse must be rooted in humaneness and a sincere desire for societal betterment, not driven by hostility or superiority. Public concern: Limit moral scrutiny to matters of public significance. Question private behavior only when it demonstrably affects society. Consensus: Ground moral critique in broadly recognized ethical principles, not in personal ideologies posing as universal righteousness.

For moral criticism to effectively sustain a healthy democracy, it must be rooted primarily in tangible, face-to-face communities, where shared relationships and contextual knowledge nurture mutual accountability and thoughtful judgment, thereby reinforcing public and legal mechanisms that curb abuses such as slander. While digital tools can supplement these interactions, online spaces—particularly unregulated social media and open publishing platforms—demand heightened vigilance as they can distort public discourse through paid influence campaigns, organized harassment, opinion manipulation, and algorithmic amplification of extreme views. By anchoring moral evaluation in real-world communities, we safeguard its ethical substance, preserve its constructive purpose, and fortify it against co-optation by bad actors. This grounded approach ensures that moral discourse remains a force for democratic renewal rather than social division.

While digital spaces already serve as platforms for moral discussion, to become truly reliable and constructive, they must blend peer-based vigilance with robust institutional safeguards. Openness to scrutiny from diverse perspectives forms a crucial first line of defense against coordinated manipulation, preserving fairness and integrity. This grassroots oversight requires reinforcement from legal and institutional structures. Key measures include refining laws to penalize paid malicious attacks and cyberviolence, establishing professional external arbitration for neutral dispute resolution, and enforcing accountability mechanisms to enhance transparency.

For long-term resilience in both real-world communities and online spaces, moral and civic education are critical. By cultivating citizenship with reasoned analysis, civic knowledge, and ethical insight, we ensure that public discourse is sustained by responsible individuals and that online and offline engagement aligns with democratic ideals.

11.4.3 The Middle Way Manifesto

Morally grounded democracy thrives on balance, moderation, and inclusivity, exemplifying the Middle Way of Confucianism and Aristotle's Golden Mean. This orientation calls for governance that carefully navigates extremes, avoiding both unchecked individualism and rigid collectivism, to harmonize individual rights with the common good. The Middle Way encourages thoughtful, measured decision-making that responds to the complexities of human life and the diverse needs of a democratic society.

The Middle Way represents not a dilution of principles but their harmonious integration—the point where distinct needs find their optimal alignment. As *The Analects* wisely state, "To go beyond is as wrong as to fall short" (11.16). Morally, moderation means recognizing when enough is enough, particularly in the pursuit of personal gain, a vital ethic for cultivating a democratic community where space and opportunity are shared equitably. While ideological extremes offer deceptively simple solutions that frequently result in unforeseen and detrimental consequences, a resilient morally grounded democracy, rooted in moderation, open-mindedness, and discernment, mitigates the divisive impact of polarized and self-righteous viewpoints, fostering resilience through understanding, balance, and openness.

Concerns often arise that the Middle Way, emphasizing consensus and harmony, clashes with the democratic principles of free speech and dissent. Yet this view conflates harmony with uniformity. True harmony does not silence differences; it creates the conditions for diverse voices to coexist meaningfully, preventing any single perspective from dominating public discourse. Nor does the Middle Way imply passivity or indecision; rather, it encourages individuals to hold firm beliefs while remaining open to thoughtful adaptation. In this way, the Middle Way strengthens democracy by transforming conflict into dialogue and polarization into mutual understanding. Most importantly, it offers a framework for balancing competing interests and carefully considering diverse perspectives—an essential foundation for a healthy democracy. By ensuring that all voices are acknowledged, it promotes participation and cooperation, leading to solutions that ensure fairness and equity. In an era of rising polarization, the Middle Way's emphasis on moderation and broad-mindedness is indispensable to the advancement of morally grounded democracy.

Next, the Middle Way should not be mistaken for ethical relativism, which blurs the line between right and wrong; rather, it seeks common ground anchored in reason, knowledge, and conscience to arrive at contextually appropriate solutions. Far from passive neutrality, it embodies an engaged, discerning approach: one that carefully weighs all perspectives, evaluates the strengths and limitations of competing views, and fosters dialectical understanding while upholding core values. Recognizing that every culture offers distinct forms of wisdom, a mature society uses the Middle Way to synthesize these insights and address shared challenges. Concord, therefore, is not the avoidance of conflict but the pursuit of principled balance. It demands courageous leadership—leaders who invite thoughtful debate and understand that true harmony arises from navigating complexity and arriving at solutions that honor both diversity and integrity.

Contrary to the stereotype of being pushover, the Middle Way embodies moral strength, principled conviction, and enduring resilience. As Ralph Waldo Emerson (1910) aptly remarks, "Your goodness must have some edge to it, —else it is none" (p. 149). True goodness demands the capacity to make difficult choices, uphold principles, and confront challenges with resolve. Without this decisive edge, goodness can become impotent: well-meaning but incapable of effecting real transformation. In this sense, the Middle Way is not simply compromise, but a holistic and discerning approach anchored in balance, inclusivity, and fairness. It requires dedication, thoughtful judgment, and persistent effort to achieve outcomes that serve the shared prosperity.

Perhaps the most vital contribution of the Middle Way today lies in its challenge to the prevailing either-or mentality, often the root of conflict, offering an integrative perspective that harmonizes competing demands. Societal conflict often arises when individuals or groups prioritize their own needs or rights at the expense of others, overlooking the principle that one's liberty ends where another's begins. Moreover, many emphasize their rights while overlooking corresponding obligations, ignoring that they are inherently linked and mutually constitutive of freedom. True harmony, therefore, is achieved not through the dominance of one side or the unilateral emphasis of one aspect over another, but through a dynamic equilibrium among opposing forces and potentially conflicting needs—a balanced consideration essential to both a stable society and a meaningful individual life.

This principle also applies to navigating majority-minority relations. It affirms the majority's right to maintain a cultural mainstream while firmly rejecting the imposition of norms that marginalize or disadvantage minority groups. Conversely, it upholds minority rights, acknowledges their specific needs, and values their unique contributions, yet resists romanticizing difference to the point of absolutism. The path forward, then, lies not in zero-sum contests but in cultivating a shared civic space, where majority norms and minority identities coexist in mutual respect and reciprocal appreciation.

The Middle Way holds significance in our time of rapid technological transformation—from artificial intelligence to genetic engineering—as a vital framework for navigating the tension between freedom and order. While freedom may drive groundbreaking innovation, without thoughtful constraints, it risks unleashing existential threats. Therefore, true wisdom lies not in ideological rigidity, but in dynamic calibration: preserving enough order to ensure collective safety while allowing sufficient freedom to sustain adaptability and progress. This is not a zero-sum tradeoff, but a symbiotic relationship, an ongoing negotiation that reframes the question from "which one?" to "where?" and "when?" Where does freedom propel us forward, and when must order, acting as a robust ethical guardrail, prevent unchecked ambition from burning everything into ashes? The challenge of our age is to develop the wisdom to continually adjust this balance, protecting core values while remaining responsive to an ever-evolving world.

In an era of rising hyperpolarization, practicing the Middle Way—with its commitment to nuance and mutual understanding—demands extraordinary moral courage. Contemporary discourse increasingly operates through reductive binaries, amplified by algorithmic echo chambers that collapse complex issues into simplistic "friend vs. foe" narratives, drowning out nuance and silencing measured perspectives. As Pan (2020) observes, "Taking a purist stance may seem easy, but adhering to the Middle Way proves challenging, as it invites alienation and criticism from both extremes" (p. 22). Yet it is precisely in such an impetuous atmosphere that the Middle Way becomes most vital, offering a crucial counterbalance to ideological rigidity. It warns against the dangers of vilifying opposing views and instead fosters genuine dialogue, attentive listening, and the pursuit of common ground, even amid deep disagreement. In doing so, the Middle Way does more than reconcile competing interests or promote reasoned thought; it revitalizes the moral foundations of democracy, transforming ideological battlegrounds into spaces of ethical, inclusive, and innovative discourse.

11.4.4 Cultural Dialogue and the Ethical Coexistence of Civilizations

Moral and democratic ideals such as equality, freedom, justice, and respect for diverse viewpoints offer a compelling path toward global unity. These values transcend national borders, enabling meaningful cross-cultural dialogue and mutual enrichment. By fostering constructive engagement, they encourage peaceful coexistence and help prevent the destructive "clashes of civilizations" that Samuel Huntington (1996) identified as "the greatest threat to world peace" (p. 338). In an era of deepening division, these principles serve not only as safeguards against conflict but as a guiding vision for a more cooperative and stable world order.

Human civilization reaches its highest expression through the dynamic interplay of cultures, where mutual learning allows each tradition to contribute its unique wisdom to the collective progress of humanity. The West's enduring legacies—liberty, equality, democratic governance, and constitutional order—find their counterpart in the East's timeless insights: the Dao, humaneness, harmony, the Golden Mean, the profound unity of Atman and Brahman, and the cultivation of moral character. These distinct yet complementary worldviews need not remain separate streams of thought. Through reciprocal learning and respectful engagement, they can converge to reveal the way toward a more enlightened global society, one that celebrates our common humanity while treasuring the diversity that gives it depth and vibrancy.

East-West dialogue holds extraordinary promise for our contemporary world, fueling innovation, addressing global challenges, and enriching our collective wisdom. As Bertrand Russell notes (2004), "If we are to feel at home in the world after the present war, we shall have to admit Asia to equality in our thoughts, not only politically, but culturally" (p. 400). For China, this vision means actively engaging as a global partner, transforming its ancient cultural heritage into bridges of mutual understanding and cooperation. For the international community, Eastern philosophical traditions offer indispensable insights toward forging global consensus. The Western emphasis on individual freedom and the Eastern focus on social harmony offer complementary perspectives on the human condition, each illuminating different dimensions of our shared humanity.

Notably, civilizational clashes arise not only from resource competition but from cognitive barriers that hinder empathy and perspective-taking. Historically, many conflicts have stemmed from seemingly irreconcilable values, whether rooted in religious doctrines or political ideologies, underscoring the vital role of dialogue, mutual understanding, and cooperation in sustaining peace. True progress requires embracing difference: just as the Dao finds harmony in opposing forces, human advancement thrives through constructive tension. Those who challenge our views need not be adversaries; they may instead reveal our blind spots and act as catalysts for growth. By transcending cycles of confrontation and retribution, we can open new possibilities for collective flourishing, building a world where diversity becomes our greatest strength and every perspective contributes.

A peaceful future requires that we embrace our shared humanity and consciously cultivate collective well-being, transcending the divisive forces of greed and short-termism. It is important to acknowledge that humans are not always rational and that selfishness and division are very powerful forces. That said, rather than succumbing to zero-sum conflicts, we can innovate to expand the "cake" of prosperity through cooperation and shared vision. True civility, the practice of mutual respect and gracious compromise, represents not weakness but the hallmark of an evolved society, embodying the ability to balance individual aspirations with communal welfare, immediate gains with enduring benefits. Ultimately, as our sense of community expands, this ethical imperative extends beyond humanity: as Earth's most influential species, we bear responsibility not merely for our own survival, but for stewarding the intricate web of life that sustains us all.

Our diverse cultures offer an invaluable repository of wisdom for addressing global challenges. While divergent values can spark conflict, universal principles like mutual respect, empathy, and understanding form the foundation for meaningful cooperation. What ultimately determines our future is the vision to recognize and the wisdom to synthesize the distinct strengths of each culture. This vision points toward a resilient world civilization—one that honors distinct cultural identities while forging deeper cohesion through joint effort or collective engagement. Though the path is undeniably challenging, this future remains a possibility, sustained by our collective will. Indeed, we stand at a critical juncture where advancements in ethical understanding and technological capacity empower us to transcend the narrow, self-serving "jungle law" mentality and embrace the ethics of the greater self—a more expansive moral vision grounded in empathy and reason inherent in our shared humanity, elevating the common future beyond primitive shadows.

In this light, this transformation is no longer a distant ideal but an existential imperative, carried forward by the timeless wisdom which holds that all beauty and goodness arise from perfect timing, appropriate measure, and heartfelt connection. While Confucius's junzi maintains virtue amidst adversity even without assurance of worldly reward, and Kant locates the ultimate reconciliation of virtue and happiness in a transcendent moral order, the concept of the greater self offers a third path: through collective agency, we strive to realize this harmony within the social world itself where virtue is rewarded not in distant transcendence but in a just and flourishing society of our own making.

References

Aurelius, M. (161–180 CE/2015). *Meditations*. Penguin.

Confucius. (2016). Analects. In J. Legge (Ed. & Trans.), *Confucianism: The four books and five classics*. Delphi Classics.

Emerson, R. W. (1910). *Essays: 1st and 2nd series* (Vol. 12). Dent.

Gandhi, M. (1958). *The collected works of Mahatma Gandhi* (Vol. 33). [Electronic edition].

Guo Dian Bamboo Slip. (n.d.). *Human nature stems from destiny*. https://ctext.org/wiki.pl?if=gb&chapter=438279&remap=gb

Huntington, S. P. (1996). *The clash of civilizations and the remaking of world order*. Simon & Schuster.

Jung, C. G. (1951/1969). *The archetypes and the collective unconscious* (R. F. C. Hull, Trans.; 2nd ed., Vol. 9). Princeton University Press.

Keltner, D., & Haidt, J. (2003). Approaching awe, a moral, spiritual, and aesthetic emotion. *Cognition and Emotion, 17*(2), 297–314.

Lao Tzu. (2010). *Daodejing*. In R. T. Ames & D. L. Hall (Eds. & Trans.), *Dao de jing: A philosophical translation*. Ballantine Books.

Li, X. (2020). The essence and limits of morality. *People's Forum, 17*, 128–131.

Maslow, A. H. (1943). A theory of human motivation. *Psychological Review, 50*(4), 370–396.

Maslow, A. H. (1971). *The farther reaches of human nature*. Viking Press.

Pan, Y. (2020). Warring states and Greece: A comparison of the roots of Chinese and Western civilizations. *Beijing Cultural Review, 3*, 14–31.

Peters, M. A., & Meier, T. (2025). Civilizational collapse and the philosophy of post-apocalyptic survival: An introduction. In M. A. Peters & T. Meier (Eds.), *Civilizational collapse and the philosophy of post-apocalyptical survival* (pp. 1–24). Peter Lang.

Piff, P. K., Dietze, P., Feinberg, M., Stancato, D. M., & Keltner, D. (2015). Awe, the small self, and prosocial behavior. *Journal of Personality and Social Psychology, 108*(6), 883–889.

Pohl, K. H. (2002). Chinese and Western values: Reflections on a cross-cultural dialogue on a universal ethics. In *Komparative Ethik: Das gute Leben zwischen den Kulturen* (pp. 213–232). Chora.

Rushing, S. (2013). What is Confucian humility? In S. Angle & M. Slote (Eds.), *Virtue ethics and Confucianism* (pp. 173–181). Routledge.

Russell, B. (2004). *A history of western philosophy*. Routledge.

Schopenhauer, A. (2016). *The world as will and representation*. Aegitas.

Schrödinger, E. (1992). *What is life?: With mind and matter and autobiographical sketches*. Cambridge University Press.

Shi, Z. (2018). *The hub: 3000 years of China*. Guangxi Normal University Press.

Shi, Z. (2020). *Breaking out of the cocoon: Isolation, trust, and the future*. Hunan Literature and Art Publishing House.

Tan, C. (2021). Three characteristics and advantages of Confucian moral education. In *Moral education and the ethics of self-cultivation: Chinese and Western perspectives* (pp. 139–150). Springer Singapore.

Tang, A. (2012). The essence, characteristics, and functions of school moral education. In W. Qi & H. Tang (Eds.), *Principles of moral education in schools*. Beijing Normal University Press.

Xu, J. (2009). The dissolution of the great self: The changing tide of individualism in modern China. *Chinese Social Science Series, 26*, 1–21.

Zhang, S. (2011). *Chinese and Western culture and self*. People's Press.

Zhuge, L. (1998). *Admonition to my son*. In X. Ouyang (Ed.), *Yiwen Leiju* (Vol. 23). Shanghai Ancient Book Press. (Original work published ca. 227–234 CE).

The manufacturer's authorised representative in the EU is Springer Nature Customer Service Centre GmbH, Europaplatz 3, 69115 Heidelberg, Germany. If you have any concerns regarding our products, please contact ProductSafety@springernature.com

Printed and bound by CPI Group (UK) Ltd, Croydon, CR0 4YY
21/09/2026
02219962-0011